Fifth Edition

The Intracoastal Waterway Chartbook

Norfolk, Virginia, to Miami, Florida

- Charts Updated to 2007
- Bridge Listings Updated to 2007
- Where to Anchor on the ICW

Chart Editors: John Kettlewell and Leslie Kettlewell

INTERNATIONAL MARINE / McGRAW-HILL

Camden, Maine ▲ New York ▲ Chicago ▲ San Francisco ▲ Lisbon ▲ London ▲ Madrid
Mexico City ▲ Milan ▲ New Delhi ▲ San Juan ▲ Seoul ▲ Singapore ▲ Sydney ▲ Toronto

The McGraw-Hill Companies

1 2 3 4 5 6 7 8 9 QPD QPD 0 9 8

Library of Congress Cataloging-in-Publication Data
Kettlewell, John.
The intracoastal waterway chartbook : Norfolk, Virginia, to Miami, Florida / chart editors,
John Kettlewell and Leslie Kettlewell. —5th ed.
p. cm.
Includes index.
ISBN 978-0-07-154579-2
1. Intracoastal waterways—South Atlantic States—Maps. 2. Atlantic Intracoastal Waterway—Maps.
3. Boats and boating—Atlantic Intracoastal Waterway—Maps. I. Kettlewell, Leslie. II. Title.
G1286.P53K4 2008
623.89'22348—dc21
2007044965

Questions regarding the content of this book should be addressed to
International Marine
P.O. Box 220
Camden, ME 04843
www.internationalmarine.com

Questions regarding the ordering of this book should be addressed to
The McGraw-Hill Companies
Customer Service Department
P.O. Box 547
Blacklick, OH 43004
Retail customers: 1-800-262-4729
Bookstores: 1-800-722-4726

Photographs by the author.

NOTICE TO MARINERS

The prudent mariner will not rely solely on any single aid to navigation. All information in this book, including daymark, light, and buoy characteristics and positions, depths, course lines, waypoints, hazards to navigation, notes, bridge information, and anchorage information, is subject to change at any time.

Much of the data in this book was obtained from official government sources. Prudent mariners will update this data by subscribing to *Local Notices to Mariners* (see appendix E), and by obtaining the latest editions of government charts where necessary. In particular, the inlet charts in this chartbook must be used in conjunction with the appropriate NOAA offshore and coastal charts. Mariners should also obtain the latest editions of tide and tidal current tables, light lists, and *Coast Pilot 4* for use with this publication.

Neither the authors nor the publisher make any guarantee of the accuracy or completeness of the information in this book, or of its suitability for any purpose. Neither the authors nor the publisher shall have any liability for errors or omissions or for any results obtained from the use of this information. Readers use this publication at their sole risk and discretion.

CONTENTS

NOTICE TO MARINERS ii

INTRODUCTION iv

INTRACOASTAL WATERWAY CHARTS: NORFOLK TO MIAMI 1–207

INLETS AND MAJOR SIDE CHANNELS

Beaufort Inlet, NC 40
Cape Fear River, NC 208–209
Winyah Bay, SC 210–211
Charleston Entrance, SC 212–213
St. Helena Sound, SC 214–215
Port Royal Sound, SC 216–217
Calibogue Sound, SC 218
Savannah River, SC/GA 219–220
Wassaw Sound, GA 221–222
St. Catherines Sound, GA 223
Sapelo Sound, GA 224
St. Simons Sound, GA 225
St. Marys River, GA/FL 226
St. Johns River, FL 227
Cape Canaveral Barge Canal, FL 228–231
Cape Canaveral Entrance, FL 232
New River, Fort Lauderdale, FL 233
Miami Beach, FL 234
Miami Inlet, FL 235
Coconut Grove, FL 236
Cape Florida Channel, FL 237

ALTERNATE ROUTES

Great Dismal Swamp Canal (Route 2) 238–248
Umbrella Cut, GA 249–250

APPENDIX A: Bridges and Locks on the Intracoastal Waterway 251–255

APPENDIX B: Anchorage List 257–261

APPENDIX C: Facilities Listings 263–268

APPENDIX D: Distance Tables and Mileage Conversion Tables 269–272

APPENDIX E: NOAA Chart Cross-Reference and Notices to Mariners Information 273

INDEX 274–275

ABOUT THE EDITORS 276

INTRODUCTION

The Intracoastal Waterway charted here is 1095 statute (not nautical) miles of "toll-free canal" from Norfolk, Viriginia, to just south of Miami, Florida. The official name of this passage is the Atlantic Intracoastal Waterway, or the AICWW, but most cruisers know it as the "Waterway," or simply the "ICW."

Seasons

The ICW can be run all year, though most boaters make the trip in the fall and/or in the spring. Southbound, leaving Norfolk in October is ideal. Many ICW travelers like to do their final gearing up at Annapolis during the boat shows, which take place during the first two weeks of October. You want to get well south of North Carolina by Thanksgiving, or the end of November, when frosts will be quite common. Seasoned ICW veterans shoot for the huge potluck Thanksgiving get-together in St. Marys, Georgia, just off the ICW near the Florida border. From December through February, frequent cold fronts sweep across the entire ICW area, bringing hat and parka weather as far south as Miami at times.

The weather pattern reverses as snowbirds migrate north in the spring. It is best to stay south of Charleston until May in order to avoid some late-winter cold snaps. Be especially careful if headed offshore in the spring. Frequent cold fronts sweep off the coast, bringing strong north winds and nasty seas, particularly in and near the Gulf Stream. Reaching Norfolk in late May or early June is ideal. By June, hot weather prevails all along the Waterway. My ideal itinerary includes an arrival in southern New England by the first half of June or July 4th at the latest.

THE SNOWBIRD'S IDEAL ITINERARY

DATE	SCHEDULE
September 1	Head southbound
October 1–31	Cruise Chesapeake Bay
November 1–30	ICW to Florida
November 30	*Hurricane season ends*
December 1–April 30	Cruise the south
May 1–31	ICW north to Norfolk
June 1	*Hurricane season begins*
June 1–August 31	Cruise north of Chesapeake Bay
September 1	Start all over again!

Bad Weather

Most winter northers won't bother boats on the protected channels of the ICW. Cold fronts arrive frequently from the north, pushing boats south with strong northwest to northeast winds. Cold, wind, and rain will last just a few days, reminding snowbirds why they're headed south. There are a few areas with open, unprotected waters where even large boats will be uncomfortable during a strong frontal passage. The wide waters of Albemarle Sound, the Pamlico River, the Neuse River, and some of the sound crossings in Georgia come to mind.

Trying to head north into the teeth of one of these northers can be wet and miserable. Some bridges may not open if the wind gets too strong. For example, the Alligator River Bridge, Mile 84.2, won't open if the wind is over 34 knots or the bridge tender thinks conditions are unsafe. Before leaving a safe anchorage, call ahead if in doubt as to storm conditions. Beware of the possibility of unusually high and low tides, or wind-driven depth changes. After heavy rains and high tides, expect to see large amounts of flotsam in the water.

The havoc wreaked by Hurricanes Hugo, Andrew, and Wilma was a grim reminder of the vulnerability of the Waterway to violent storms. During hurricane season (June through November) monitor VHF weather radio every day. The months of greatest storm activity are generally August and September. Plot the progress of approaching storms on a small-scale (large area) chart. Television weather reports often give a better view of the large picture and tend to be updated more frequently than NOAA weather radio. An excellent source of information is the National Hurricane Center Web site: www.nhc.noaa.gov.

While the area covered in this book will often be hit by several tropical storms each year, there are literally hundreds of protected hurricane holes just off the ICW. The best defense is to run as far and as fast as possible from the predicted track of the storm. Don't wait until the last minute! There should be several days of warnings for any major storm. Most boats can cover more than 100 miles in two days, and some can cover much greater distances. Try to get to a safe harbor at least a day before the storm is predicted to hit, as many bridges over the ICW will not open in order to facilitate the evacuation of those on land.

Unfortunately, hurricane landfall predictions are imprecise. Many of the storms approach from the east or the southeast, which means they cross the Gulf Stream just prior to landfall. This often alters a hurricane's track at the last minute. Other storms approach from the Gulf of Mexico, passing over Florida or Georgia before hopping back into the Atlantic Ocean. Don't stop monitoring a storm just because it has made landfall—it may double back and get you. Also, be aware that the damage inflicted by a major hurricane takes many months or years to fix. Even if your boat was not directly impacted, you may have to wait for the repair of bridges, marinas, and fuel docks.

Daily Runs

Mileage on the ICW is measured in statute miles (land miles). A conversion table for miles, nautical miles, meters, and feet is found in appendix D, and a sidebar provides a quick reference here. The charts, and the borders of these pages, are marked every five statute miles. In this guide, and in many others, bridges, anchorages, marinas, towns, and channels are described as being located at, or near, a particular "Mile." The ICW in North Carolina is marked with signposts corresponding to the mile markers on the charts.

CONVERSIONS
1 Statute Mile = 0.869 Nautical Mile
1 Nautical Mile = 1.151 Statute Miles
1 Statute Mile = 5,280 Feet
1 Statute Mile = 1,609.35 Meters

The average auxiliary sailboat will travel up to 50 statute miles per day. Some powerful auxiliaries and motorsailers manage 80 miles per day or more. Our best one-day run on the ICW in our 38-foot motorsailer, *Minke*, was 99 miles, during the long days of June. Power craft can travel farther, but keep in mind possible delays at locks, bridges, fuel stops, and "No-Wake" zones. In recent years we have seen more and more slow-speed zones, and more and more enforcement of these zones. There are many more places where courteous boaters will slow down of their own accord.

No-Wake Zones and Passing

It is simple courtesy to slow down when your wake will cause discomfort or danger to another boat on the water or ones tied to docks. Small craft are particularly vulnerable when large wakes grow steep and break as they roll out of the deep channel into shallow water. Keep a watchful eye out for small fishing craft found all along the channels of the ICW. Many docks on the Waterway are vulnerable to wake action, as are the boats moored to them.

Captains of slow boats should follow a few simple rules to allow fast boats to pass with minimum wake. The slow boat must reduce throttle to idle as the fast boat approaches. Then the fast boat can slip past at a good clip, but below its maximum wake speed. If the slow boat continues at six or seven knots, a fast boat must go eight or 10 knots to get by, throwing a huge wake in the process.

Most cruisers monitor VHF channel 16 (see Communications, below), which facilitates these passing situations. A few quick words back and forth (keep your radio on low power) can make a passing situation clear to both parties. Very few pleasure boaters know or use proper horn signals. If you hear a horn signal that sounds legitimate, try to contact the other boat on the VHF before making any sudden changes in direction or speed. When in doubt, it is usually safe to slow up and move to starboard, keeping in mind the shoal waters that often line the sides of the ICW.

Communications

Commercial boats rarely use horn signals except in emergency situations, communicating on VHF channel 13 or 16 instead. Commercial boats will often hail you on channel 16 if you might get in their way—something to avoid if at all possible! If you ask, they will suggest the best course of action. Once you've conferred and decided on a course of action, the tug will usually respond with something like this: "Roger, skipper, that's two whistles," which means he'll pass you on the port side. This way everyone avoids actual horn blasting and knows exactly what is going on.

One blast would be the signal if the tug wished to pass you to starboard. Keep in mind the amount of room needed to maneuver three or four barges lashed together, and give way if in any doubt as to what is happening. At turning points in the channel, tows will often need the whole width of the ICW.

Cruisers also use VHF radios to communicate in passing situations. Monitor VHF channel 16 when underway, and listen to channel 13 for commercial boat traffic or bridge communications. All South Carolina, Georgia, and Florida bridge tenders communicate on VHF channels 09 and 16, but commercial traffic continues to use channel 13 for safety communications. Pleasure boaters often switch to channels 68, 69, 71, and 72 after making contact, but these same channels are often used by waterside businesses. It is a good idea to listen for open channels before making any radio call.

Channel 70 must be kept free for digital selective calling (DSC), though at this writing (2007) there are few users of the system. In an emergency, you might want to try flipping the "Mayday" button on your DSC radio, which can transmit your position information to listeners and the Coast Guard. However, I strongly suggest making additional emergency calls on VHF channel 16 in order to have the best chance of making contact with others.

The FCC has designated channel 09 as an alternate recreational hailing channel for use by non-commercial boaters. Use of 09 for hailing is voluntary in some parts of the country, but it is not being used this way on the ICW, and in South Carolina, Georgia, and Florida this channel must be kept clear for bridge communications.

Boaters often listen to the cocktail hour VHF radio show around 5 P.M. and many also tune in for a breakfast chat. The VHF radio has become both a party line and the Waterway's indispensable "grapevine" for news. Though the airwaves are less crowded in the Carolinas and Georgia, you'll find plenty of people trying to share this limited resource all up and down the ICW. Try to limit your chats to the essentials and avoid prohibited channels.

Calling Bridges

Most bridge and lock tenders monitor VHF channel 13 in Virginia and North Carolina. As noted above, bridge tenders in South Carolina, Georgia, and Florida monitor channels 09 and 16. Try channel 09 or 13 first, to avoid the congestion on 16. If your radio can't be heard in the cockpit, try using a handheld radio that can be recharged at night from the boat's batteries. Bridges often call boats to provide advice or warnings. Call ahead, or call a passing boat to confirm a bridge's opening times. Check with lock tenders for the best placement of fenders and suggestions on which side to tie to.

If the bridge tender doesn't respond to a call on VHF channel 09, 13, or 16, the proper signal is one prolonged blast on a horn followed quickly by one short blast. The bridge tender should return your horn signal if the bridge will open shortly, but this rarely happens (the tender usually responds on the radio). For an emergency opening, try the danger signal of five short blasts on the horn (if a call on the VHF doesn't work), but don't expect miracles. Even in an emergency, most bridges need five or ten minutes to open. See the following section on bridges for more information.

Bridges

There are more than eighty opening bridges between Norfolk and Miami on the main ICW channel. Many of the older opening bridges have been replaced by fixed spans or newer, faster-opening bridges. The official lower limit for fixed bridges is 65 feet, but several have been reported to be lower than specifications. Some of these low bridges are noted in appendix A. Three of the bridges in this category are the Wilkerson Bridge (Mile 125.9), the Atlantic Beach Highway Bridge (Mile 206.7), and the Blue Heron Bridge (Mile 1017.2). The lowest fixed bridge over the ICW is the Julia Tuttle Bridge in Miami (Mile 1087.1), with 56 feet of vertical clearance.

Many bridges have clearance gauges attached to the wooden fendering at their bases. The gauges are designed so fluctuating water levels will give a true reading as to the available clearance under the bridge. These gauges appear to be accurate, but prudence suggests giving yourself a couple of feet to spare when in doubt. The bridge tender can be called (at opening bridges) for clearance information, but always check the gauge with your own eyes. The law prohibits boats from requesting unnecessary bridge openings. Boats with easily lowered antennas, outriggers, biminis, or other appurtenances must take them down. Bridge tenders have become stricter on this matter in recent years.

As mentioned earlier, the best method for requesting a bridge opening is via VHF channel 09, 13, or 16. Always stay well back from the bridge until your boat can pass through safely. Some bridge tenders may insist you get very close before the bridge opens, but keep in mind the strong currents along certain parts of the Waterway and the possible effects of wind on your boat. There is often little room to maneuver near a bridge. Every boat should keep an anchor ready to go at a moment's notice.

Bridge tenders generally follow the published schedule quite strictly, but they occasionally delay an opening (usually no more than ten minutes) to allow stragglers to catch up. They are trying to minimize unnecessary openings while maintaining a comfortable flow of boat traffic. The bridge may have to delay its opening for land traffic, emergency vehicles, or repairs. Also, schedules change frequently, and special events modify the usual routine.

NOTE: *Boats have been struck by closing bridges. Always make sure the bridge tender knows you are coming.*

There are several types of opening bridges on the ICW. Swing bridges are becoming less common as they are replaced by high-level bridges and faster-opening bascule bridges. Most swing bridges are located in the Carolinas. These bridges pivot on a central turning point. There will usually be two channels available—one on either side of the pivot. Appendix A lists some bridges that have a preferred channel, but check with the bridge tender if in doubt. If there is a current running, its speed may increase as it squeezes through the constricted channel under the bridge.

At some bridges, a crosscurrent will pull or push boats toward the wooden fenders. Always pass through the center of the opening if possible, and do not try to negotiate the channel when a boat is coming the other way—boats traveling with the current have the right-of-way. Commercial vessels may not be able to stop or maneuver in the narrow ICW channel, so always give them plenty of room at bridges. Keep in contact with the bridge and any commercial craft on VHF channel 09 or 13 until well clear of the bridge.

Though some may disagree, we feel that fast boats should move to the head of the line if there are several boats waiting for a bridge opening. With everyone stopped, or proceeding at idle speed, it is the ideal time for fast boats to slip by slow craft, avoiding difficult, and potentially uncomfortable, passing situations later.

Bascule bridges are very common, particularly in Florida. With a bascule, a portion of the roadway will hinge straight up into a near-vertical position. Double bascules have two portions of roadway hinged up from opposite sides of the channel. Sometimes two sets of double bascules will service a divided highway, but all of the bridge portions should open together. However, if the bridge is undergoing repairs one or more sections may not open. On occasion the bridge tender will halt the bridge opening before the bascule is in the full upright position—sailors, watch your mastheads! These bridges tend to open faster than swing bridges, but still require several minutes.

Lift bridges have two towers with the movable roadway slung between them. The center portion of the bridge lifts vertically until there is enough clearance for your boat. This type of bridge is often used for railroad tracks. Always request plenty of height for your boat (add a couple of feet for safety). The bridge tender will usually give you more than enough clearance, but check if in doubt. This type of bridge tends to be slower to open than swing or bascule types.

There is one remaining pontoon bridge, the Sunset Beach Highway bridge at Mile 337.9, near the North Carolina–South Carolina border. The roadway floats on several barges attached to cables across the channel. By pulling the barges off to one side an opening is created. After the channel is clear, boaters must wait for the cable to drop to the bottom of the channel before proceeding through the opening. The bridge tender will signal when to proceed. Because it takes so long to open and close, this bridge opens only on the hour, and it is slow to open. There is no clearance under the roadway, so even the smallest craft must request an opening.

Locks

On the main route there is one lock in Great Bridge, Virginia (Mile 11.5), and there are two locks on the Dismal Swamp Canal alternate route. Check pages 228 and 239 for the lock schedules and call on VHF channel 13 or 16 for an opening. If there is no response, try two long and two short blasts of a horn. If there is still no response, tie up to the bulkhead before the lock and call again a bit later. Chances are the lock tender is off doing something or is between lock houses. The lock tenders may also open the nearby bridges.

The Great Bridge Lock is easy to negotiate, with only a foot or two of rise and fall—the movement may be undetectable. There are places to tie up on either side of the lock while waiting. The south side of the lock is fendered with very slippery plastic bumpers that allow pleasure boats to slide smoothly up and down. Whether north- or southbound, try to tie up along the south side of the lock, but be prepared to switch to the other side if the lock becomes crowded. The lock tender will assist you when docking on the slightly rougher north side.

The Dismal Swamp locks have about a 12-foot rise or fall, so they require longer lines for your tie-up. Very small boats might get by with one person handling the lines, but most cruisers will want to have strong crew at both bow and stern. The lock tender will indicate where to tie up, but be prepared with fenders and lines before entering. Have fenders on both sides of the boat in case of last-minute changes in the docking plan. Have bow and stern lines ready, too. Fender boards are not necessary.

The lock will show a green light when it is safe to enter. The gates to the lock should be fully open before you proceed into the lock at idle speed. The gate area of the lock may have swirling currents, which can swing your boat into the lock wall. Stay in the middle of the opening until inside the lock, and listen for the lock tender's instructions on where to tie up. There may be several other boats inside. You will probably be instructed to tie up on one side or the other, but you may have to raft off another boat if the lock is very full.

The lock tender will often secure your lines at the top of the lock wall, or loop them around a bollard so you can control both ends. The tender will usually ask you for your registration or documentation number and your hailing port. As the water level rises or falls you will have to adjust the length of your lines to keep the boat near the wall. Usually, the up-locks are a bit trickier than the down-locks. In an up-lock, water flowing into the lock pushes boats away from the wall, while boats are pulled toward the wall when the water is exiting.

Keep bow and stern lines snug, but not tight. Pulling too hard on either the bow or stern will force the other end of the boat away from the lock wall. Then the person on the other end pulls harder to compensate, and you pull even harder. Pretty soon you are both pulling your backs out of line, because you're working against each other. Keep the lines snug until you are completely ready to leave the lock with your engine running and your boat in gear.

Don't run your engine while in the lock, as the lock will quickly fill up with fumes, and the extra noise makes it difficult to relay instructions or talk to other boats. When pulling away from the lock wall try to use low power to avoid pushing the boat behind you into the wall. Again, stay in the middle of the opening when passing through the gates. The area around a lock is always a slow-speed No-Wake zone.

The Dismal Swamp Canal (Route 2)

The locks in this canal are discussed in the previous section. The canal was partly surveyed by George Washington, as portions of it passed over some land he owned. It is a very narrow passage—in places the trees arch overhead from each bank until they almost touch. Sailors must watch their masthead as much as their depth-sounder. Controlling depth was about six feet in 2007, but in dry periods there may be less water, and in very dry periods the canal may be closed entirely. Call ahead to the lock tenders (see page 239 for the phone numbers) for the latest depth and regulation information. Each lock opening requires a tremendous quantity of water, and there may be a reduced schedule of openings in a dry season.

From the beginning of the Dismal Swamp route to Elizabeth City, North Carolina, is about 43 miles. From Norfolk to the South Mills Lock is a distance of about 33 miles. If you catch the first lock opening at Deep Creek, you should be able to exit the canal at South Mills before dark, but you may not be able to make it all the way to Elizabeth City.

The lock tenders frequently open the bridge at South Mills 10 or 15 minutes before the scheduled lock opening, so it pays to arrive a bit early. If you miss the bridge you can't catch the lock opening. There is usually room along the wooden bulkheads just before the bridges for those who need to tie up overnight.

Depths

The federal project depths for the Waterway are 12 feet from Norfolk, Virginia, Mile 0, to Fort Pierce, Florida, Mile 965.6. From Fort Pierce to Miami, Mile 1089, the project calls for 10-foot depths. The Dismal Swamp Route is safe for boats with up to six-foot drafts, but occasionally someone makes it through drawing up to seven feet.

Unfortunately, the project depths are not always available. Those who draw less than six feet should have little trouble. Boats drawing six to eight feet will probably be able to make it through, though they will find some high spots in certain sections. Boats needing more than eight feet of water will probably want to avoid the Waterway as much as possible, unless they carry dredging equipment. In recent years there has been severe shoaling in several places, particularly in South Carolina and Georgia. Low-tide depths of only a foot or two have been found in some areas, but luckily those same areas have rather large tidal ranges allowing careful boaters to proceed.

In 2005, 2006, and 2007 areas to be especially careful include the waters between Charleston and Beaufort, South Carolina, Fields Cut just before the Savannah River, north and south around the Savannah River crossing in Georgia, the Little Mud River north of Mile 655, and Jekyll Creek in Georgia. Monitor the VHF radio during the day and you'll hear warnings about upcoming shoal spots.

Depths tend to be greatest in the center of the Waterway, and the channel markers are often set in shallow water. Stay at least 20 feet from any navigation aid for safety and best water. If you must pull over to let a barge pass, do so at slow speed with one eye on the depth-sounder, especially in the "Rockpile," a section dredged through solid rock between Miles 347 and 365.

When traveling long straight stretches, periodically look over your stern to be sure you are not being pushed out of the channel. Crosswinds and currents may be setting your boat toward the shoaler edges of the channel. With this chartbook you'll be able to follow your progress closely on the charts. It is critical to have charts at the helm station where you can see them. Many groundings occur when boaters misinterpret buoys or daymarks at channel junctions.

In some places it is tempting to cut corners, but do so with caution. Charted depths outside the charted channels are unreliable, and these areas are more prone to having snags or sunken debris.

The best method to escape from a grounding is to use the tide (if available). Often a wait of half an hour can raise a boat enough to let it float off easily—a falling tide can put a boat hard aground rapidly. While waiting for help from the tide, always put a kedge anchor out toward deep water, especially if the wind and current are pushing the boat toward the shoal. Tides run over nine feet in South Carolina and Georgia—a complete set of tide tables is a necessity for these areas.

Aids to Navigation

All types of navigation aids are found on the ICW. The typical marker is either a red triangular daymark or a green square daymark. The red marks are to starboard and the green to port when headed south. ICW markers are further identified by a fluorescent yellow triangle on starboard-hand markers and a fluorescent yellow square on port-hand marks. The yellow marks help to prevent confusion when another channel coincides with the Waterway channel. For example, the upper reaches of the Pungo River have red marks to port and green to starboard when you are heading south. The marks are correct for the river, but opposite the normal color scheme for the Waterway; however, the yellow squares on the red marks and the yellow triangles on the green marks identify them for the ICW boater. There are several places on the ICW where the navigation marks of a river reverse the normal color scheme you might expect. Note these areas on the charts before they cause confusion.

Ranges are unfamiliar to many boaters, but they are frequently found on the Waterway. A range consists of two marks (usually towers or multi-pile structures) that will keep you in the channel when they are brought into alignment. Usually, the front mark in a range will be below the rear mark when the two are in alignment. Ranges often have vertical orange stripes to aid in daytime identification. When the front and back marks are aligned, the orange stripes are aligned. Most ranges are lit at night, and the daymarks are fluorescent. An example of a range is found in the mouth of Adams Creek, just after Mile 185. Unfortunately, many ranges we have used in the past have not been maintained and may be in disrepair or unusable.

Navigation

Most of the time you will be using "eyeball navigation"—simply following the red and green marks. Occasionally, you will need to plot a compass course across a sound or large bay, but most of these passages have been preplotted in this chartbook. You can also use a GPS unit to navigate on these open stretches, and we have included important waypoints on the charts. Use plotted courses or your GPS when visibility is poor, or when caught out at night.

Your depth-sounder should be on constantly. Calibrate the unit by dropping a measured line over the side while at anchor. Some units allow the user to input a correction to the displayed reading.

The position-finding capability of GPS is of little value most of the time, though it can be very handy if caught in a thunderstorm while crossing Albemarle Sound. Use your GPS to keep track of speed over the ground by setting the unit to read in statute miles per hour. This GPS ground speed can indicate the presence of favorable or unfavorable currents. Used in conjunction with the mile markings on the charts (and the mileage posts in some areas), this speed information allows you to accurately predict arrival at a restricted bridge. The latitude/longitude readout from a GPS can be useful at times. For example, the long Rockpile section has few distinguishing landmarks for almost 18 miles. However, longitude lines cross the canal at regular intervals, allowing precise position determination when using a GPS. The same situation applies in the Dismal Swamp Canal.

Some boaters report great faith in radar, but along much of the ICW there are few distinct landmarks or structures. The low, marshy banks of Georgia and South Carolina make very poor targets. Many aids to navigation are made of wood and also give poor returns. However, radar could be very useful in the more open stretches: the Cape Fear River, Albemarle Sound, or the Pamlico River crossing.

Night Travel

Noting the many lighted aids to navigation, a cruiser might assume a run after dark will be easy; however, these aids tend to be far apart and difficult to use for the uninitiated. Some of the lights may not be working. The deep-water channel is narrow and it is easy to blunder out of it. Floating hazards (logs, stumps, oil barrels, etc.) will go unseen until they bang up your prop. Commercial vessels manage to navigate these channels aided by huge spotlights and thick steel hulls, but they frequently go aground or miss the channel—you'll see dents in marshes where they missed turns. The average pleasure boater will find the experience less than pleasant, if not dangerous. Don't travel at night.

To avoid getting caught out, plan on stopping at least an hour before dark. In October, this may mean pulling over by 4 P.M. or 5 P.M. Delays can often destroy the best-laid plans, so review your schedule as the day progresses. Try to decide on an anchorage or marina early in the day. Sometimes, you need to settle for an unusually short day to avoid getting caught out. For example, you don't want to enter the Alligator-Pungo Canal, Miles 105 to 126, unless you can make it out the other end before dark. Similarly, don't enter the canal if you're low on fuel. There is no safe place to stop in the 21-mile-long canal, and you can't anchor in the middle of the channel—huge barges are pushed through day and night.

Anchorages

There are hundreds of fabulous gunkholes all along the ICW, and only Florida has significant restrictions on anchoring out. To assist in planning your trip, a list of more than a hundred popular anchorages is in appendix B. Each anchorage is marked by an anchor symbol and a corresponding mileage reading on the chart border. These mileage numbers correspond to the brief notes in the anchorage list in the appendix.

Anchorages are frequent enough to let dedicated gunkholers anchor every night. There are some stretches where the anchoring possibilities are less frequent, and other areas where there are more anchorages than can be listed.

Proper anchor tackle for your home waters will likely be appropriate for the ICW, too. Many anchorages are less than 8 feet deep so you won't need a lot of scope out. Having plenty of chain on the bottom reduces your scope requirements, increases holding power, and dampens out any swinging. There are few spots you'll have to anchor in more than 20 feet of water.

Many anchorages have reversing currents due to the effects of tide, and you may need a second anchor to limit your swinging room. When headed south, this problem will first be encountered in Beaufort, North Carolina. The anchorage in Taylor Creek is always crowded, and the channel must be kept clear for local traffic. Most cruisers use two anchors there.

Most of the places listed here are not coast guard–designated Special Anchorages. Always display a proper anchor light when not in a designated anchorage. Some local authorities have been known to enforce this sensible rule. An anchor light near deck level can be seen by the low skiffs and dinghies likely to be blasting through the anchorage at night. A masthead light can disappear against a background of stars, and boats traveling at high speed do not look up at the sky as they scream along.

Marinas

This book does not pretend to be a marina guide, but a copy of the government facilities listings is included in appendix C. The numbers correspond to numbers on the appropriate chart page. These listings provide basic information on available services, though we've found this type of list becomes dated quickly. In general, most major towns along the coasts have at least one marina that will take transient boaters. Most, but not all, marinas have diesel fuel, gas, electricity on the docks, and water, and many also have showers, laundry facilities, wifi and/or Internet access, cable TV, and other amenities. Those planning to tie up frequently would be well advised to get one of the privately published, annually updated facilities listings.

Even if you are planning on spending most nights in marinas, you should be prepared to anchor. During the peak migrating seasons some marinas fill up quickly in the evening, and there may not be another for many miles. Also, you may be running behind schedule due to a bridge failure or a problem with your boat. For this reason it is wise to carry a dinghy, even if you are a dedicated marina user. Every boat should also be prepared to anchor at a moment's notice in case of engine failure.

Inside Out

Many boaters like to combine ocean runs with their Intracoastal trips. Most inlets can be rough or dangerous when an onshore sea piles up against an outgoing current. Even the "all-weather" inlets should be avoided in strong onshore winds. Study the charts carefully, as the inlets are often protected by long submerged jetties extending well out to sea. Shoals may surround the marked entrance channels, causing large areas of breaking seas in heavy weather.

When the chart shows no buoys for an inlet, you know it demands "local knowledge." Another tip-off to use great care is the note, "Buoys are not charted as they are frequently shifted in position." Examples include St. Augustine Inlet and St. Andrew Sound. Such an inlet can be tempting in settled weather, but be prepared to retreat if you can't sort out the buoyage. Many of these secondary channels have a controlling depth of six feet or less. Beware of big swells from some distant storm breaking heavily even though the local weather may be calm.

Heading south, your first chance to jump outside is Beaufort, North Carolina. This is a convenient inlet if you are heading offshore to Bermuda or the Caribbean, but plan your trip to cross the Gulf Stream well ahead of any bad weather. If you are headed south to Florida, a better choice is to proceed down the ICW to Cape Fear. It is not worth rounding outside of Frying Pan Shoals, as you often have to go all the way out to the Gulf Stream before heading back in. The area around Frying Pan Shoals is notorious for bad weather.

Cape Fear, North Carolina, is the next really good inlet south of Beaufort, though in moderate weather many boats use Masonboro Inlet at Wrightsville Beach. The problem with Masonboro is it is north of Frying Pan Shoals again. The current pouring through the inlet can create dangerous sea conditions at the entrance.

Winyah Bay, South Carolina, is the next good inlet. The town of Georgetown is about 15 miles upstream, and is a popular stop for ICW cruisers. Charleston, South Carolina, has one of the best inlets on the southeast coast. It is heavily used by commercial shipping and naval vessels. Just south of Charleston you'll see local boats using Stono Inlet, the North Edisto River, South Edisto River, and St. Helena Sound. These all have a controlling depth of around six feet, if you can find the deep water with the help of local knowledge. These inlets are for use in good weather only. The next "all-weather" inlet is Port Royal Sound, south of Beaufort, South

Carolina. Calibogue Sound, leading to Hilton Head, can be a bit tricky, especially if you haven't run it before—study the charts carefully. The channel begins at the range lights for the Bloody Point Range in the Savannah River entrance channel.

The Savannah River channel is excellent, but has very strong currents. A coast guard station is located along the New Channel Range. Other possible inlets in Georgia include Wassaw Sound, Ossabaw Sound, St. Catherines Sound, Sapelo Sound, Doboy Sound, St. Simons Sound, St. Andrew Sound, and the St. Marys River on the Florida border. Wassaw Sound is frequented by tall-masted boats wishing to use the marine facilities at Thunderbolt. Of these Georgia inlets, only St. Simons Sound and the St. Marys River are really deep and well marked. The others are fair-weather inlets only, though they are heavily used by fishing boats and other local traffic.

Florida's east coast has few good inlets. From north to south they are: St. Marys River, St. Johns River, Cape Canaveral, Ft. Pierce, Palm Beach (Lake Worth Inlet), Ft. Lauderdale, and Miami. St. Augustine Inlet should only be attempted in good weather, with local knowledge. The buoys in the channel are constantly shifted with the ever-changing sands. If you should wish to attempt the inlet, seek local knowledge. Local Sea Tow and TowBoatU.S. services can provide advice. Ponce de Leon Inlet at New Smyrna Beach is used heavily by local boaters, and there is a coast guard station for assistance, but it should be considered a fair-weather inlet only. St. Lucie inlet can be very rough. Jupiter Inlet is another "local knowledge only" place, with the buoys constantly shifted around. Boynton Inlet, Boca Raton Inlet, Hillsboro Inlet, and Bakers Haulover Inlet are mainly used by small, local fishing craft. Larger sportfishermen (that can clear a 32-foot fixed bridge) frequent Bakers Haulover.

South of Miami you'll find Bahamas-bound cruisers using Cape Florida Channel and Biscayne Channel to get out to the Gulf Stream. These are good channels in decent weather, but beware the many shoal spots. The markers in the channels tend to be perplexing to the first-timer, and can be confused with other navigation aids in the area. Study the charts carefully before venturing out. Obtain the latest NOAA offshore charts when venturing outside.

How to Use This Book

Though the use of this chartbook should be self-explanatory, a few hints may be in order. The charts are arranged in geographic order starting with Norfolk, Virginia, on page 1, proceeding south down the Intracoastal Waterway to Miami, Florida, on pages 205–206, and continuing on to Key Biscayne on page 207. Details of many inlets, rivers, and alternate routes appear on pages 208–250, including the popular Dismal Swamp Canal on pages 238–248.

The table of contents and index should be used to locate particular places. Several appendices include further information: appendix A is a list of important bridge information, appendix B lists many popular anchorages, appendix C contains the government facilities listings, appendix D provides distance tables and a mileage conversion chart, and appendix E cross-references this book with NOAA charts and tells you where to obtain *Local Notices to Mariners.*

Each chart page has useful notations in the right-hand border, and sometimes on the charts themselves. Statute miles are labeled every five miles. Bridges are labeled by name and a mileage designation. Locks are labeled with mileage, and anchorages are marked with an anchor symbol. Refer to the appropriate mileage designation in one of the appendices to get more information on bridges, locks, and anchorages. Open bodies of water feature charted courses (magnetic) and latitude/longitude waypoints.

If you are planning an offshore trip, you should obtain the proper charts to join the inlet and Waterway charts in this book.

Have a great trip!

NOTE: *The charts and mileage scales in this book have been reproduced at full size. Most ICW charts (pages 1–207) are at 1:40,000 scale. Most of the inlet and alternate route charts (pages 208–250) are at either 1:40,000 or 1:80,000. Several detailed charts are at a scale of 1:24,000, and the Canaveral Barge Canal is mostly 1:10,000. Whenever possible, mileage scales have been included.*

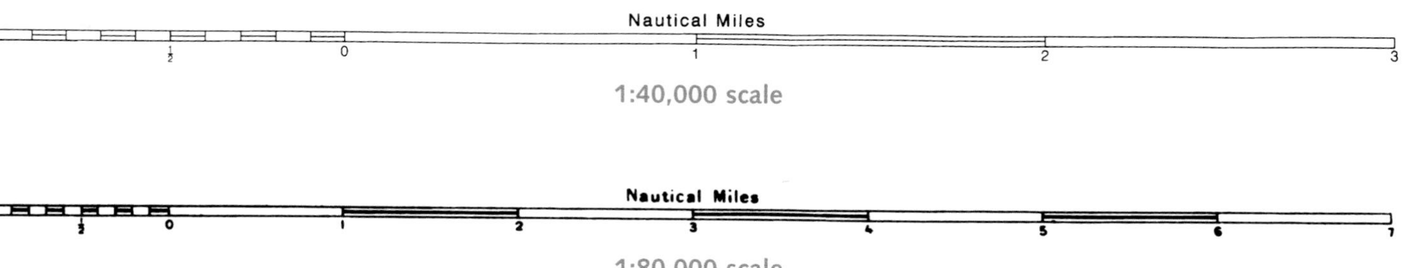

Chesapeake Bay
VIRGINIA
Cape Charles
Norfolk
Albemarle Sound
NORTH CAROLINA
Cape Hatteras
Beaufort/Morehead City
Pamlico Sound
Cape Lookout
Wilmington
SOUTH CAROLINA
Cape Fear
Georgetown
Charleston
GEORGIA
Port Royal
Beaufort
Savannah
Hilton Head
Atlantic
Brunswick
Ocean
Jacksonville
St. Augustine
Daytona Beach
FLORIDA
Cape Canaveral
Tampa
Melbourne
Fort Pierce
West Palm Beach
Fort Lauderdale
Miami
Bahama Islands
Florida Keys
Key West
Intracoastal Waterway

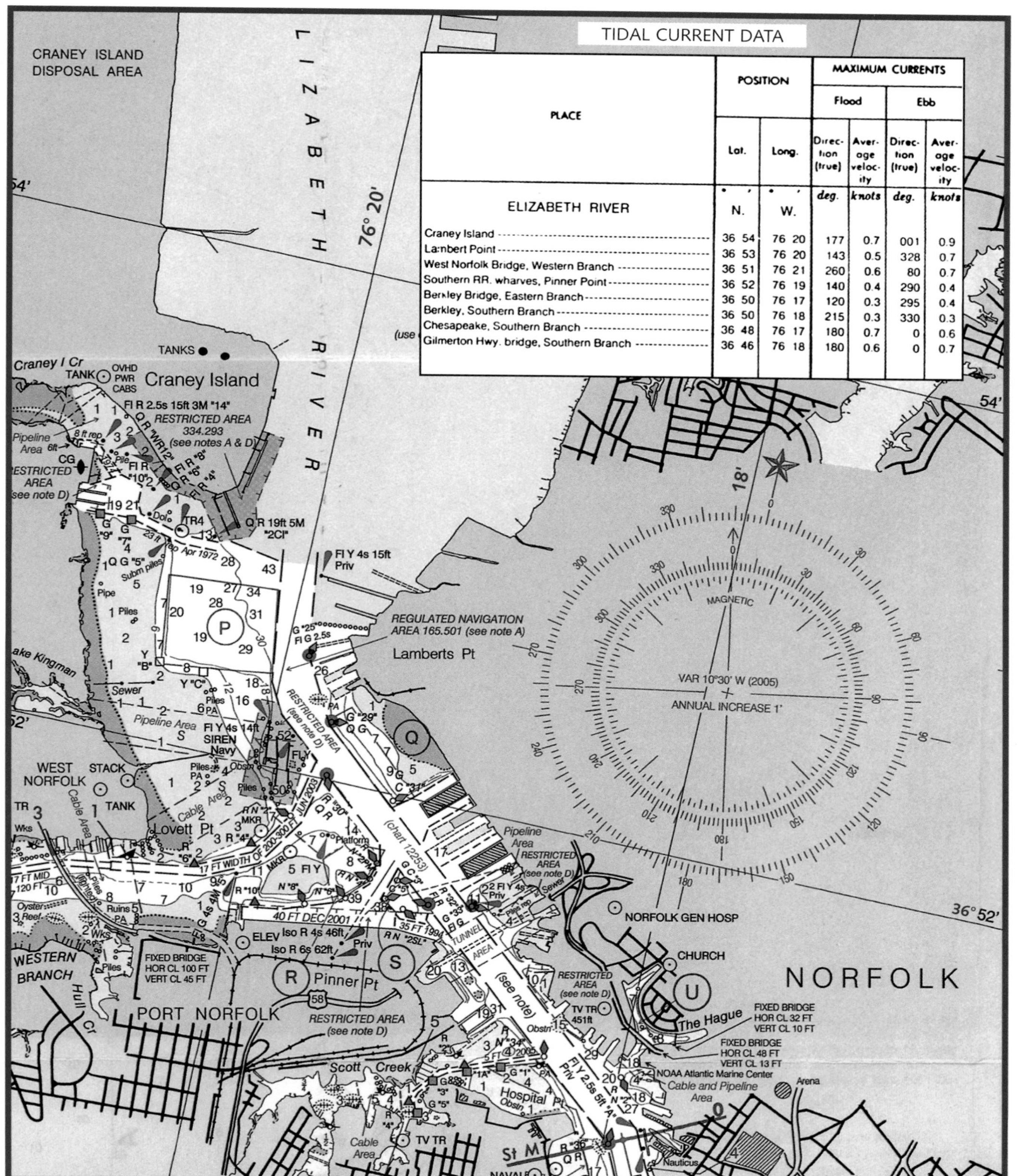

TIDAL CURRENT DATA

PLACE	POSITION		MAXIMUM CURRENTS			
			Flood		Ebb	
	Lat.	Long.	Direction (true)	Average velocity	Direction (true)	Average velocity
ELIZABETH RIVER	° ′ N.	° ′ W.	deg.	knots	deg.	knots
Craney Island	36 54	76 20	177	0.7	001	0.9
Lambert Point	36 53	76 20	143	0.5	328	0.7
West Norfolk Bridge, Western Branch	36 51	76 21	260	0.6	80	0.7
Southern RR. wharves, Pinner Point	36 52	76 19	140	0.4	290	0.4
Berkley Bridge, Eastern Branch	36 50	76 17	120	0.3	295	0.4
Berkley, Southern Branch	36 50	76 18	215	0.3	330	0.3
Chesapeake, Southern Branch	36 48	76 17	180	0.7	0	0.6
Gilmerton Hwy. bridge, Southern Branch	36 46	76 18	180	0.6	0	0.7

2

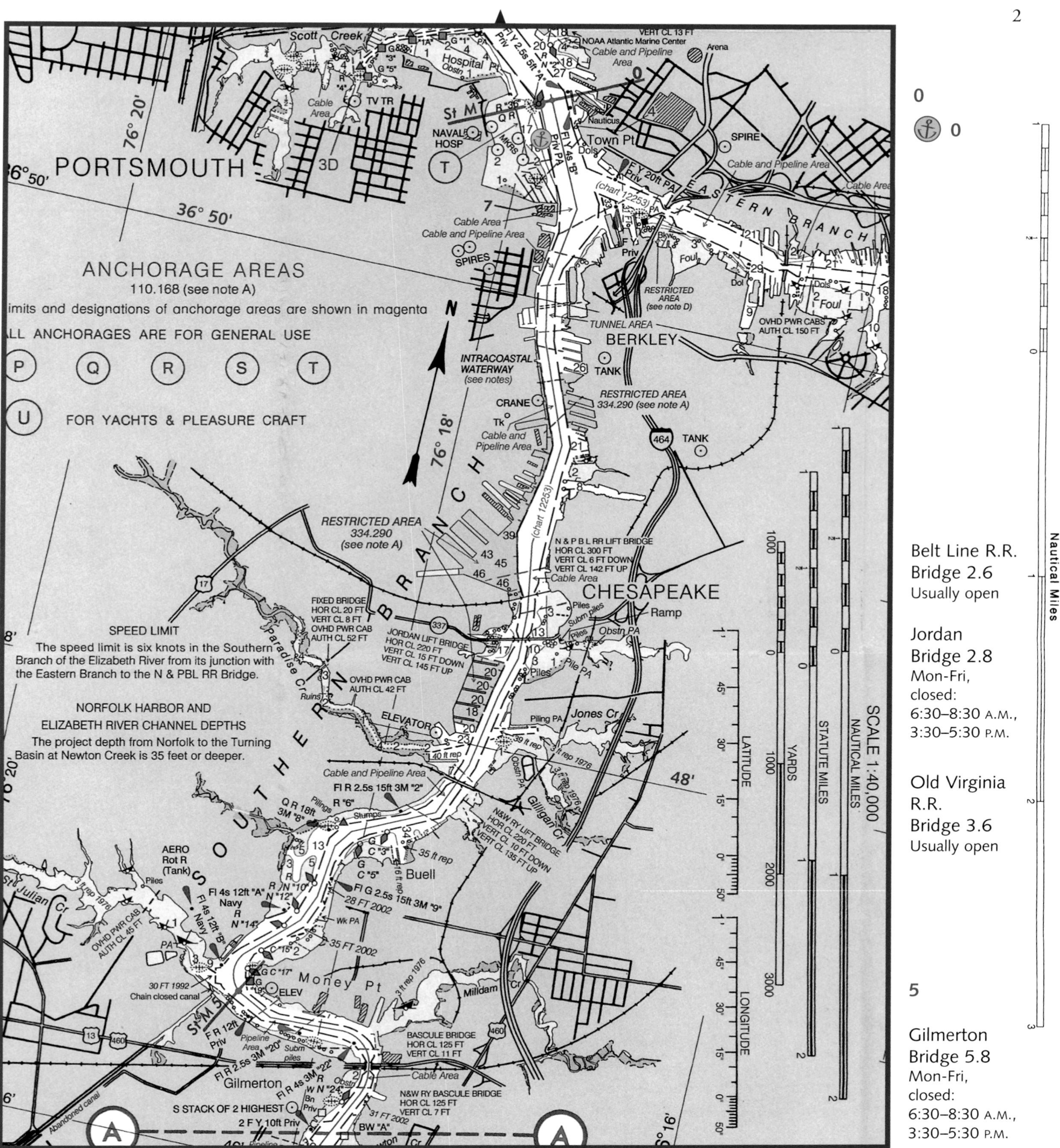

0

0

Belt Line R.R.
Bridge 2.6
Usually open

Jordan
Bridge 2.8
Mon-Fri,
closed:
6:30–8:30 A.M.,
3:30–5:30 P.M.

Old Virginia
R.R.
Bridge 3.6
Usually open

5

Gilmerton
Bridge 5.8
Mon-Fri,
closed:
6:30–8:30 A.M.,
3:30–5:30 P.M.

Nautical Miles

Joins Page 238 For Great Dismal Swamp Canal (Route 2)

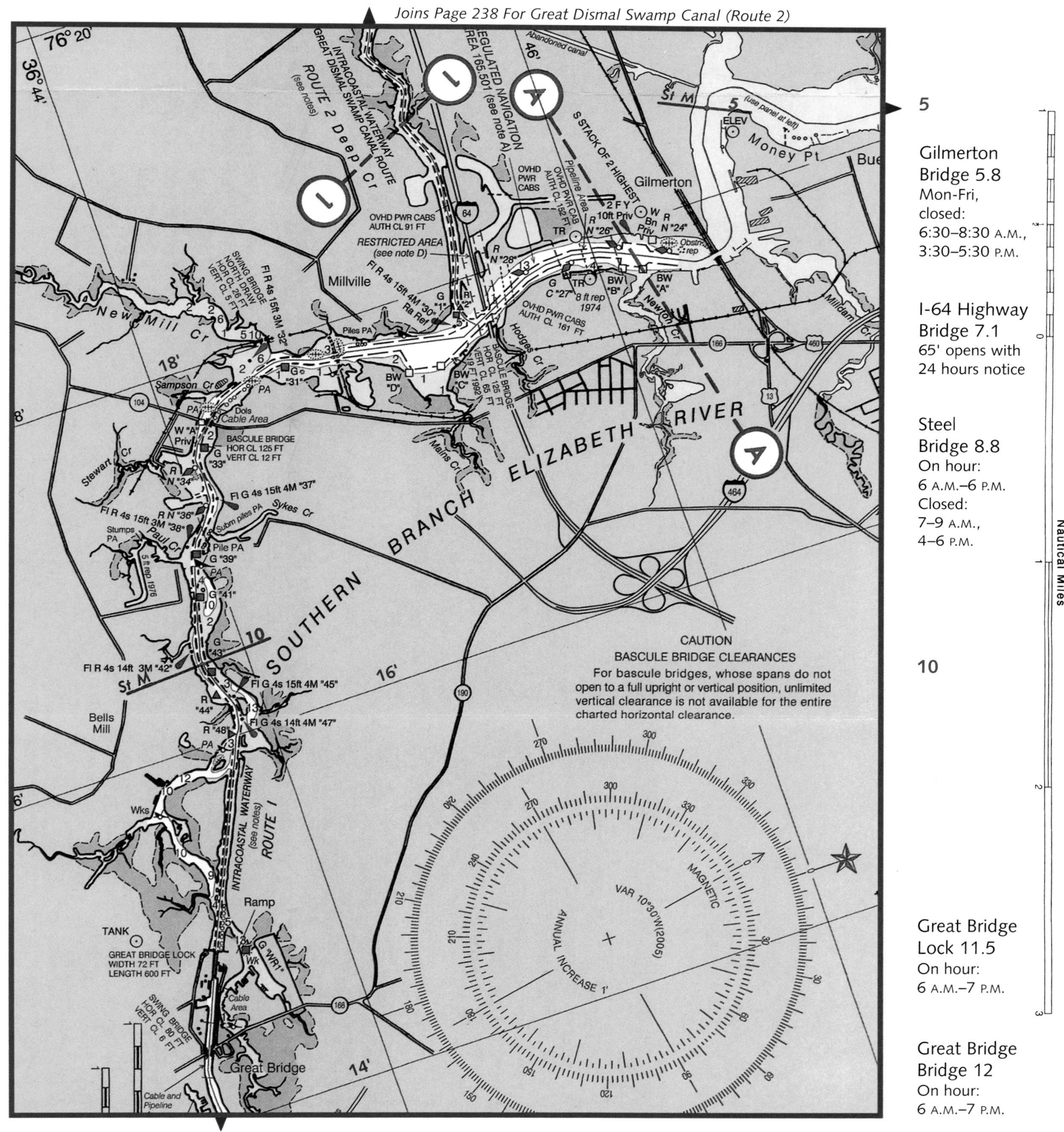

5

Gilmerton Bridge 5.8
Mon-Fri, closed:
6:30–8:30 A.M.,
3:30–5:30 P.M.

I-64 Highway Bridge 7.1
65' opens with 24 hours notice

Steel Bridge 8.8
On hour:
6 A.M.–6 P.M.
Closed:
7–9 A.M.,
4–6 P.M.

10

Great Bridge Lock 11.5
On hour:
6 A.M.–7 P.M.

Great Bridge Bridge 12
On hour:
6 A.M.–7 P.M.

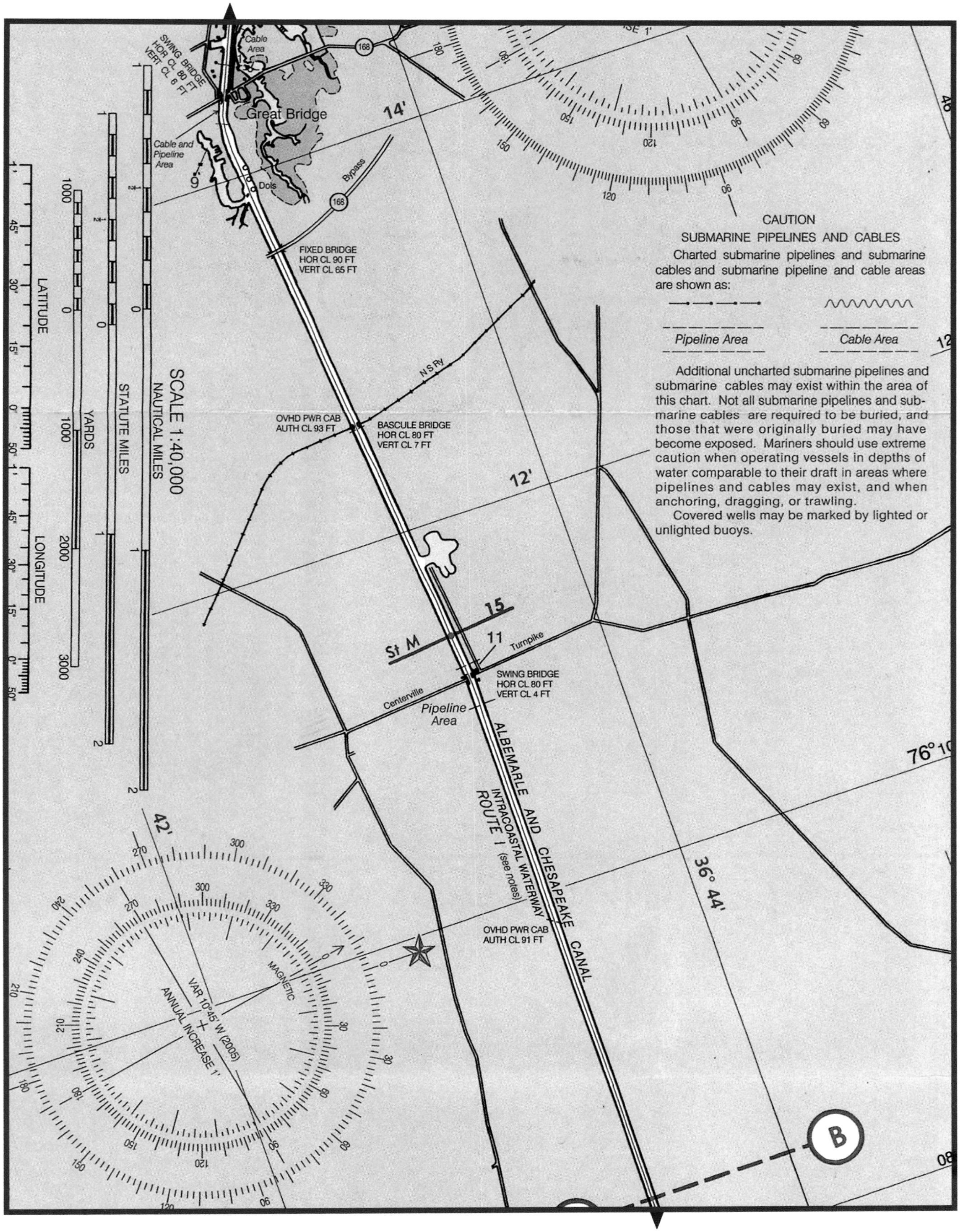
SWING BRIDGE
HOR CL 80 FT
VERT CL 6 FT
Cable Area
Great Bridge
14'
Cable and Pipeline Area
Dols
Bypass
168
FIXED BRIDGE
HOR CL 90 FT
VERT CL 65 FT
CAUTION
SUBMARINE PIPELINES AND CABLES
Charted submarine pipelines and submarine cables and submarine pipeline and cable areas are shown as:
Pipeline Area
Cable Area
Additional uncharted submarine pipelines and submarine cables may exist within the area of this chart. Not all submarine pipelines and submarine cables are required to be buried, and those that were originally buried may have become exposed. Mariners should use extreme caution when operating vessels in depths of water comparable to their draft in areas where pipelines and cables may exist, and when anchoring, dragging, or trawling.
Covered wells may be marked by lighted or unlighted buoys.
N S Ry
OVHD PWR CAB
AUTH CL 93 FT
BASCULE BRIDGE
HOR CL 80 FT
VERT CL 7 FT
12'
SCALE 1:40,000
NAUTICAL MILES
STATUTE MILES
YARDS
LATITUDE
LONGITUDE
St M
15
11
Turnpike
Centerville
SWING BRIDGE
HOR CL 80 FT
VERT CL 4 FT
Pipeline Area
ALBEMARLE AND CHESAPEAKE CANAL
INTRACOASTAL WATERWAY
ROUTE 1 (see notes)
76° 10
36° 44'
42'
OVHD PWR CAB
AUTH CL 91 FT
MAGNETIC
VAR 10°45' W (2005)
ANNUAL INCREASE 1'
B

Great Bridge
Bridge 12
On hour:
6 A.M.–7 P.M.

Norfolk
Southern R.R.
Bridge 13.9
Usually open

15

Centerville
Turnpike
Bridge 15.2
On hour and
half-hour:
8:30 A.M.–4 P.M.
Closed:
6:30–8:30 A.M.,
4–6 P.M.

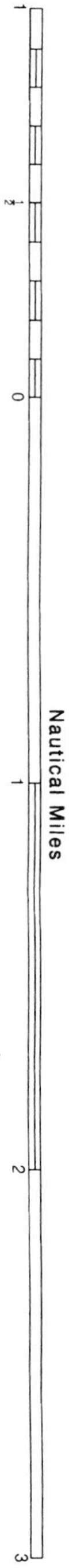
Nautical Miles

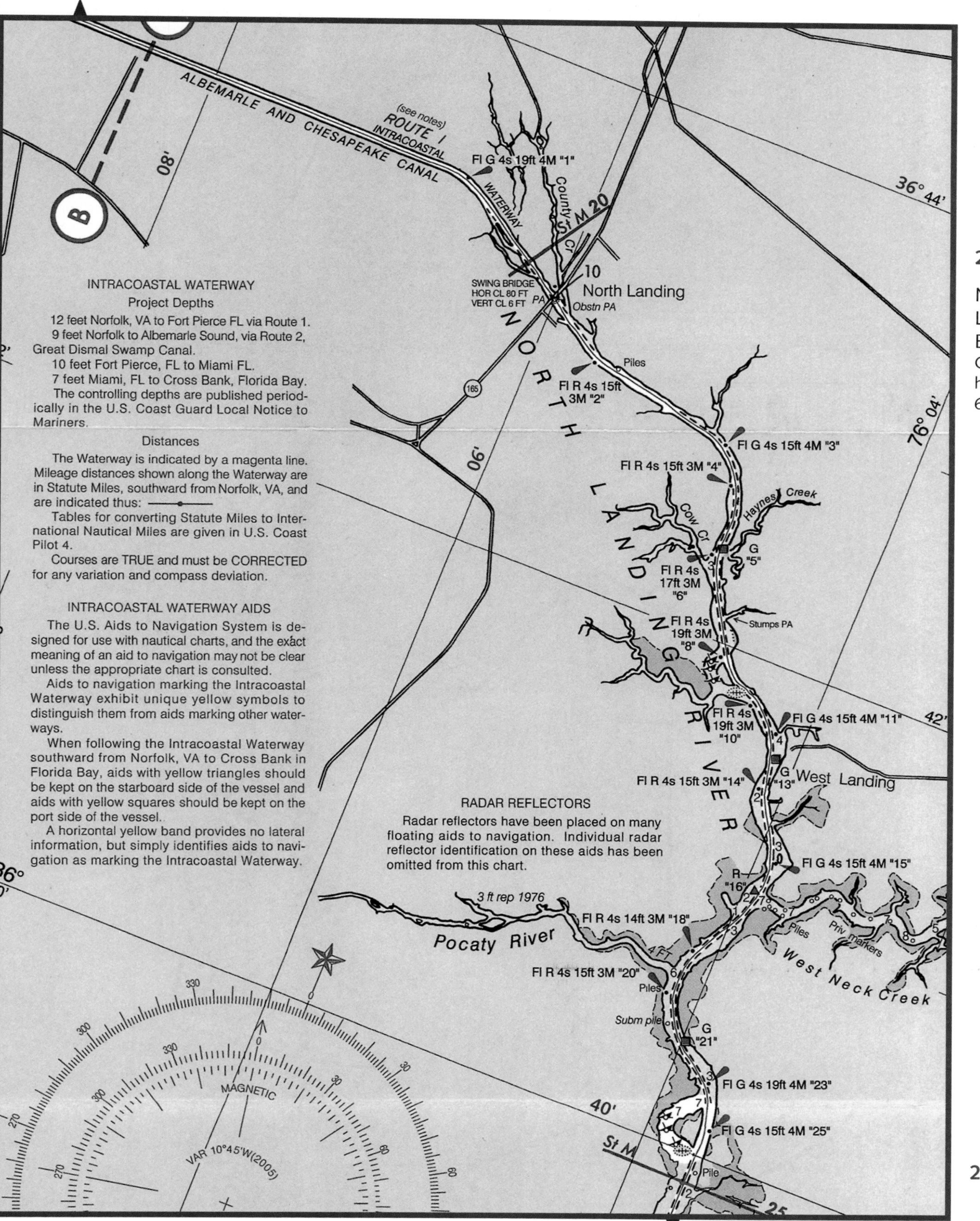

20

North Landing Bridge 20.2
On hour and half-hour:
6 A.M.–7 P.M.

25

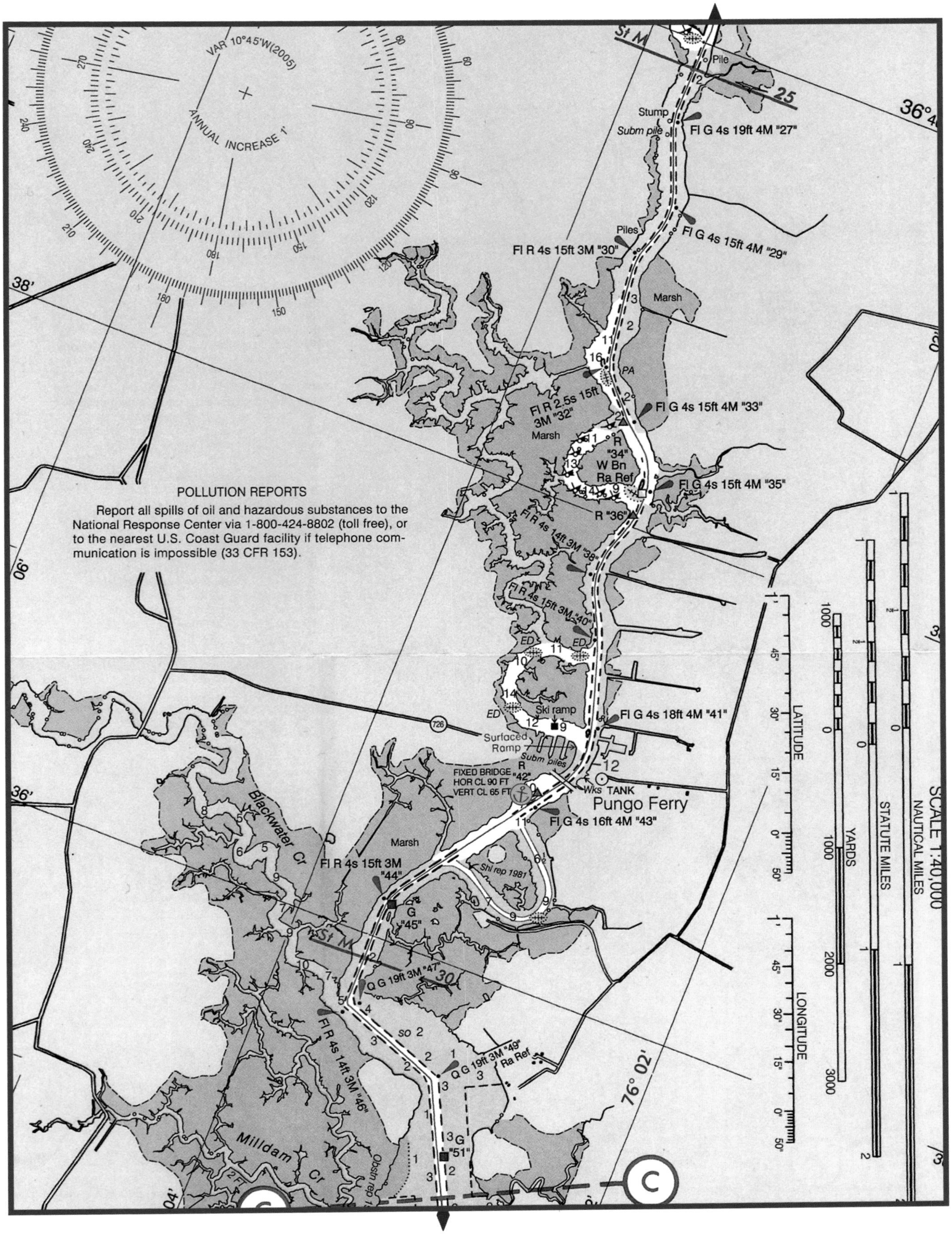

25

29

30

POLLUTION REPORTS

Report all spills of oil and hazardous substances to the National Response Center via 1-800-424-8802 (toll free), or to the nearest U.S. Coast Guard facility if telephone communication is impossible (33 CFR 153).

SCALE 1:40,000

NAUTICAL MILES

STATUTE MILES

YARDS

LATITUDE

LONGITUDE

Nautical Miles

VAR 10°45'W(2005)

ANNUAL INCREASE 1'

Pungo Ferry

FIXED BRIDGE "42" HOR CL 90 FT VERT CL 65 FT

Fl G 4s 19ft 4M "27"

Fl G 4s 15ft 4M "29"

Fl R 4s 15ft 3M "30"

Fl G 4s 15ft 4M "33"

Fl R 2.5s 15ft 3M "32"

R "34" W Bn Ra Ref

Fl G 4s 15ft 4M "35"

R "36"

Fl R 4s 14ft 3M "38"

Fl R 4s 15ft 3M "40"

Fl G 4s 18ft 4M "41"

Fl G 4s 16ft 4M "43"

Fl R 4s 15ft 3M "44"

G "45"

Q G 19ft 3M "47"

Q G 19ft 3M "49" Ra Ref

Fl R 4s 14ft 3M "46"

G "51"

Blackwater Cr

Milldam Cr

Marsh

Ski ramp

Surfaced Ramp

Subm piles

Shl rep 1981

Obstn rep

Stump

Subm pile

Piles

Pile

Wks TANK

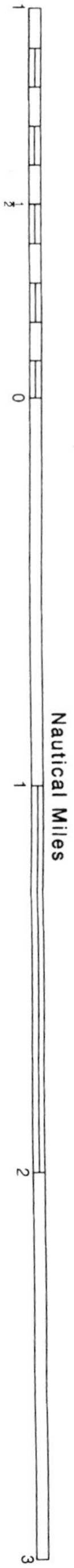

76° 02'

36° 38'

36° 36'

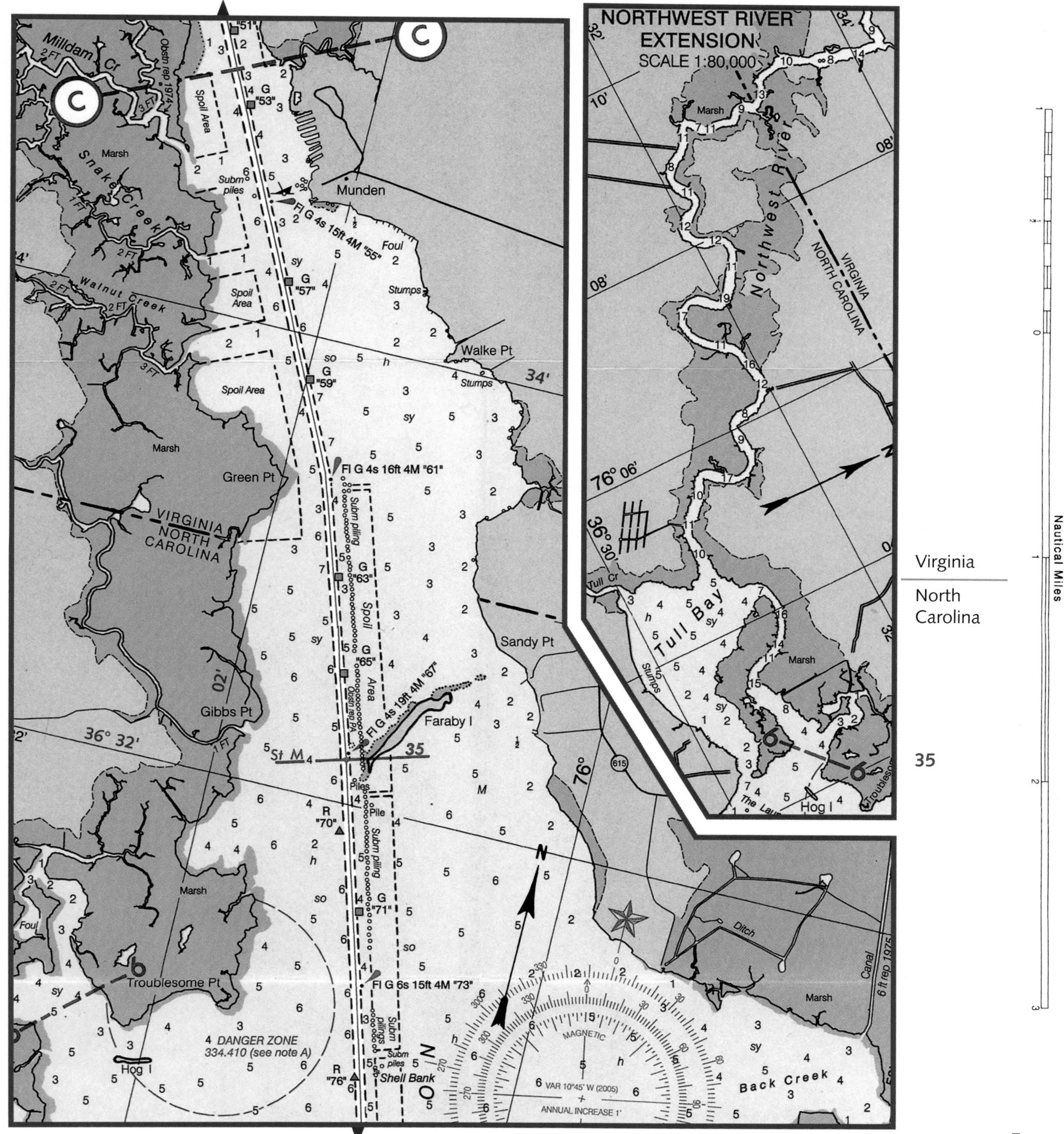

Virginia

North Carolina

35

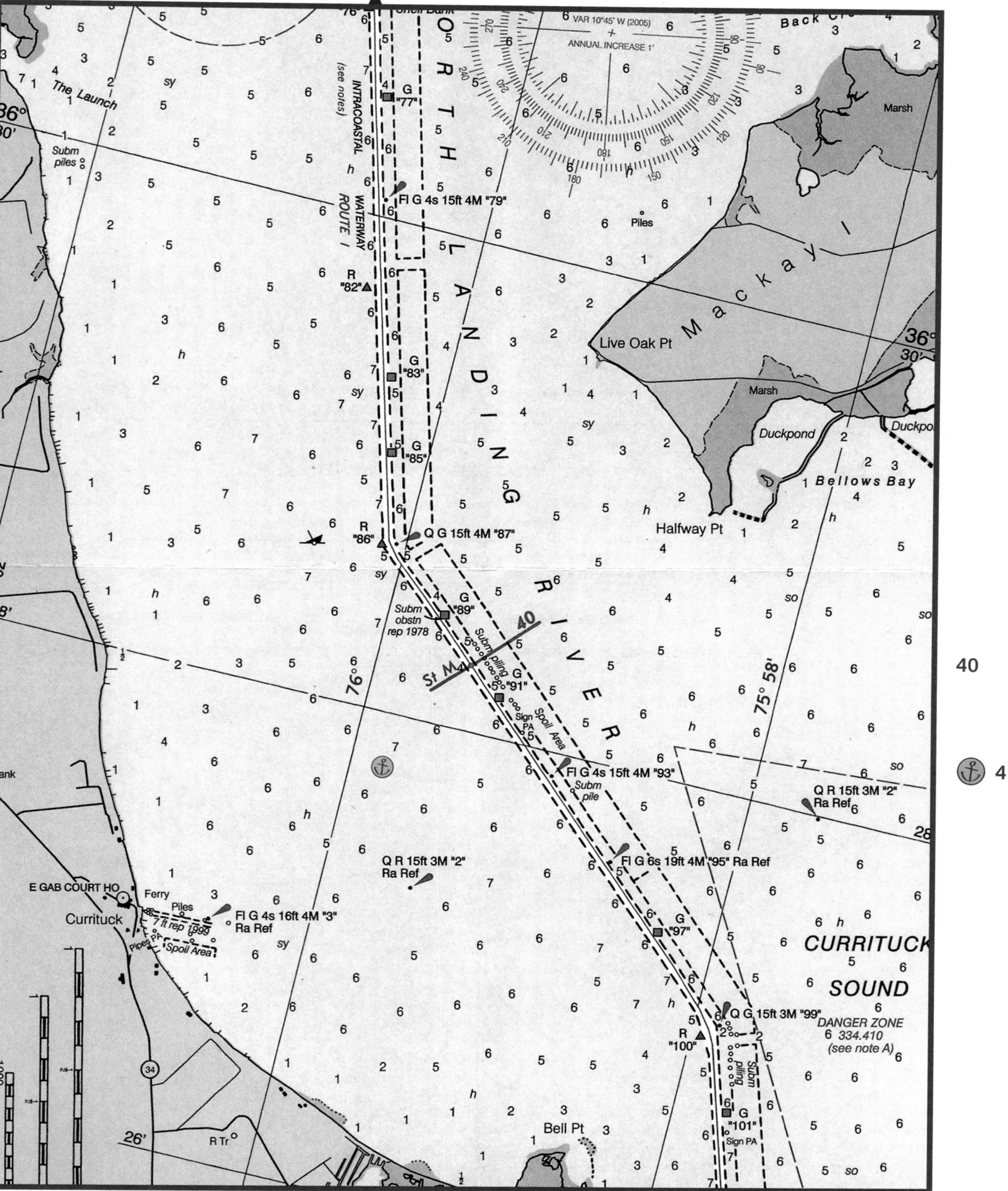

NORTH LANDING RIVER
INTRACOASTAL WATERWAY ROUTE I
(see notes)
CURRITUCK SOUND
Mackay I
Live Oak Pt
Marsh
Duckpond
Bellows Bay
Halfway Pt
Bell Pt
The Launch
Back Cr
Currituck
E GAB COURT HO
Ferry
Piles
Tank
Subm piles
Fl G 4s 15ft 4M "79"
R "82"
G "77"
G "83"
G "85"
R "86"
Q G 15ft 4M "87"
G "89"
Subm obstn rep 1978
Subm piling
G "91"
Sign PA
Spoil Area
Fl G 4s 15ft 4M "93"
Subm pile
Q R 15ft 3M "2" Ra Ref
Fl G 6s 19ft 4M "95" Ra Ref
Fl G 4s 16ft 4M "3" Ra Ref
7 ft rep 1999
Pipes PA
G "97"
Q G 15ft 3M "99"
DANGER ZONE 334.410 (see note A)
R "100"
G "101"
St M
VAR 10°45' W (2005)
ANNUAL INCREASE 1'
76°
75° 58'
36° 30'
28'
26'
Nautical Miles
40
41

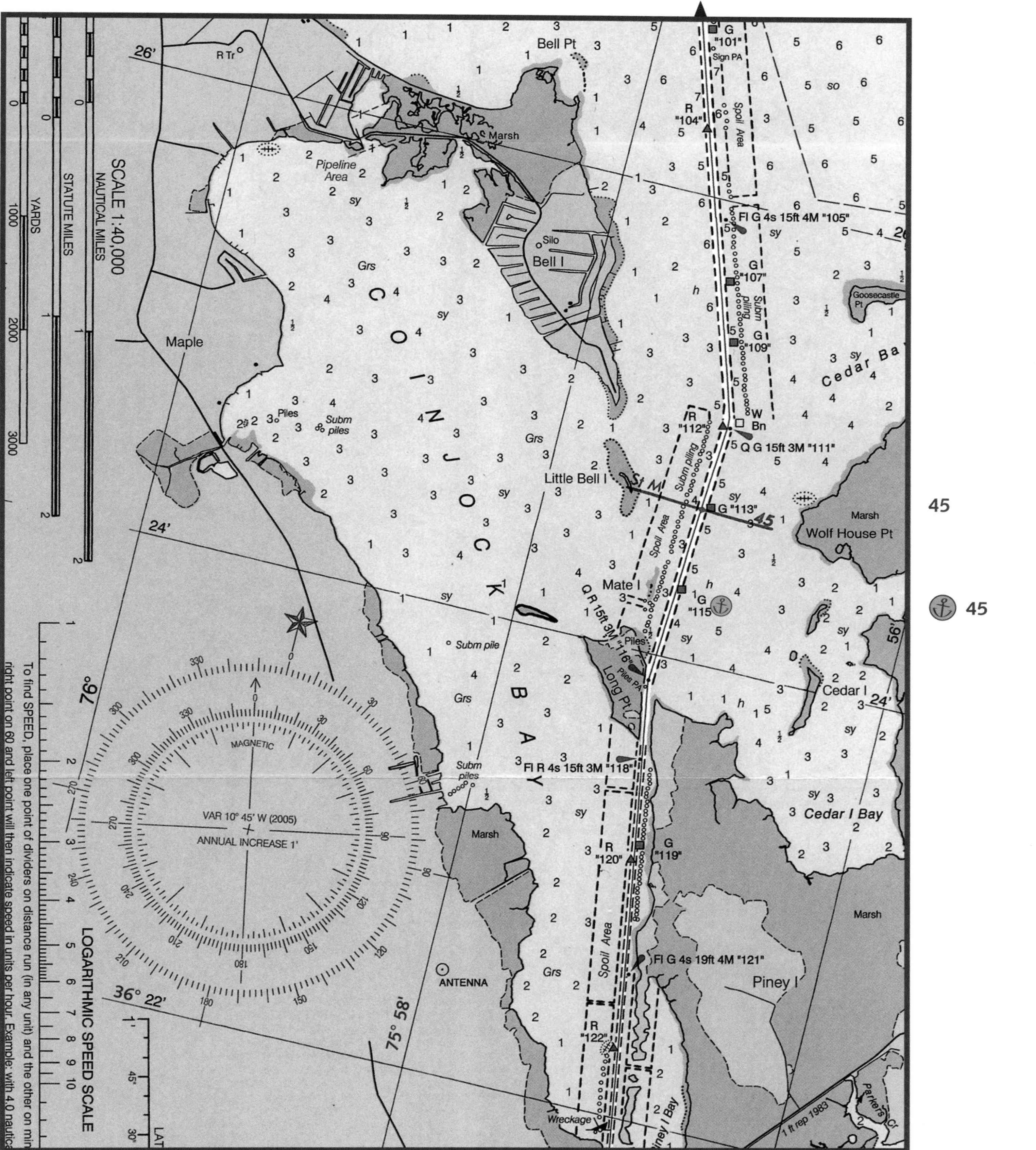

North Carolina

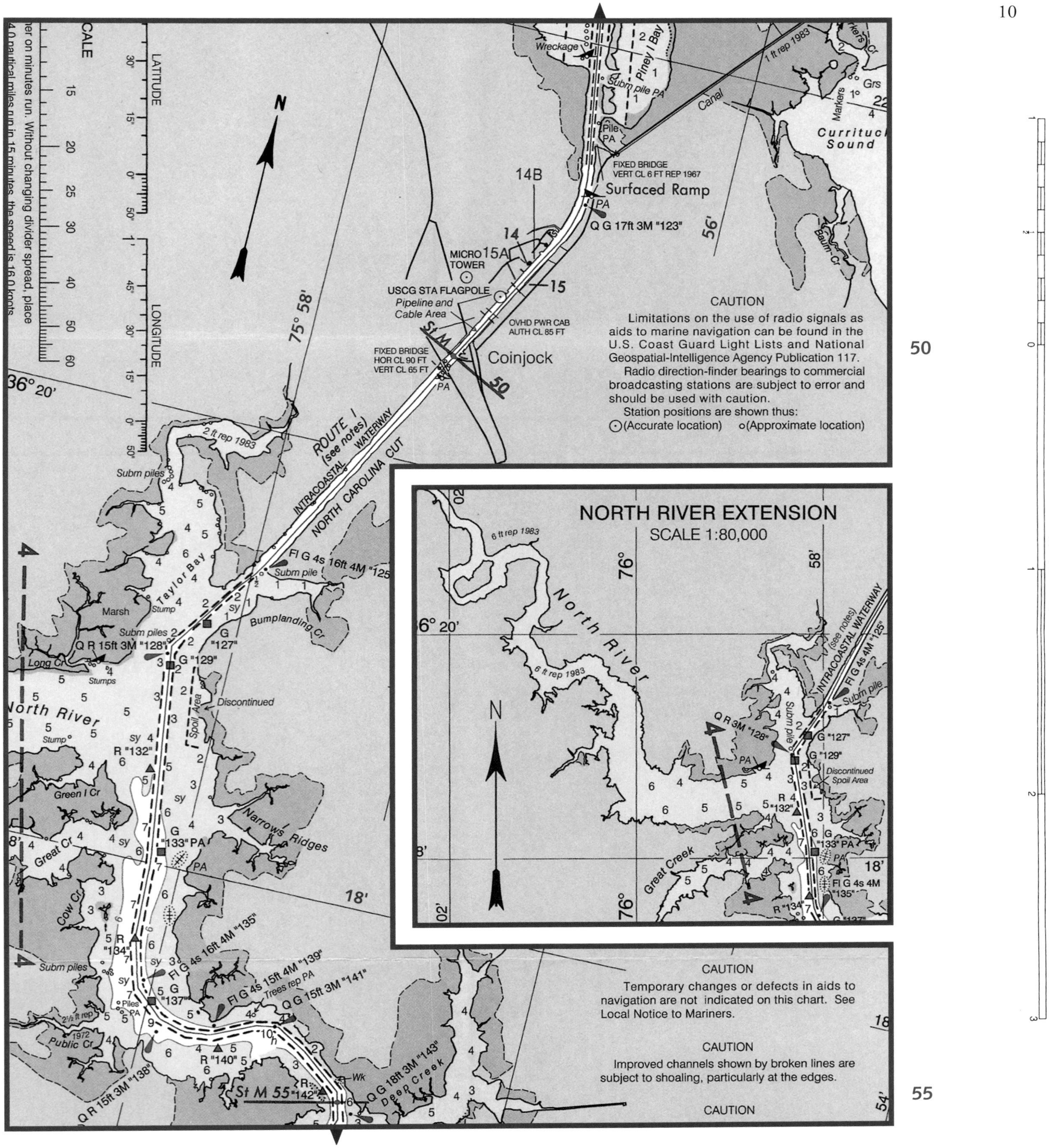

CAUTION

Limitations on the use of radio signals as aids to marine navigation can be found in the U.S. Coast Guard Light Lists and National Geospatial-Intelligence Agency Publication 117. Radio direction-finder bearings to commercial broadcasting stations are subject to error and should be used with caution.

Station positions are shown thus:

⊙(Accurate location) ∘(Approximate location)

NORTH RIVER EXTENSION

SCALE 1:80,000

CAUTION

Temporary changes or defects in aids to navigation are not indicated on this chart. See Local Notice to Mariners.

CAUTION

Improved channels shown by broken lines are subject to shoaling, particularly at the edges.

CAUTION

50

55

Nautical Miles

Coinjock

Currituck Sound

North River

Taylor Bay

Narrows Ridges

Bumplanding Cr

Great Cr

Cow Cr

Public Cr

Deep Creek

Long Cr

Green I Cr

Piney I Bay

Baum Cr

Great Creek

INTRACOASTAL WATERWAY

NORTH CAROLINA CUT

ROUTE 1 (see notes)

FIXED BRIDGE VERT CL 6 FT REP 1967

Surfaced Ramp

Q G 17ft 3M "123"

USCG STA FLAGPOLE

MICRO TOWER

Pipeline and Cable Area

OVHD PWR CAB AUTH CL 85 FT

FIXED BRIDGE HOR CL 90 FT VERT CL 65 FT

Fl G 4s 16ft 4M "125"

Q R 15ft 3M "128"

Fl G 4s 16ft 4M "135"

Fl G 4s 15ft 4M "139"

Q G 15ft 3M "141"

Q G 18ft 3M "143"

Q R 15ft 3M "138"

St M 55

Discontinued Spoil Area

LATITUDE

LONGITUDE

...er on minutes run. Without changing divider spread, place ... 4.0 nautical miles run in 15 minutes, the speed is 16.0 knots

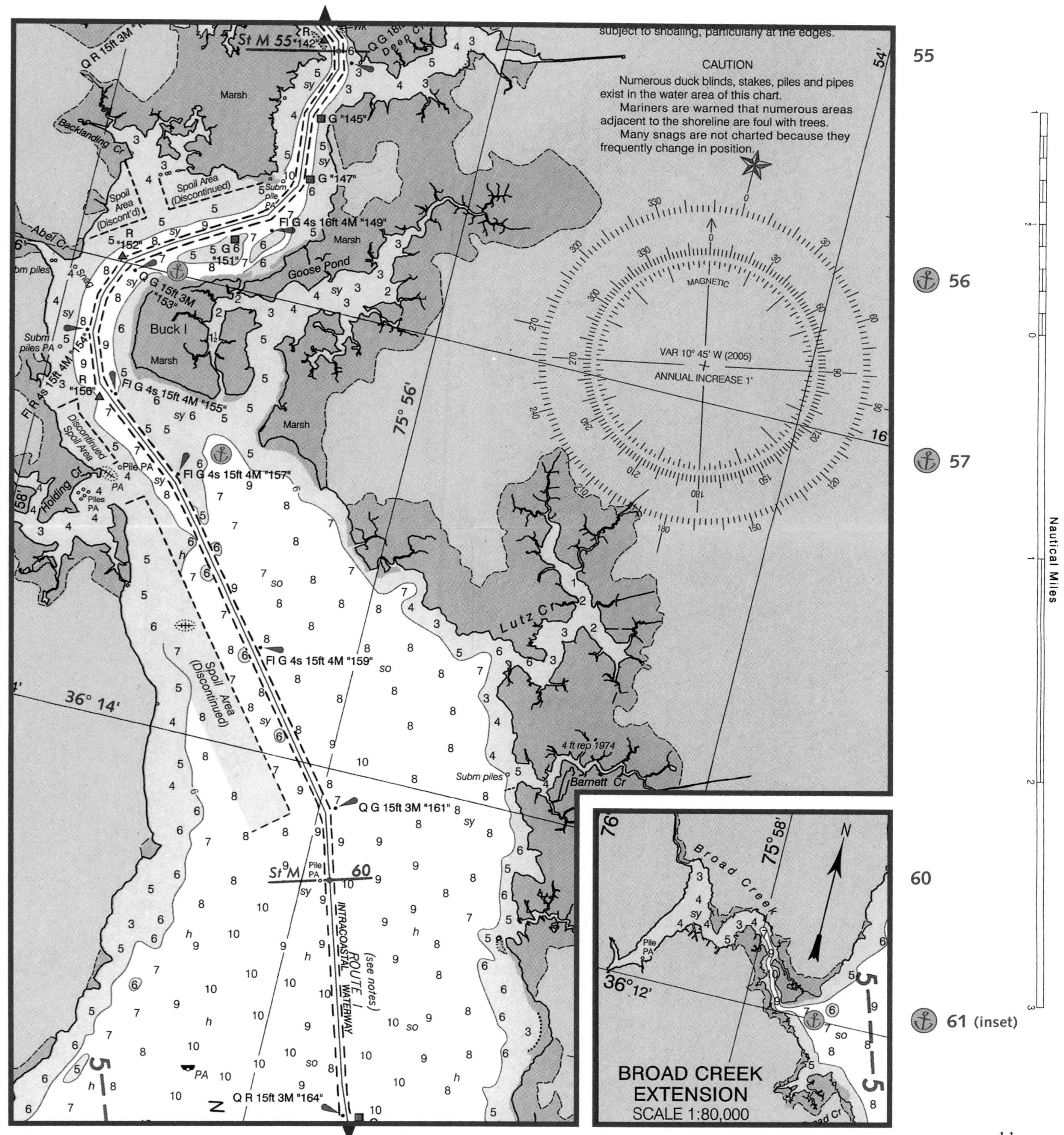
subject to shoaling, particularly at the edges.
CAUTION
Numerous duck blinds, stakes, piles and pipes exist in the water area of this chart.
Mariners are warned that numerous areas adjacent to the shoreline are foul with trees.
Many snags are not charted because they frequently change in position.
St M 55
"142"
Q G 18ft
Deep Cr
Q R 15ft 3M
Marsh
G "145"
Backlanding Cr
Spoil Area (Discontinued)
Spoil Area (Discont'd)
Subm pile PA
G "147"
Fl G 4s 16ft 4M "149"
Abel Cr
R "152"
G "151"
Goose Pond
Q G 15ft 3M "153"
Snag
Buck I
Subm piles PA
Fl R 4s 15ft 4M "154"
R "156"
Fl G 4s 15ft 4M "155"
Discontinued Spoil Area
Pile PA
Holding Cr
Piles PA
Fl G 4s 15ft 4M "157"
75° 56'
MAGNETIC
VAR 10° 45' W (2005)
ANNUAL INCREASE 1'
Lutz Cr
Fl G 4s 15ft 4M "159"
36° 14'
Spoil Area (Discontinued)
4 ft rep 1974
Subm piles
Barnett Cr
Q G 15ft 3M "161"
St M 60
INTRACOASTAL WATERWAY
ROUTE 1
(see notes)
Q R 15ft 3M "164"
54'
16'
58'
55
56
57
60
61 (inset)
Nautical Miles
Broad Creek
75°58'
76'
36°12'
BROAD CREEK EXTENSION
SCALE 1:80,000

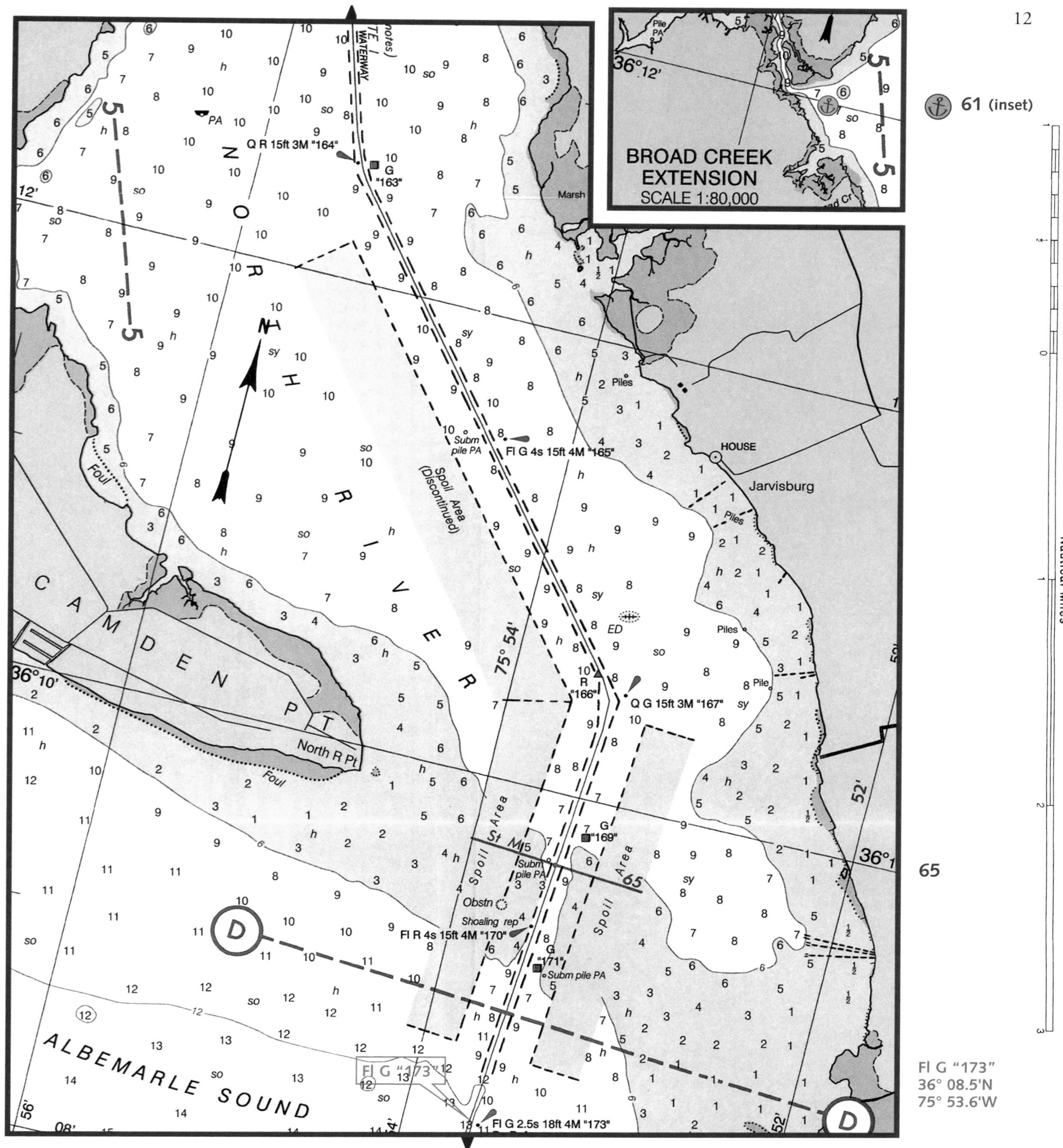
BROAD CREEK
EXTENSION
SCALE 1:80,000
61 (inset)
NORTH RIVER
CAMDEN PT
North R Pt
ALBEMARLE SOUND
Jarvisburg
HOUSE
Marsh
Spoil Area (Discontinued)
Spoil Area
Q R 15ft 3M "164"
G "163"
Fl G 4s 15ft 4M "165"
R "166"
Q G 15ft 3M "167"
G "169"
Fl R 4s 15ft 4M "170"
G "171"
Fl G 2.5s 18ft 4M "173"
Fl G "173"
Shoaling rep
Obstn
Subm pile PA
St M
75° 54'
36°10'
36°12'
52'
65
Nautical Miles
0
1
2
3
Fl G "173"
36° 08.5'N
75° 53.6'W

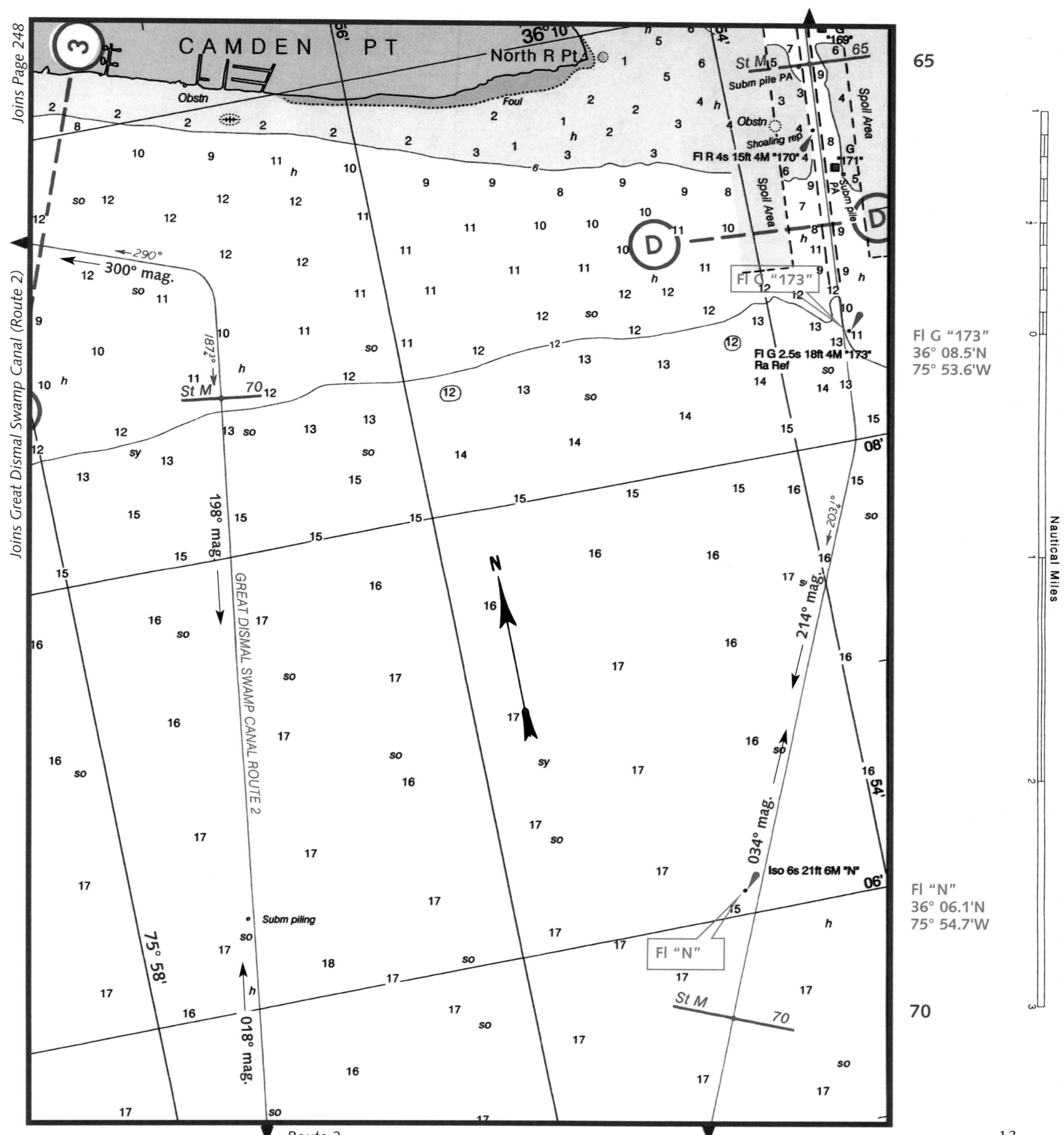
CAMDEN PT
North R Pt
Joins Page 248
Joins Great Dismal Swamp Canal (Route 2)
GREAT DISMAL SWAMP CANAL ROUTE 2
300° mag.
198° mag.
018° mag.
214° mag.
034° mag.
Spoil Area
Subm pile PA
Shoaling rep
Fl R 4s 15ft 4M "170" 4
Fl G 2.5s 18ft 4M "173"
Ra Ref
Iso 6s 21ft 6M "N"
Subm piling
Fl G "173"
Fl "N"
Fl G "173"
36° 08.5'N
75° 53.6'W
Fl "N"
36° 06.1'N
75° 54.7'W
75° 58'
Nautical Miles
Route 2

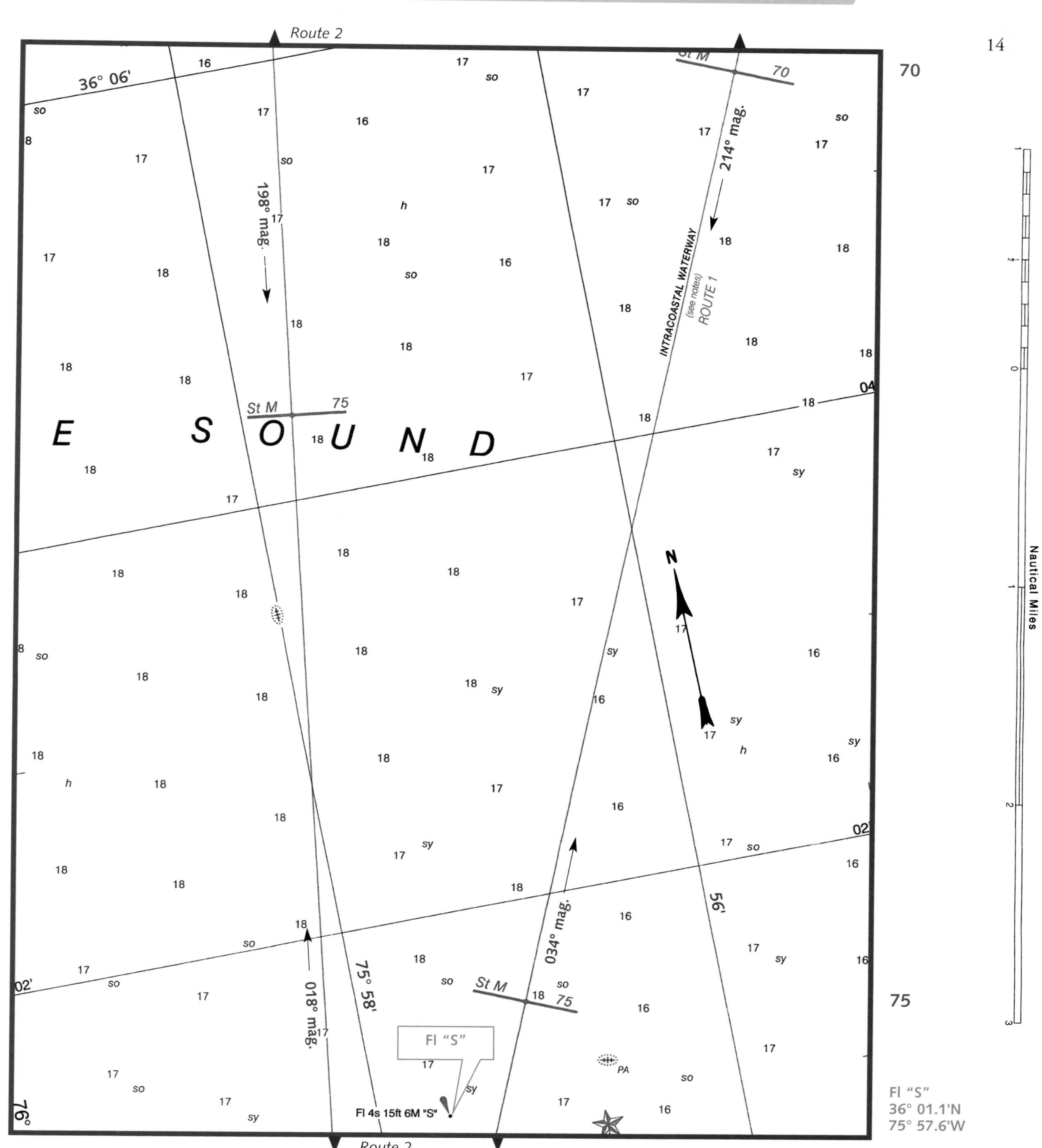
Route 2
36° 06'
198° mag.
214° mag.
INTRACOASTAL WATERWAY
(see notes)
ROUTE 1
St M 75
St M 70
E S O U N D
N
034° mag.
018° mag.
75° 58'
56'
St M 75
Fl "S"
Fl 4s 15ft 6M "S"
PA
76°
02'
04
70
75
Nautical Miles
Fl "S"
36° 01.1'N
75° 57.6'W

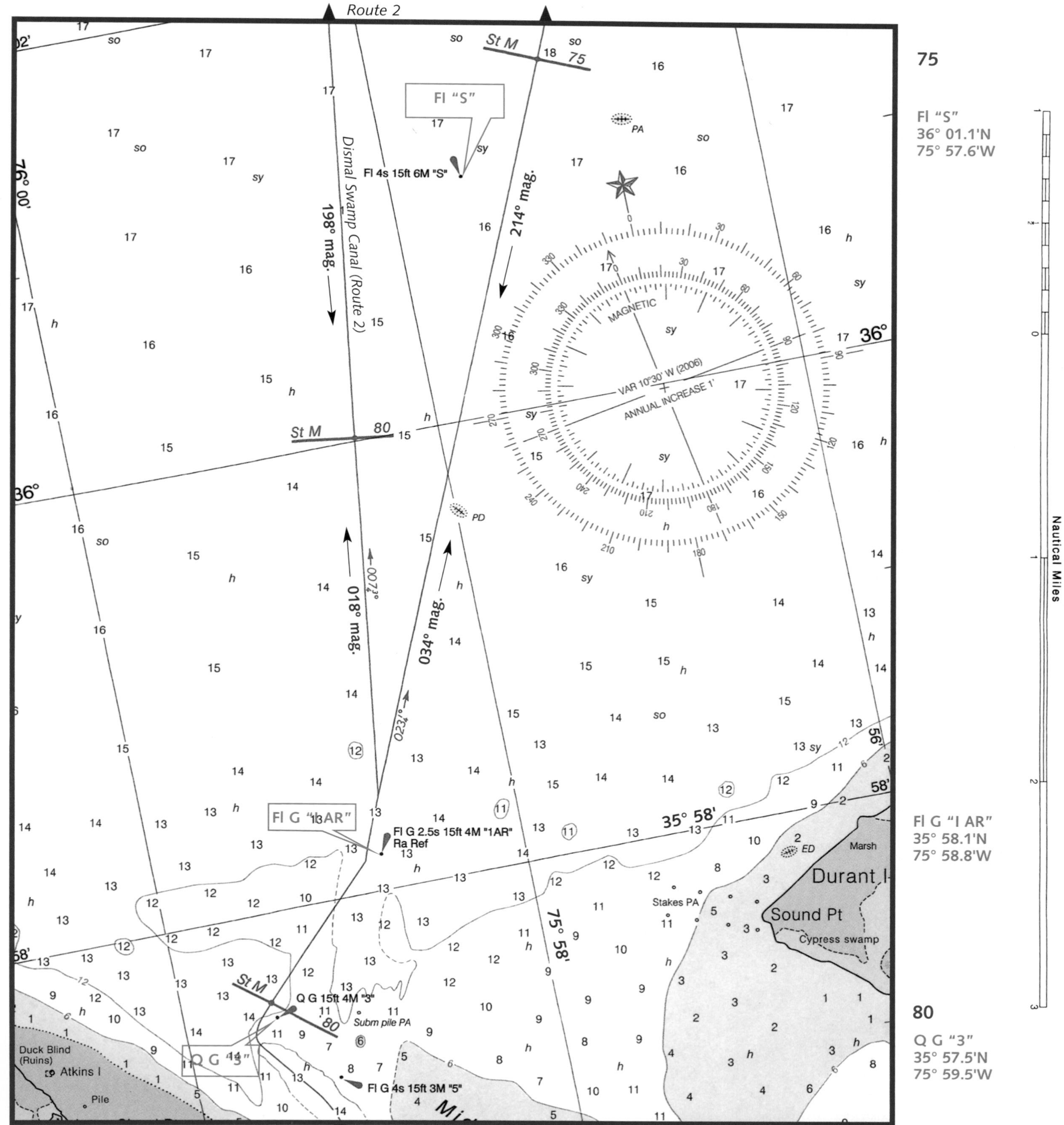
Route 2
Dismal Swamp Canal (Route 2)
St M 75
St M 80
Fl "S"
Fl 4s 15ft 6M "S"
198° mag.
214° mag.
018° mag.
034° mag.
007¾°
023¼°
MAGNETIC
VAR 10°30' W (2006)
ANNUAL INCREASE 1'
76° 00'
36°
35° 58'
75° 58'
Fl G "1AR"
Fl G 2.5s 15ft 4M "1AR"
Ra Ref
Q G 15ft 4M "3"
Q G "3"
Subm pile PA
Fl G 4s 15ft 3M "5"
Stakes PA
Durant I
Sound Pt
Marsh
Cypress swamp
Duck Blind (Ruins)
Atkins I
Pile
75
Fl "S"
36° 01.1'N
75° 57.6'W
Fl G "1 AR"
35° 58.1'N
75° 58.8'W
80
Q G "3"
35° 57.5'N
75° 59.5'W
Nautical Miles

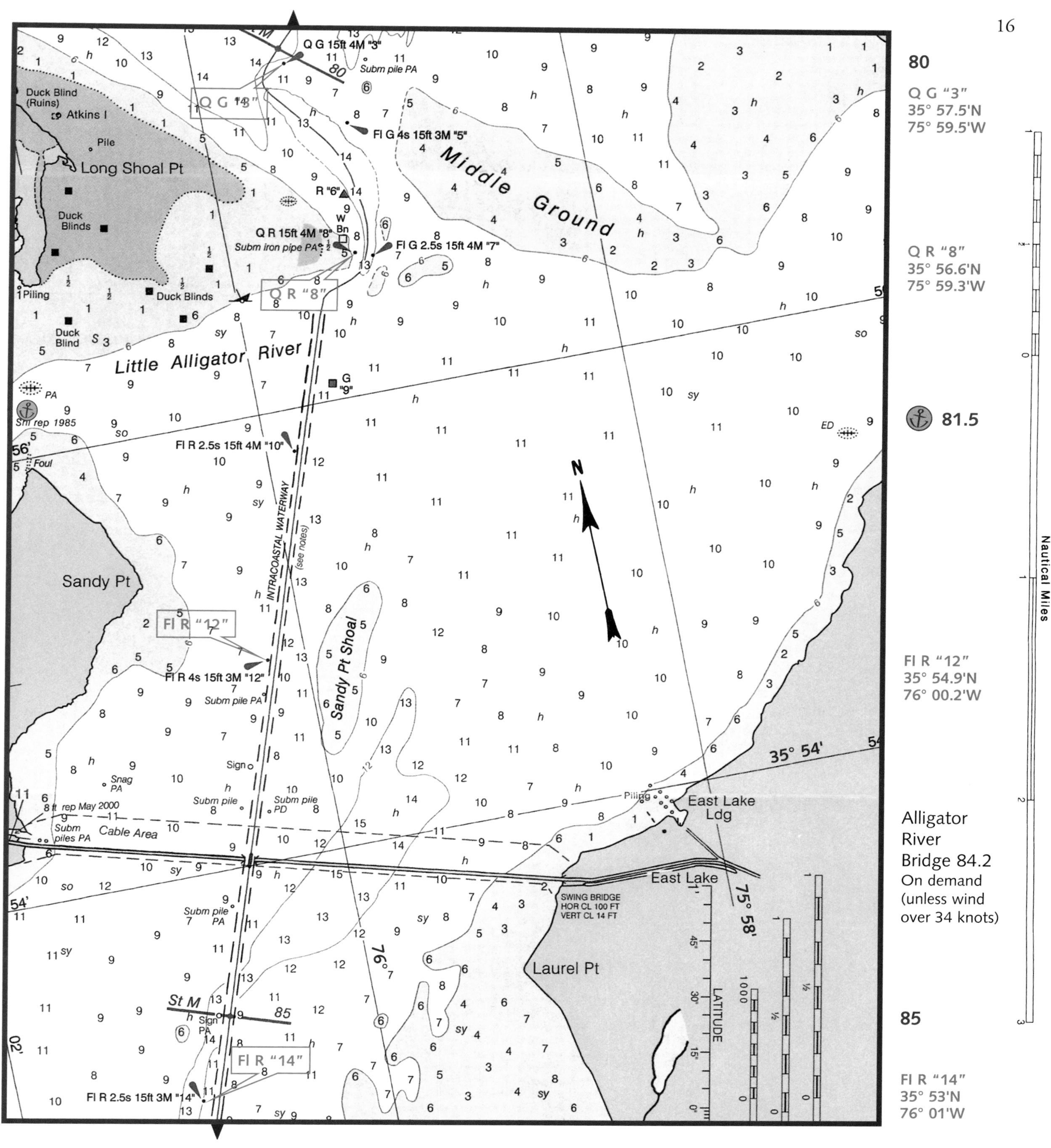

80

Q G "3"
35° 57.5'N
75° 59.5'W

Q R "8"
35° 56.6'N
75° 59.3'W

81.5

Fl R "12"
35° 54.9'N
76° 00.2'W

Alligator River Bridge 84.2
On demand (unless wind over 34 knots)

85

Fl R "14"
35° 53'N
76° 01'W

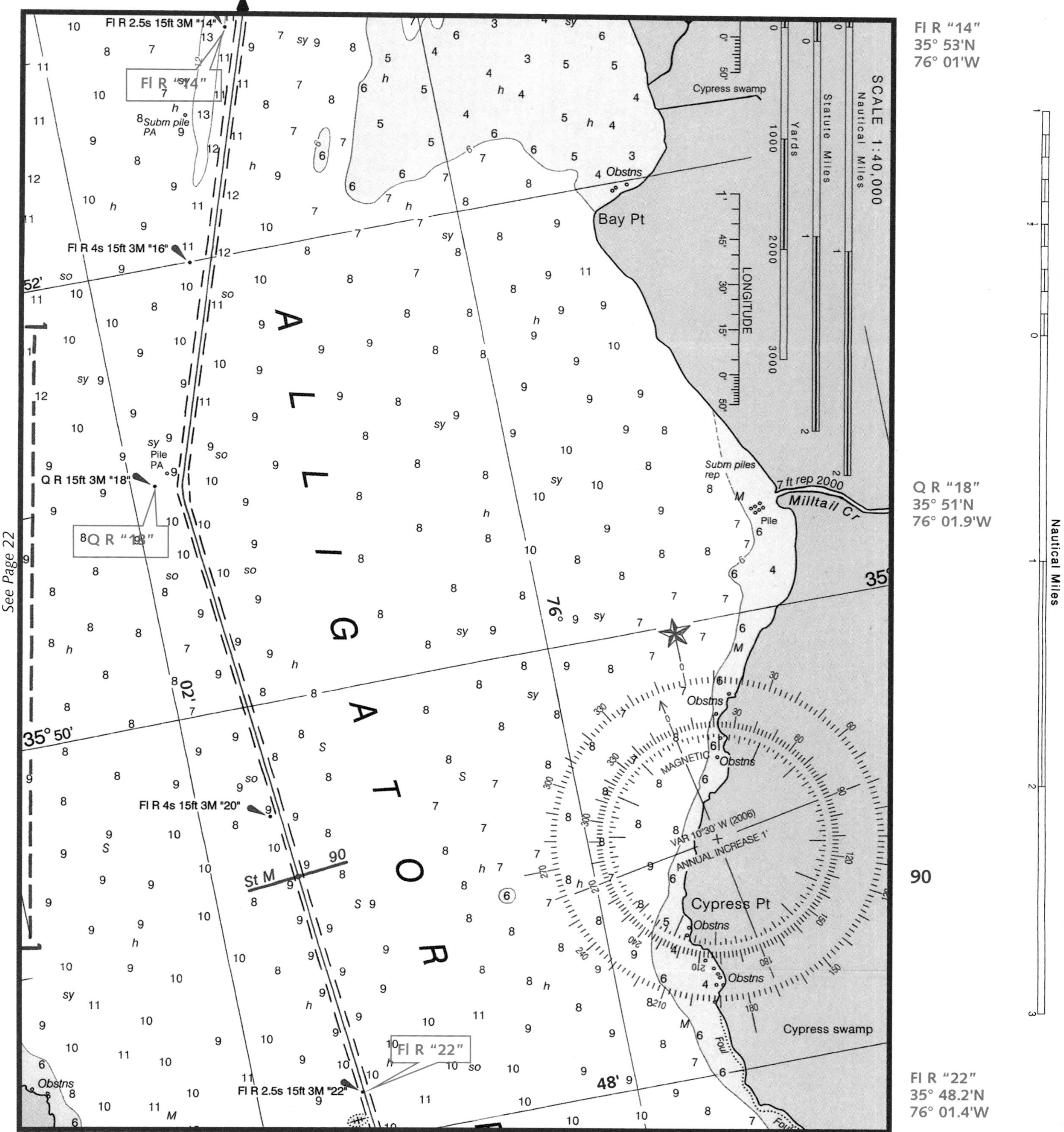

Fl R 2.5s 15ft 3M "14"
Fl R "14"
Subm pile
PA
Cypress swamp
SCALE 1:40,000
Nautical Miles
Statute Miles
Yards
LONGITUDE
Obstns
Bay Pt
Fl R 4s 15ft 3M "16"
52'
ALLIGATOR
Pile
PA
Q R 15ft 3M "18"
Q R "18"
See Page 22
Subm piles
rep
7 ft rep 2000
Milltail Cr
Pile
35°
76°
02'
35° 50'
MAGNETIC
VAR 10°30' W (2006)
ANNUAL INCREASE 1'
Fl R 4s 15ft 3M "20"
St M
90
Cypress Pt
Cypress swamp
Fl R "22"
Fl R 2.5s 15ft 3M "22"
48'
Foul
Fl R "14"
35° 53'N
76° 01'W
Q R "18"
35° 51'N
76° 01.9'W
90
Fl R "22"
35° 48.2'N
76° 01.4'W
Nautical Miles

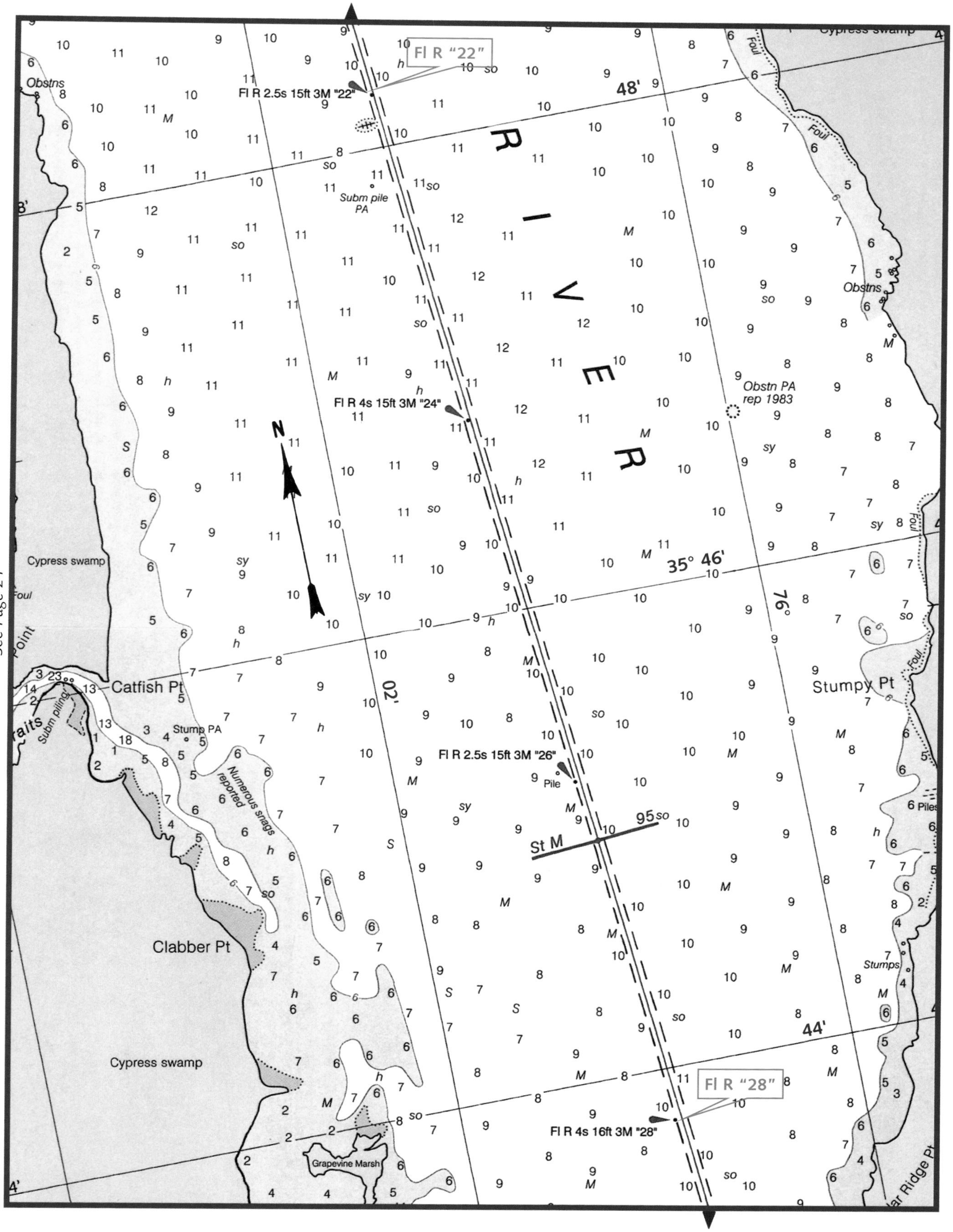

See Page 24

Fl R "22"
35° 48.2'N
76° 01.4'W

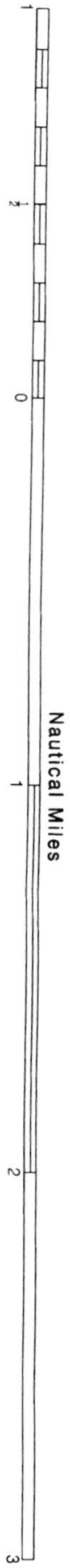

95

Fl R "28"
35° 43.8'N
76° 00.9'W

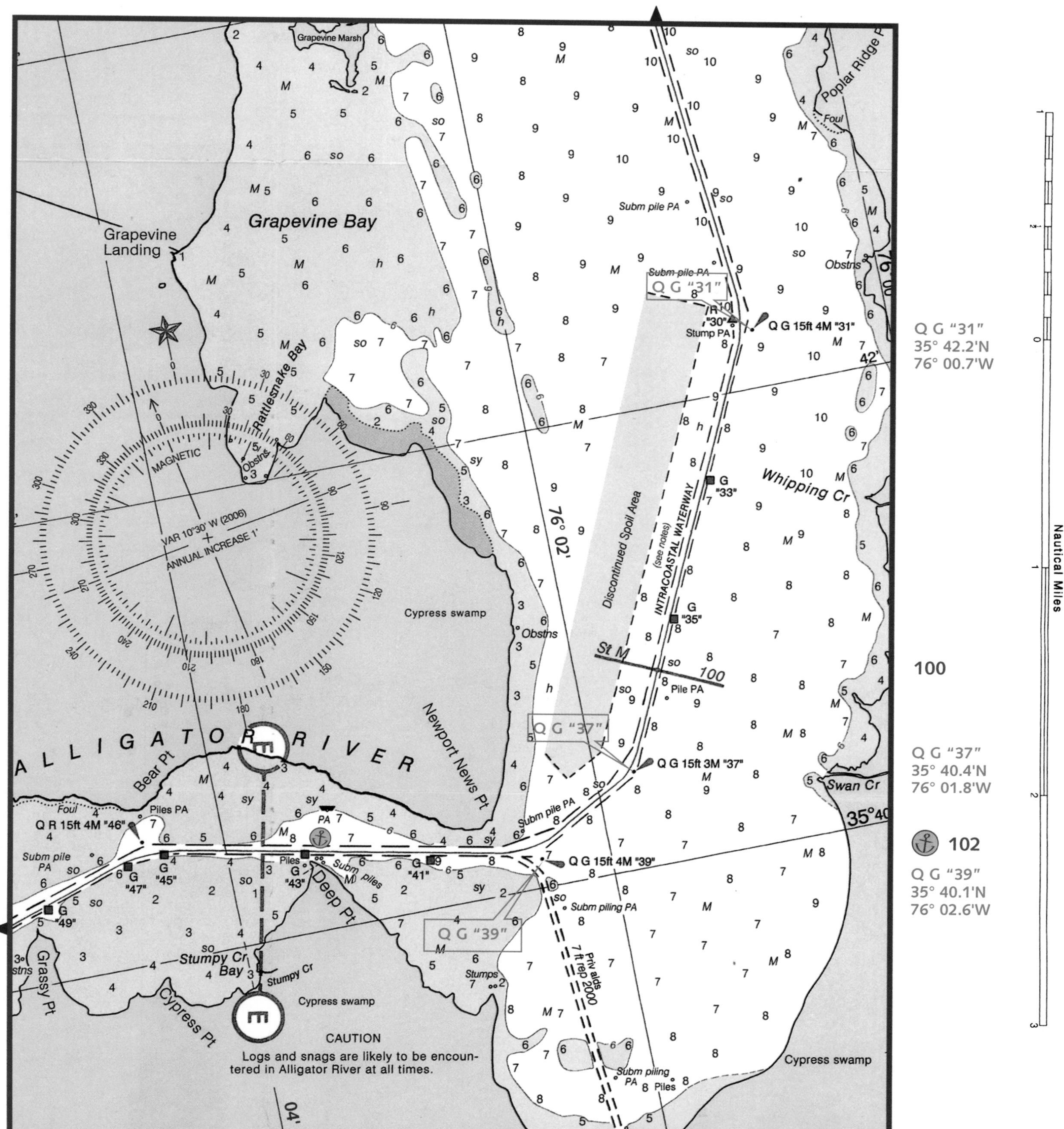

Grapevine Marsh
Grapevine Bay
Grapevine Landing
Rattlesnake Bay
Poplar Ridge Pt
Whipping Cr
Swan Cr
ALLIGATOR RIVER
Bear Pt
Newport News Pt
Deep Pt
Stumpy Cr Bay
Stumpy Cr
Grassy Pt
Cypress Pt
Cypress swamp
Discontinued Spoil Area
INTRACOASTAL WATERWAY
(see notes)
MAGNETIC
VAR 10°30' W (2006)
ANNUAL INCREASE 1'
76° 02'
76° 00'
35° 40'
42'
04'
Subm pile PA
Stump PA
Obstns
Piles PA
Subm piling PA
Pile PA
Priv aids
7 ft rep 2000
Q G 15ft 4M "31"
Q G 15ft 3M "37"
Q G 15ft 4M "39"
Q R 15ft 4M "46"
Q G "31"
Q G "37"
Q G "39"
CAUTION
Logs and snags are likely to be encountered in Alligator River at all times.
Q G "31"
35° 42.2'N
76° 00.7'W
100
Q G "37"
35° 40.4'N
76° 01.8'W
102
Q G "39"
35° 40.1'N
76° 02.6'W
Nautical Miles

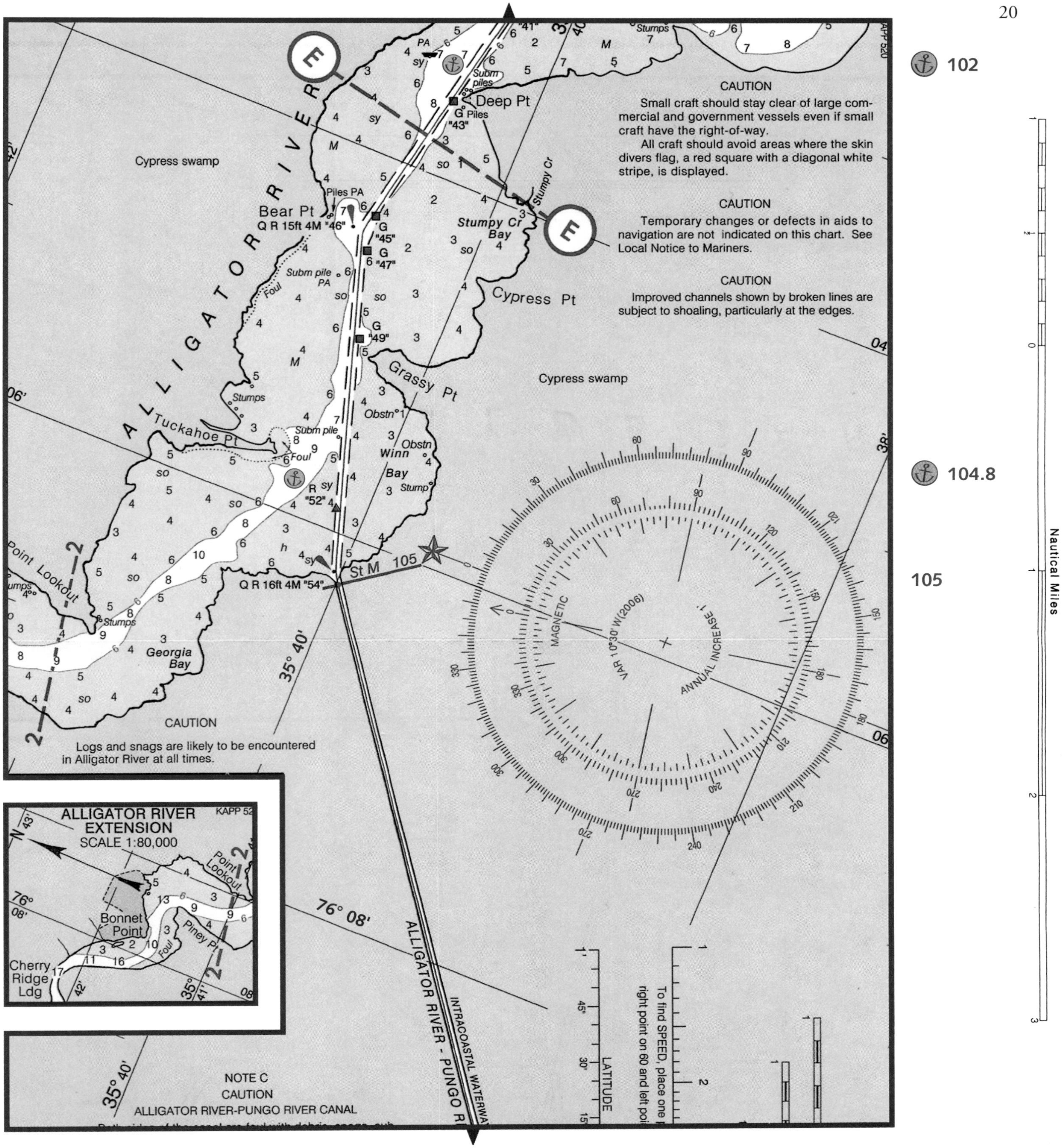

ALLIGATOR RIVER

CAUTION

Small craft should stay clear of large commercial and government vessels even if small craft have the right-of-way.

All craft should avoid areas where the skin divers flag, a red square with a diagonal white stripe, is displayed.

CAUTION

Temporary changes or defects in aids to navigation are not indicated on this chart. See Local Notice to Mariners.

CAUTION

Improved channels shown by broken lines are subject to shoaling, particularly at the edges.

CAUTION

Logs and snags are likely to be encountered in Alligator River at all times.

Deep Pt

Bear Pt

Q R 15ft 4M "46"

Stumpy Cr Bay

Cypress Pt

Grassy Pt

Tuckahoe Pt

Winn Bay

Georgia Bay

Point Lookout

Cypress swamp

St M 105

Q R 16ft 4M "54"

VAR 10°30' W(2006)

ANNUAL INCREASE 1'

MAGNETIC

76° 08'

35° 40'

ALLIGATOR RIVER - PUNGO RIVER

INTRACOASTAL WATERWAY

ALLIGATOR RIVER EXTENSION

SCALE 1:80,000

Bonnet Point

Cherry Ridge Ldg

Piney Pt

NOTE C

CAUTION

ALLIGATOR RIVER-PUNGO RIVER CANAL

LATITUDE

To find SPEED, place one right point on 60 and left poi

102

104.8

105

Nautical Miles

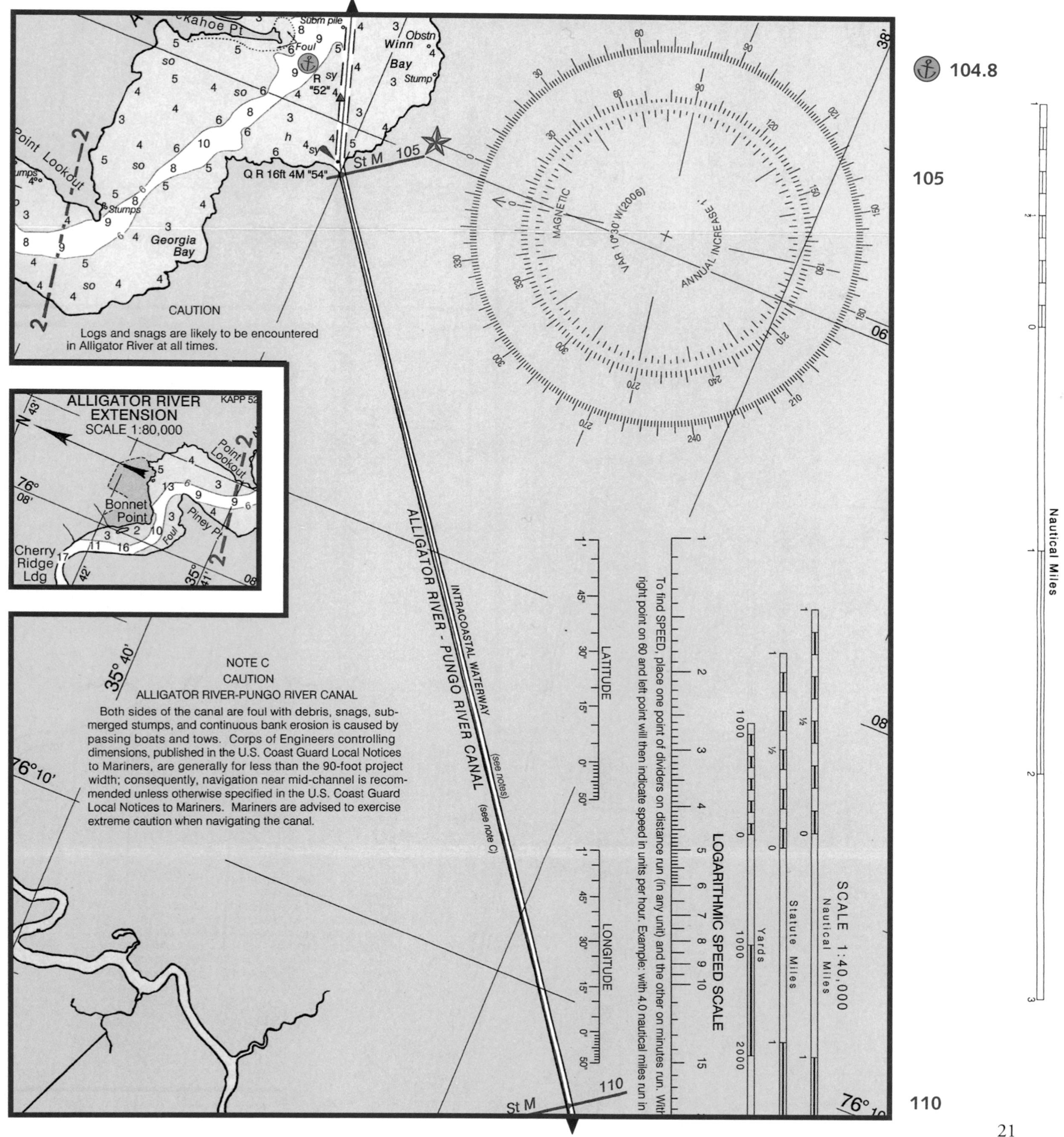

CAUTION
Logs and snags are likely to be encountered in Alligator River at all times.
ALLIGATOR RIVER EXTENSION
SCALE 1:80,000
NOTE C
CAUTION
ALLIGATOR RIVER-PUNGO RIVER CANAL
Both sides of the canal are foul with debris, snags, submerged stumps, and continuous bank erosion is caused by passing boats and tows. Corps of Engineers controlling dimensions, published in the U.S. Coast Guard Local Notices to Mariners, are generally for less than the 90-foot project width; consequently, navigation near mid-channel is recommended unless otherwise specified in the U.S. Coast Guard Local Notices to Mariners. Mariners are advised to exercise extreme caution when navigating the canal.
ALLIGATOR RIVER - PUNGO RIVER CANAL
INTRACOASTAL WATERWAY
Q R 16ft 4M "54"
St M 105
St M 110
Georgia Bay
Winn Bay
Point Lookout
LOGARITHMIC SPEED SCALE
To find SPEED, place one point of dividers on distance run (in any unit) and the other on minutes run. With right point on 60 and left point will then indicate speed in units per hour. Example: with 4.0 nautical miles run in
SCALE 1:40,000
Nautical Miles
Statute Miles
Yards
LATITUDE
LONGITUDE
VAR 10°30'W(2006)
ANNUAL INCREASE 1'
MAGNETIC
Nautical Miles

104.8

105

110

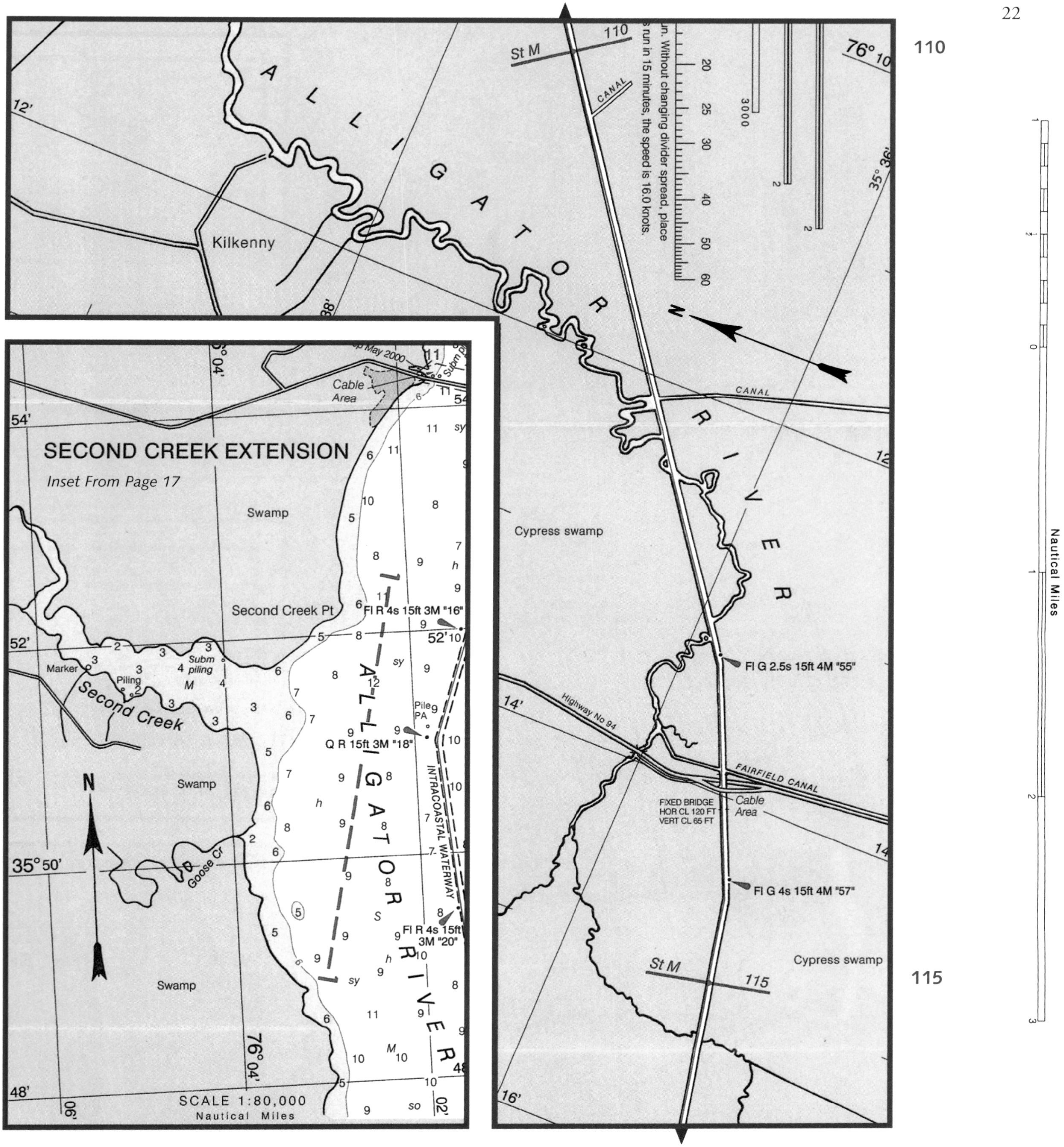

ALLIGATOR RIVER
Kilkenny
St M 110
St M 115
CANAL
76° 10'
35° 36'
12'
14'
16'
Cypress swamp
Highway No 94
FAIRFIELD CANAL
FIXED BRIDGE
HOR CL 120 FT
VERT CL 65 FT
Cable Area
Fl G 2.5s 15ft 4M "55"
Fl G 4s 15ft 4M "57"
N
un. Without changing divider spread, place
s run in 15 minutes, the speed is 16.0 knots.
20 25 30 40 50 60
3000
110
115
Nautical Miles
SECOND CREEK EXTENSION
Inset From Page 17
Swamp
Second Creek Pt
Second Creek
Goose Cr
Marker
Piling
Subm piling
Pile PA
Cable Area
Fl R 4s 15ft 3M "16"
Q R 15ft 3M "18"
Fl R 4s 15ft 3M "20"
INTRACOASTAL WATERWAY
35° 50'
52'
54'
48'
76° 04'
SCALE 1:80,000
Nautical Miles

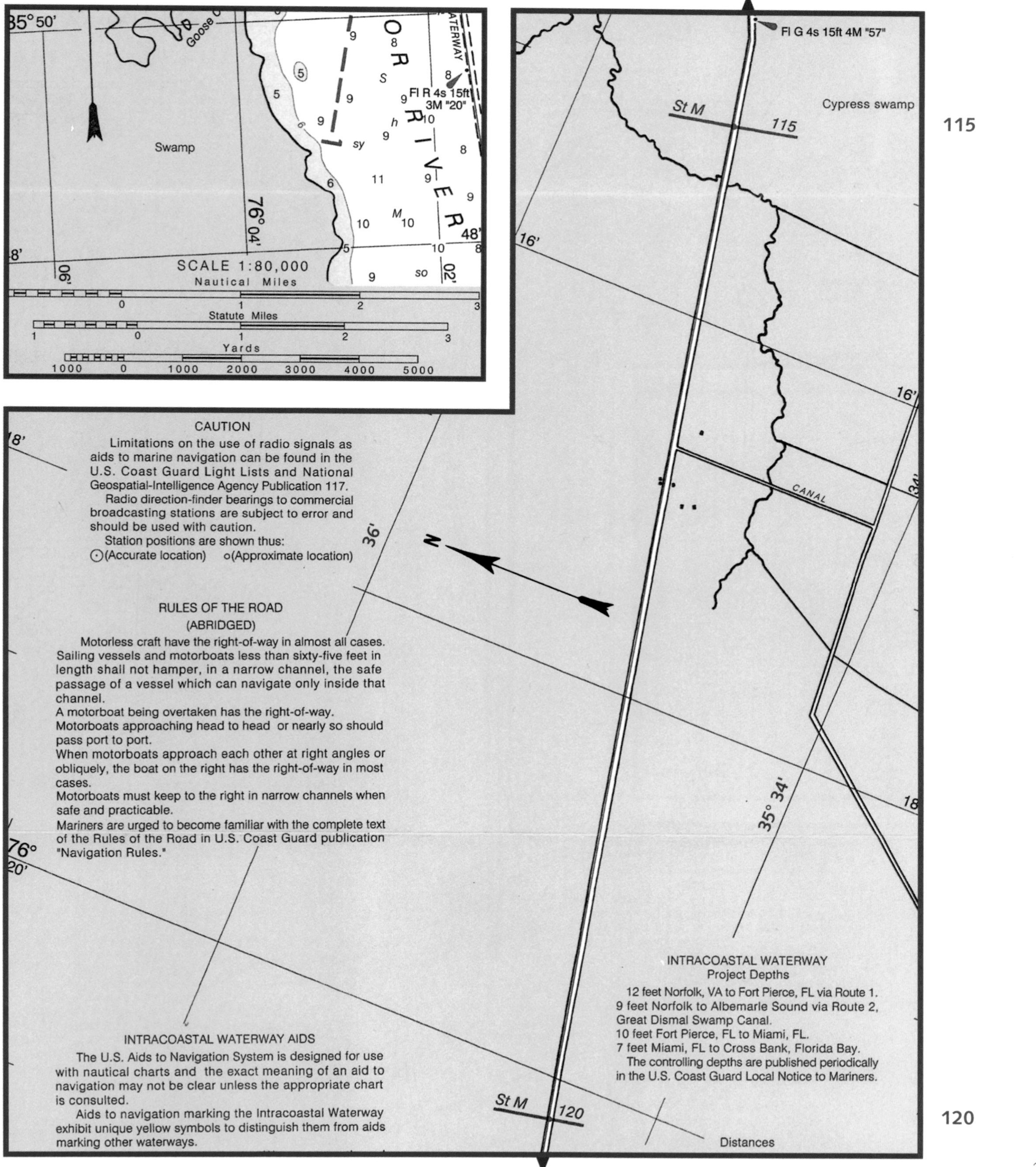
35°50'
Goose
Swamp
76°04'
48'
02'
SCALE 1:80,000
Nautical Miles
Statute Miles
Yards
Fl R 4s 15ft 3M "20"
Fl G 4s 15ft 4M "57"
Cypress swamp
St M 115
16'
CANAL
36'
N
35° 34'
18
76°
20'
St M 120
115
120
Nautical Miles
Distances
CAUTION
Limitations on the use of radio signals as aids to marine navigation can be found in the U.S. Coast Guard Light Lists and National Geospatial-Intelligence Agency Publication 117.
Radio direction-finder bearings to commercial broadcasting stations are subject to error and should be used with caution.
Station positions are shown thus:
⊙(Accurate location) o(Approximate location)
RULES OF THE ROAD
(ABRIDGED)
Motorless craft have the right-of-way in almost all cases.
Sailing vessels and motorboats less than sixty-five feet in length shall not hamper, in a narrow channel, the safe passage of a vessel which can navigate only inside that channel.
A motorboat being overtaken has the right-of-way.
Motorboats approaching head to head or nearly so should pass port to port.
When motorboats approach each other at right angles or obliquely, the boat on the right has the right-of-way in most cases.
Motorboats must keep to the right in narrow channels when safe and practicable.
Mariners are urged to become familiar with the complete text of the Rules of the Road in U.S. Coast Guard publication "Navigation Rules."
INTRACOASTAL WATERWAY
Project Depths
12 feet Norfolk, VA to Fort Pierce, FL via Route 1.
9 feet Norfolk to Albemarle Sound via Route 2, Great Dismal Swamp Canal.
10 feet Fort Pierce, FL to Miami, FL.
7 feet Miami, FL to Cross Bank, Florida Bay.
The controlling depths are published periodically in the U.S. Coast Guard Local Notice to Mariners.
INTRACOASTAL WATERWAY AIDS
The U.S. Aids to Navigation System is designed for use with nautical charts and the exact meaning of an aid to navigation may not be clear unless the appropriate chart is consulted.
Aids to navigation marking the Intracoastal Waterway exhibit unique yellow symbols to distinguish them from aids marking other waterways.

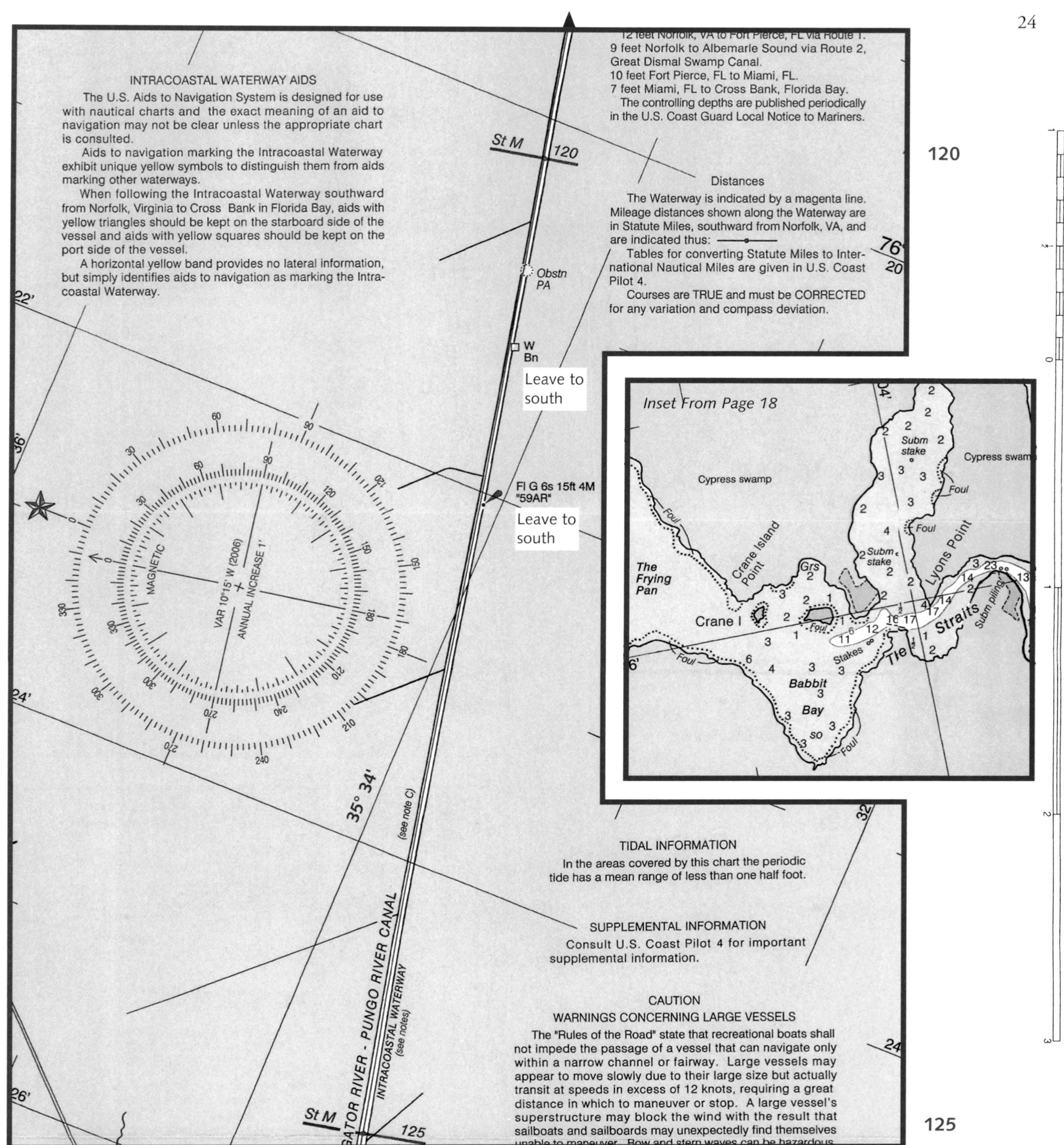
12 feet Norfolk, VA to Fort Pierce, FL via Route 1.
9 feet Norfolk to Albemarle Sound via Route 2, Great Dismal Swamp Canal.
10 feet Fort Pierce, FL to Miami, FL.
7 feet Miami, FL to Cross Bank, Florida Bay.
The controlling depths are published periodically in the U.S. Coast Guard Local Notice to Mariners.
INTRACOASTAL WATERWAY AIDS
The U.S. Aids to Navigation System is designed for use with nautical charts and the exact meaning of an aid to navigation may not be clear unless the appropriate chart is consulted.
Aids to navigation marking the Intracoastal Waterway exhibit unique yellow symbols to distinguish them from aids marking other waterways.
When following the Intracoastal Waterway southward from Norfolk, Virginia to Cross Bank in Florida Bay, aids with yellow triangles should be kept on the starboard side of the vessel and aids with yellow squares should be kept on the port side of the vessel.
A horizontal yellow band provides no lateral information, but simply identifies aids to navigation as marking the Intracoastal Waterway.
Distances
The Waterway is indicated by a magenta line. Mileage distances shown along the Waterway are in Statute Miles, southward from Norfolk, VA, and are indicated thus:
Tables for converting Statute Miles to International Nautical Miles are given in U.S. Coast Pilot 4.
Courses are TRUE and must be CORRECTED for any variation and compass deviation.
St M
120
Obstn
PA
W
Bn
Leave to south
Fl G 6s 15ft 4M
"59AR"
Leave to south
MAGNETIC
VAR 10°15' W (2006)
ANNUAL INCREASE 1'
35° 34'
(see note C)
GATOR RIVER - PUNGO RIVER CANAL
INTRACOASTAL WATERWAY
(see notes)
St M
125
Inset From Page 18
Cypress swamp
The Frying Pan
Crane Island Point
Crane I
Grs
Foul
Lyons Point
Subm stake
The Straits
Subm piling
Stakes
Babbit
Bay
TIDAL INFORMATION
In the areas covered by this chart the periodic tide has a mean range of less than one half foot.
SUPPLEMENTAL INFORMATION
Consult U.S. Coast Pilot 4 for important supplemental information.
CAUTION
WARNINGS CONCERNING LARGE VESSELS
The "Rules of the Road" state that recreational boats shall not impede the passage of a vessel that can navigate only within a narrow channel or fairway. Large vessels may appear to move slowly due to their large size but actually transit at speeds in excess of 12 knots, requiring a great distance in which to maneuver or stop. A large vessel's superstructure may block the wind with the result that sailboats and sailboards may unexpectedly find themselves
120
125
Nautical Miles

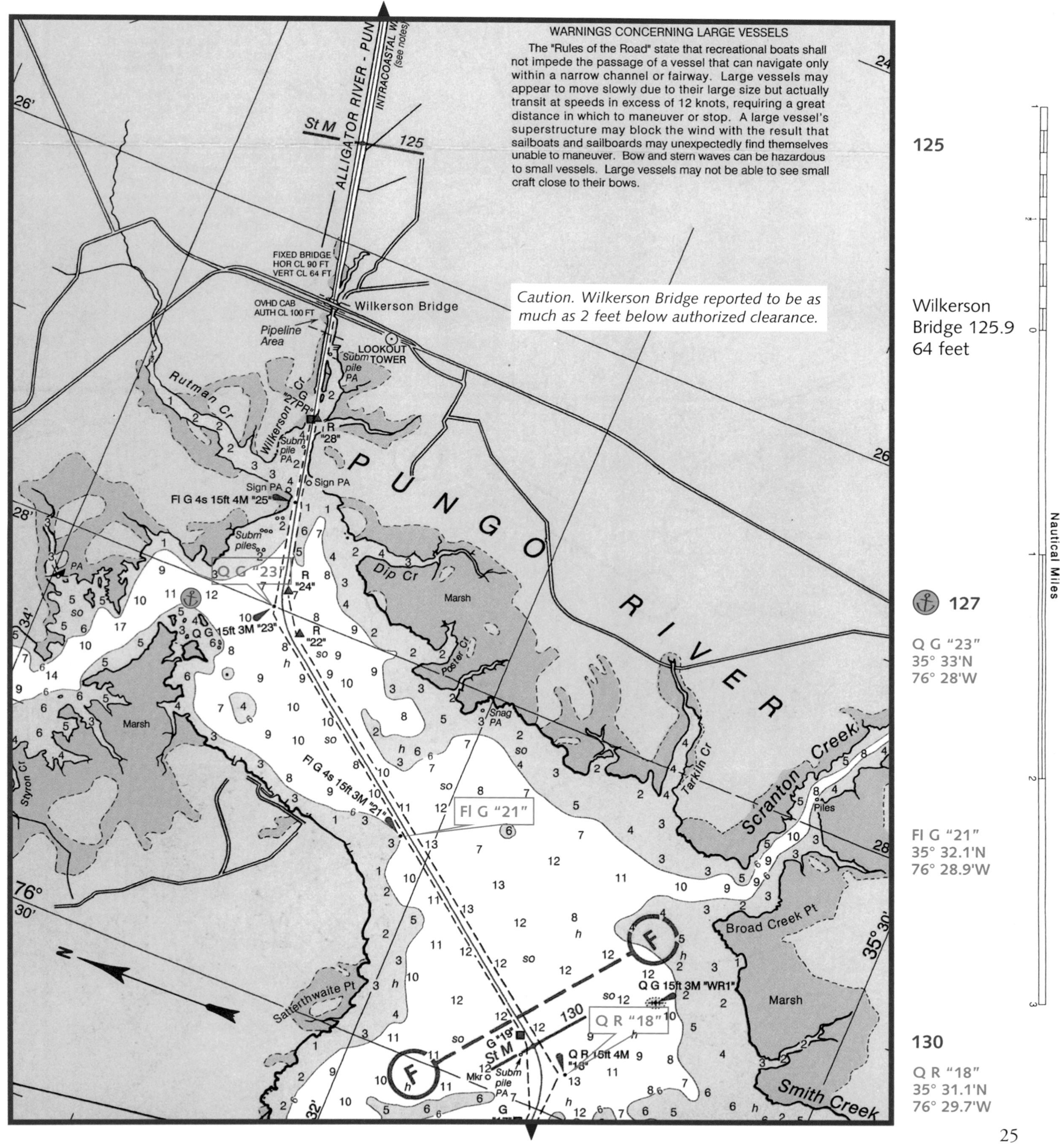
WARNINGS CONCERNING LARGE VESSELS
The "Rules of the Road" state that recreational boats shall not impede the passage of a vessel that can navigate only within a narrow channel or fairway. Large vessels may appear to move slowly due to their large size but actually transit at speeds in excess of 12 knots, requiring a great distance in which to maneuver or stop. A large vessel's superstructure may block the wind with the result that sailboats and sailboards may unexpectedly find themselves unable to maneuver. Bow and stern waves can be hazardous to small vessels. Large vessels may not be able to see small craft close to their bows.
Caution. Wilkerson Bridge reported to be as much as 2 feet below authorized clearance.
ALLIGATOR RIVER - PUN
INTRACOASTAL W
(see notes)
St M
125
FIXED BRIDGE
HOR CL 90 FT
VERT CL 64 FT
OVHD CAB
AUTH CL 100 FT
Wilkerson Bridge
Pipeline Area
LOOKOUT TOWER
Rutman Cr
Wilkerson Cr
PUNGO RIVER
Dip Cr
Marsh
Poster Cr
Tarkiln Cr
Scranton Creek
Broad Creek Pt
Smith Creek
Satterthwaite Pt
Styron Cr
Fl G 4s 15ft 4M "25"
Q G 15ft 3M "23"
Fl G 4s 15ft 3M "21"
Q G 15ft 3M "WR1"
Q R 15ft 4M "18"
Q G "23"
Fl G "21"
Q R "18"
130
125
Wilkerson Bridge 125.9 64 feet
127
Q G "23" 35° 33'N 76° 28'W
Fl G "21" 35° 32.1'N 76° 28.9'W
130
Q R "18" 35° 31.1'N 76° 29.7'W
Nautical Miles

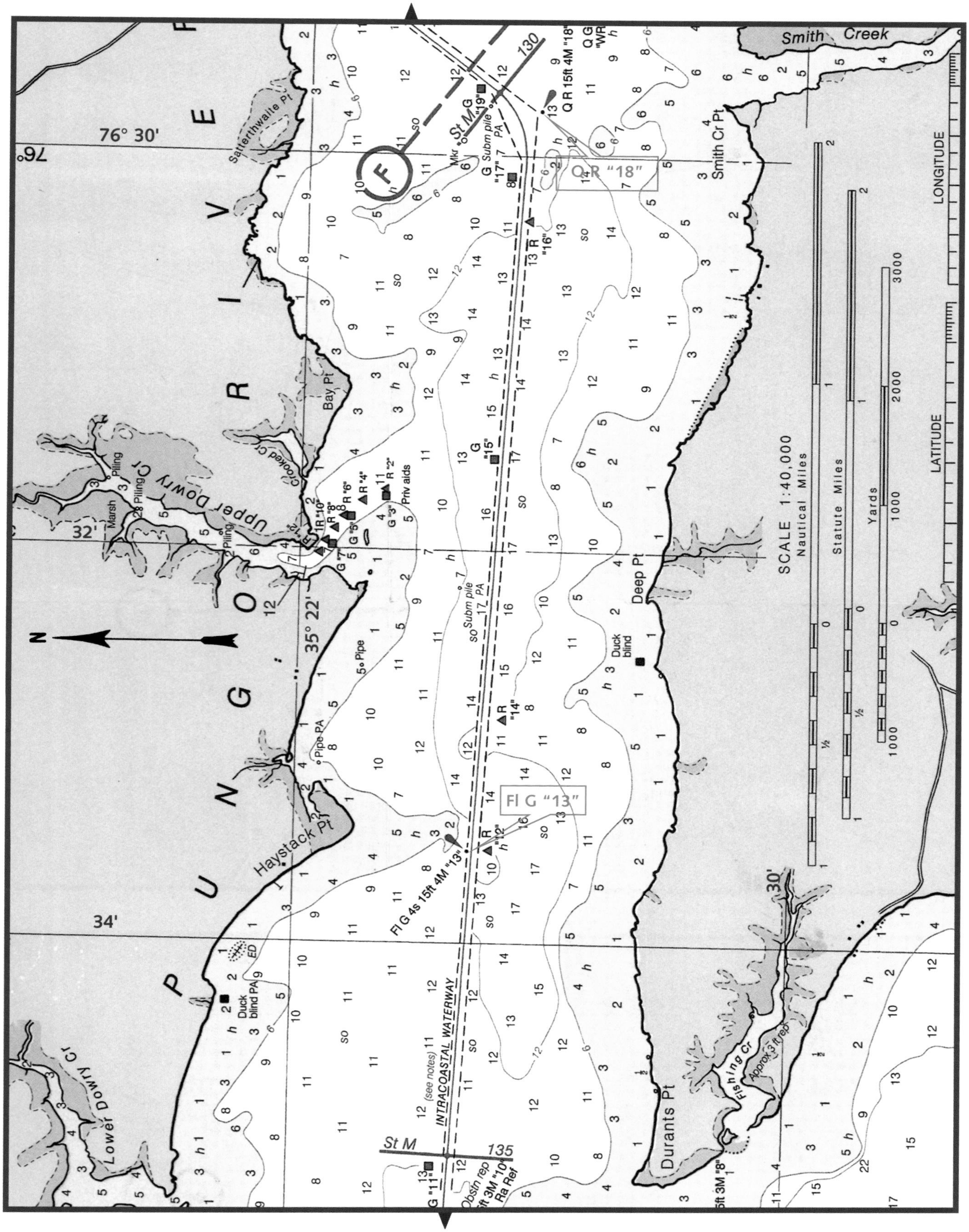
PUNGO RIVER
Upper Dowry Cr
Lower Dowry Cr
Crooked Cr
Haystack Pt
Bay Pt
Satterthwaite Pt
Durants Pt
Deep Pt
Smith Cr Pt
Smith Creek
Fishing Cr
INTRACOASTAL WATERWAY
(see notes)
Fl G 4s 15ft 4M "13"
Q R 15ft 4M "18"
Fl G "13"
Q R "18"
Duck blind
Duck blind PA
Pipe PA
Pipe
Subm pile 17 PA
Subm pile 7 PA
Priv aids
Marsh
Piling
St M
130
135
35° 22'
76° 30'
76°
34'
32'
30'
SCALE 1:40,000
Nautical Miles
Statute Miles
Yards
LATITUDE
LONGITUDE

130

Q R "18"
35° 31.1'N
76° 29.7'W

Fl G "13"
35° 31.3'N
76° 33.6'W

135

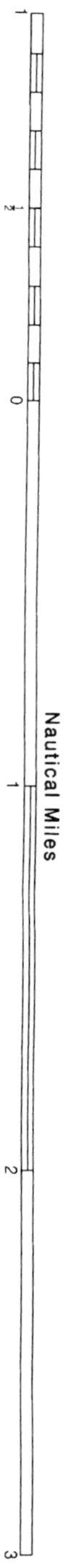
Nautical Miles

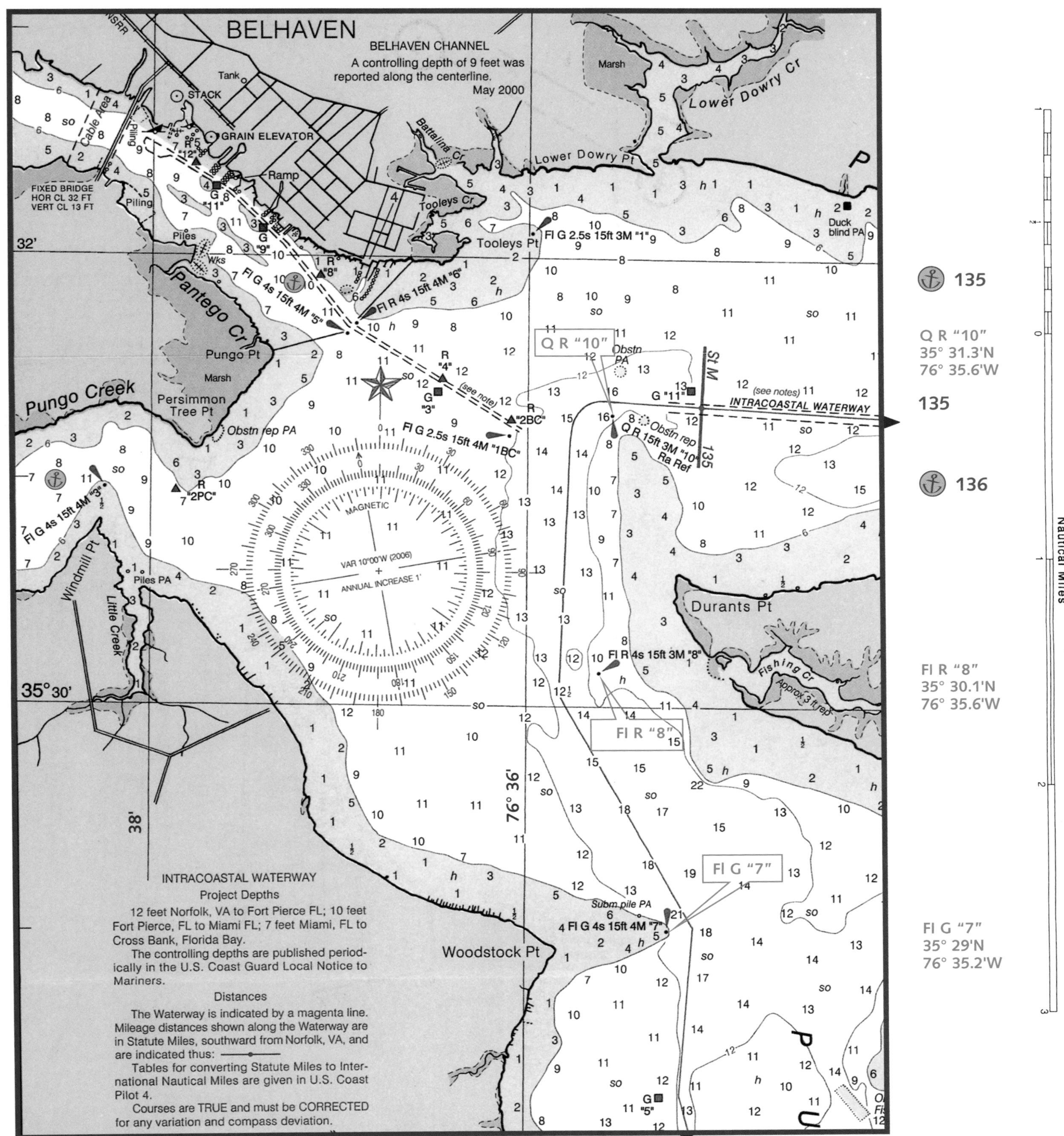

BELHAVEN
BELHAVEN CHANNEL
A controlling depth of 9 feet was reported along the centerline.
May 2000
Tank
STACK
GRAIN ELEVATOR
Ramp
Cable Area
Piling
FIXED BRIDGE
HOR CL 32 FT
VERT CL 13 FT
Piles
Wks
Marsh
Lower Dowry Cr
Lower Dowry Pt
Battalina Cr
Tooleys Cr
Tooleys Pt
Duck blind PA
Fl G 2.5s 15ft 3M "1"
Fl G 4s 15ft 4M "5"
Fl R 4s 15ft 4M "6"
Pantego Cr
Pungo Pt
Marsh
Pungo Creek
Persimmon Tree Pt
Obstn rep PA
Q R "10"
Obstn PA
G "11"
St M
INTRACOASTAL WATERWAY
Q R 15ft 3M "10" Ra Ref
Obstn rep
135
Fl G 2.5s 15ft 4M "1BC"
R "2BC"
R "4"
G "3"
(see note)
(see notes)
R "2PC"
Fl G 4s 15ft 4M "3"
MAGNETIC
VAR 10°00'W (2006)
ANNUAL INCREASE 1'
Windmill Pt
Little Creek
Piles PA
Durants Pt
Fl R 4s 15ft 3M "8"
Fishing Cr
Approx 3 ft rep
Fl R "8"
32'
35°30'
38'
76°36'
Fl G "7"
Subm pile PA
Fl G 4s 15ft 4M "7"
Woodstock Pt
G "5"
INTRACOASTAL WATERWAY
Project Depths
12 feet Norfolk, VA to Fort Pierce FL; 10 feet Fort Pierce, FL to Miami FL; 7 feet Miami, FL to Cross Bank, Florida Bay.
The controlling depths are published periodically in the U.S. Coast Guard Local Notice to Mariners.
Distances
The Waterway is indicated by a magenta line. Mileage distances shown along the Waterway are in Statute Miles, southward from Norfolk, VA, and are indicated thus:
Tables for converting Statute Miles to International Nautical Miles are given in U.S. Coast Pilot 4.
Courses are TRUE and must be CORRECTED for any variation and compass deviation.
135
135
136
Q R "10"
35° 31.3'N
76° 35.6'W
Fl R "8"
35° 30.1'N
76° 35.6'W
Fl G "7"
35° 29'N
76° 35.2'W
Nautical Miles

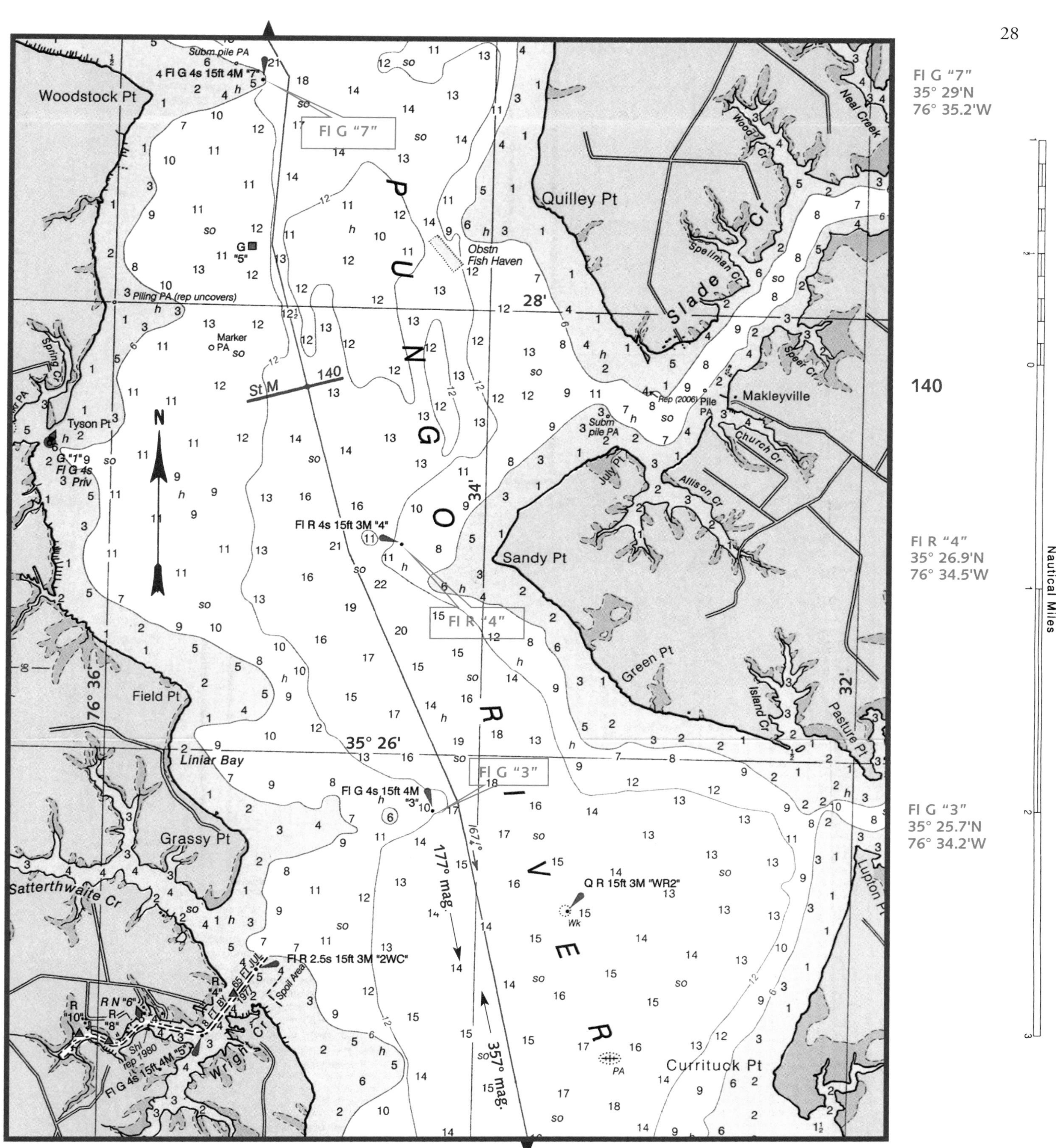

Fl G "7"
35° 29'N
76° 35.2'W

140

Fl R "4"
35° 26.9'N
76° 34.5'W

Fl G "3"
35° 25.7'N
76° 34.2'W

Nautical Miles

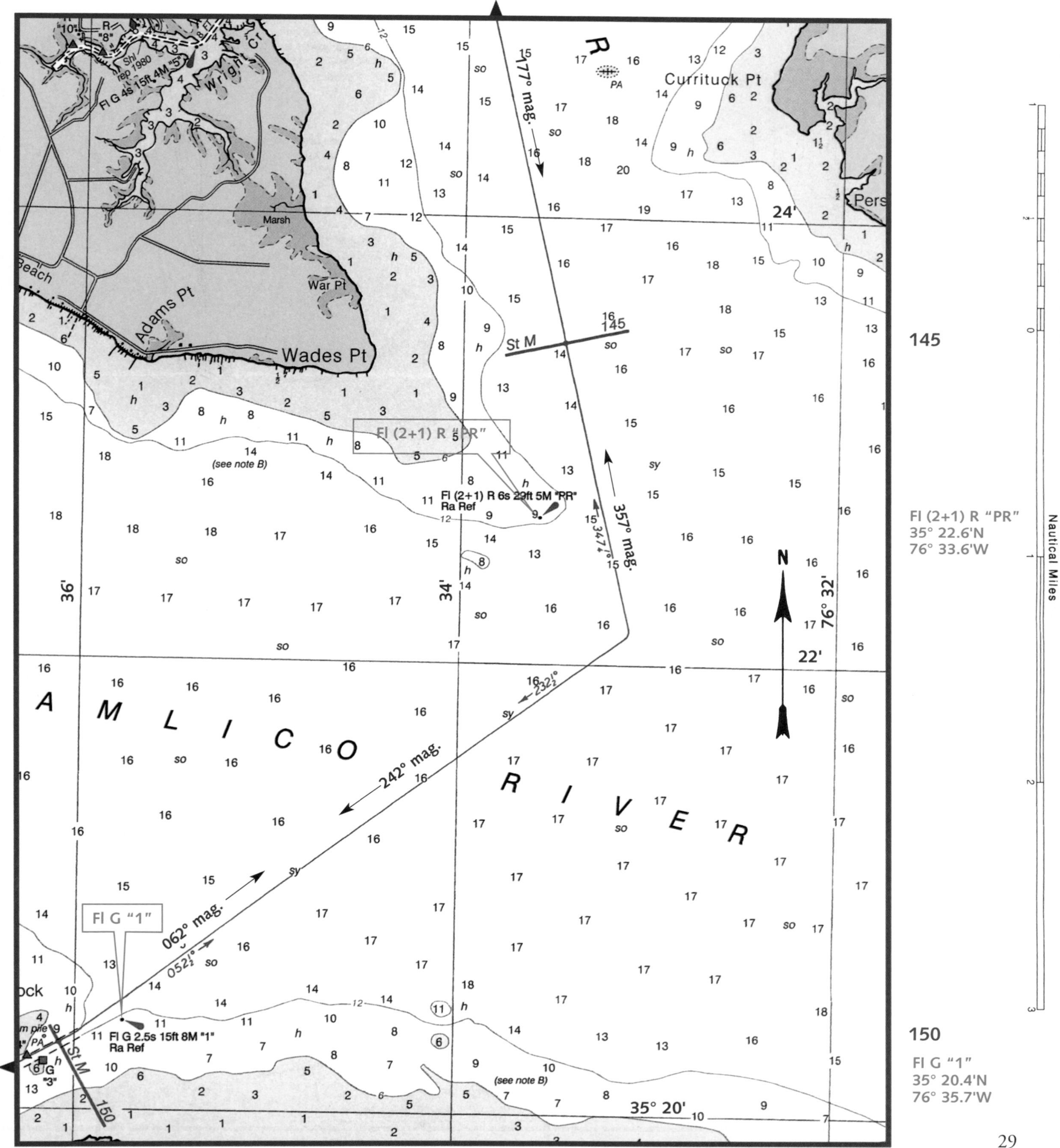
Currituck Pt
Wright Cr
Marsh
War Pt
Adams Pt
Wades Pt
Beach
Fl G 4s 15ft 4M "5"
Shl rep 1980
St M
145
177° mag.
357° mag.
347¼°
232½°
242° mag.
062° mag.
052½°
Fl (2+1) R "PR"
Fl (2+1) R 6s 23ft 5M "PR"
Ra Ref
(see note B)
PAMLICO RIVER
Fl G "1"
Fl G 2.5s 15ft 8M "1"
Ra Ref
150
35° 20'
36'
34'
22'
24'
76° 32'
N
145
Fl (2+1) R "PR"
35° 22.6'N
76° 33.6'W
150
Fl G "1"
35° 20.4'N
76° 35.7'W
Nautical Miles

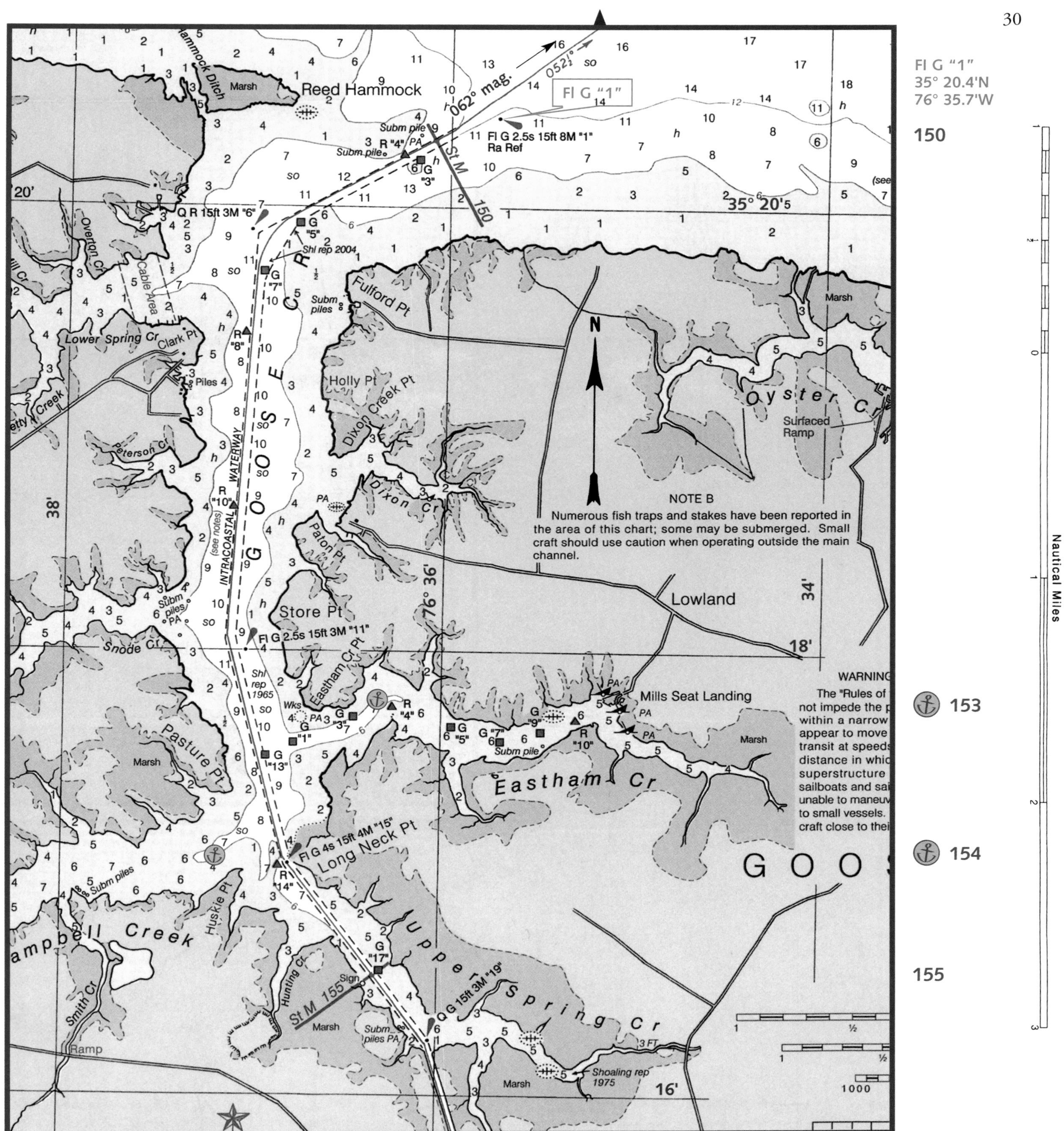
Reed Hammock
Fl G "1"
062° mag.
052½° so
Fl G 2.5s 15ft 8M "1"
Ra Ref
St M 150
Q R 15ft 3M "6"
Shl rep 2004
Fulford Pt
Lower Spring Cr
Clark Pt
Cable Area
Overton Cr
Holly Pt
Dixon Creek Pt
Peterson Cr
INTRACOASTAL WATERWAY
G O O S E C R
Dixon Cr
Paton Pt
Store Pt
Fl G 2.5s 15ft 3M "11"
Snode Cr
Eastham Cr Pt
Pasture Pt
Fl G 4s 15ft 4M "15"
Long Neck Pt
Huskie Pt
Campbell Creek
Hunting Cr
St M 155
Smith Cr
Upper Spring Cr
Q G 15ft 3M "19"
Shoaling rep 1975
Eastham Cr
Mills Seat Landing
Lowland
Oyster Cr
Surfaced Ramp
Marsh
76° 36'
34'
38'
18'
16'
20'
35° 20'5
NOTE B
Numerous fish traps and stakes have been reported in the area of this chart; some may be submerged. Small craft should use caution when operating outside the main channel.
WARNING
The "Rules of
not impede the p
within a narrow
appear to move
transit at speeds
distance in whic
superstructure
sailboats and sai
unable to maneuv
to small vessels.
craft close to thei
Fl G "1"
35° 20.4'N
76° 35.7'W
150
153
154
155
Nautical Miles

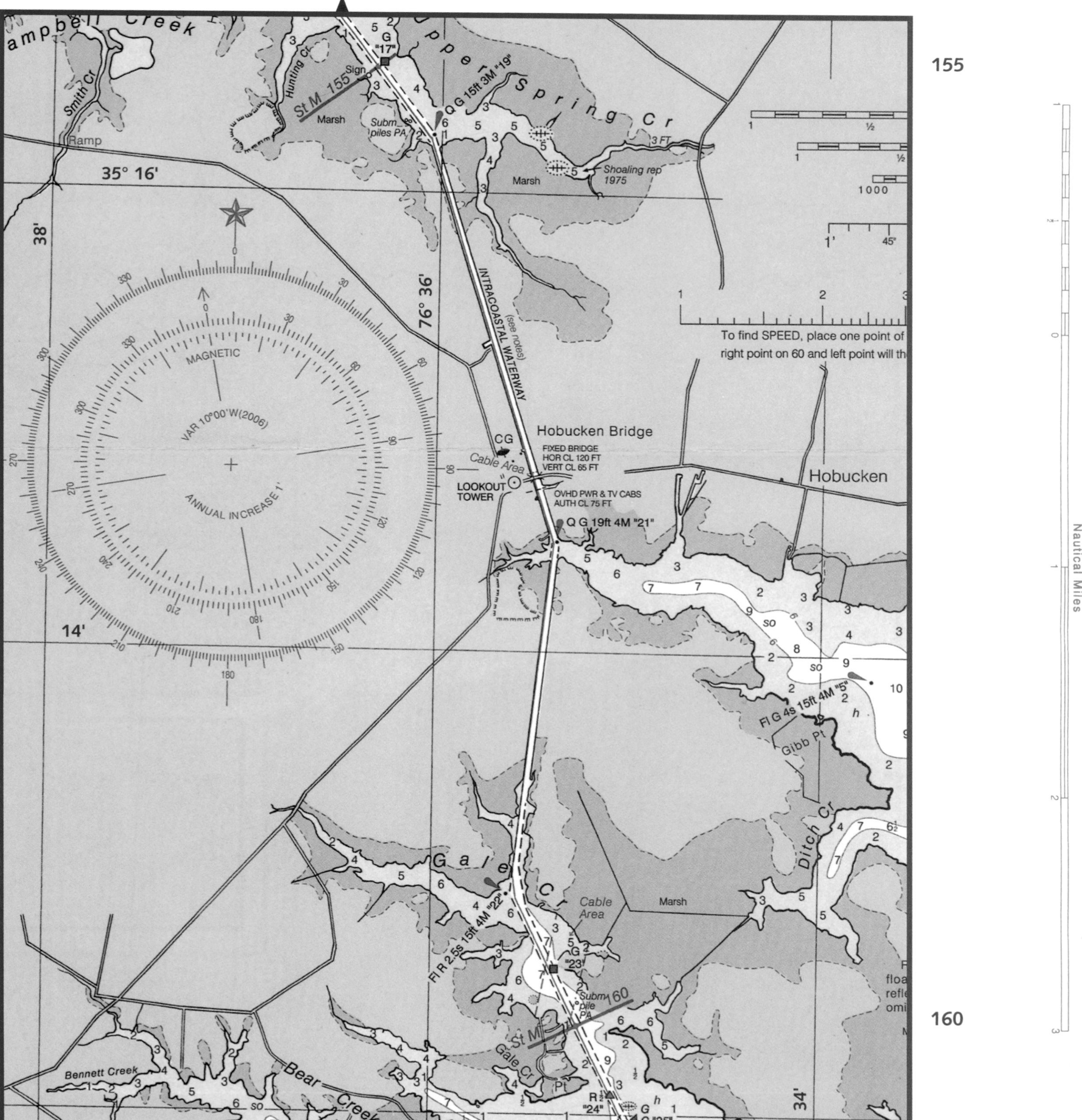

Campbell Creek
Smith Cr
Hunting Cr
Upper Spring Cr
St M 155
Sign
G "17"
Q G 15ft 3M "19"
Marsh
Subm piles PA
Ramp
Shoaling rep 1975
35° 16'
38'
76° 36'
INTRACOASTAL WATERWAY
(see notes)
MAGNETIC
VAR 10°00'W(2006)
ANNUAL INCREASE 1'
Hobucken Bridge
FIXED BRIDGE
HOR CL 120 FT
VERT CL 65 FT
CG
Cable Area
LOOKOUT TOWER
OVHD PWR & TV CABS
AUTH CL 75 FT
Q G 19ft 4M "21"
Hobucken
To find SPEED, place one point of
right point on 60 and left point will th
14'
Fl G 4s 15ft 4M "5"
Gibb Pt
Ditch Cr
Gale Cr
Cable Area
Marsh
Fl R 2.5s 15ft 4M "22"
G "23"
Subm pile PA
St M 160
Gale Cr Pt
R "24"
G C "25"
Bennett Creek
Bear Creek
34'
155
160
Nautical Miles

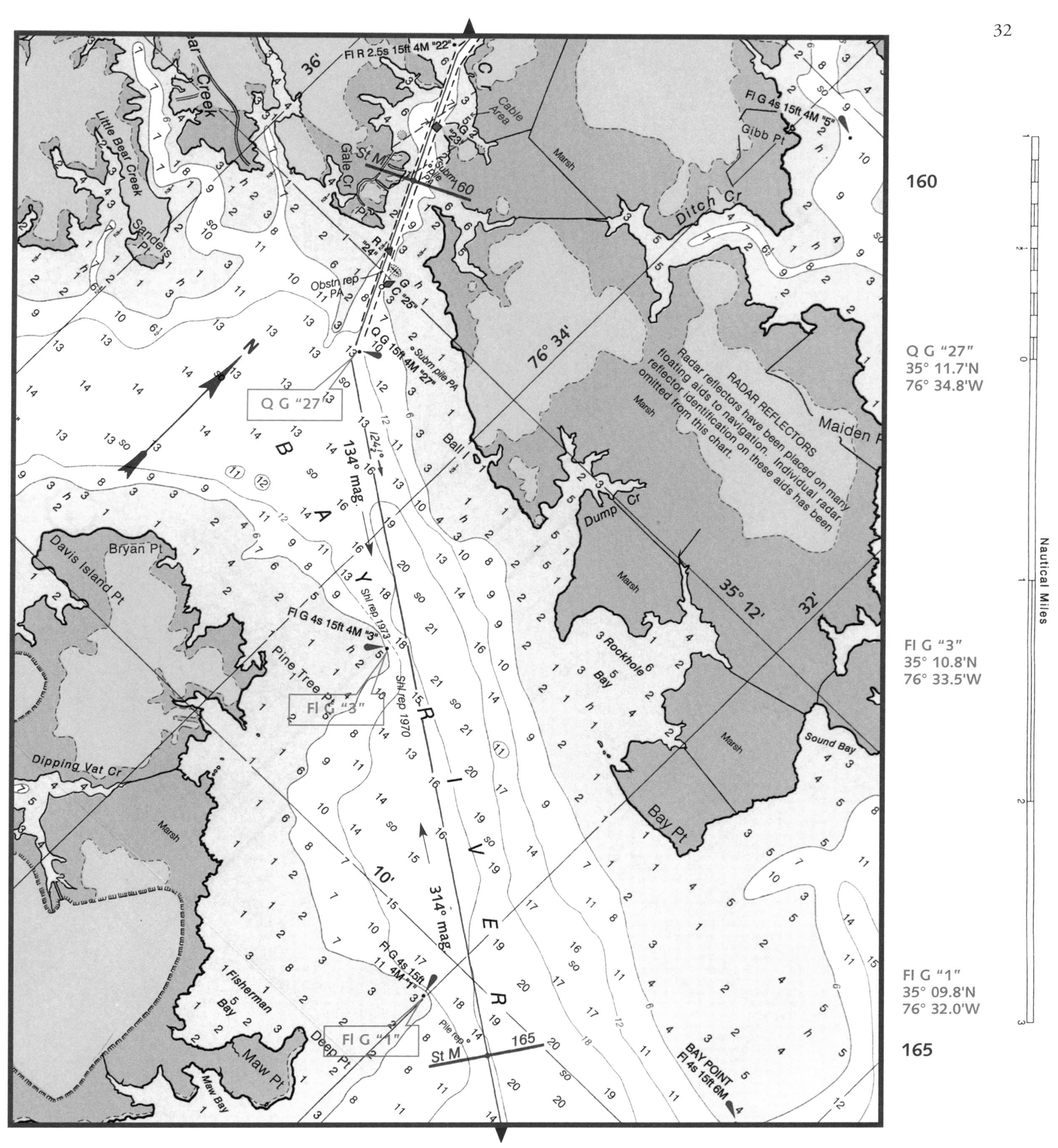

160

Q G "27"
35° 11.7'N
76° 34.8'W

Fl G "3"
35° 10.8'N
76° 33.5'W

Fl G "1"
35° 09.8'N
76° 32.0'W

165

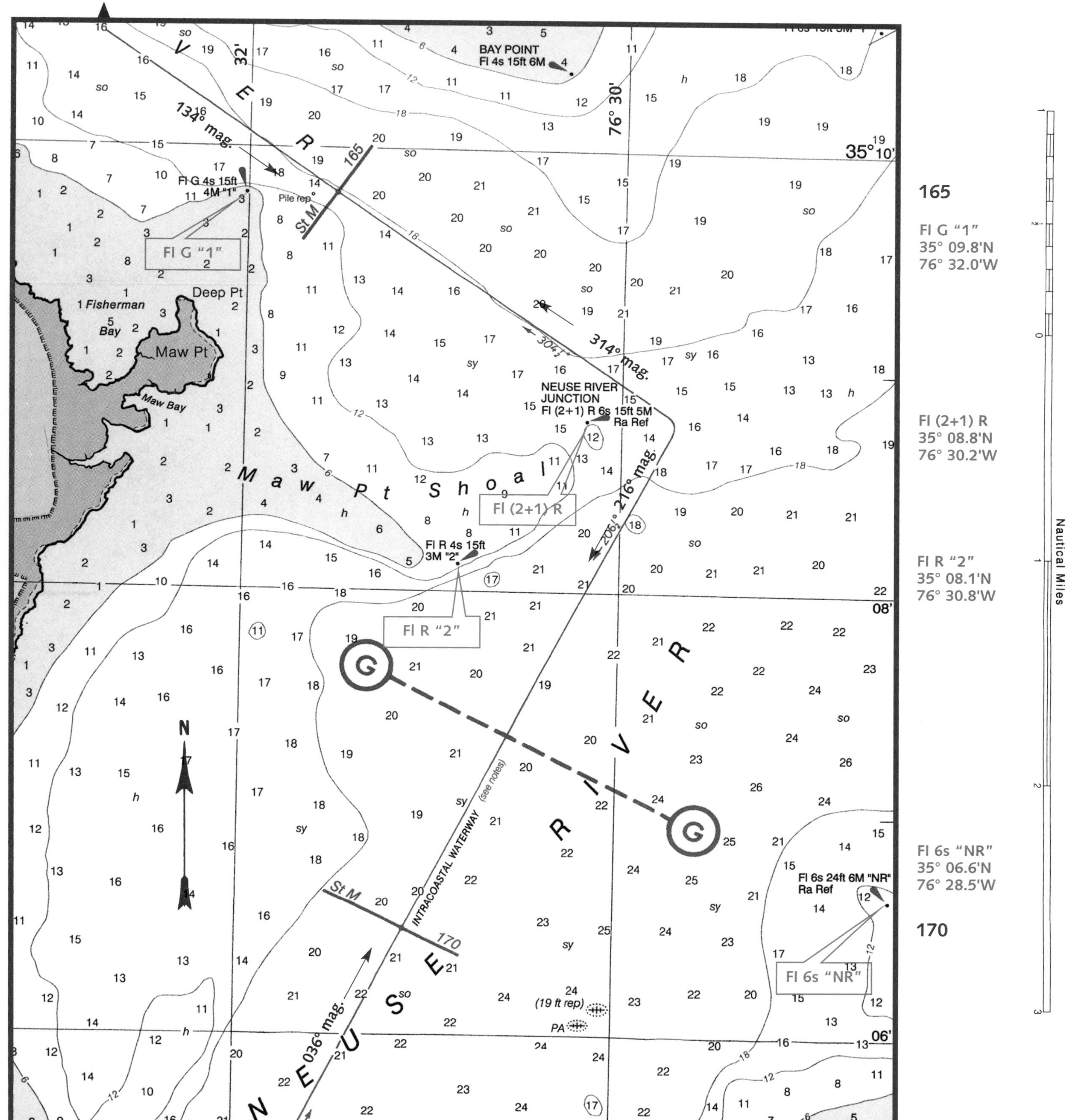

BAY POINT
Fl 4s 15ft 6M
Fl G 4s 15ft 4M "1"
Pile rep
Fl G "1"
Deep Pt
Fisherman Bay
Maw Pt
Maw Bay
Maw Pt Shoal
NEUSE RIVER JUNCTION
Fl (2+1) R 6s 15ft 5M
Ra Ref
Fl (2+1) R
Fl R 4s 15ft 3M "2"
Fl R "2"
Fl 6s 24ft 6M "NR"
Ra Ref
Fl 6s "NR"
134° mag.
314° mag.
216° mag.
036° mag.
INTRACOASTAL WATERWAY
(see notes)
(19 ft rep)
PA
NEUSE RIVER
St M
165
170
32'
76° 30'
35° 10'
08'
06'
N
165
Fl G "1"
35° 09.8'N
76° 32.0'W
Fl (2+1) R
35° 08.8'N
76° 30.2'W
Fl R "2"
35° 08.1'N
76° 30.8'W
Fl 6s "NR"
35° 06.6'N
76° 28.5'W
170
Nautical Miles

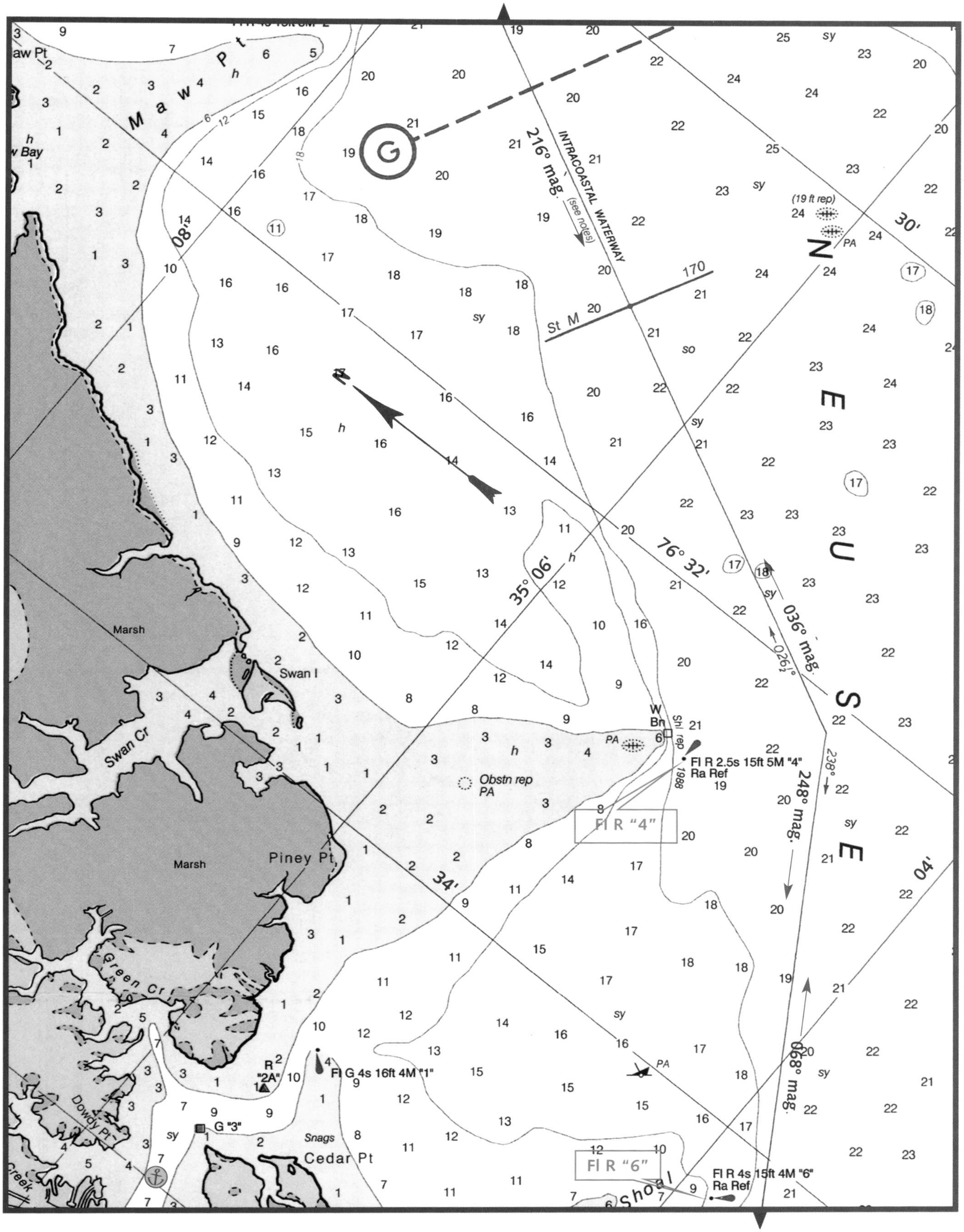

170

Fl R "4"
35° 05.1'N
76° 32.7'W

Fl R "6"
35° 03.8'N
76° 34.4'W

174

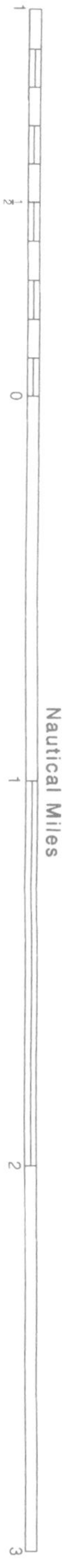

Nautical Miles

NEUSE

INTRACOASTAL WATERWAY (see notes)

216° mag.

036° mag.

248° mag.

068° mag.

Maw Pt

Swan I

Swan Cr

Piney Pt

Green Cr

Dowdy Pt

Cedar Pt

Shoal

Marsh

Obstn rep PA

Fl R 2.5s 15ft 5M "4" Ra Ref

Fl R 4s 15ft 4M "6" Ra Ref

Fl G 4s 16ft 4M "1"

G "3"

R "2A"

W Bn

St M 20

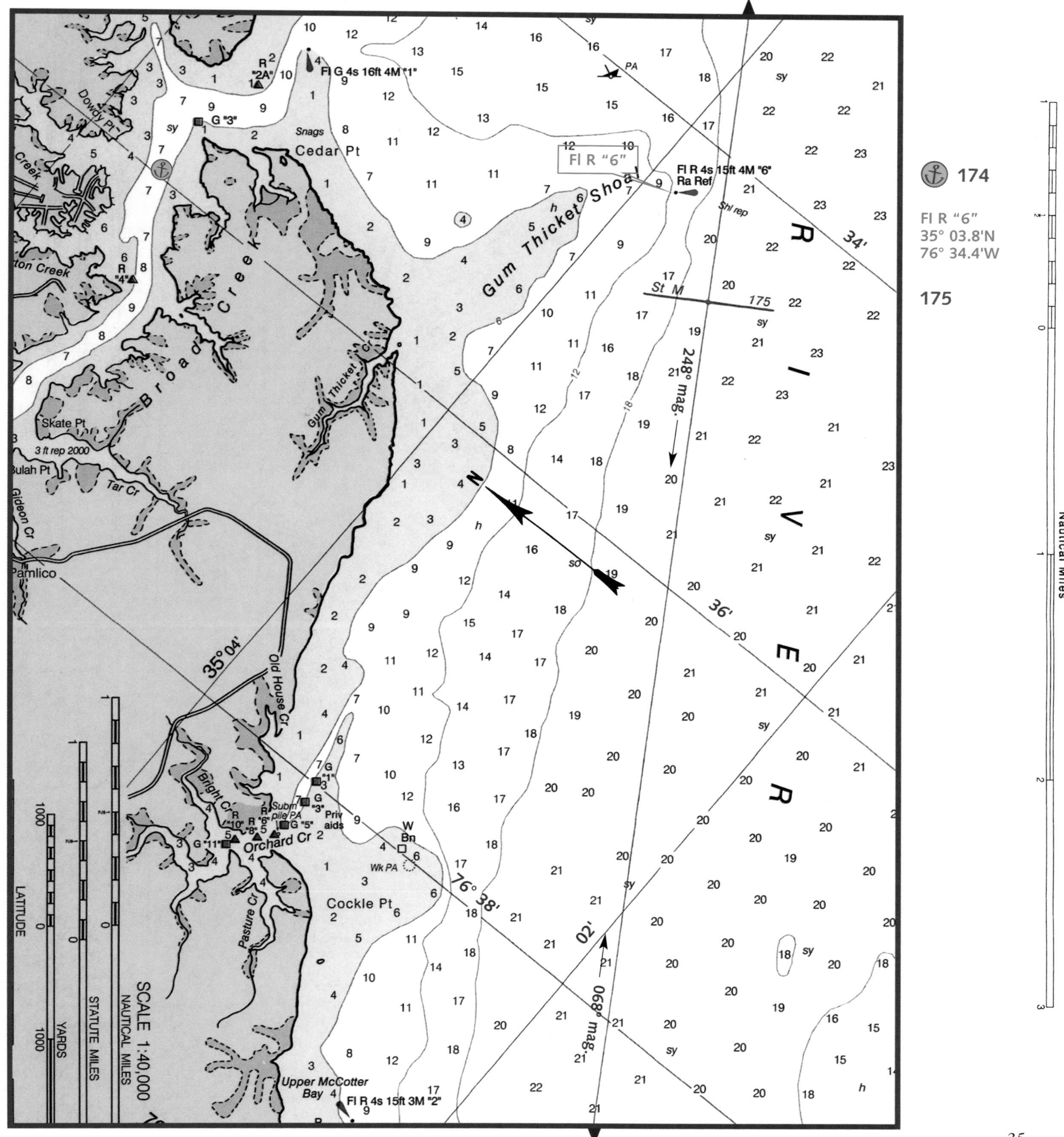
Fl G 4s 16ft 4M "1"
R "2A"
G "3"
Snags
Cedar Pt
Dowdy Pt
Creek
Broad Creek
ton Creek
R "4"
Skate Pt
3 ft rep 2000
Bulah Pt
Tar Cr
Gideon Cr
Pamlico
Gum Thicket Shoal
Gum Thicket Cr
Fl R "6"
Fl R 4s 15ft 4M "6" Ra Ref
Shl rep
St M
175
248° mag.
068° mag.
R I V E R
34'
36'
35°04'
76° 38'
02'
Old House Cr
Bright Cr
G "1"
G "3"
G "5"
G "11"
R "10"
R "8"
R "6"
Subm pile PA
Priv aids
W Bn
Wk PA
Orchard Cr
Pasture Cr
Cockle Pt
Upper McCotter Bay
Fl R 4s 15ft 3M "2"
SCALE 1:40,000
NAUTICAL MILES
STATUTE MILES
YARDS
LATITUDE
Nautical Miles
174
Fl R "6"
35° 03.8'N
76° 34.4'W
175

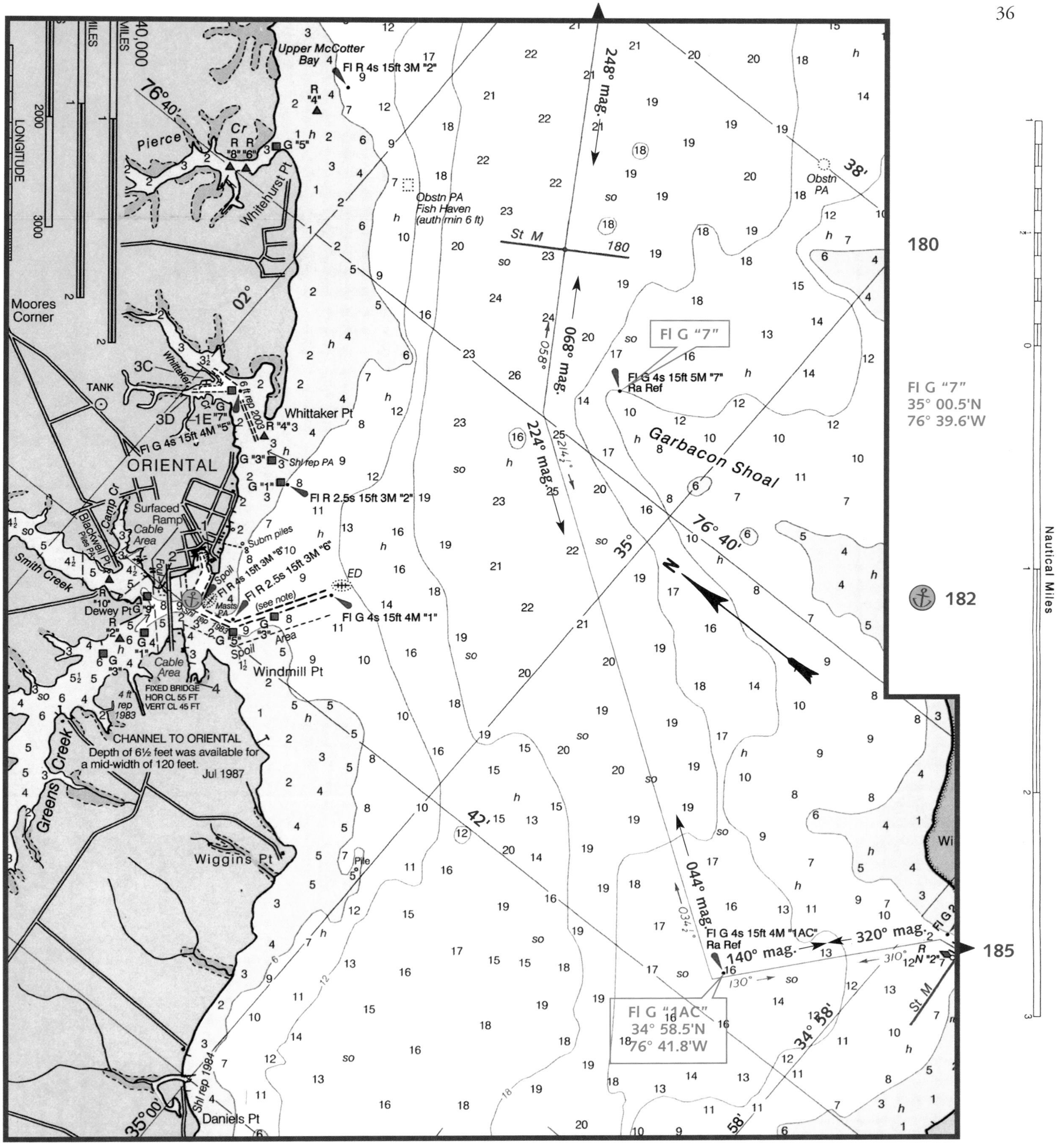

Upper McCotter Bay
Fl R 4s 15ft 3M "2"
R "4"
Pierce Cr
R "8" R "6"
G "5"
Whitehurst Pt
Obstn PA
Fish Haven
(auth min 6 ft)
Obstn PA
76° 40'
38'
02°
St M
180
248° mag.
068° mag.
224° mag.
044° mag.
Moores Corner
LONGITUDE
TANK
3C
3D
1E
Whittaker Cr
Whittaker Pt
6 ft rep 2003
Fl G 4s 15ft 4M "5"
R "4"
ORIENTAL
G "3"
Shl rep PA
G "1"
Fl R 2.5s 15ft 3M "2"
Camp Cr
Surfaced Ramp
Cable Area
Blackwell Pt
Piles PA
Smith Creek
Subm piles
Fl R 4s 15ft 3M "8"
Fl R 2.5s 15ft 3M "6"
ED
Spoil
Masts PA
(see note)
Fl G 4s 15ft 4M "1"
Dewey Pt
R "10"
G "9"
R "2"
G "1"
G "3"
Shl rep 1983
G "5"
G "3"
Spoil Area
Cable Area
Windmill Pt
FIXED BRIDGE
HOR CL 55 FT
VERT CL 45 FT
4 ft rep 1983
CHANNEL TO ORIENTAL
Depth of 6½ feet was available for a mid-width of 120 feet.
Jul 1987
Greens Creek
Wiggins Pt
Pile
42'
35°
N
Fl G "7"
Fl G 4s 15ft 5M "7"
Ra Ref
Fl G "7"
35° 00.5'N
76° 39.6'W
Garbacon Shoal
76° 40'
180
182
185
Nautical Miles
Fl G 4s 15ft 4M "1AC"
Ra Ref
140° mag.
320° mag.
310°
130°
12N "2"
Fl G 2
Fl G "1AC"
34° 58.5'N
76° 41.8'W
34° 58'
58'
Shl rep 1984
35° 00'
Daniels Pt

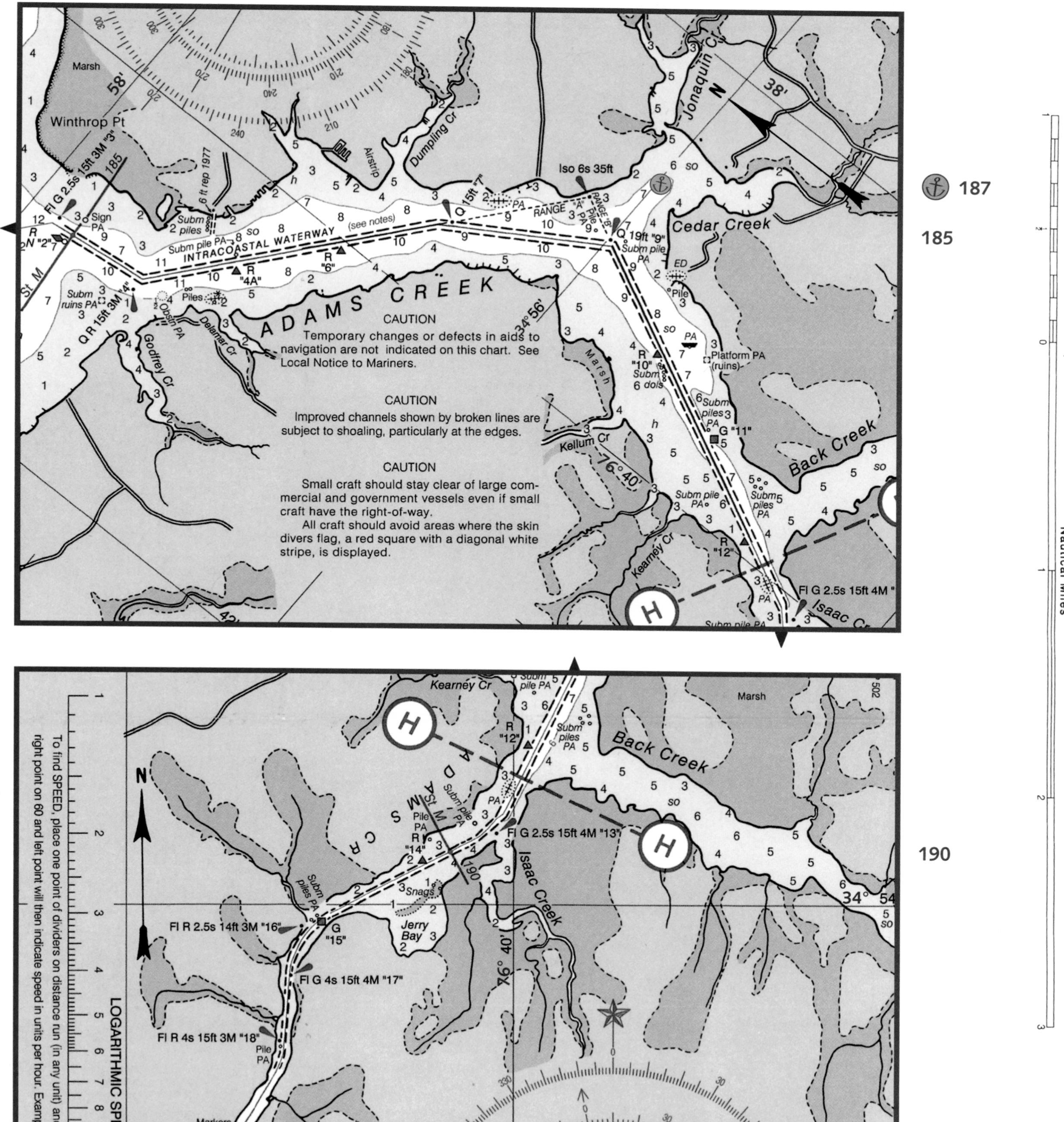
Winthrop Pt
Marsh
Jonaquin Cr
Dumpling Cr
Airstrip
Iso 6s 35ft
Q 15ft "7"
RANGE "A"
RANGE "B"
Cedar Creek
Q 19ft "9"
INTRACOASTAL WATERWAY
(see notes)
Fl G 2.5s 15ft 3M "3"
Q R 15ft 3M "4"
ADAMS CREEK
Godfrey Cr
Delamar Cr
CAUTION
Temporary changes or defects in aids to navigation are not indicated on this chart. See Local Notice to Mariners.
CAUTION
Improved channels shown by broken lines are subject to shoaling, particularly at the edges.
CAUTION
Small craft should stay clear of large commercial and government vessels even if small craft have the right-of-way.
All craft should avoid areas where the skin divers flag, a red square with a diagonal white stripe, is displayed.
Platform PA (ruins)
Kellum Cr
Back Creek
Kearney Cr
Fl G 2.5s 15ft 4M "13"
Isaac Creek
Jerry Bay
Snags
Fl R 2.5s 14ft 3M "16"
Fl G 4s 15ft 4M "17"
Fl R 4s 15ft 3M "18"
Markers
LOGARITHMIC SPEED
To find SPEED, place one point of dividers on distance run (in any unit) and the right point on 60 and left point will then indicate speed in units per hour. Example:
187
185
190
Nautical Miles

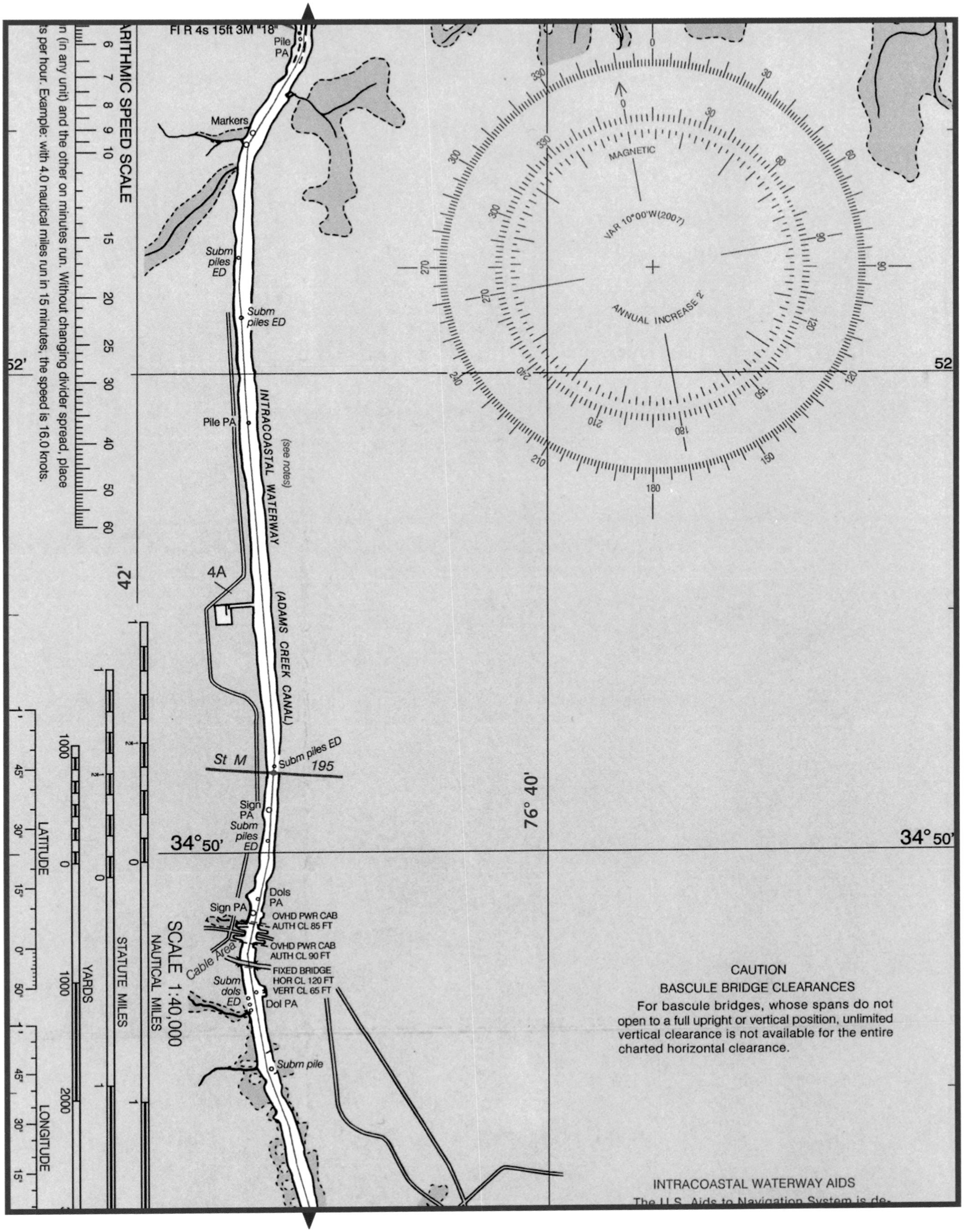

195

Fl R 4s 15ft 3M "18"

Pile PA

Markers

Subm piles ED

Subm piles ED

Pile PA

INTRACOASTAL WATERWAY

(see notes)

4A

(ADAMS CREEK CANAL)

St M

Subm piles ED

195

Sign PA

Subm piles ED

Dols PA

Sign PA

OVHD PWR CAB AUTH CL 85 FT

OVHD PWR CAB AUTH CL 90 FT

Cable Area

FIXED BRIDGE HOR CL 120 FT VERT CL 65 FT

Subm dols ED

Dol PA

Subm pile

52'

52

34°50'

34°50'

76° 40'

42'

MAGNETIC

VAR 10°00'W(2007)

ANNUAL INCREASE 2'

...ARITHMIC SPEED SCALE

...n (in any unit) and the other on minutes run. Without changing divider spread, place ...ts per hour. Example: with 4.0 nautical miles run in 15 minutes, the speed is 16.0 knots.

SCALE 1:40,000

NAUTICAL MILES

STATUTE MILES

YARDS

LATITUDE

LONGITUDE

CAUTION

BASCULE BRIDGE CLEARANCES

For bascule bridges, whose spans do not open to a full upright or vertical position, unlimited vertical clearance is not available for the entire charted horizontal clearance.

INTRACOASTAL WATERWAY AIDS

The U.S. Aids to Navigation System is de-

Nautical Miles

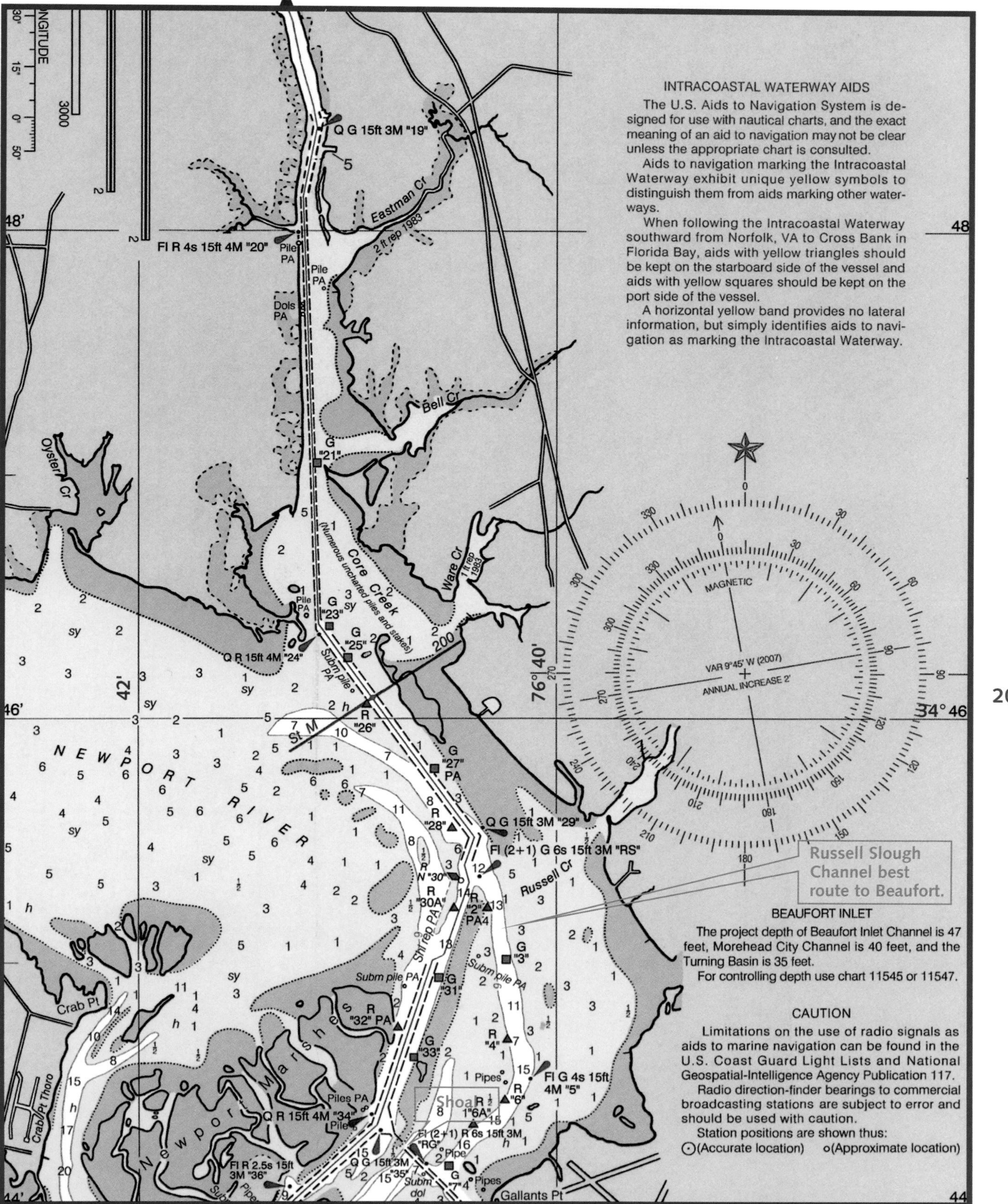
INTRACOASTAL WATERWAY AIDS
The U.S. Aids to Navigation System is designed for use with nautical charts, and the exact meaning of an aid to navigation may not be clear unless the appropriate chart is consulted.
Aids to navigation marking the Intracoastal Waterway exhibit unique yellow symbols to distinguish them from aids marking other waterways.
When following the Intracoastal Waterway southward from Norfolk, VA to Cross Bank in Florida Bay, aids with yellow triangles should be kept on the starboard side of the vessel and aids with yellow squares should be kept on the port side of the vessel.
A horizontal yellow band provides no lateral information, but simply identifies aids to navigation as marking the Intracoastal Waterway.
Russell Slough Channel best route to Beaufort.
BEAUFORT INLET
The project depth of Beaufort Inlet Channel is 47 feet, Morehead City Channel is 40 feet, and the Turning Basin is 35 feet.
For controlling depth use chart 11545 or 11547.
CAUTION
Limitations on the use of radio signals as aids to marine navigation can be found in the U.S. Coast Guard Light Lists and National Geospatial-Intelligence Agency Publication 117.
Radio direction-finder bearings to commercial broadcasting stations are subject to error and should be used with caution.
Station positions are shown thus:
(Accurate location) (Approximate location)
Q G 15ft 3M "19"
Eastman Cr
Fl R 4s 15ft 4M "20"
Bell Cr
Oyster Cr
Core Creek
(numerous uncharted piles and stakes)
Ware Cr
Q R 15ft 4M "24"
NEWPORT RIVER
Q G 15ft 3M "29"
Fl (2+1) G 6s 15ft 3M "RS"
Russell Cr
Fl G 4s 15ft 4M "5"
Q R 15ft 4M "34"
Fl R 2.5s 15ft 3M "36"
Fl (2+1) R 6s 15ft 3M "RG"
Q G 15ft 3M "35"
Newport Marshes
Crab Pt
Gallants Pt
Shoal
MAGNETIC
VAR 9°45' W (2007)
ANNUAL INCREASE 2'
76°40'
34°46'
200
Nautical Miles

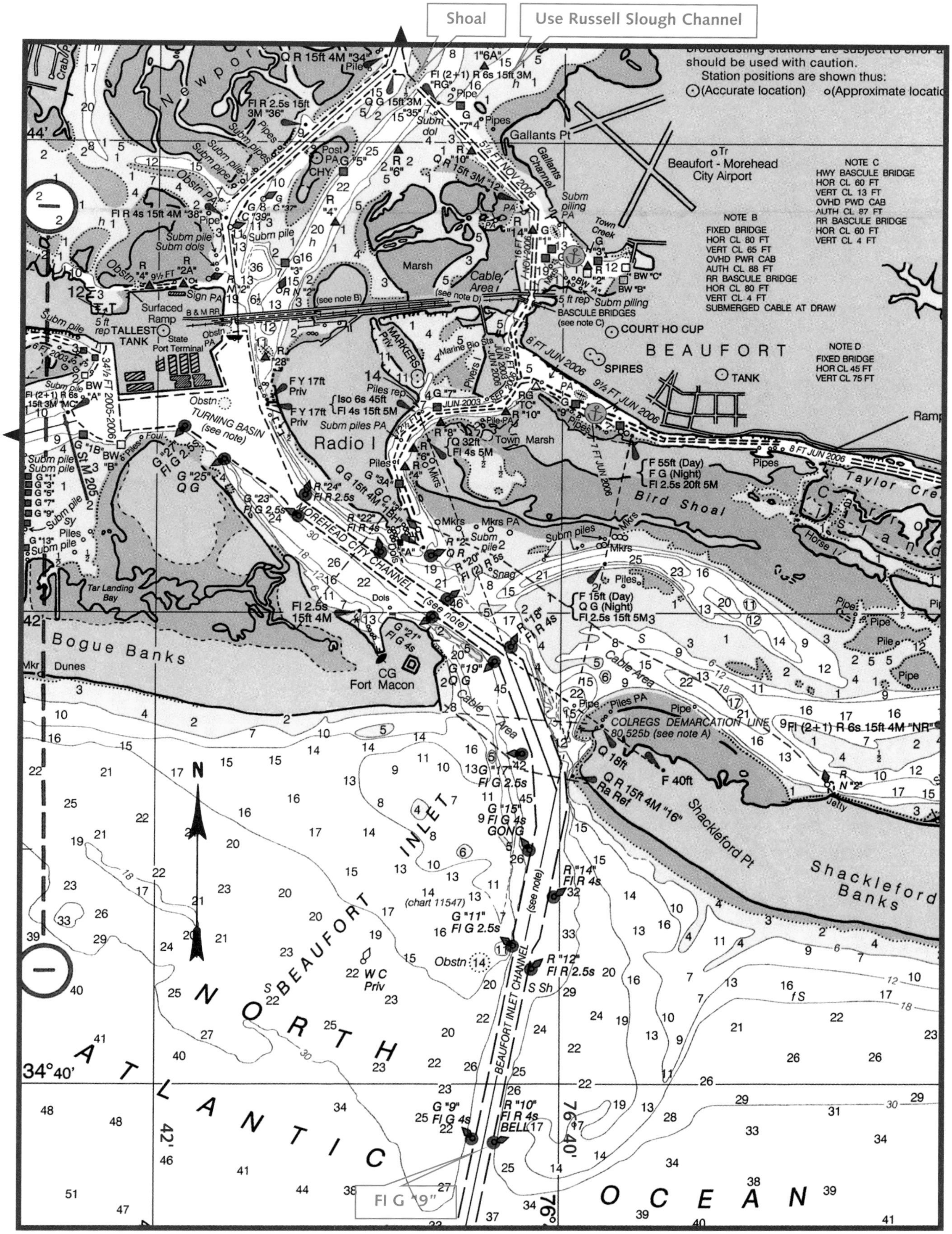

Shoal

Use Russell Slough Channel

Broadcasting stations are subject to error and should be used with caution.
Station positions are shown thus:
⊙(Accurate location) o(Approximate location)

NOTE C
HWY BASCULE BRIDGE
HOR CL 60 FT
VERT CL 13 FT
OVHD PWD CAB
AUTH CL 87 FT
RR BASCULE BRIDGE
HOR CL 60 FT
VERT CL 4 FT

NOTE B
FIXED BRIDGE
HOR CL 80 FT
VERT CL 65 FT
OVHD PWR CAB
AUTH CL 88 FT
RR BASCULE BRIDGE
HOR CL 80 FT
VERT CL 4 FT
SUBMERGED CABLE AT DRAW

NOTE D
FIXED BRIDGE
HOR CL 45 FT
VERT CL 75 FT

BEAUFORT

Radio I

Bird Shoal

Bogue Banks

Shackleford Banks

Fort Macon

MOREHEAD CITY CHANNEL

BEAUFORT INLET CHANNEL

BEAUFORT INLET

NORTH ATLANTIC OCEAN

Fl G "9"

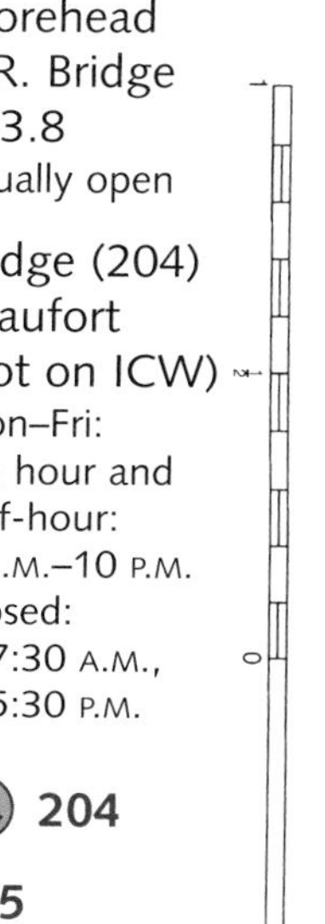

203

Beaufort and Morehead R.R. Bridge 203.8
Usually open

Bridge (204) Beaufort (not on ICW)
Mon–Fri:
On hour and half-hour:
6 A.M.–10 P.M.
Closed:
7–7:30 A.M.,
5–5:30 P.M.

204

205

Nautical Miles

Fl G "9"
34° 39.7'N
76° 40.4'W

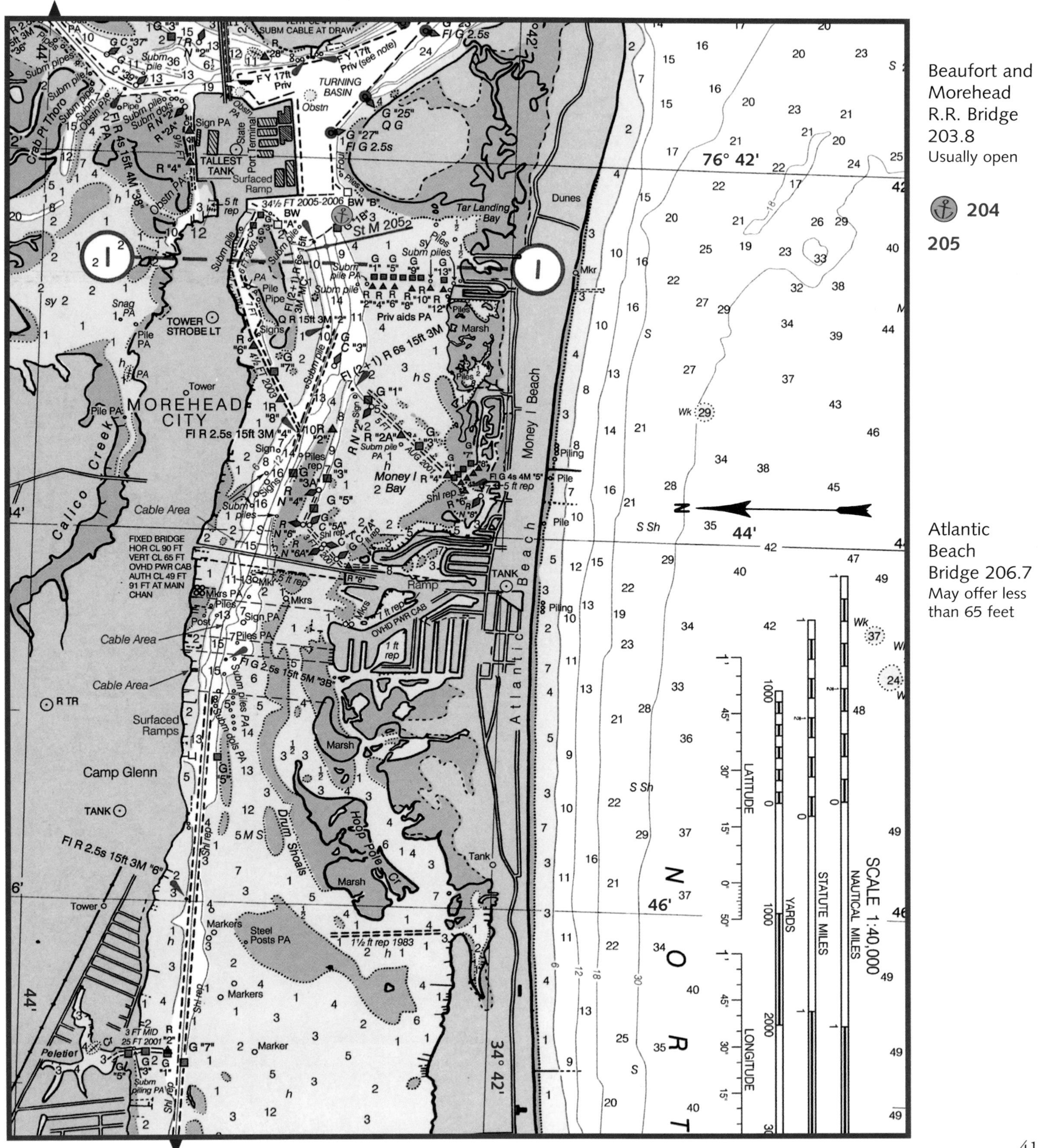

Beaufort and Morehead R.R. Bridge 203.8
Usually open
204
205
Atlantic Beach Bridge 206.7
May offer less than 65 feet
MOREHEAD CITY
Calico Creek
Camp Glenn
TURNING BASIN
TALLEST TANK
State Port Terminal
Surfaced Ramp
TOWER STROBE LT
Money I Beach
Atlantic Beach
Money I Bay
Tar Landing Bay
Dunes
Marsh
Drum Shoals
Hoop Pole Cr
Peletier
Cable Area
FIXED BRIDGE HOR CL 90 FT VERT CL 65 FT OVHD PWR CAB AUTH CL 49 FT 91 FT AT MAIN CHAN
SUBM CABLE AT DRAW
Surfaced Ramps
TANK
Tower
Steel Posts PA
Markers
76° 42'
44'
46'
34° 42'
NORT
SCALE 1:40,000
NAUTICAL MILES
STATUTE MILES
YARDS
LATITUDE
LONGITUDE
Nautical Miles

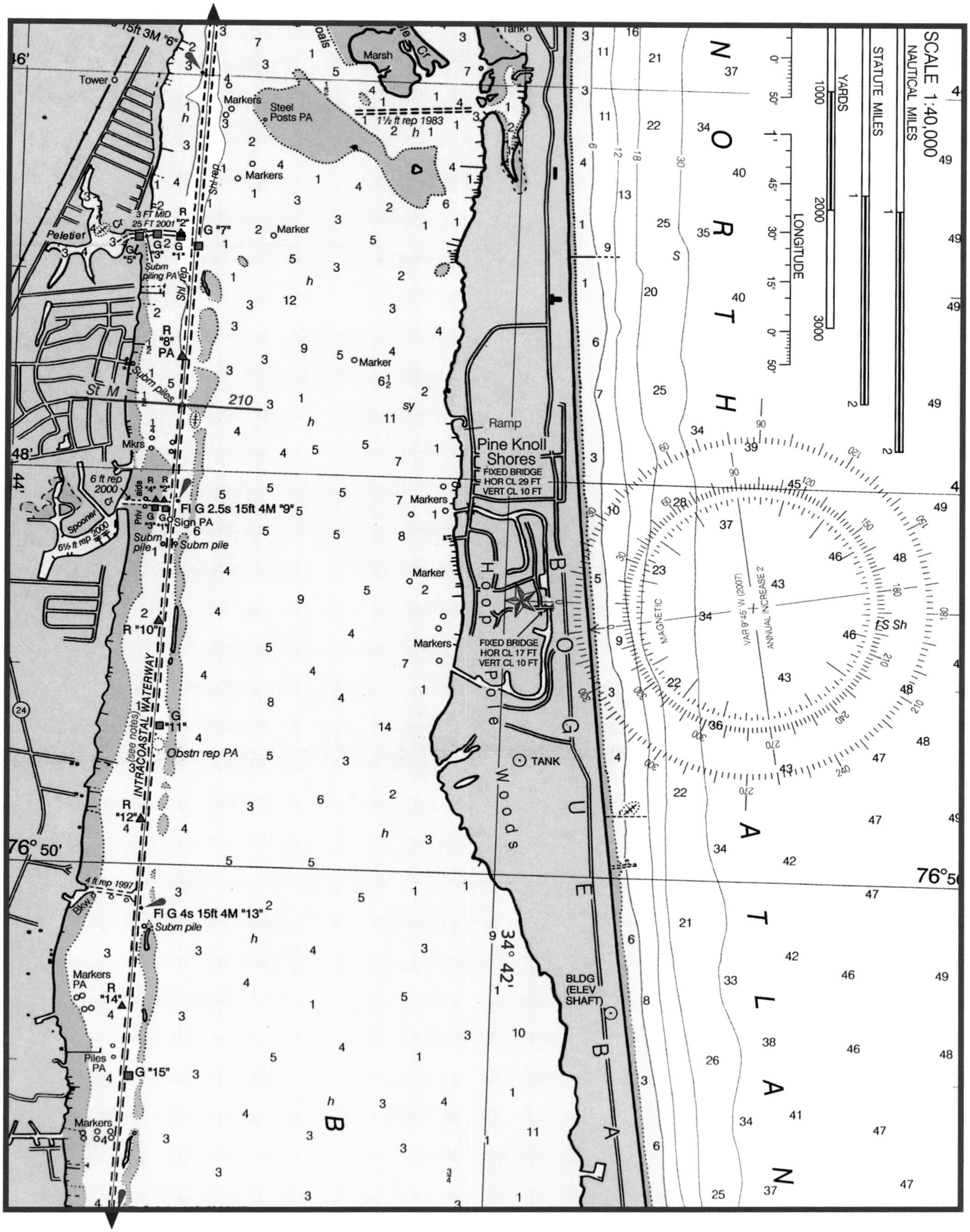

SCALE 1:40,000
NAUTICAL MILES
STATUTE MILES
YARDS
LONGITUDE
NORTH ATLANTIC
BOGUE BANKS
BOGUE
Pine Knoll Shores
FIXED BRIDGE HOR CL 29 FT VERT CL 10 FT
FIXED BRIDGE HOR CL 17 FT VERT CL 10 FT
Hoop Pole Woods
TANK
Ramp
BLDG (ELEV SHAFT)
INTRACOASTAL WATERWAY (see notes)
Fl G 2.5s 15ft 4M "9"
Fl G 4s 15ft 4M "13"
Obstn rep PA
Subm pile
Subm piles
Markers
Marker
Steel Posts PA
Marsh
Tower
Peletier
Spooner
3 FT MID 25 FT 2001
6 ft rep 2000
6½ ft rep 2000
4 ft rep 1997
1½ ft rep 1983
76° 50'
34° 42'
VAR 9°45' W (2007) ANNUAL INCREASE 2'
MAGNETIC
210
Nautical Miles

210

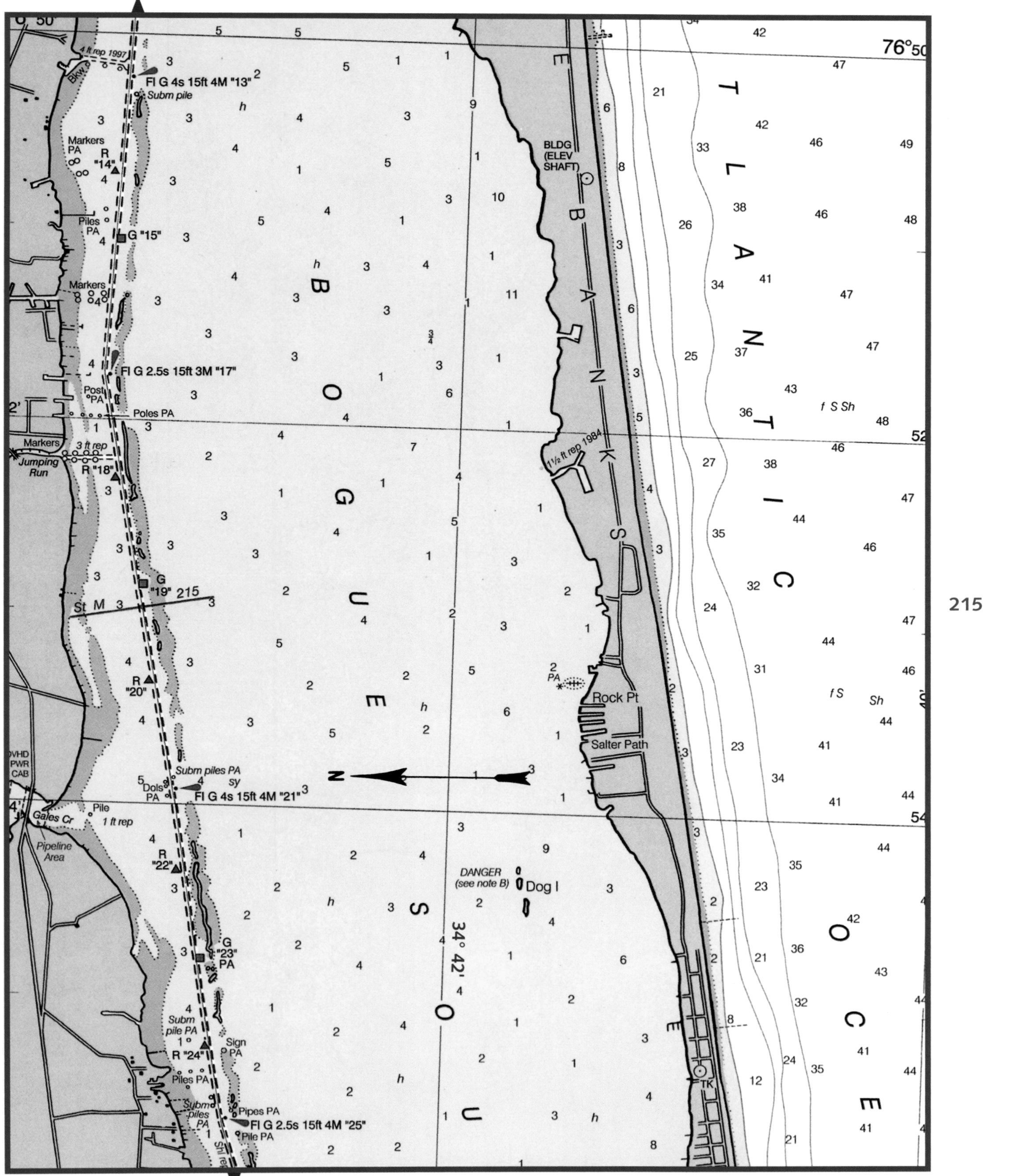

76°50
BOGUE SOUND
BANKS
ATLANTIC OCEAN
34° 42'
Fl G 4s 15ft 4M "13"
Subm pile
4 ft rep 1997
Markers PA
R "14"
Piles PA
G "15"
Markers
Fl G 2.5s 15ft 3M "17"
Post PA
Poles PA
Markers
3 ft rep
Jumping Run
R "18"
G "19"
215
St M
R "20"
Subm piles PA
Dols PA
Fl G 4s 15ft 4M "21"
OVHD PWR CAB
Gales Cr
Pile
1 ft rep
Pipeline Area
R "22"
G "23" PA
Subm pile PA
Sign PA
R "24"
Piles PA
Subm piles PA
Pipes PA
Fl G 2.5s 15ft 4M "25"
Pile PA
Shl rep
BLDG (ELEV SHAFT)
1½ ft rep 1984
Rock Pt
Salter Path
DANGER (see note B)
Dog I
TK
f S Sh
fS Sh
N
Nautical Miles

215

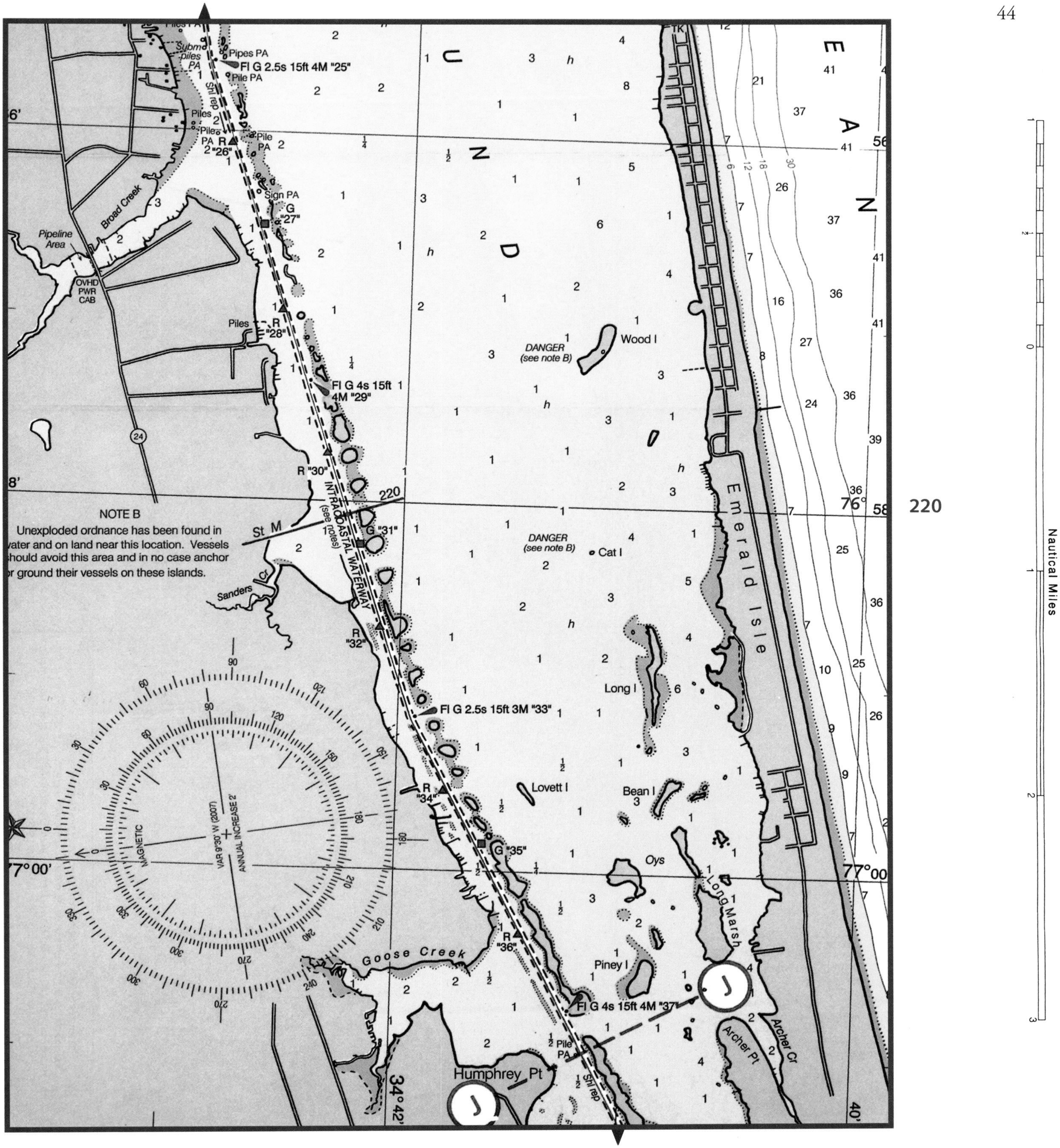

NOTE B
Unexploded ordnance has been found in water and on land near this location. Vessels should avoid this area and in no case anchor or ground their vessels on these islands.

Fl G 2.5s 15ft 4M "25"
R "26"
G "27"
R "28"
Fl G 4s 15ft 4M "29"
R "30"
G "31"
R "32"
Fl G 2.5s 15ft 3M "33"
R "34"
G "35"
R "36"
Fl G 4s 15ft 4M "37"

INTRACOASTAL WATERWAY (see notes)
220
St M
Sanders Cr
Broad Creek
Pipeline Area
OVHD PWR CAB
Goose Creek
Humphrey Pt
Archer Pt
Archer Cr
Long Marsh
Piney I
Oys
Bean I
Lovett I
Long I
Cat I
Wood I
DANGER (see note B)
Emerald Isle
OCEAN
SOUND
76° 58'
77° 00'
34° 42'
40'
56'
MAGNETIC
VAR 9°30' W (2007)
ANNUAL INCREASE 2'

Nautical Miles

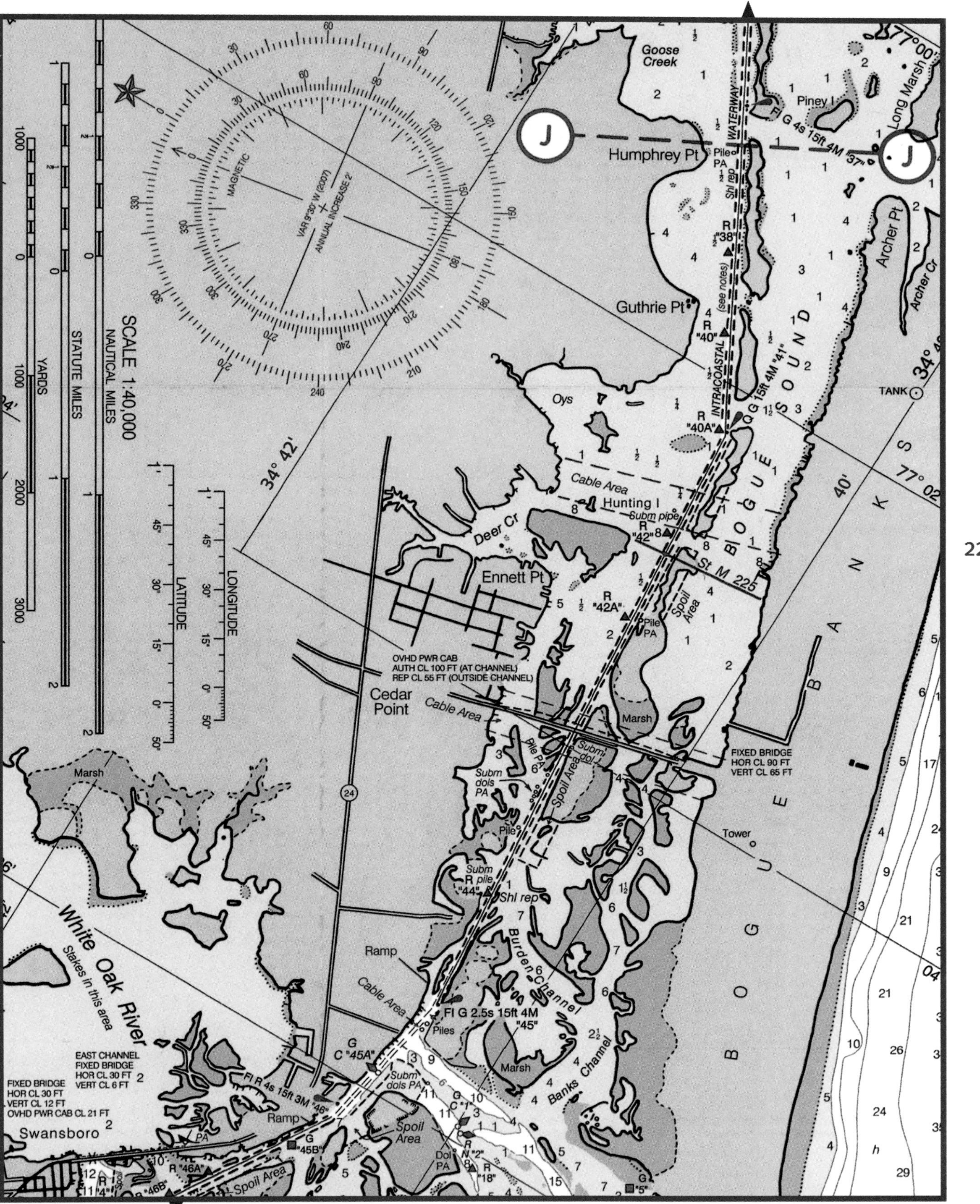

Goose Creek
Humphrey Pt
Piney I
Long Marsh
Archer Pt
Archer Cr
Guthrie Pt
INTRACOASTAL WATERWAY
BOGUE SOUND
BOGUE BANKS
Oys
Cable Area
Hunting I
Subm pipe
Deer Cr
Ennett Pt
St M 225
Spoil Area
OVHD PWR CAB
AUTH CL 100 FT (AT CHANNEL)
REP CL 55 FT (OUTSIDE CHANNEL)
Cedar Point
Marsh
FIXED BRIDGE
HOR CL 90 FT
VERT CL 65 FT
Tower
TANK
White Oak River
Stakes in this area
Ramp
Burden Channel
Banks Channel
Fl G 2.5s 15ft 4M "45"
EAST CHANNEL
FIXED BRIDGE
HOR CL 30 FT
VERT CL 6 FT
FIXED BRIDGE
HOR CL 30 FT
VERT CL 12 FT
OVHD PWR CAB CL 21 FT
Swansboro
SCALE 1:40,000
NAUTICAL MILES
STATUTE MILES
YARDS
LATITUDE
LONGITUDE
MAGNETIC
VAR 9°30'W (2007)
ANNUAL INCREASE 2'
34° 42'
77° 02'
77° 00'
Nautical Miles

225

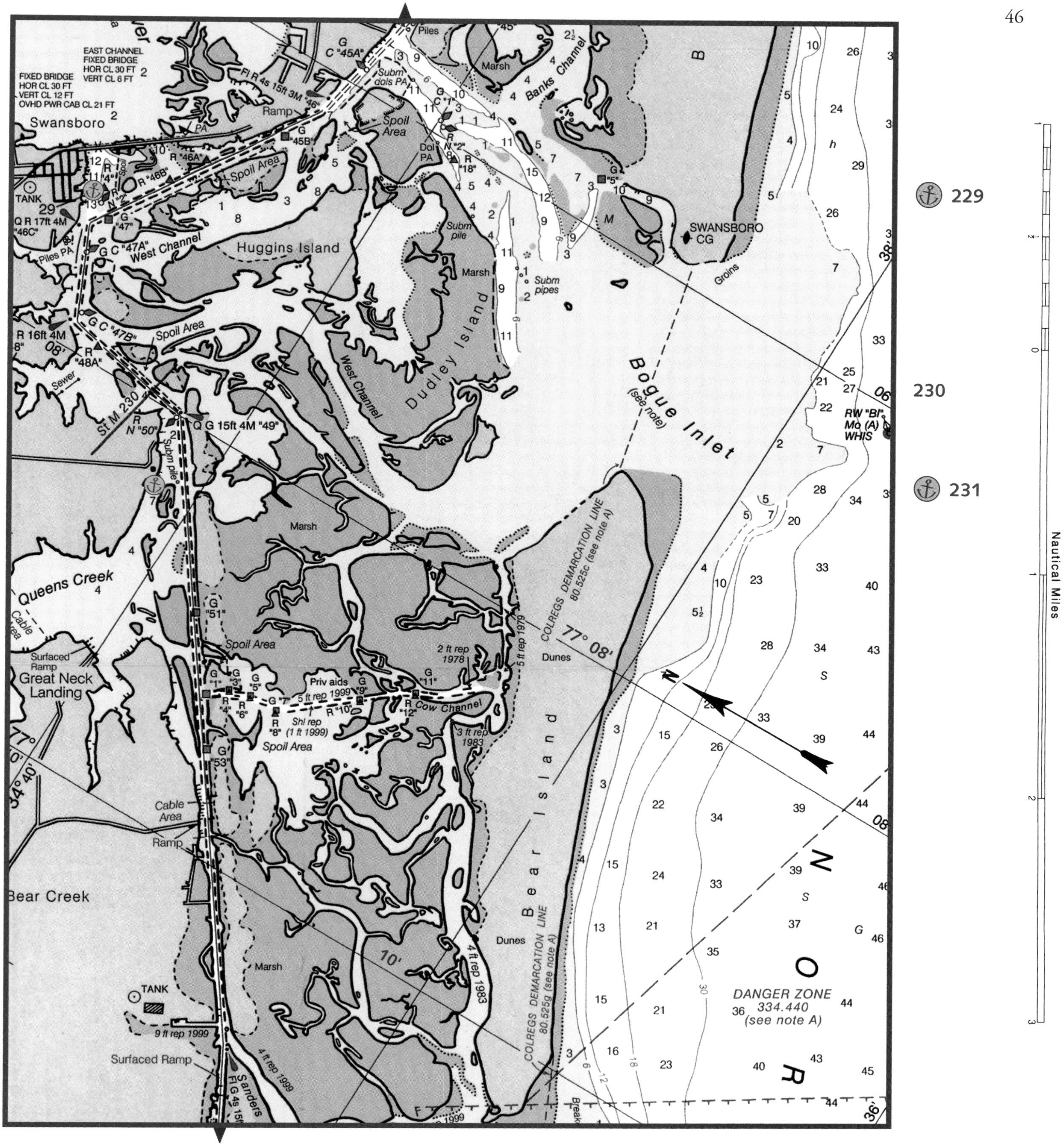
EAST CHANNEL FIXED BRIDGE HOR CL 30 FT VERT CL 6 FT
FIXED BRIDGE HOR CL 30 FT VERT CL 12 FT OVHD PWR CAB CL 21 FT
Swansboro
Huggins Island
West Channel
Spoil Area
Dudley Island
Bogue Inlet
(see note)
SWANSBORO CG
Groins
Banks Channel
Marsh
Queens Creek
Great Neck Landing
Surfaced Ramp
Cable Area
Ramp
Bear Creek
Bear Island
Cow Channel
Priv aids
Dunes
COLREGS DEMARCATION LINE 80.525c (see note A)
COLREGS DEMARCATION LINE 80.525g (see note A)
77° 08'
DANGER ZONE 334.440 (see note A)
RW "BI" Mo (A) WHIS
Q G 15ft 4M "49"
St M 230
TANK
Surfaced Ramp
Sanders
229
230
231
Nautical Miles

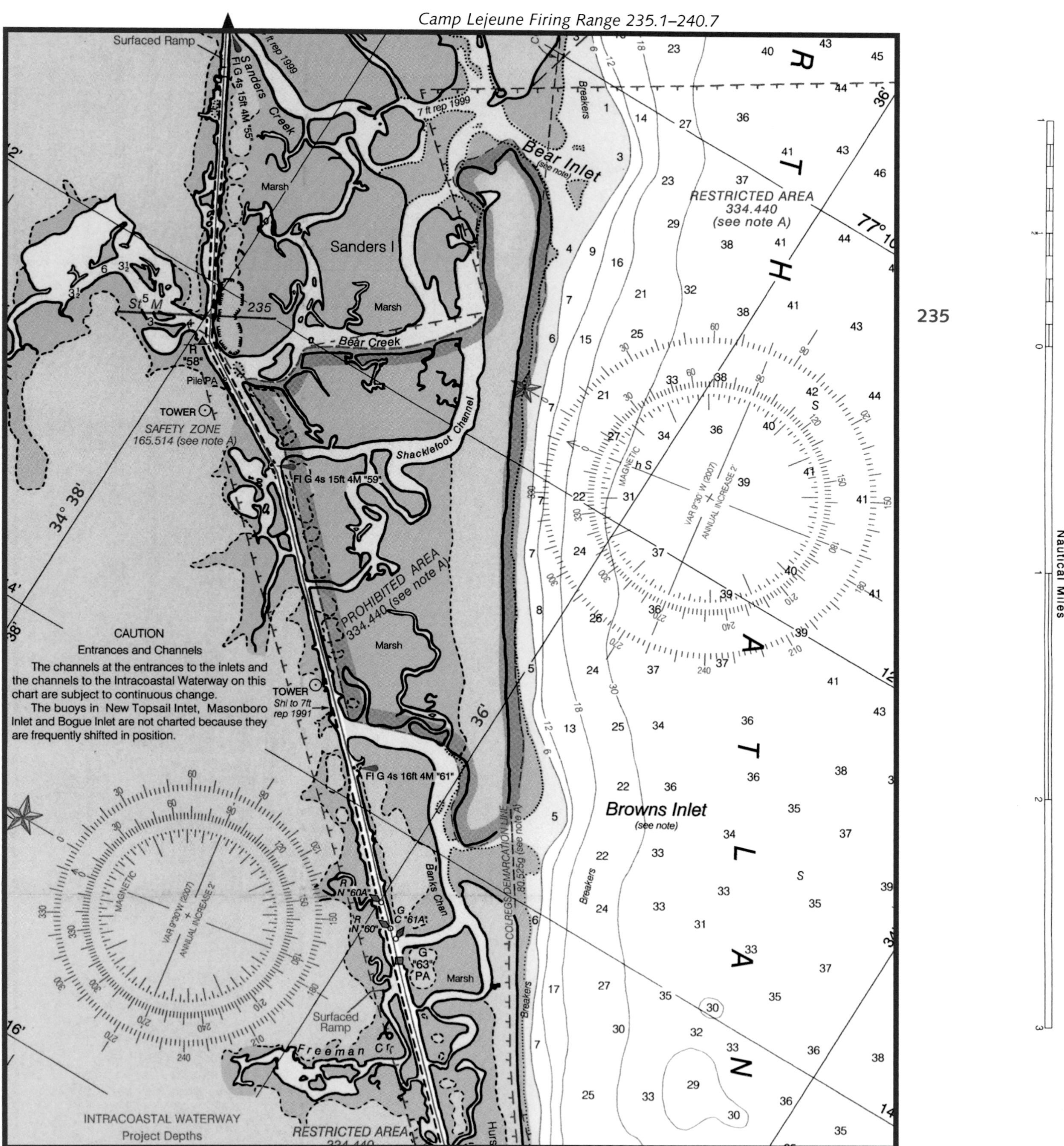

Surfaced Ramp
Sanders Creek
Fl G 4s 15ft 4M "55"
Bear Inlet
(see note)
Marsh
Sanders I
Bear Creek
Shackleloot Channel
TOWER
SAFETY ZONE
165.514 (see note A)
34° 38'
Fl G 4s 15ft 4M "59"
PROHIBITED AREA
334.440 (see note A)
RESTRICTED AREA
334.440
(see note A)
CAUTION
Entrances and Channels
The channels at the entrances to the inlets and the channels to the Intracoastal Waterway on this chart are subject to continuous change.
The buoys in New Topsail Intet, Masonboro Inlet and Bogue Inlet are not charted because they are frequently shifted in position.
TOWER
Shl to 7ft rep 1991
Fl G 4s 16ft 4M "61"
Browns Inlet
(see note)
Banks Chan
COLREGS DEMARCATION LINE
80.525g (see note A)
Breakers
Surfaced Ramp
Freeman Cr
INTRACOASTAL WATERWAY
Project Depths
ATLANTIC
NORTH
77° 10'
36'
235
Nautical Miles

235

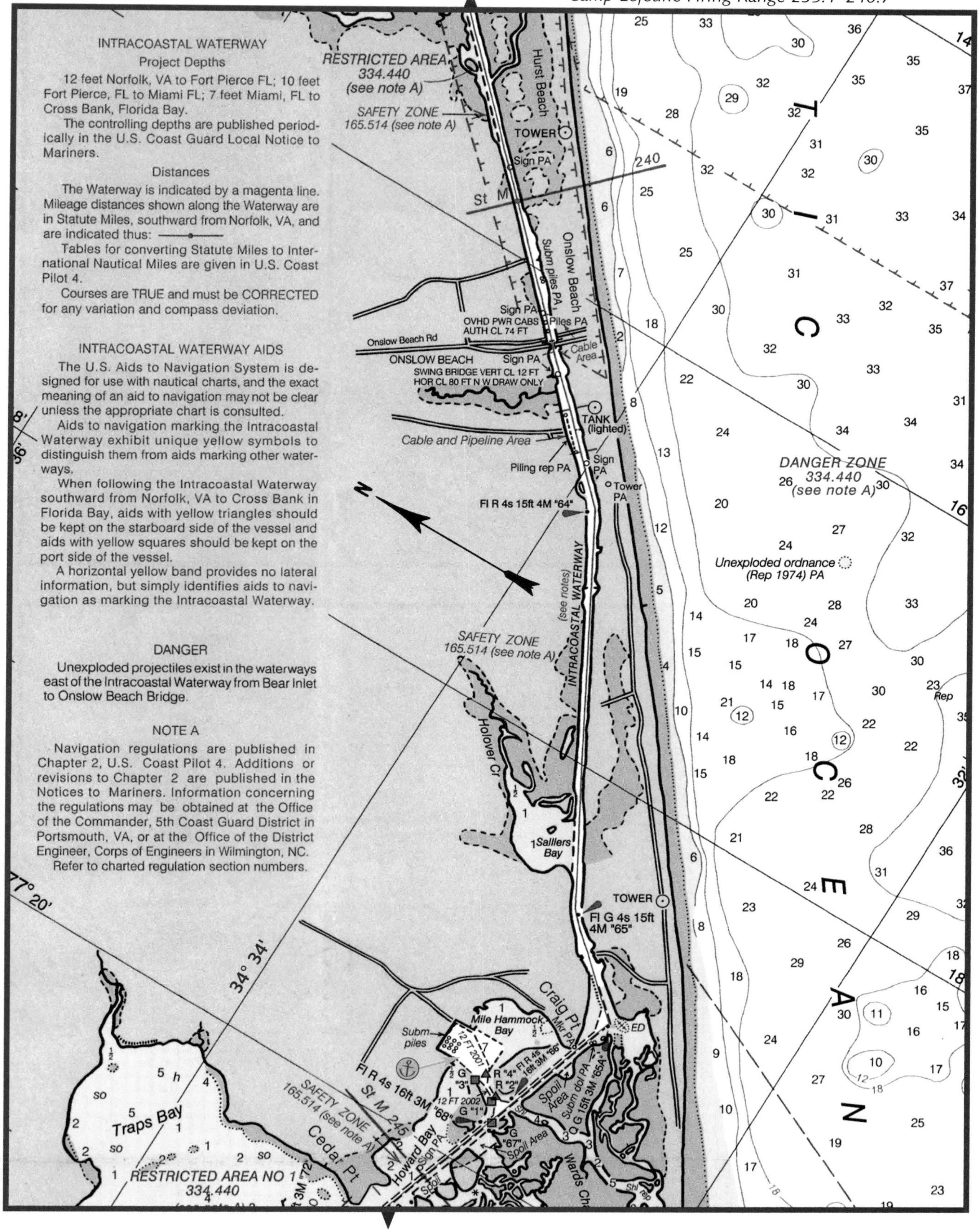

Camp Lejeune Firing Range 235.1–240.7

INTRACOASTAL WATERWAY

Project Depths

12 feet Norfolk, VA to Fort Pierce FL; 10 feet Fort Pierce, FL to Miami FL; 7 feet Miami, FL to Cross Bank, Florida Bay.

The controlling depths are published periodically in the U.S. Coast Guard Local Notice to Mariners.

Distances

The Waterway is indicated by a magenta line. Mileage distances shown along the Waterway are in Statute Miles, southward from Norfolk, VA, and are indicated thus: ———•———

Tables for converting Statute Miles to International Nautical Miles are given in U.S. Coast Pilot 4.

Courses are TRUE and must be CORRECTED for any variation and compass deviation.

INTRACOASTAL WATERWAY AIDS

The U.S. Aids to Navigation System is designed for use with nautical charts, and the exact meaning of an aid to navigation may not be clear unless the appropriate chart is consulted.

Aids to navigation marking the Intracoastal Waterway exhibit unique yellow symbols to distinguish them from aids marking other waterways.

When following the Intracoastal Waterway southward from Norfolk, VA to Cross Bank in Florida Bay, aids with yellow triangles should be kept on the starboard side of the vessel and aids with yellow squares should be kept on the port side of the vessel.

A horizontal yellow band provides no lateral information, but simply identifies aids to navigation as marking the Intracoastal Waterway.

DANGER

Unexploded projectiles exist in the waterways east of the Intracoastal Waterway from Bear Inlet to Onslow Beach Bridge.

NOTE A

Navigation regulations are published in Chapter 2, U.S. Coast Pilot 4. Additions or revisions to Chapter 2 are published in the Notices to Mariners. Information concerning the regulations may be obtained at the Office of the Commander, 5th Coast Guard District in Portsmouth, VA, or at the Office of the District Engineer, Corps of Engineers in Wilmington, NC.

Refer to charted regulation section numbers.

RESTRICTED AREA
334.440
(see note A)

SAFETY ZONE
165.514 (see note A)

Hurst Beach

TOWER

Sign PA

St M 240

Onslow Beach

Subm piles PA

OVHD PWR CABS AUTH CL 74 FT

Piles PA

Onslow Beach Rd

ONSLOW BEACH

SWING BRIDGE VERT CL 12 FT HOR CL 80 FT N W DRAW ONLY

Cable Area

TANK (lighted)

Cable and Pipeline Area

Piling rep PA

Tower PA

Fl R 4s 15ft 4M "64"

INTRACOASTAL WATERWAY (see notes)

SAFETY ZONE
165.514 (see note A)

Holover Cr

Salliers Bay

TOWER

Fl G 4s 15ft 4M "65"

Craig Pt

Mile Hammock Bay

Subm piles

12 FT 2001

12 FT 2002

Fl R 4s 16ft 3M "68"

St M 245

SAFETY ZONE
165.514 (see note A)

Cedar Pt

Howard Bay

Spoil Area

Subm dol PA

Fl G 15ft 3M "65A"

Wards Ch

Traps Bay

RESTRICTED AREA NO 1
334.440

DANGER ZONE
334.440
(see note A)

Unexploded ordnance
(Rep 1974) PA

O C E A N   A T L A N T I C

77° 20′

34° 34′

N

240

Onslow Beach Bridge 240.7
On hour and half-hour:
7 A.M.–7 P.M.

244.5

245

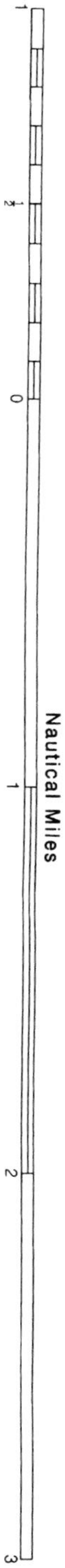

Nautical Miles
0 1 2 3

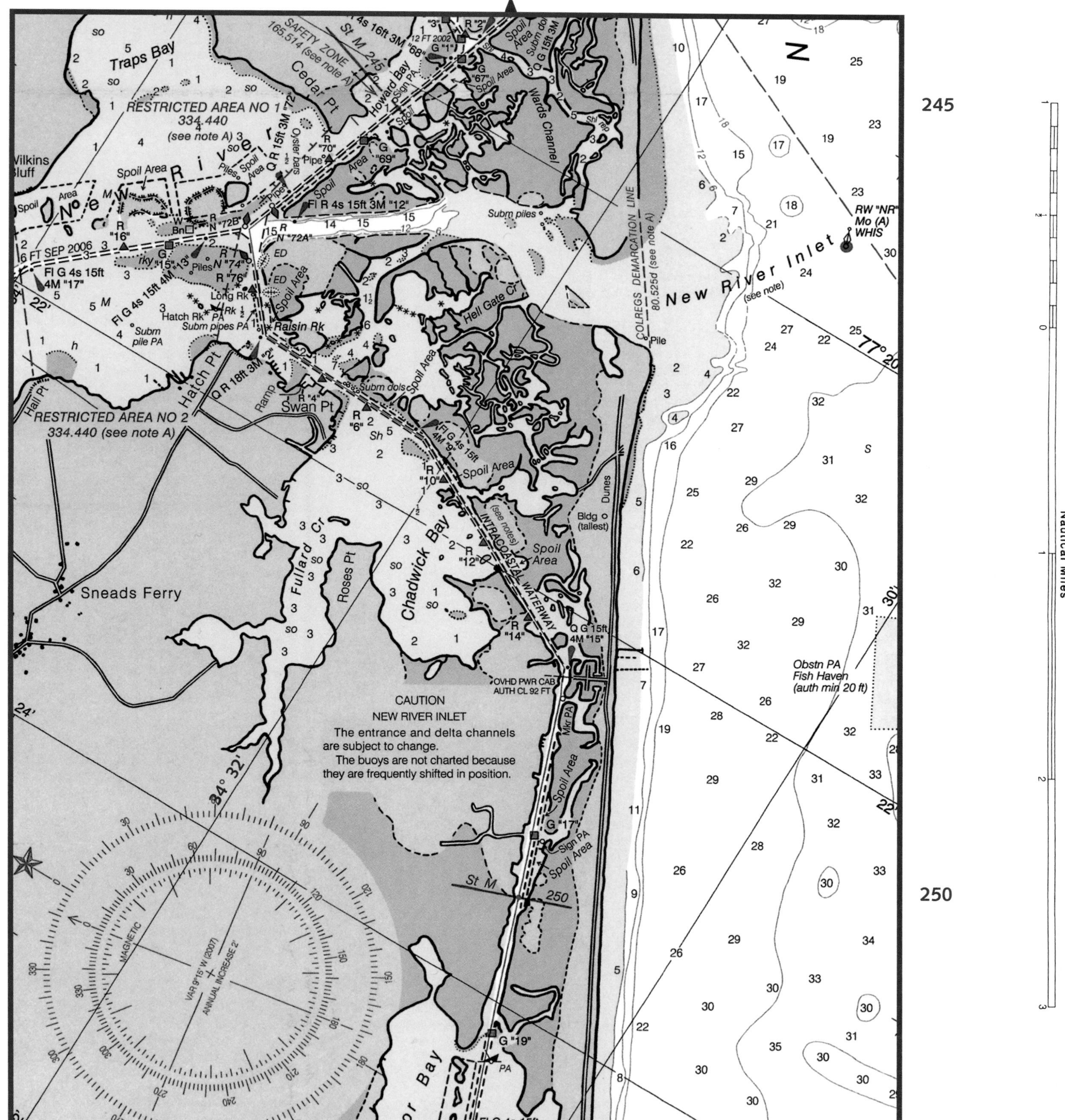
Traps Bay
RESTRICTED AREA NO 1
334.440
(see note A)
SAFETY ZONE
165.514 (see note A)
Cedar Pt
Howard Bay
Wilkins
Bluff
Spoil Area
New River
Wards Channel
Subm piles
Hell Gate Cr
COLREGS DEMARCATION LINE
80.525d (see note A)
New River Inlet
(see note)
RW "NR"
Mo (A)
WHIS
Long Rk
Hatch Rk
Raisin Rk
Subm pipes PA
Subm
pile PA
Hatch Pt
Swan Pt
Ramp
Subm dols
Hall Pt
RESTRICTED AREA NO 2
334.440 (see note A)
Chadwick Bay
Fullard Cr
Roses Pt
Sneads Ferry
INTRACOASTAL WATERWAY
(see notes)
Bldg
(tallest)
Dunes
Pile
OVHD PWR CAB
AUTH CL 92 FT
Obstn PA
Fish Haven
(auth min 20 ft)
CAUTION
NEW RIVER INLET
The entrance and delta channels
are subject to change.
The buoys are not charted because
they are frequently shifted in position.
Mkr PA
Sign PA
St M
250
VAR 9°15' W (2007)
ANNUAL INCREASE 2'
MAGNETIC
245
250
Nautical Miles

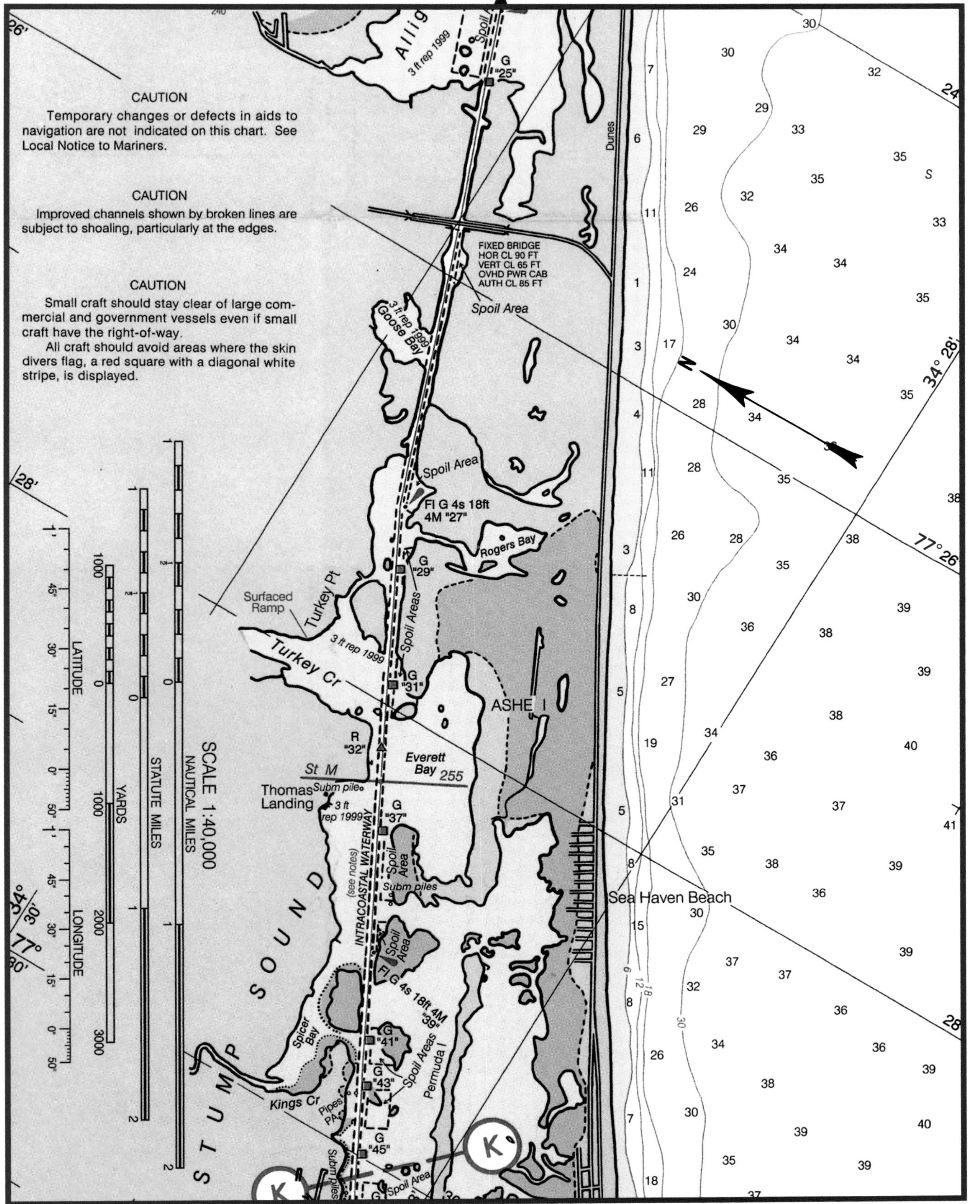

CAUTION
Temporary changes or defects in aids to navigation are not indicated on this chart. See Local Notice to Mariners.
CAUTION
Improved channels shown by broken lines are subject to shoaling, particularly at the edges.
CAUTION
Small craft should stay clear of large commercial and government vessels even if small craft have the right-of-way.
All craft should avoid areas where the skin divers flag, a red square with a diagonal white stripe, is displayed.
FIXED BRIDGE
HOR CL 90 FT
VERT CL 65 FT
OVHD PWR CAB
AUTH CL 85 FT
Spoil Area
Goose Bay
3 ft rep 1999
Fl G 4s 18ft
4M "27"
Rogers Bay
G "29"
Spoil Areas
Surfaced Ramp
Turkey Pt
Turkey Cr
G "31"
ASHE I
R "32"
Everett Bay 255
St M
Thomas Landing
Subm pile
G "37"
Spoil Area
Subm piles
INTRACOASTAL WATERWAY
(see notes)
Sea Haven Beach
Fl G 4s 18ft 4M "39"
G "41"
G "43"
G "45"
Spicer Bay
Kings Cr
Pipes PA
Permuda I
STUMP SOUND
Dunes
SCALE 1:40,000
NAUTICAL MILES
STATUTE MILES
YARDS
LATITUDE
LONGITUDE
34° 28'
77° 26'
34° 30'
77° 30'
Nautical Miles

255

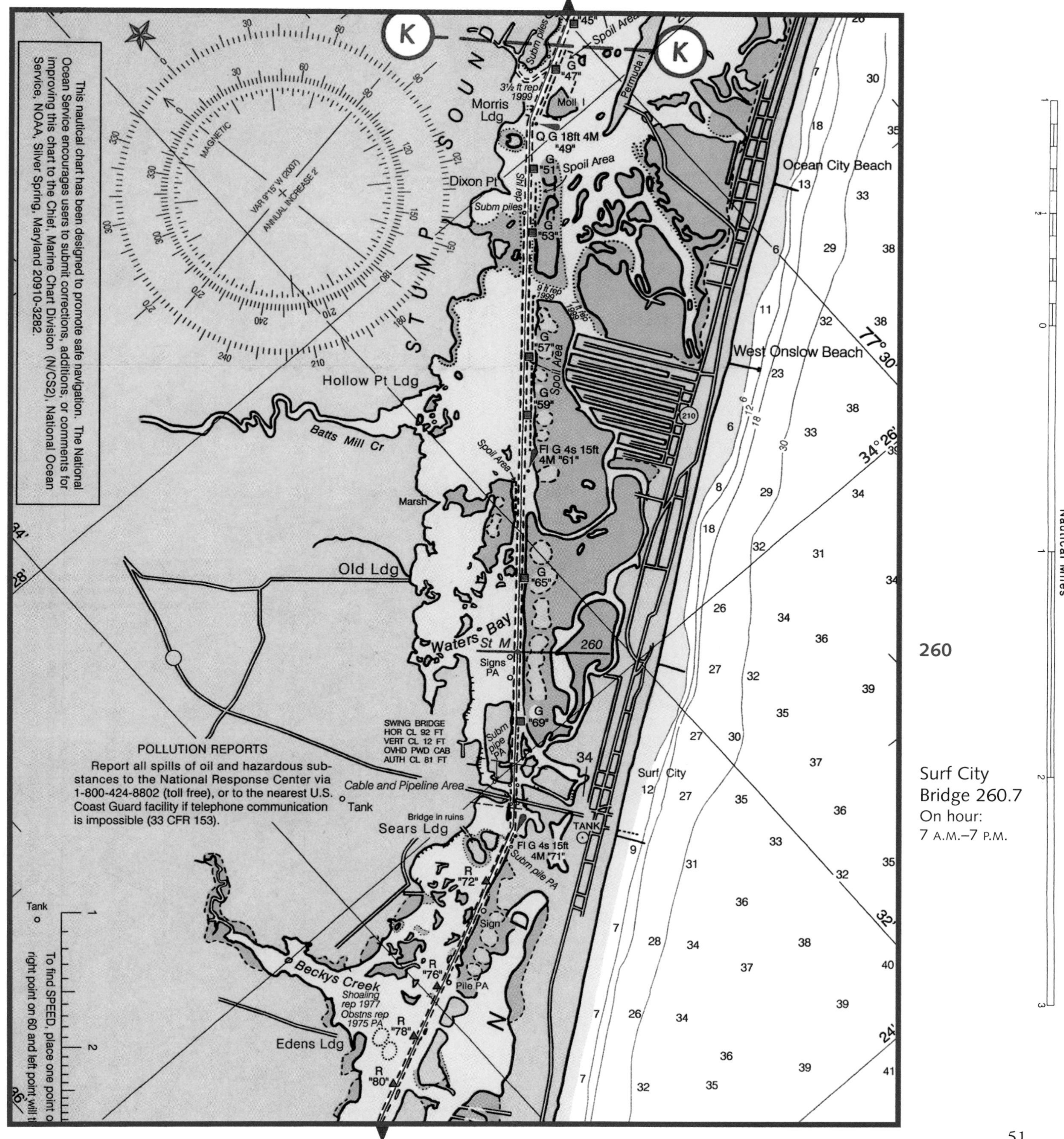

260

Surf City Bridge 260.7
On hour:
7 A.M.–7 P.M.

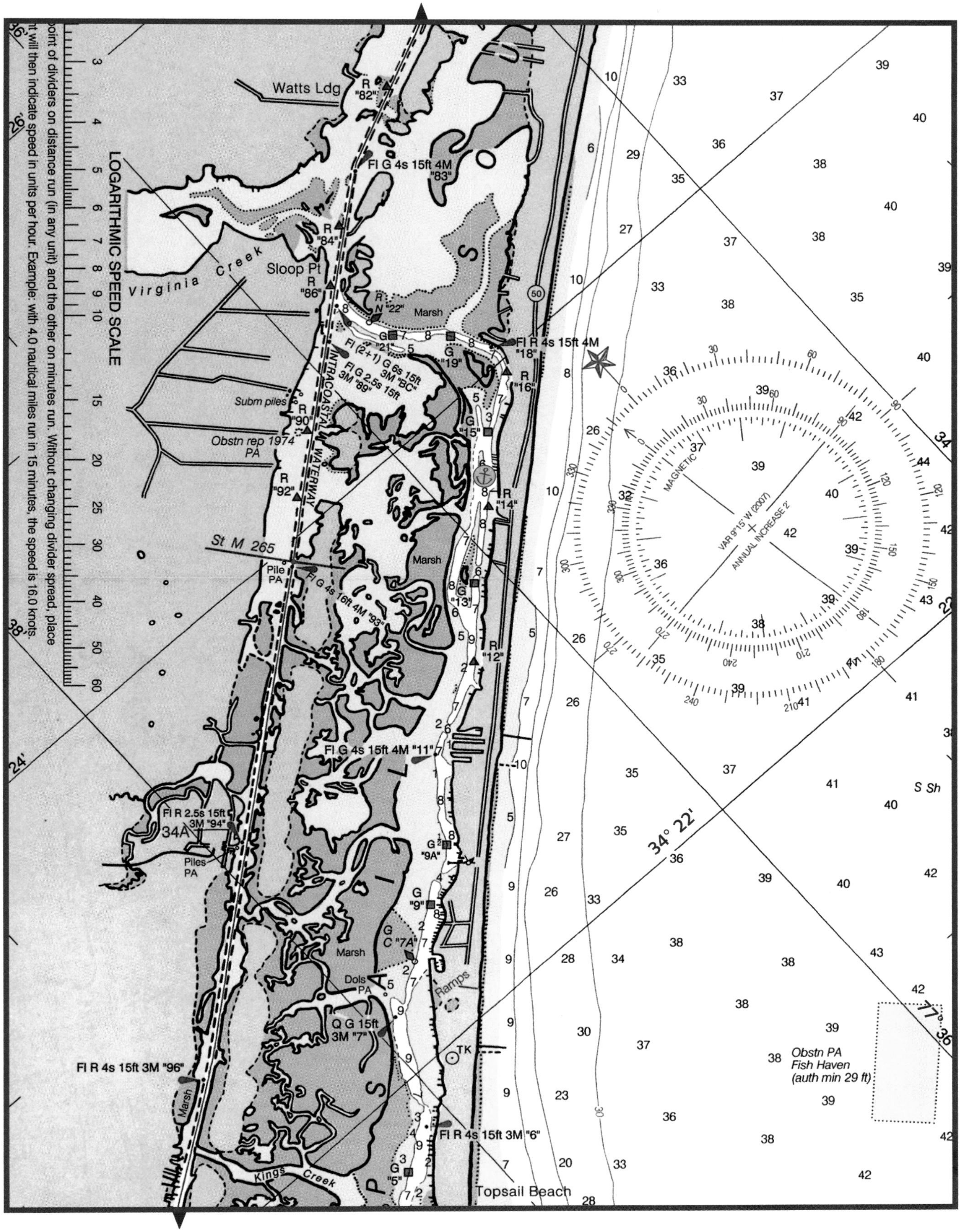

Watts Ldg
R "82"
Fl G 4s 15ft 4M "83"
R "84"
Virginia Creek
Sloop Pt
R "86"
R N "22"
Marsh
G "21"
Fl (2+1) G 6s 15ft 3M "BC"
Fl G 2.5s 15ft 3M "89"
G "19"
Fl R 4s 15ft 4M "18"
R "16"
INTRACOASTAL WATERWAY
Subm piles
R "90"
Obstn rep 1974 PA
G "15"
R "14"
R "92"
St M 265
Pile PA
Fl G 4s 16ft 4M "93"
Marsh
G "13"
R "12"
Fl G 4s 15ft 4M "11"
Fl R 2.5s 15ft 3M "94"
34A
Piles PA
G "9A"
G "9"
G C "7A"
Marsh
Dols PA
Ramps
Q G 15ft 3M "7"
TK
Fl R 4s 15ft 3M "96"
Marsh
Fl R 4s 15ft 3M "6"
Kings Creek
G "5"
Topsail Beach
MAGNETIC
VAR 9°15' W (2007)
ANNUAL INCREASE 2'
34° 22'
77° 36'
S Sh
Obstn PA
Fish Haven
(auth min 29 ft)

264.5

265

LOGARITHMIC SPEED SCALE

3 4 5 6 7 8 9 10 15 20 25 30 40 50 60

point of dividers on distance run (in any unit) and the other on minutes run. Without changing divider spread, place
nt will then indicate speed in units per hour. Example: with 4.0 nautical miles run in 15 minutes, the speed is 16.0 knots.

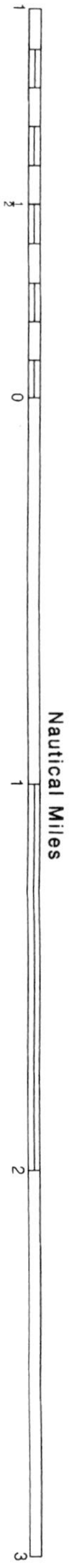

Nautical Miles

1 ½ 0 1 2 3

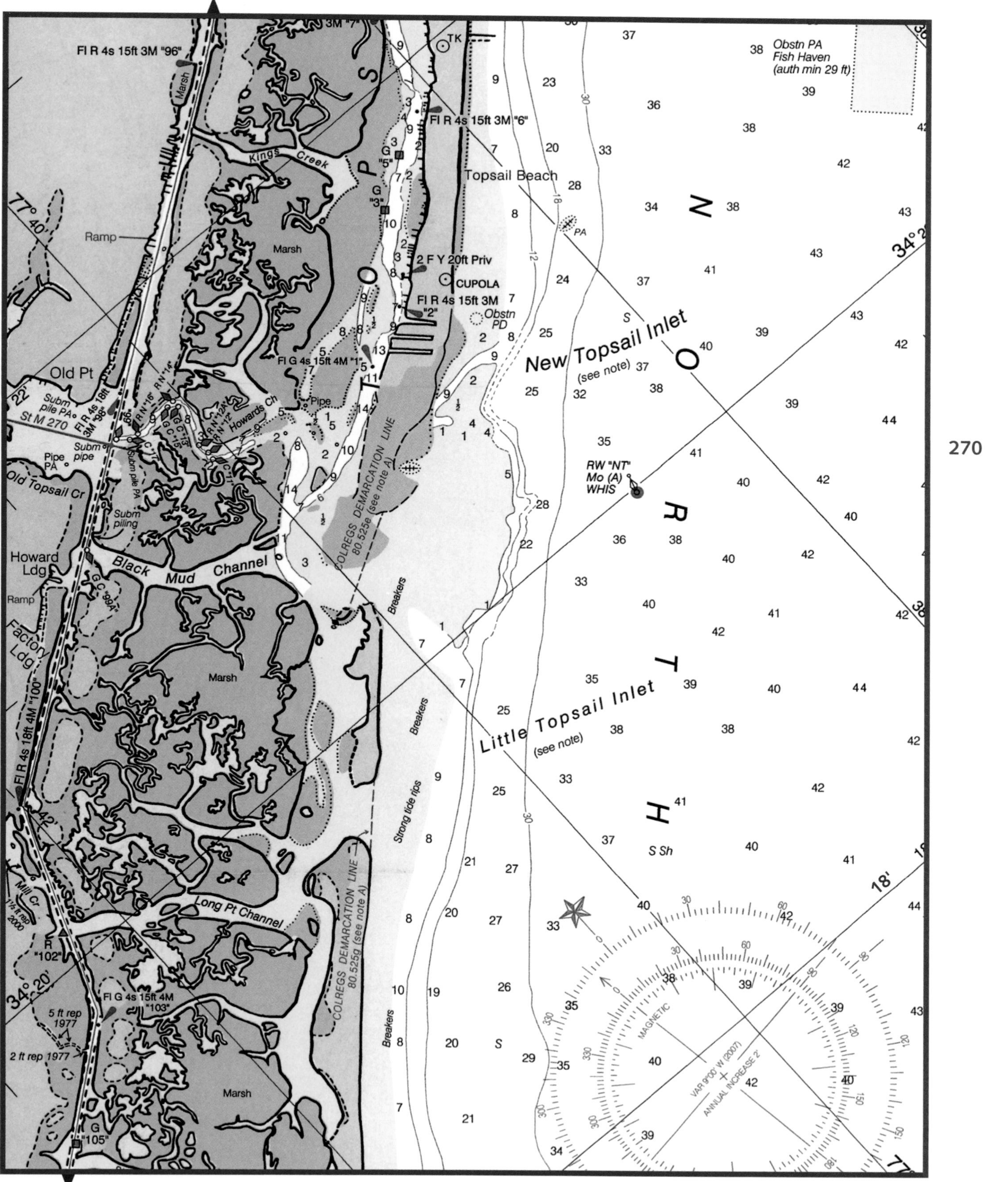

Nautical Miles

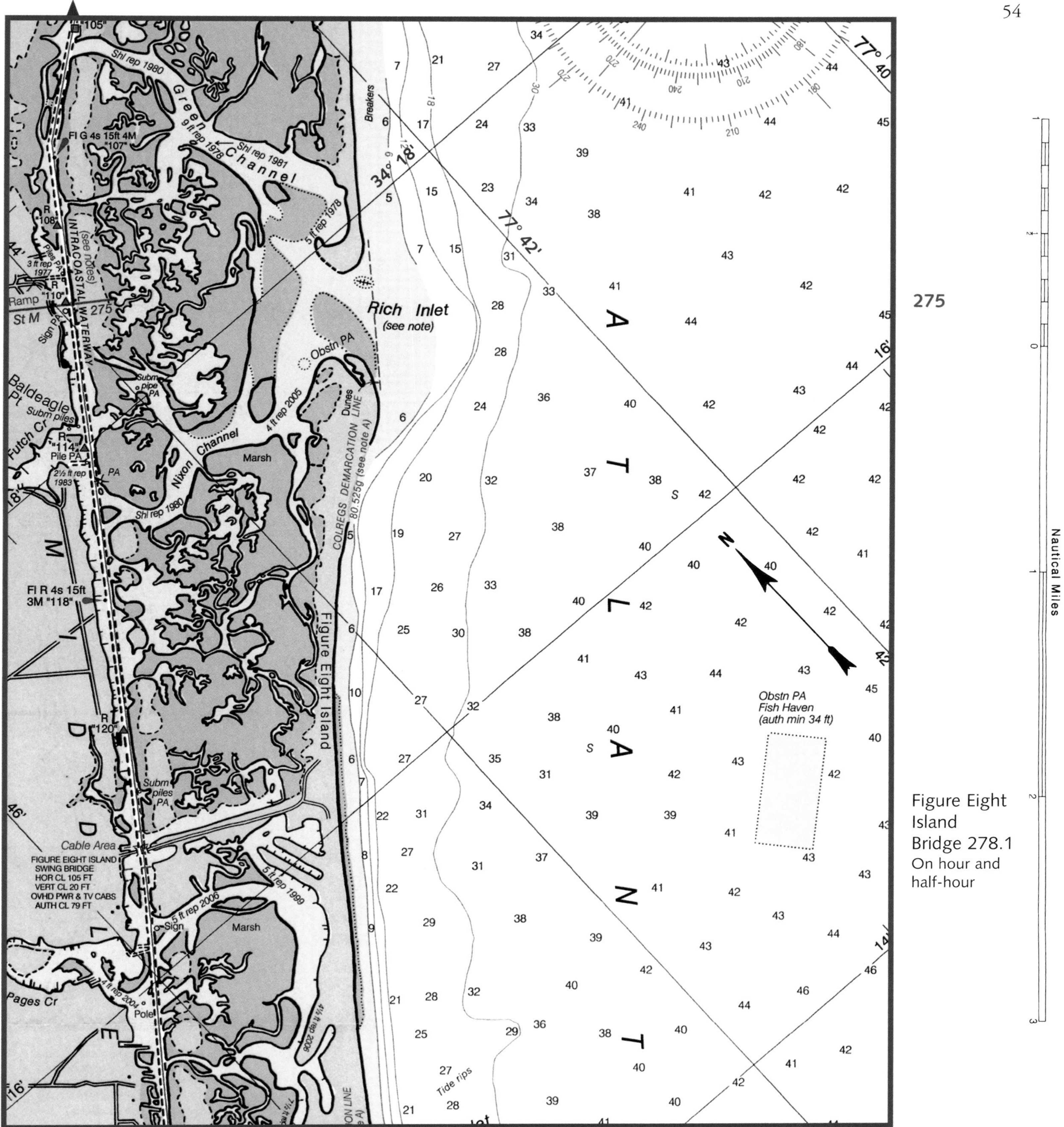

275

Figure Eight
Island
Bridge 278.1
On hour and
half-hour

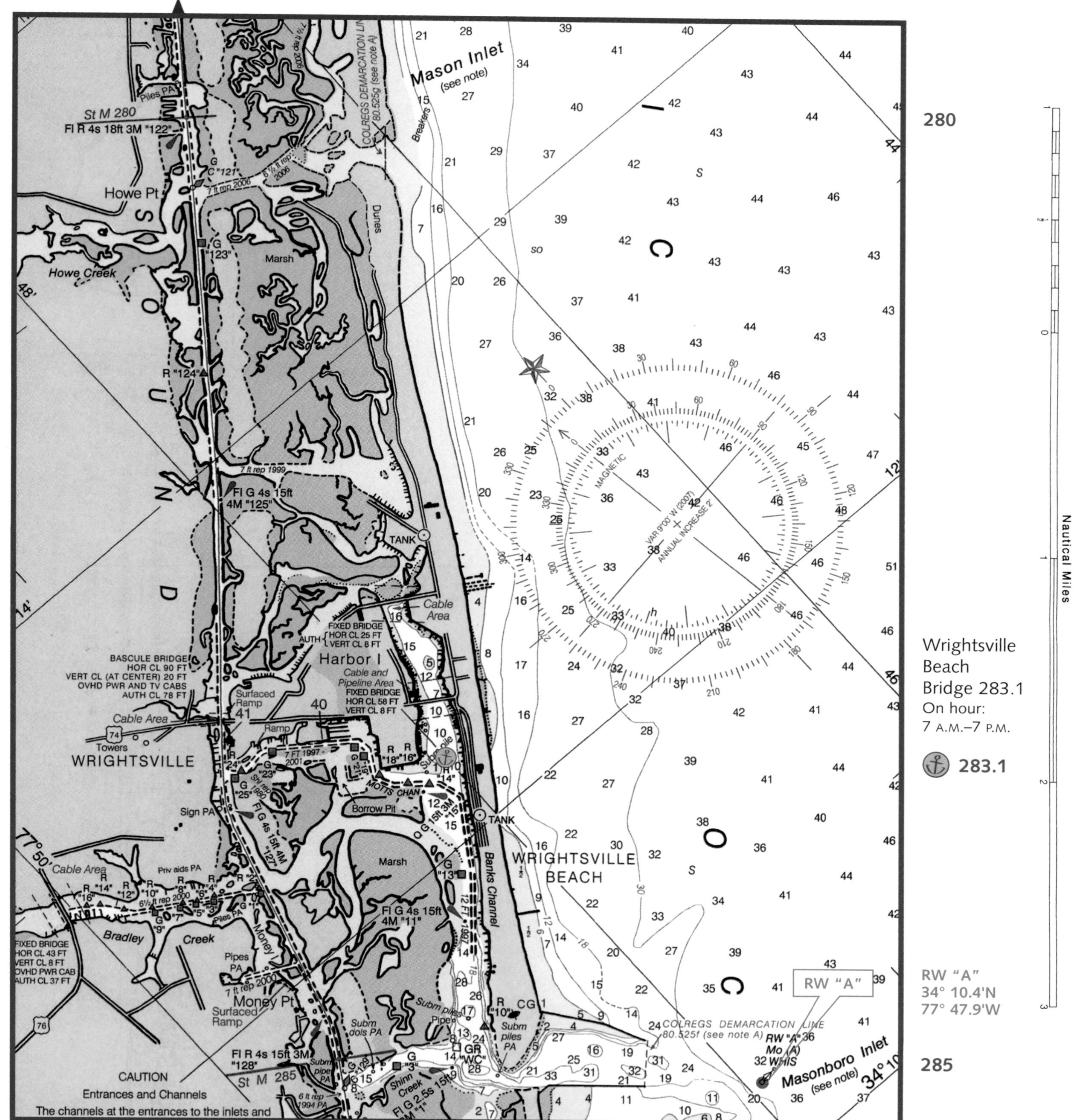

280
Wrightsville Beach Bridge 283.1
On hour: 7 A.M.–7 P.M.
283.1
RW "A"
34° 10.4'N
77° 47.9'W
285
Nautical Miles
Mason Inlet
(see note)
Breakers
COLREGS DEMARCATION LINE
St M 280
Fl R 4s 18ft 3M "122"
Howe Pt
Howe Creek
Marsh
Dunes
R "124"
7 ft rep 1999
Fl G 4s 15ft
4M "125"
TANK
Cable Area
FIXED BRIDGE
HOR CL 25 FT
VERT CL 8 FT
Harbor I
Cable and
Pipeline Area
FIXED BRIDGE
HOR CL 58 FT
VERT CL 8 FT
BASCULE BRIDGE
HOR CL 90 FT
VERT CL (AT CENTER) 20 FT
OVHD PWR AND TV CABS
AUTH CL 78 FT
Surfaced
Ramp
Cable Area
Towers
WRIGHTSVILLE
Sign PA
MOTTS CHAN
Borrow Pit
Marsh
Banks Channel
WRIGHTSVILLE
BEACH
Fl G 4s 15ft
4M "11"
Cable Area
Bradley
Creek
FIXED BRIDGE
HOR CL 43 FT
VERT CL 8 FT
OVHD PWR CAB
AUTH CL 37 FT
Pipes
PA
Money Pt
Surfaced
Ramp
Fl R 4s 15ft 3M
"128"
St M 285
Shinn
Creek
CAUTION
Entrances and Channels
The channels at the entrances to the inlets and
COLREGS DEMARCATION LINE
80.525f (see note A)
RW "A"
Mo (A)
WHIS
Masonboro Inlet
(see note)

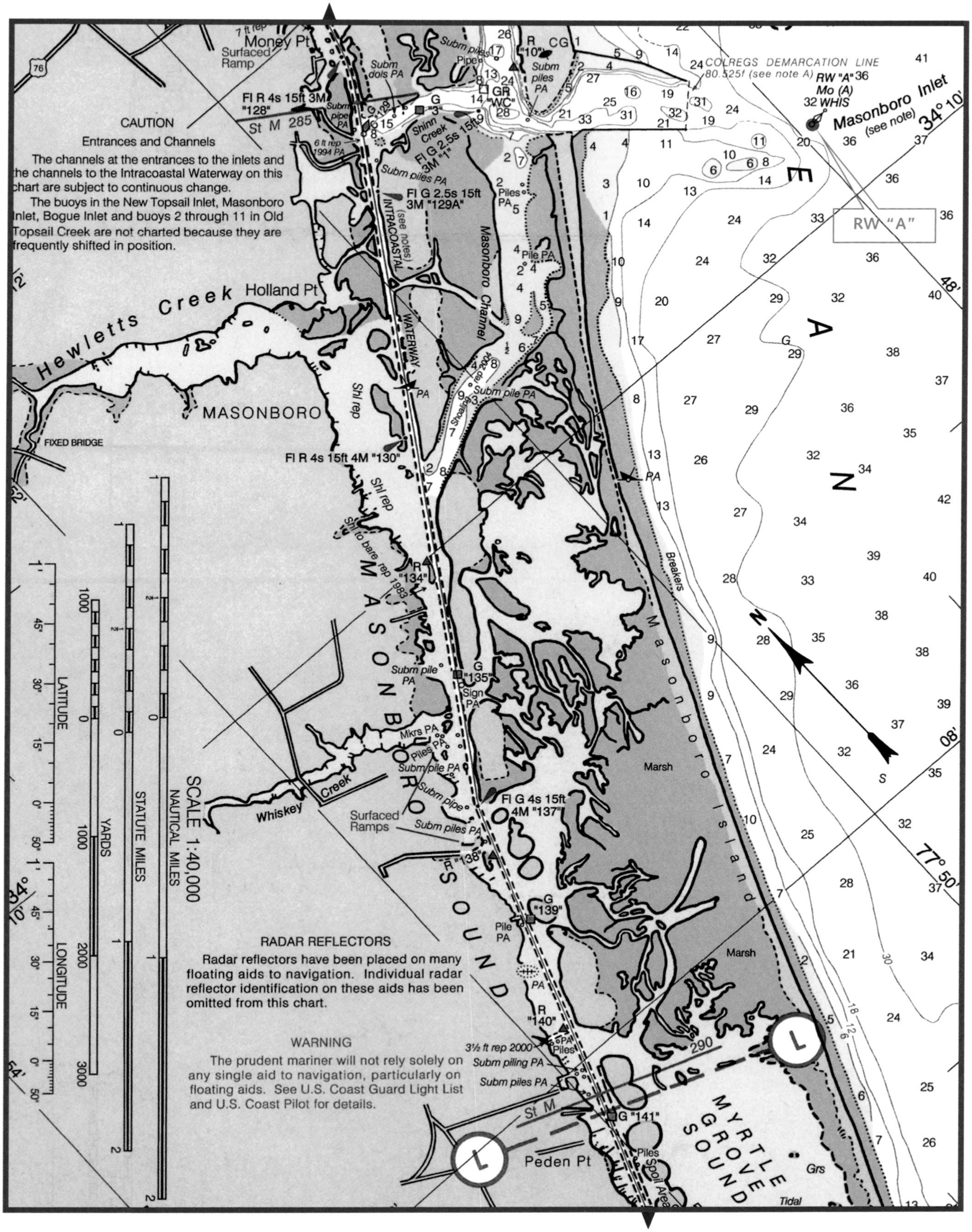

285

RW "A"
34° 10.4'N
77° 47.9'W

290

CAUTION

Entrances and Channels

The channels at the entrances to the inlets and the channels to the Intracoastal Waterway on this chart are subject to continuous change.

The buoys in the New Topsail Inlet, Masonboro Inlet, Bogue Inlet and buoys 2 through 11 in Old Topsail Creek are not charted because they are frequently shifted in position.

RADAR REFLECTORS

Radar reflectors have been placed on many floating aids to navigation. Individual radar reflector identification on these aids has been omitted from this chart.

WARNING

The prudent mariner will not rely solely on any single aid to navigation, particularly on floating aids. See U.S. Coast Guard Light List and U.S. Coast Pilot for details.

SCALE 1:40,000
NAUTICAL MILES
STATUTE MILES
YARDS
LATITUDE
LONGITUDE

Nautical Miles

COLREGS DEMARCATION LINE
80.525f (see note A)
RW "A" 36
Mo (A)
32 WHIS
Masonboro Inlet
(see note)

Money Pt
Surfaced Ramp
Fl R 4s 15ft 3M "128"
St M 285
Fl G 2.5s 15ft 3M "1"
Shinn Creek
Fl G 2.5s 15ft 3M "129A"
INTRACOASTAL (see notes) WATERWAY
Masonboro Channel
Hewletts Creek
Holland Pt
MASONBORO
FIXED BRIDGE
Fl R 4s 15ft 4M "130"
Shl rep
Shl to bare rep 1983
R "134"
G "135"
MASONBORO SOUND
Whiskey Creek
Surfaced Ramps
Fl G 4s 15ft 4M "137"
"138"
G "139"
R "140"
3½ ft rep 2000
Subm piling PA
Subm piles PA
G "141"
St M 290
Peden Pt
MYRTLE GROVE SOUND
Spoil Area
Masonboro Island
Breakers
Marsh
OCEAN

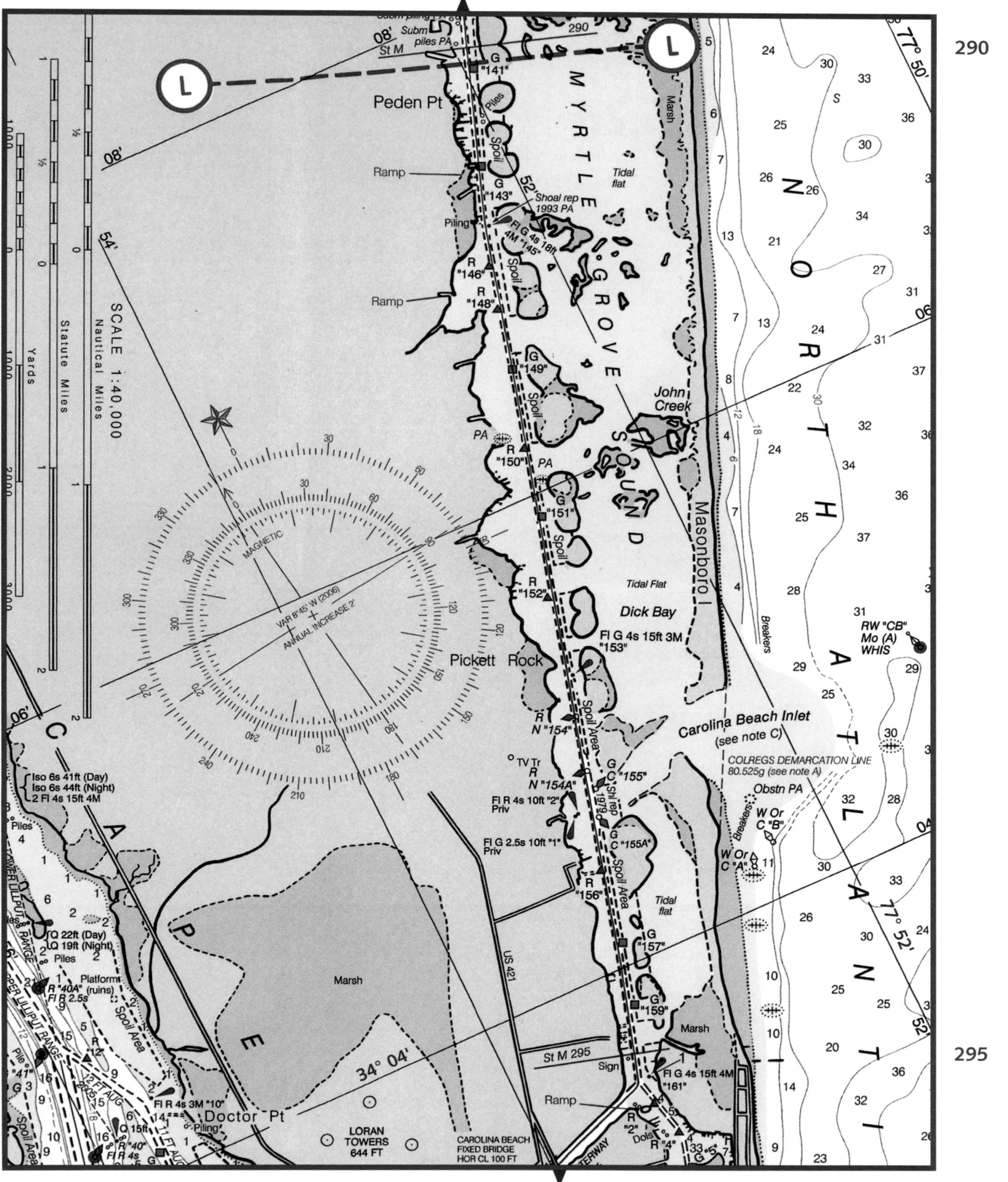
Peden Pt
Ramp
Piling
MYRTLE GROVE SOUND
Tidal flat
Shoal rep 1993 PA
Fl G 4s 18ft 4M "145"
John Creek
Masonboro I
Tidal Flat
Dick Bay
Fl G 4s 15ft 3M "153"
Pickett Rock
Carolina Beach Inlet
(see note C)
COLREGS DEMARCATION LINE
80.525g (see note A)
Obstn PA
RW "CB" Mo (A) WHIS
Breakers
NORTH ATLANTIC
CAPE
Marsh
Doctor Pt
LORAN TOWERS 644 FT
CAROLINA BEACH FIXED BRIDGE HOR CL 100 FT
Fl G 4s 15ft 4M "161"
St M 295
Iso 6s 41ft (Day)
Iso 6s 44ft (Night)
2 Fl 4s 15ft 4M
SCALE 1:40,000
Nautical Miles
Statute Miles
Yards
VAR 8°45' W (2006)
ANNUAL INCREASE 2'
MAGNETIC
34° 04'
77° 50'
77° 52'
Nautical Miles
290
295

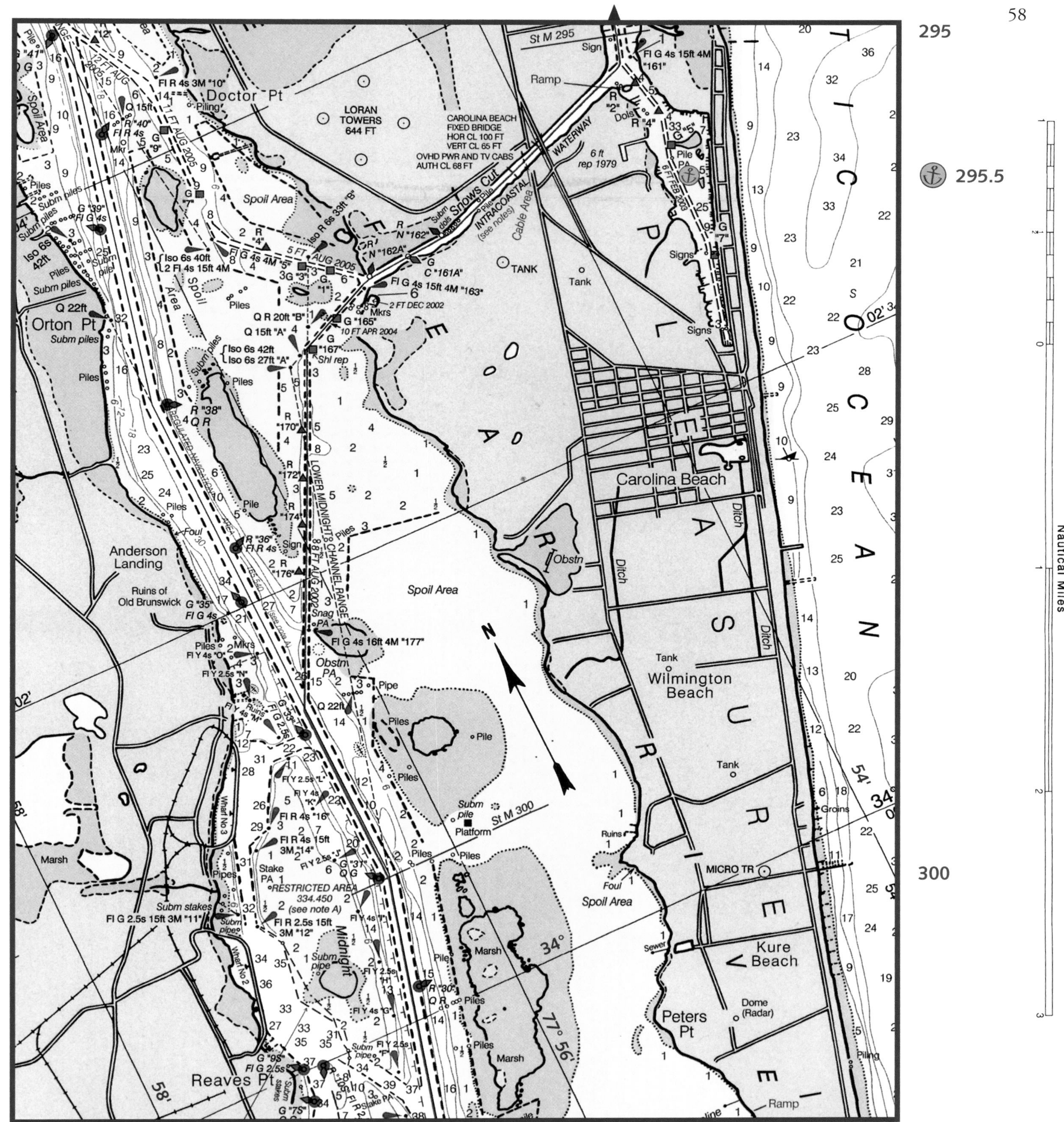

295
295.5
300
Nautical Miles
Doctor Pt
LORAN TOWERS 644 FT
CAROLINA BEACH FIXED BRIDGE HOR CL 100 FT VERT CL 65 FT
OVHD PWR AND TV CABS AUTH CL 68 FT
Snows Cut
INTRACOASTAL WATERWAY
Cable Area
Spoil Area
Orton Pt
Anderson Landing
Ruins of Old Brunswick
LOWER MIDNIGHT CHANNEL RANGE
Carolina Beach
Wilmington Beach
Kure Beach
Peters Pt
Reaves Pt
Midnight
RESTRICTED AREA 334.450 (see note A)
Marsh
Platform
St M 295
St M 300
MICRO TR
Dome (Radar)
TANK
Tank
Wharf No 3
Wharf No 2
PLEASURE ISLAND
ATLANTIC OCEAN

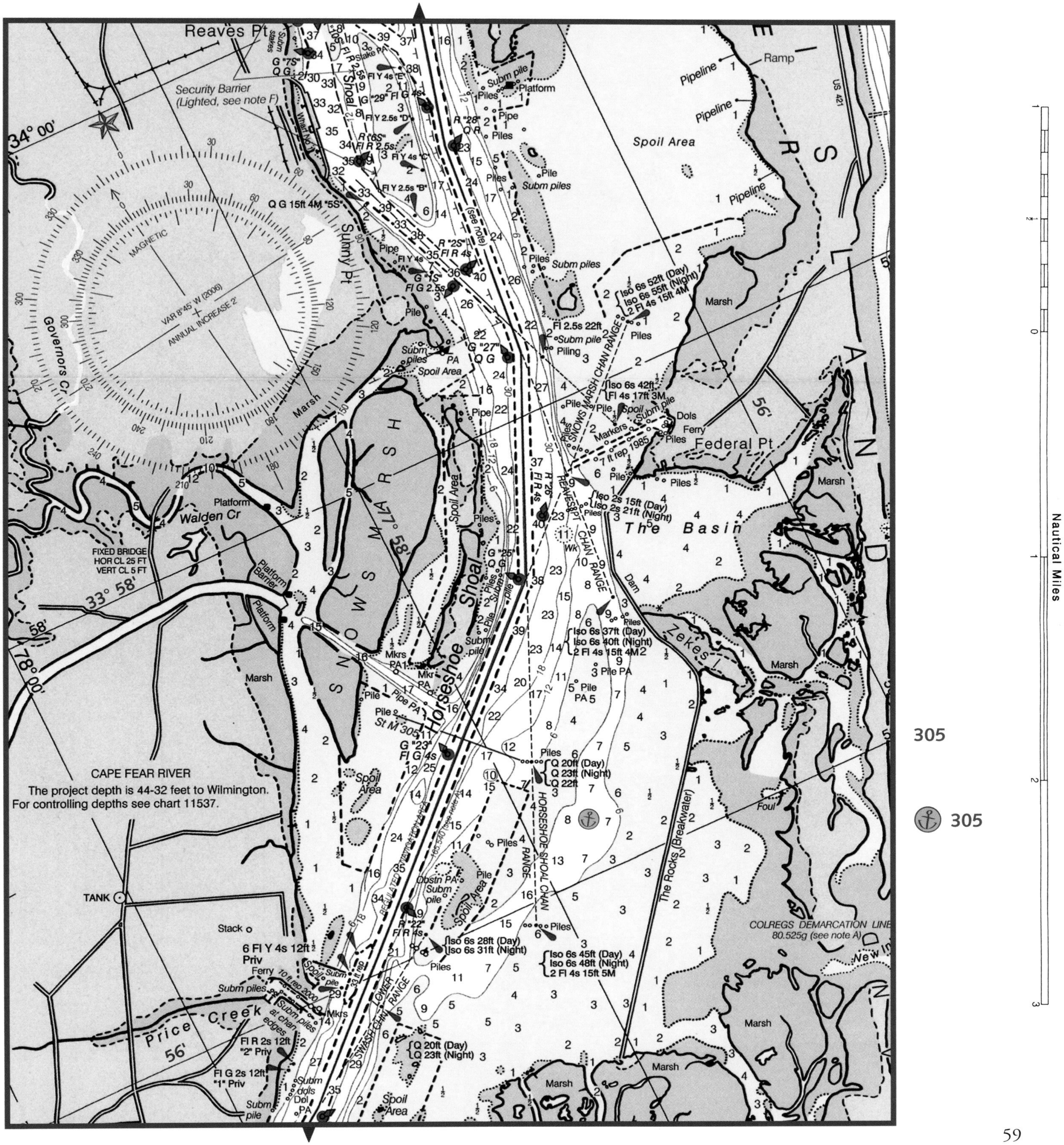
Reaves Pt
Security Barrier
(Lighted, see note F)
34° 00'
Sunny Pt
Governors Cr
MAGNETIC
VAR 8°45' W (2006)
ANNUAL INCREASE 2'
Spoil Area
Pipeline
Ramp
US 421
Marsh
Snows Marsh
Walden Cr
Platform
FIXED BRIDGE
HOR CL 25 FT
VERT CL 5 FT
33° 58'
78° 00'
Horseshoe Shoal
Federal Pt
Dols
Ferry
The Basin
Zekes I
SNOWS MARSH CHAN RANGE
REAVES PT CHAN RANGE
HORSESHOE SHOAL CHAN RANGE
LOWER SWASH CHAN RANGE
The Rocks (Breakwater)
COLREGS DEMARCATION LINE
80.525g (see note A)
New Inlet
CAPE FEAR RIVER
The project depth is 44-32 feet to Wilmington.
For controlling depths see chart 11537.
TANK
Stack
Price Creek
56'
Foul
305
305
Nautical Miles
0
1
2
3

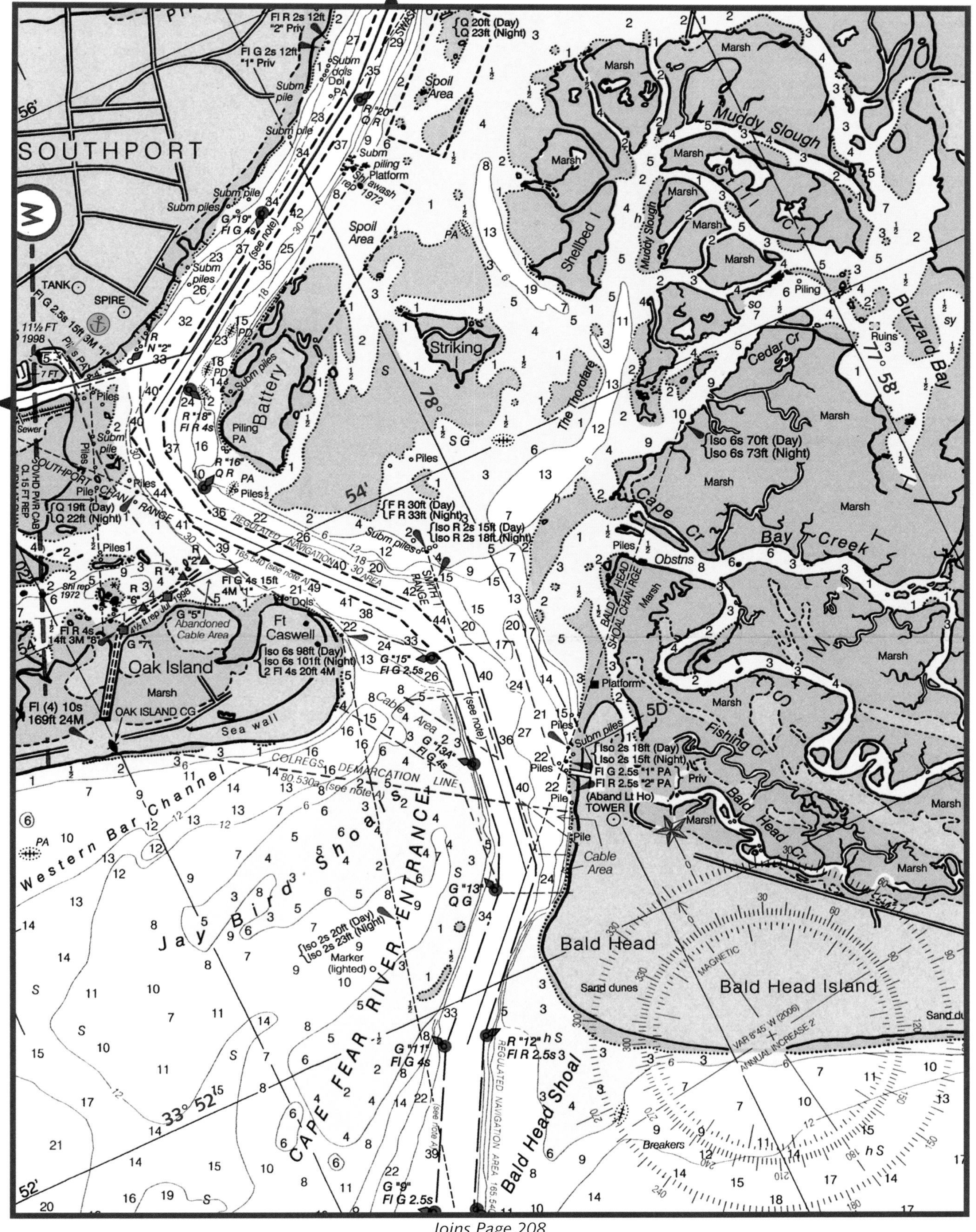

Joins Page 208

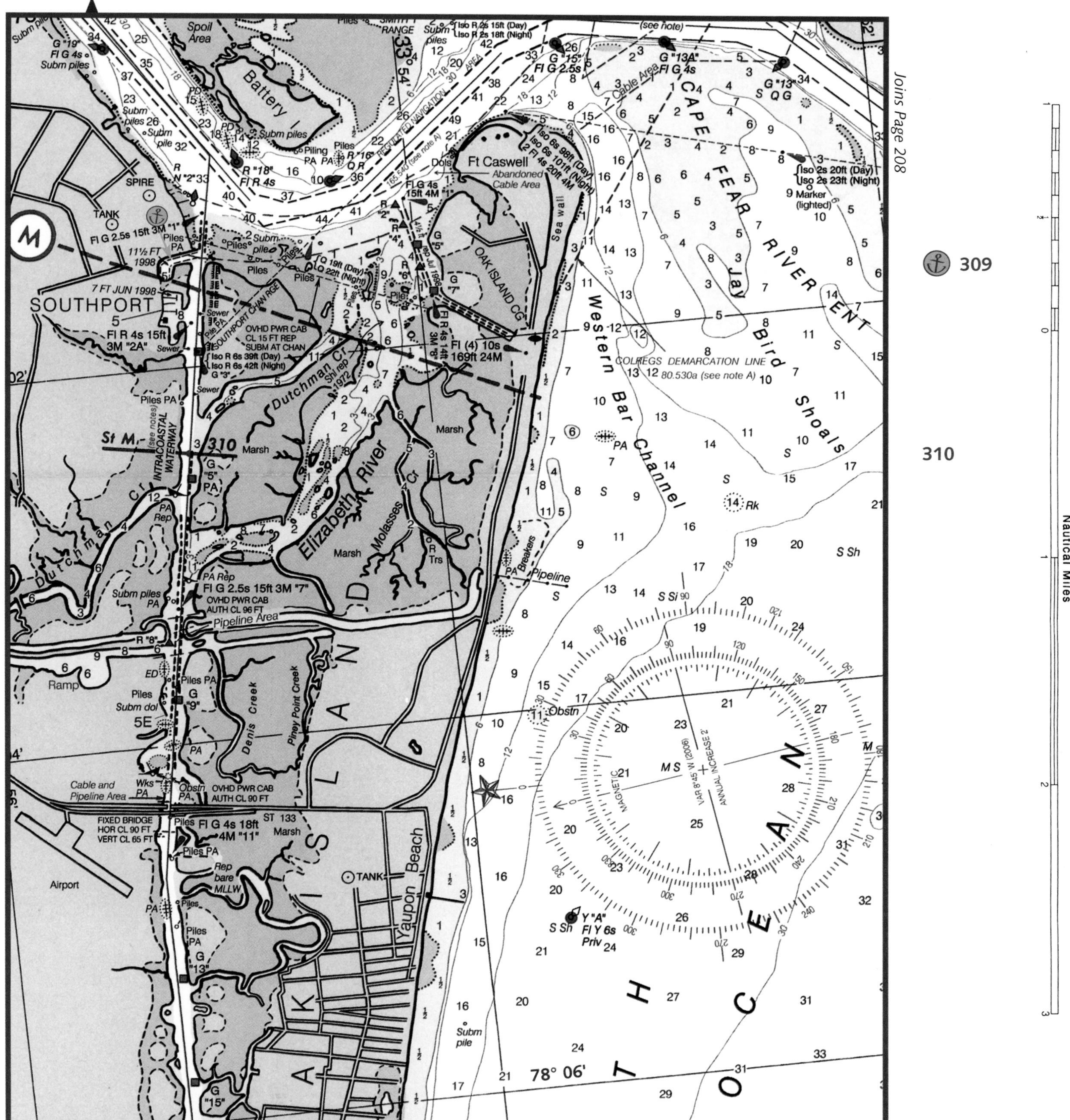

Joins Page 208
309
310
SOUTHPORT
Ft Caswell
CAPE FEAR RIVER ENT
Jay Bird Shoals
Western Bar Channel
OAK ISLAND CG
Elizabeth River
Dutchman Cr
Molasses Cr
Denis Creek
Piney Point Creek
Battery
Yaupon Beach
OAK ISLAND
ATLANTIC OCEAN
COLREGS DEMARCATION LINE 80.530a (see note A)
INTRACOASTAL WATERWAY
FIXED BRIDGE HOR CL 90 FT VERT CL 65 FT
Airport
78° 06'
Nautical Miles

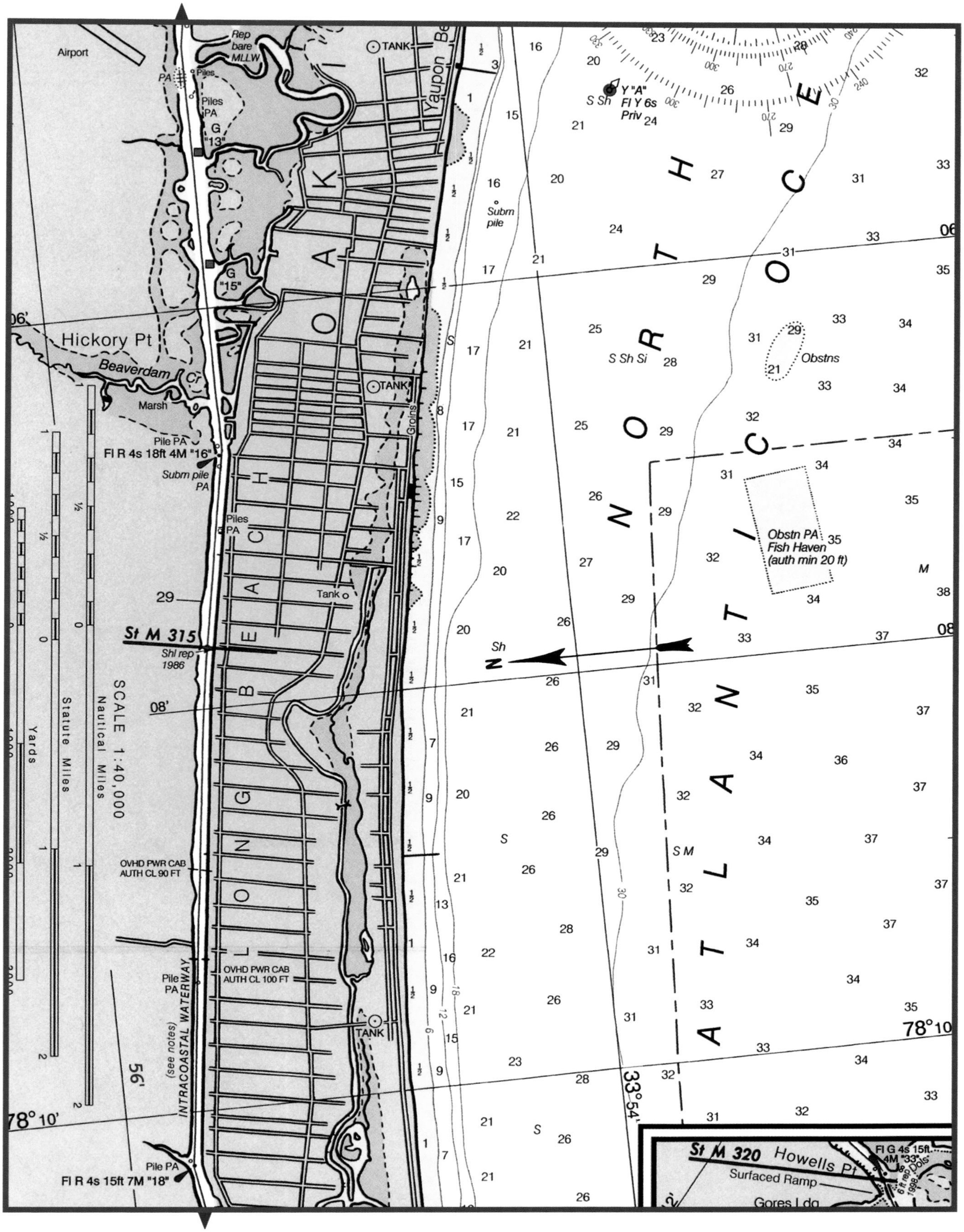
NORTH ATLANTIC OCEAN
LONG BEACH
OAK
Yaupon Be
Airport
Rep bare MLLW
Piles PA
G "13"
G "15"
Hickory Pt
Beaverdam Cr
Marsh
Pile PA
Fl R 4s 18ft 4M "16"
Subm pile PA
Piles PA
Tank
TANK
Groins
St M 315
Shl rep 1986
SCALE 1:40,000
Nautical Miles
Statute Miles
Yards
OVHD PWR CAB AUTH CL 90 FT
OVHD PWR CAB AUTH CL 100 FT
Pile PA
INTRACOASTAL WATERWAY
(see notes)
56'
78°10'
08'
06'
33°54'
Fl R 4s 15ft 7M "18"
Y "A" Fl Y 6s Priv
S Sh
S Sh Si
Obstns
Obstn PA Fish Haven (auth min 20 ft)
Subm pile
S M
St M 320
Howells Pt
Surfaced Ramp
Gores Ldg
Fl G 4s 15ft 4M "33"

315

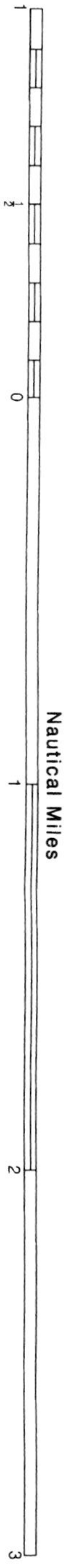
Nautical Miles

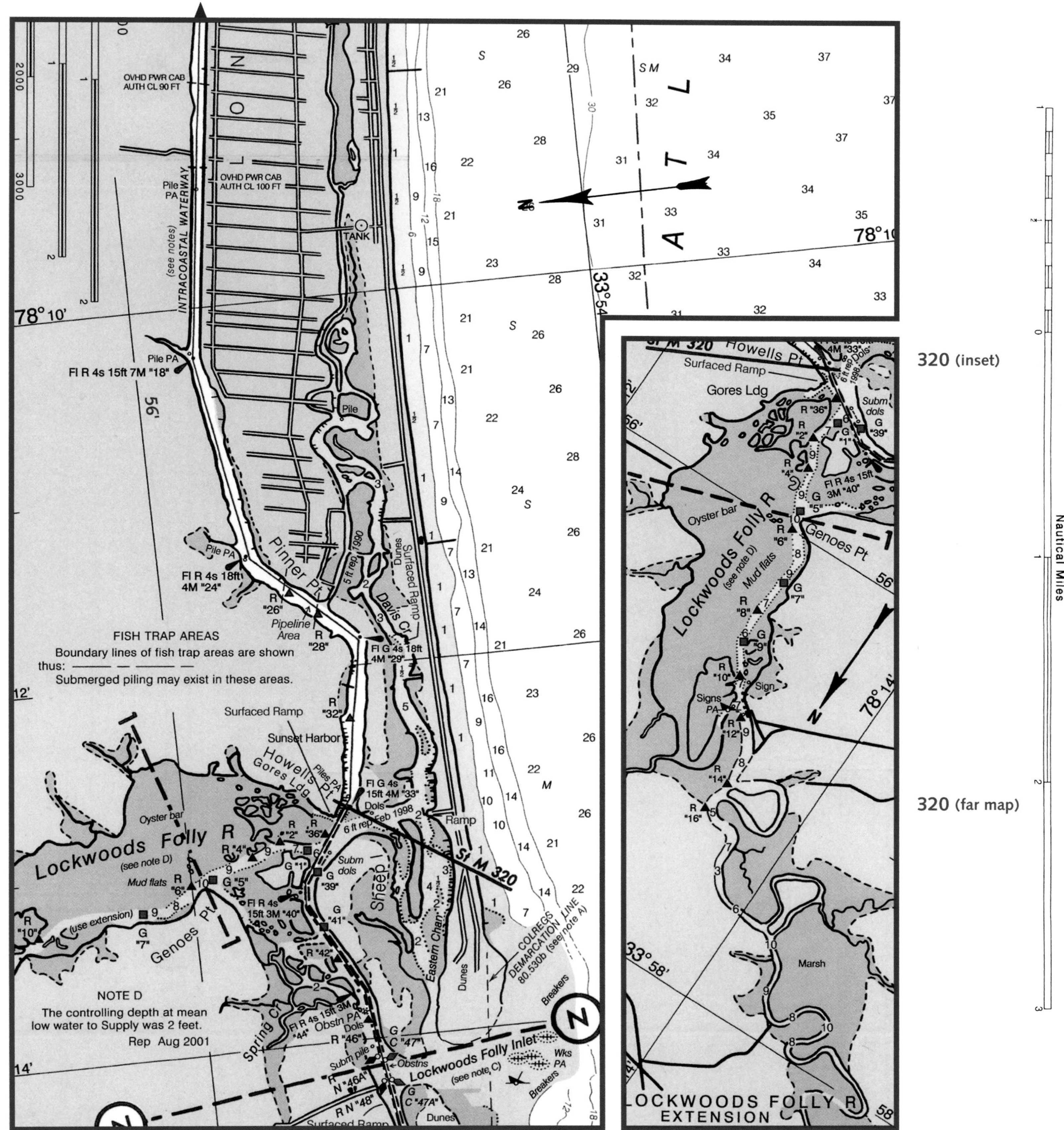

FISH TRAP AREAS
Boundary lines of fish trap areas are shown thus: ——— — ——— —
Submerged piling may exist in these areas.
NOTE D
The controlling depth at mean low water to Supply was 2 feet.
Rep Aug 2001
INTRACOASTAL WATERWAY
(see notes)
OVHD PWR CAB AUTH CL 90 FT
OVHD PWR CAB AUTH CL 100 FT
Lockwoods Folly R
Lockwoods Folly Inlet
Genoes Pt
Howells Pt
Gores Ldg
Sunset Harbor
Pinner Pt
Davis Cr
Spring Cr
Eastern Chan
Sheep
Surfaced Ramp
Pipeline Area
COLREGS DEMARCATION LINE 80.530b (see note A)
St M 320
LOCKWOODS FOLLY R EXTENSION
Nautical Miles
320 (inset)
320 (far map)

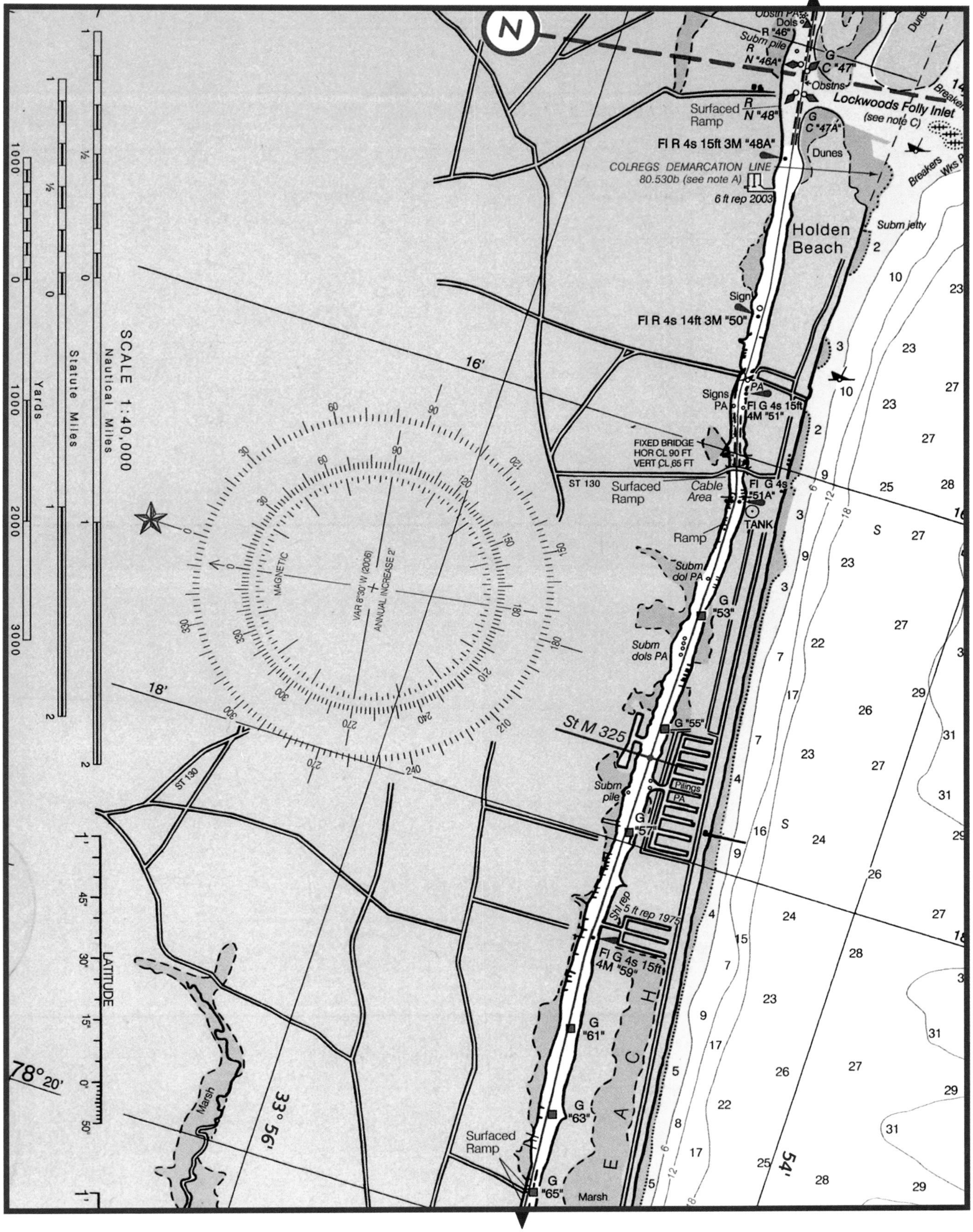
Lockwoods Folly Inlet
(see note C)
Holden Beach
COLREGS DEMARCATION LINE
80.530b (see note A)
6 ft rep 2003
Fl R 4s 15ft 3M "48A"
Fl R 4s 14ft 3M "50"
Fl G 4s 15ft 4M "51"
Fl G 4s "51A"
Fl G 4s 15ft 4M "59"
FIXED BRIDGE
HOR CL 90 FT
VERT CL 65 FT
St M 325
Surfaced Ramp
Cable Area
TANK
Subm dols PA
Subm pile
Pilings PA
Shl rep 5 ft rep 1975
ST 130
Marsh
Dunes
Subm jetty
Breakers
SCALE 1:40,000
Nautical Miles
Statute Miles
Yards
LATITUDE
VAR 8°30'W (2006)
ANNUAL INCREASE 2'
MAGNETIC
78°20'
33° 56'
54'
16'
18'
Nautical Miles

325

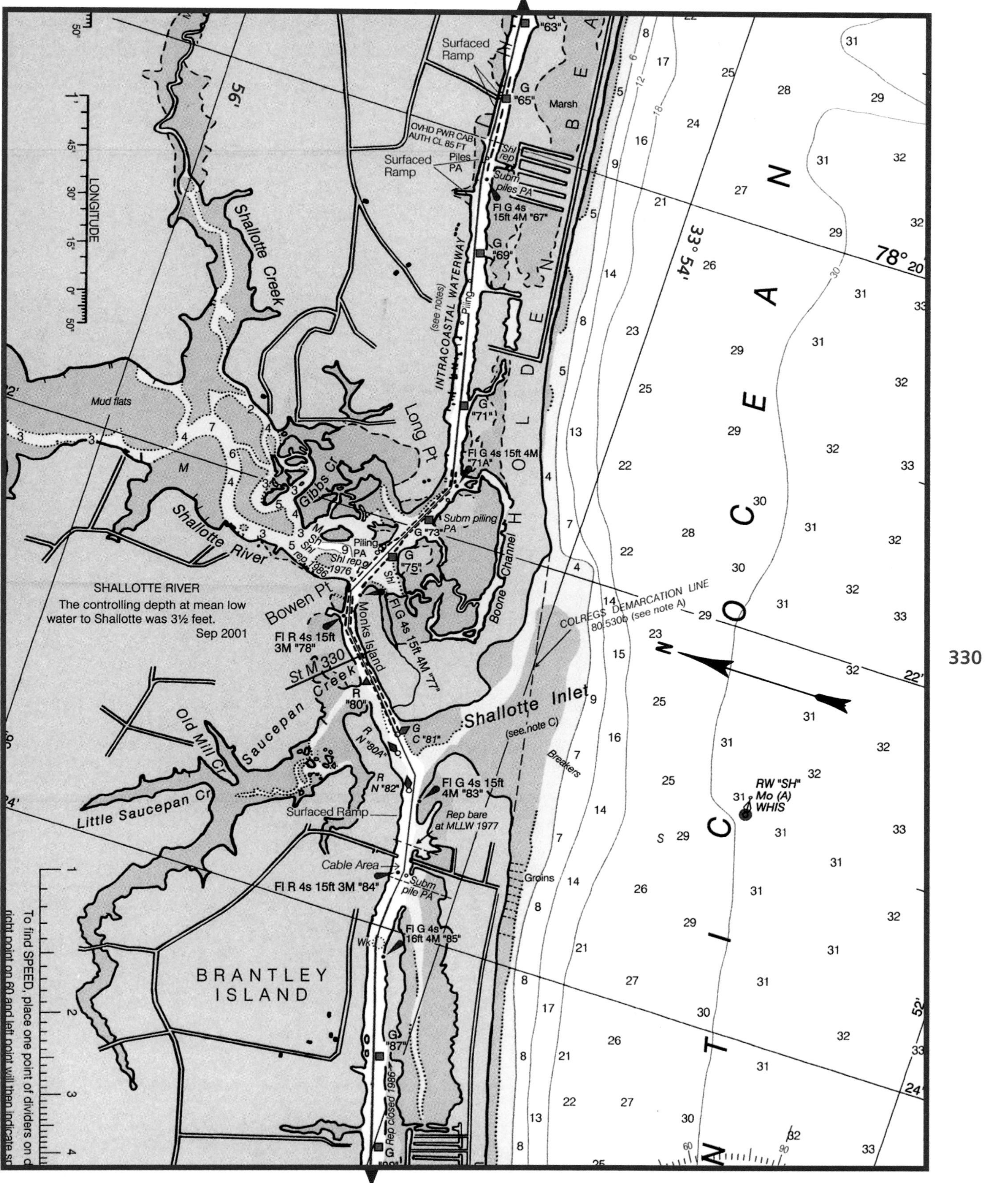

SHALLOTTE RIVER
The controlling depth at mean low water to Shallotte was 3½ feet.
Sep 2001
Shallotte Creek
Shallotte River
Shallotte Inlet
INTRACOASTAL WATERWAY
Long Pt
Gibbs Cr
Bowen Pt
Monks Island
Boone Channel
Saucepan Creek
Old Mill Cr
Little Saucepan Cr
BRANTLEY ISLAND
HOLDEN BEACH
ATLANTIC OCEAN
Mud flats
Surfaced Ramp
Marsh
OVHD PWR CAB AUTH CL 85 FT
COLREGS DEMARCATION LINE 80.530b (see note A)
St M 330
Cable Area
Groins
Breakers
Rep bare at MLLW 1977
RW "SH" Mo (A) WHIS
LONGITUDE
Nautical Miles
330

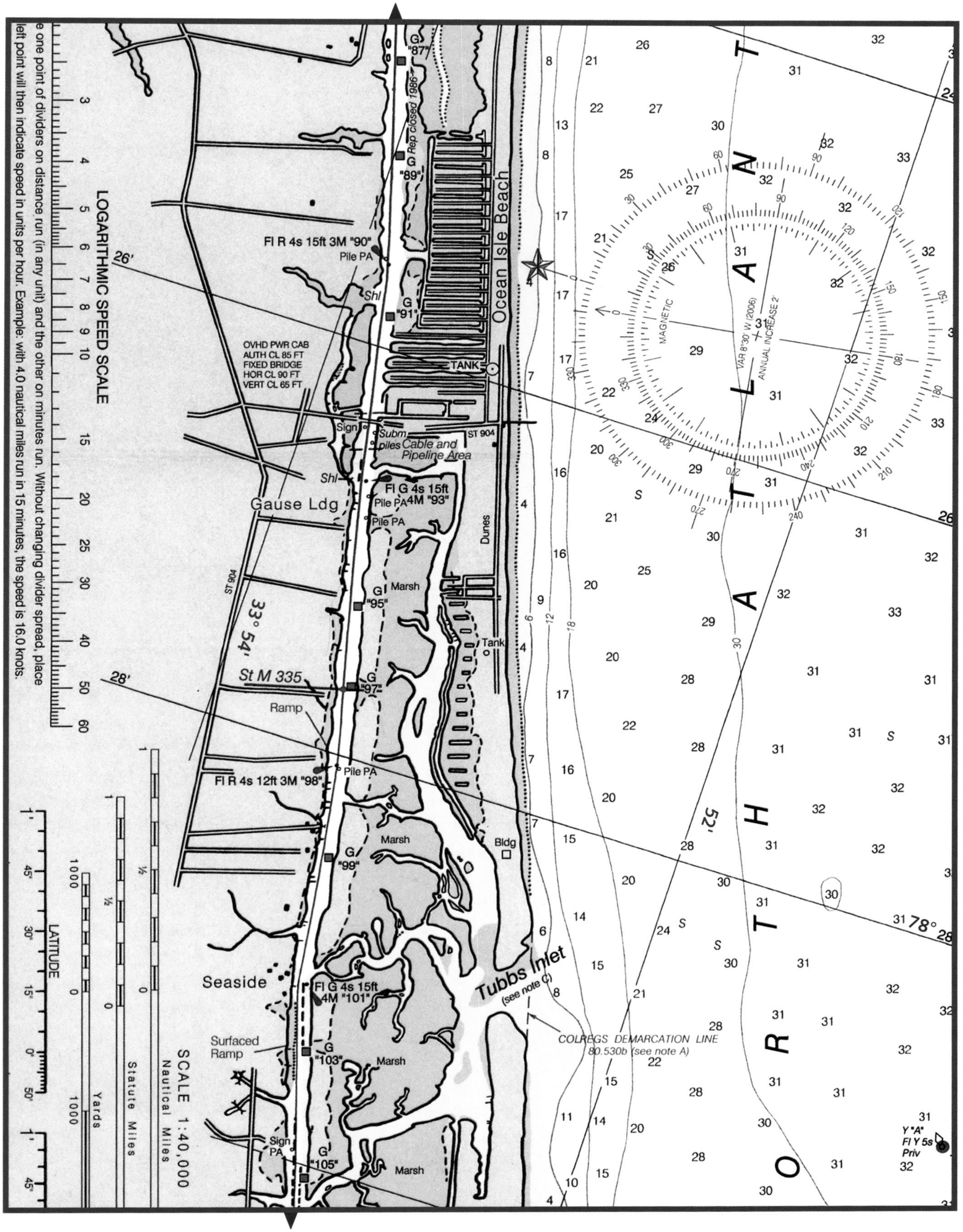

335

LOGARITHMIC SPEED SCALE

...e one point of dividers on distance run (in any unit) and the other on minutes run. Without changing divider spread, place left point will then indicate speed in units per hour. Example: with 4.0 nautical miles run in 15 minutes, the speed is 16.0 knots.

SCALE 1:40,000
Nautical Miles
Statute Miles
Yards
LATITUDE

NORTH ATLANTIC

Ocean Isle Beach
Tubbs Inlet (see note C)
COLREGS DEMARCATION LINE 80.530b (see note A)
Seaside
Surfaced Ramp
Gause Ldg
St M 335
ST 904
Dunes
Tank
TANK
Bldg
Ramp
Marsh
Sign
Pile PA
Shl
Subm piles
Cable and Pipeline Area
Rep closed 1986

OVHD PWR CAB
AUTH CL 85 FT
FIXED BRIDGE
HOR CL 90 FT
VERT CL 65 FT

G "87"
G "89"
Fl R 4s 15ft 3M "90"
G "91"
Fl G 4s 15ft 4M "93"
G "95"
G "97"
Fl R 4s 12ft 3M "98"
G "99"
Fl G 4s 15ft 4M "101"
G "103"
G "105"
Y "A" Fl Y 5s Priv

33° 54'
52'
78° 28'
26'
28'

VAR 8°30' W (2006)
ANNUAL INCREASE 2'
MAGNETIC

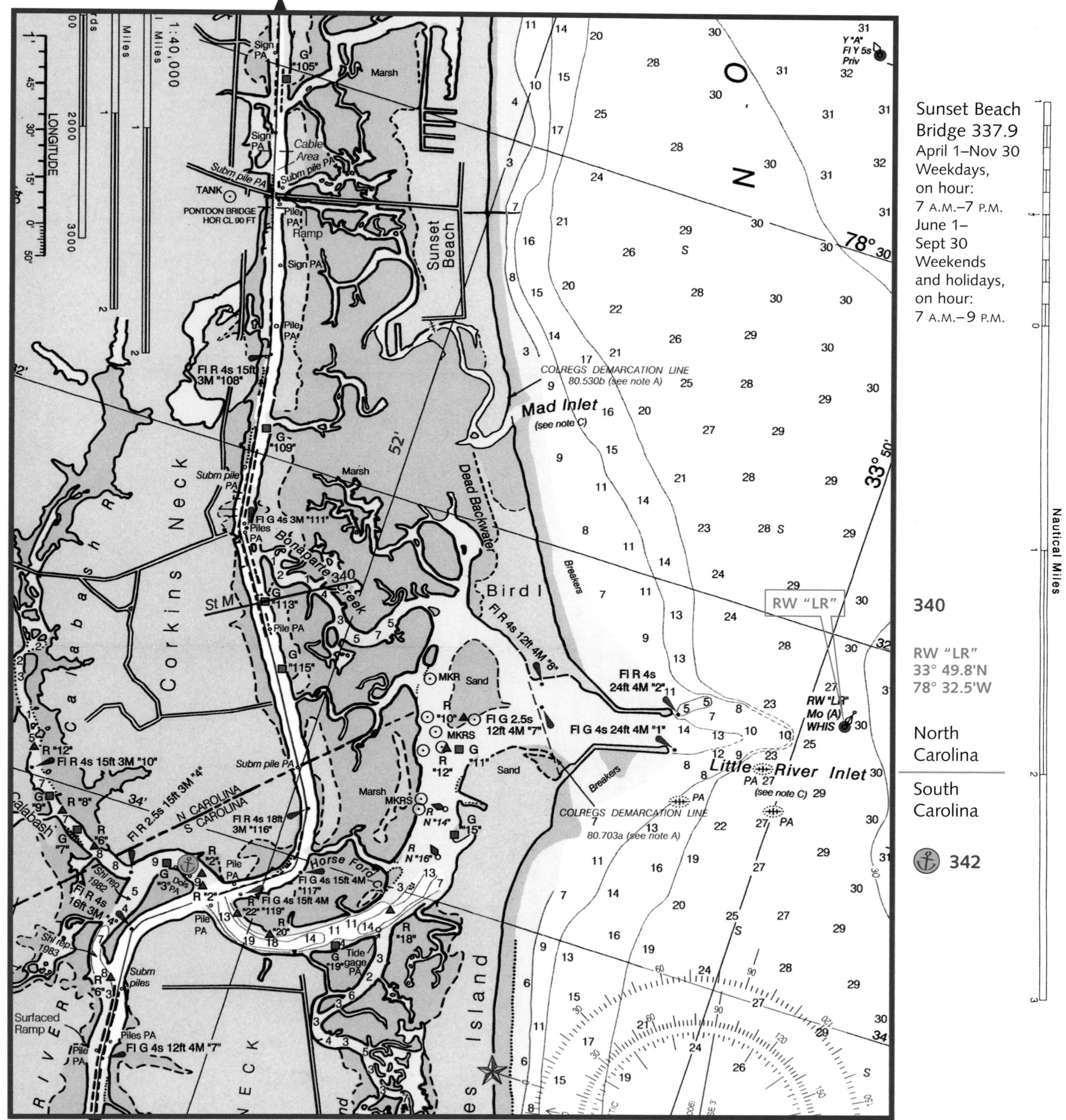

Sunset Beach Bridge 337.9
April 1–Nov 30
Weekdays,
on hour:
7 A.M.–7 P.M.
June 1–
Sept 30
Weekends
and holidays,
on hour:
7 A.M.–9 P.M.
340
RW "LR"
33° 49.8'N
78° 32.5'W
North Carolina
South Carolina
342
Nautical Miles
1:40,000
LONGITUDE
Miles
Sunset Beach
Marsh
Cable Area
Submerged pile PA
TANK
PONTOON BRIDGE
HOR CL 90 FT
Ramp
Fl R 4s 15ft 3M "108"
G "109"
G "105"
Corkins Neck
Bonaparte Creek
Fl G 4s 3M "111"
St M
G "113"
G "115"
Dead Backwater
Bird I
Mad Inlet
(see note C)
COLREGS DEMARCATION LINE
80.530b (see note A)
Fl R 4s 12ft 4M "8"
Fl R 4s 24ft 4M "2"
Fl G 4s 24ft 4M "1"
Fl G 2.5s 12ft 4M "7"
Breakers
Little River Inlet
(see note C)
COLREGS DEMARCATION LINE
80.703a (see note A)
RW "LR" Mo (A) WHIS
Y "A" Fl Y 5s Priv
Sand
N CAROLINA
S CAROLINA
Fl R 2.5s 15ft 3M "4"
Fl R 4s 15ft 3M "10"
Fl R 4s 18ft 3M "116"
Fl G 4s 15ft 4M "117"
Fl G 4s 15ft 4M "119"
Horse Ford C
Calabash
Calabash R
Fl R 4s 16ft 3M "4"
Shl rep. 1982
Shl rep. 1983
Surfaced Ramp
Fl G 4s 12ft 4M "7"
Tide gage PA
Island
78° 30'
33° 50'

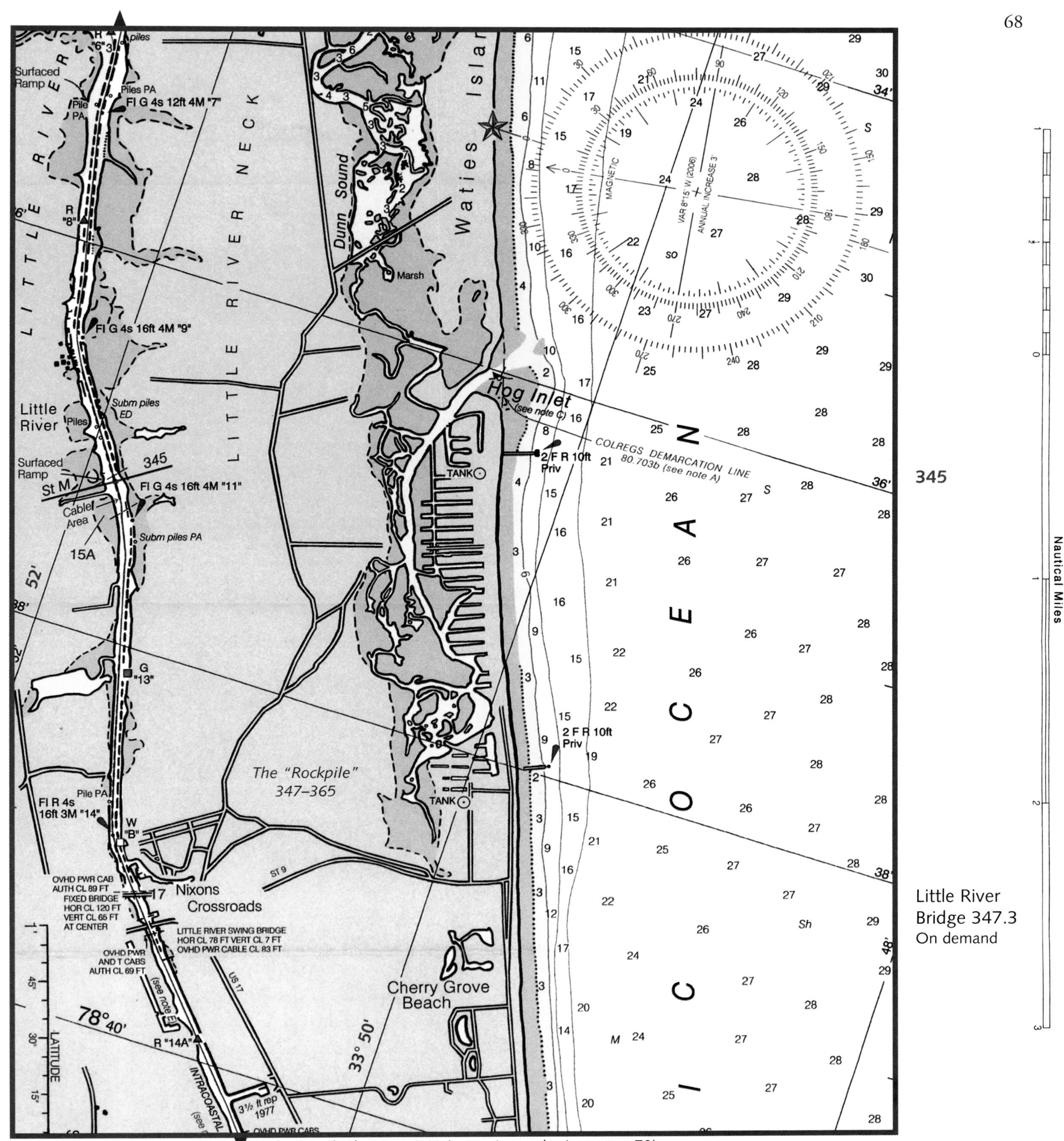

345

Little River
Bridge 347.3
On demand

The "Rockpile" 347–365 (see note on chart on page 70)

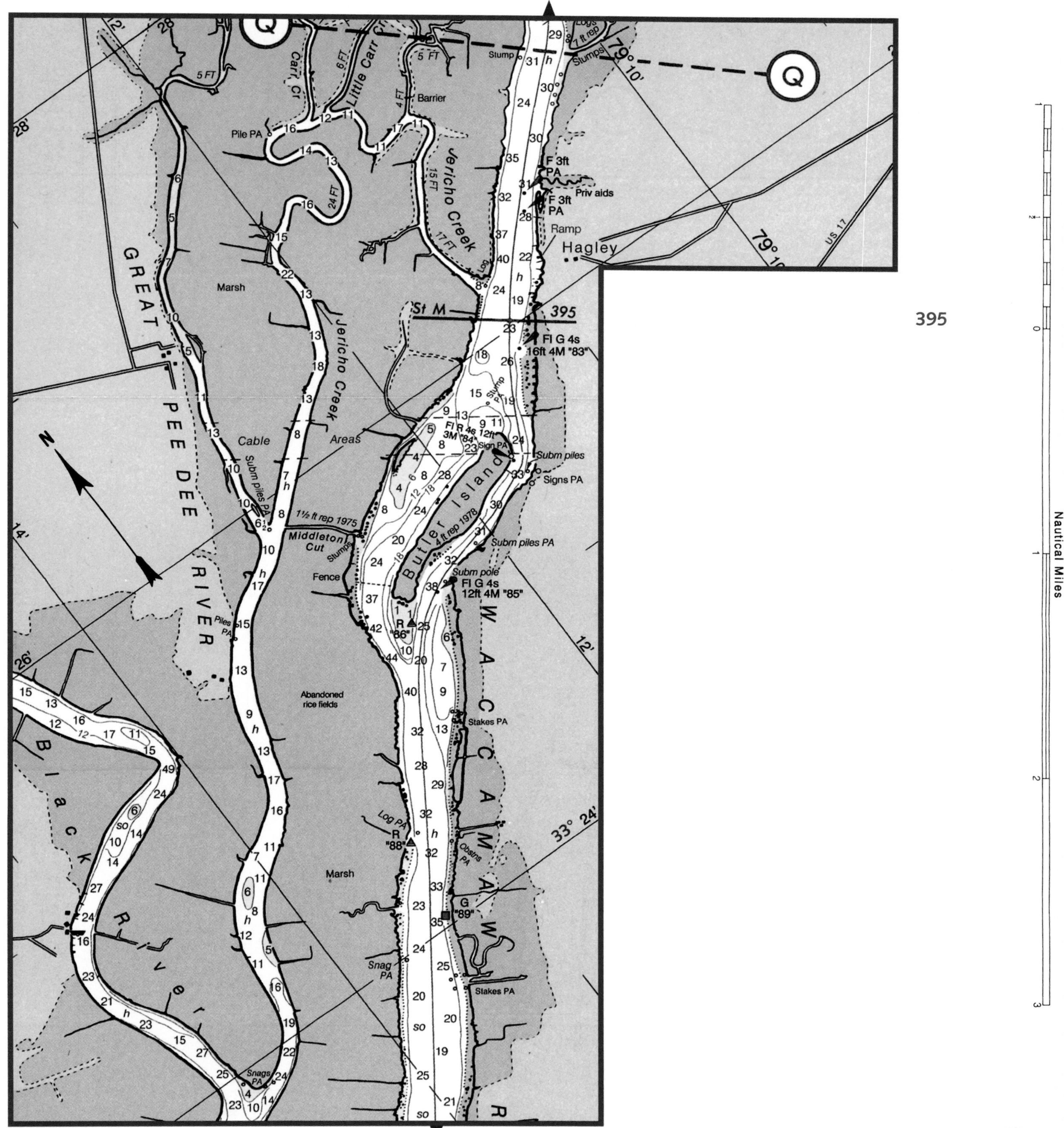

GREAT PEE DEE RIVER
Jericho Creek
Little Carr Cr
Carr Cr
Marsh
Hagley
Ramp
Priv aids
St M
395
Middleton Cut
Butler Island
Abandoned rice fields
Black River
WACCAMAW R
Cable Areas
Fence
Nautical Miles

395

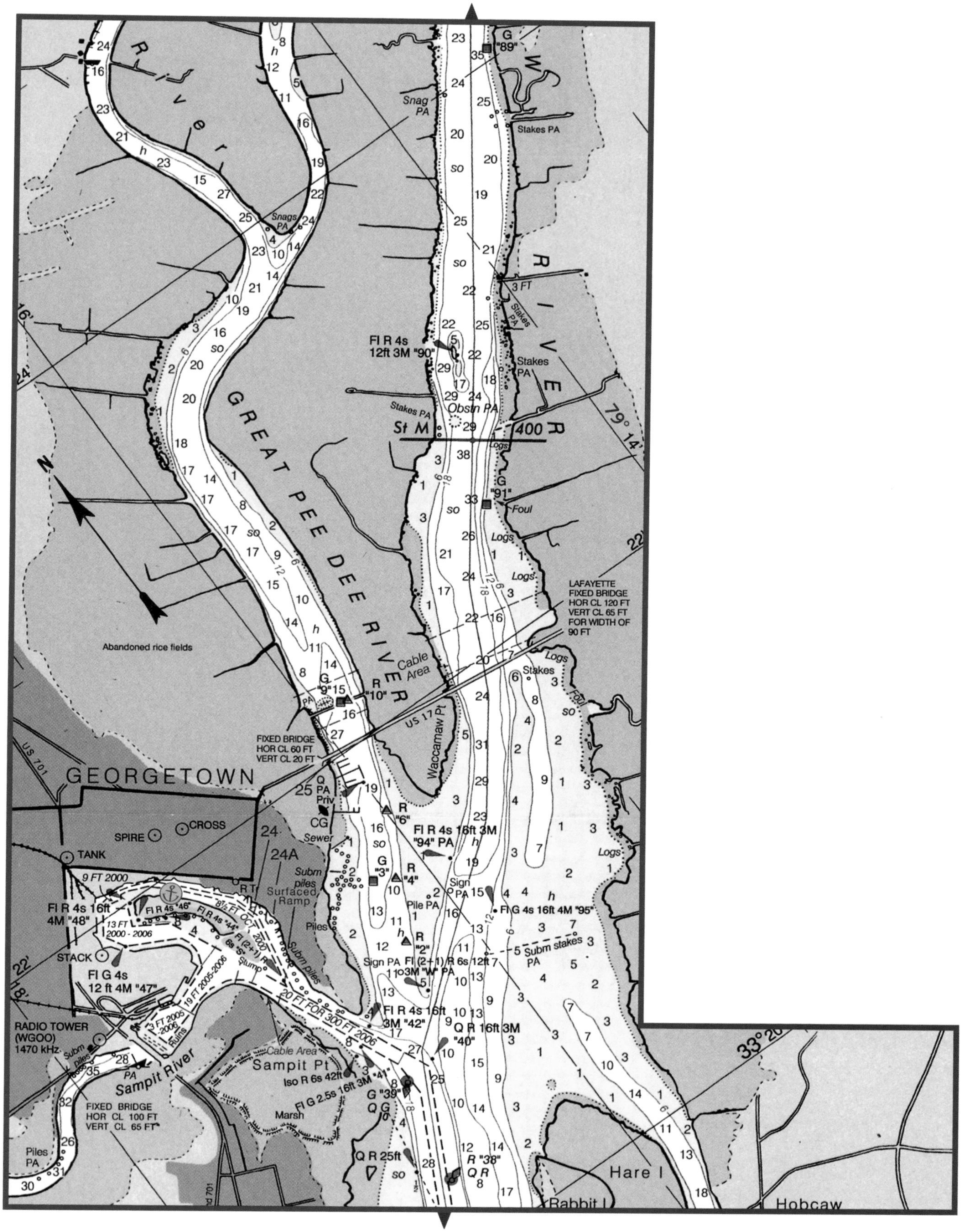

GREAT PEE DEE RIVER
W R I V E R
GEORGETOWN
Waccamaw Pt
Sampit Pt
Sampit River
Hare I
Rabbit I
Hobcaw
Abandoned rice fields
LAFAYETTE
FIXED BRIDGE
HOR CL 120 FT
VERT CL 65 FT
FOR WIDTH OF
90 FT
FIXED BRIDGE
HOR CL 60 FT
VERT CL 20 FT
FIXED BRIDGE
HOR CL 100 FT
VERT CL 65 FT
RADIO TOWER
(WGOO)
1470 kHz
SPIRE
CROSS
TANK
STACK
Fl R 4s
12ft 3M "90"
Fl R 4s 16ft 3M
"94" PA
Fl G 4s 16ft 4M "95"
Fl R 4s 16ft
4M "48"
Fl G 4s
12 ft 4M "47"
Fl R 4s 16ft
3M "42"
Q R 16ft 3M
"40"
Iso R 6s 42ft
Fl G 2.5s 16ft 3M "41"
Q R 25ft
20 FT FOR 300 FT 2006
St M
400
79° 14'
33° 20'
Nautical Miles
400
402.5

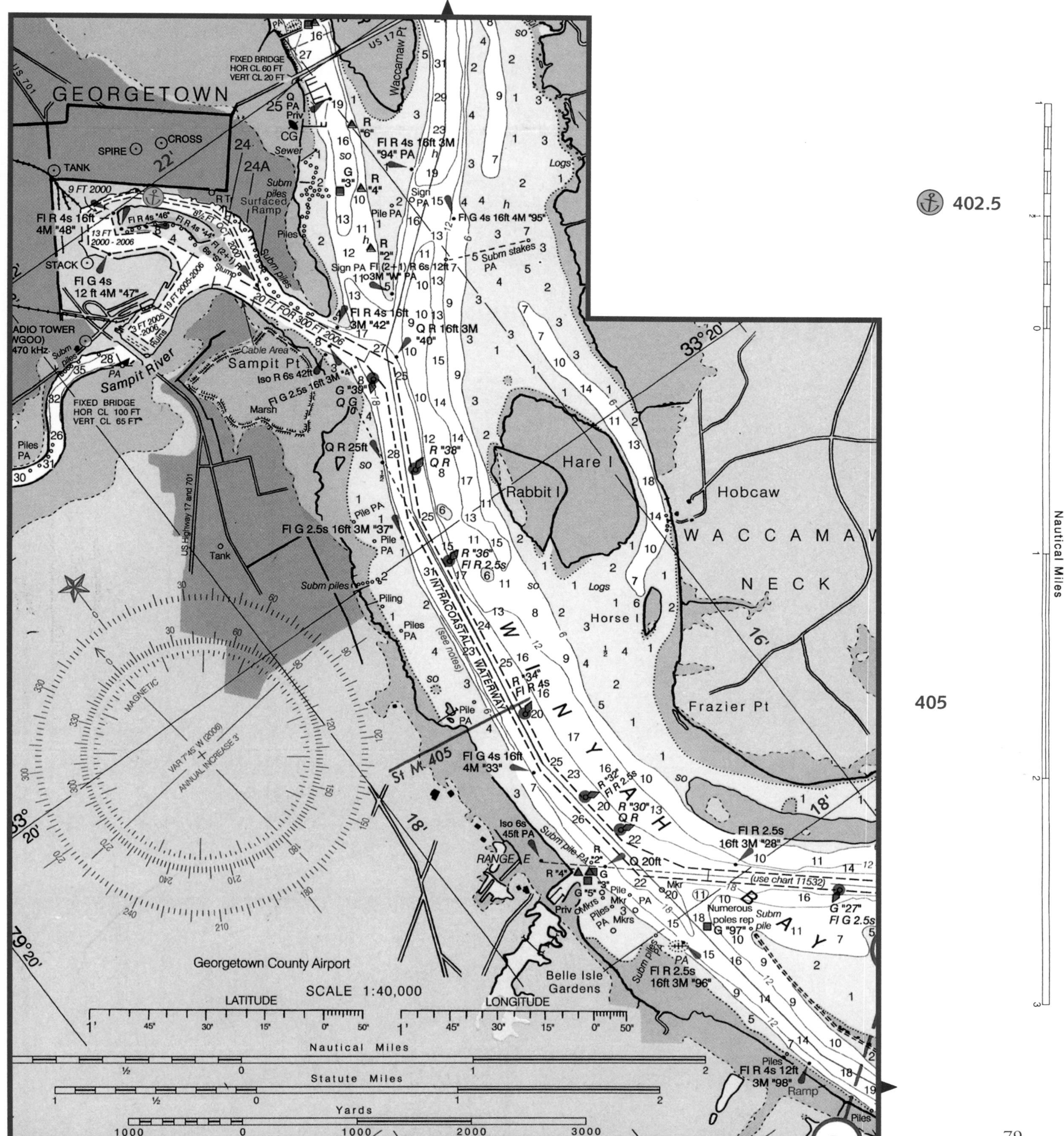
GEORGETOWN
FIXED BRIDGE HOR CL 60 FT VERT CL 20 FT
US 17 Pt
Waccamaw Pt
SPIRE
CROSS
TANK
STACK
CG
Sewer
Subm piles
Surfaced Ramp
Piles
9 FT 2000
13 FT 2000 - 2006
Fl R 4s 16ft 4M "48"
Fl G 4s 12 ft 4M "47"
20 FT FOR 300 FT 2006
Fl R 4s 16ft 3M "42"
Q R 16ft 3M "40"
Fl R 4s 16ft 3M "94" PA
Fl G 4s 16ft 4M "95"
Fl (2+1) R 6s 12ft 3M "W" PA
Subm stakes PA
Logs
Sign PA
Pile PA
RADIO TOWER (WGOO) 1470 kHz
Sampit River
Sampit Pt
Cable Area
Marsh
Iso R 6s 42ft
Fl G 2.5s 16ft 3M "41"
G "39" Q G
Q R 25ft
R "38" Q R
FIXED BRIDGE HOR CL 100 FT VERT CL 65 FT
Piles PA
US Highway 17 and 701
Tank
Fl G 2.5s 16ft 3M "37"
R "36" Fl R 2.5s
Subm piles
Piling
Hare I
Rabbit I
Horse I
Hobcaw
WACCAMAW NECK
Frazier Pt
33°20'
16'
18'
INTRACOASTAL WATERWAY (see notes)
WINYAH BAY
R "34" Fl R 4s
Fl G 4s 16ft 4M "33"
R "32" Fl R 2.5s
R "30" Q R
St M 405
Iso 6s 45ft PA
RANGE E
Subm pile PA
R "2" Q 20ft
R "4"
G "5"
G "3"
Priv
Mkrs
Piles PA
Mkr
Fl R 2.5s 16ft 3M "28"
(use chart 11532)
G "27" Fl G 2.5s
Numerous poles rep
G "97"
Subm pile
Fl R 2.5s 16ft 3M "96"
Belle Isle Gardens
Georgetown County Airport
Fl R 4s 12ft 3M "98"
Piles
Ramp
MAGNETIC
VAR 7°45' W (2006) ANNUAL INCREASE 3'
33° 20'
79° 20'
SCALE 1:40,000
LATITUDE
LONGITUDE
Nautical Miles
Statute Miles
Yards
402.5
405

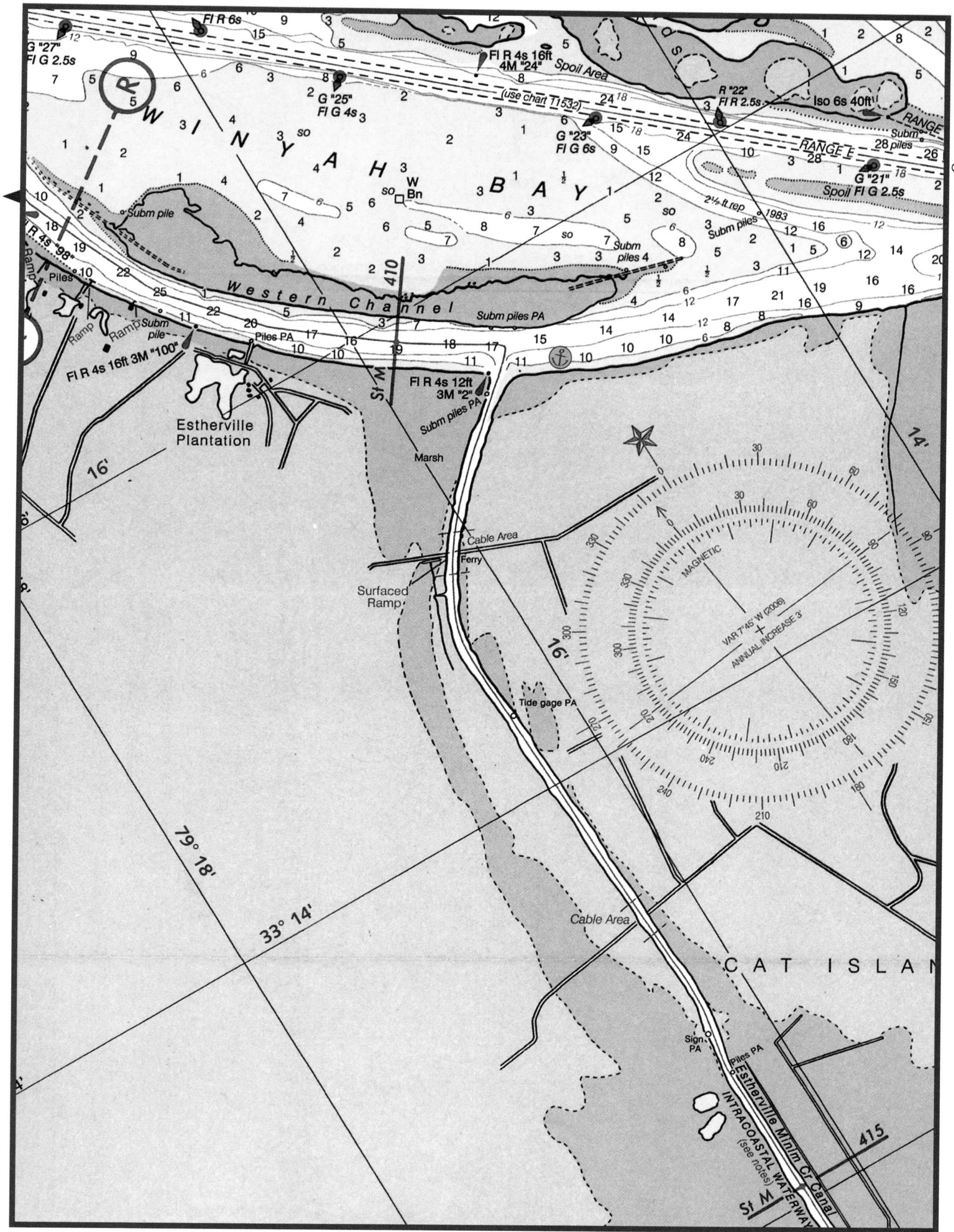

Joins Page 210

410

415

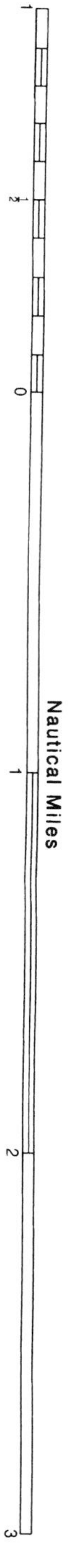

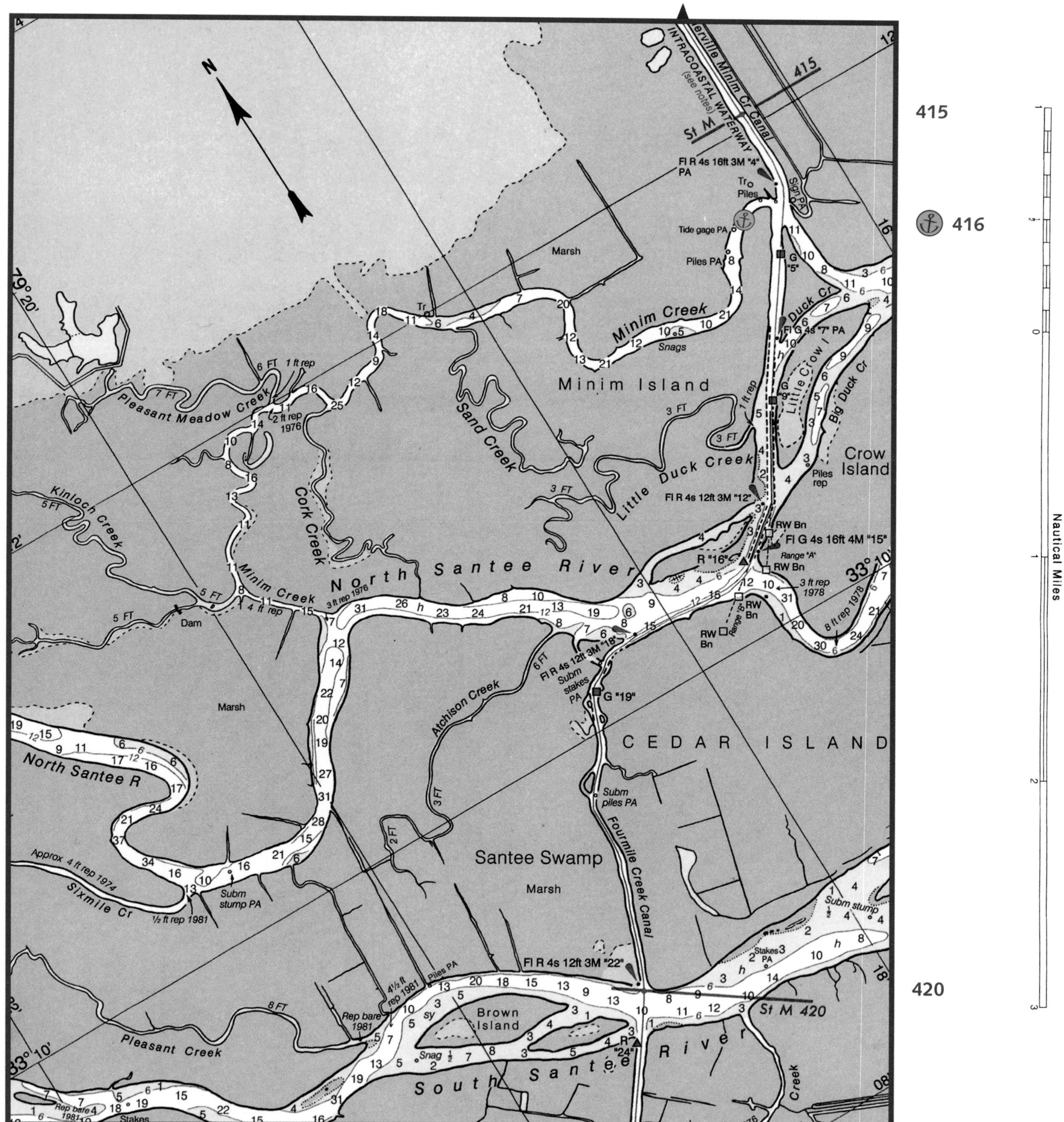

Minim Island
North Santee River
CEDAR ISLAND
Santee Swamp
Marsh
Brown Island
South Santee River
Crow Island
Minim Creek
Sand Creek
Cork Creek
Little Duck Creek
Kinloch Creek
Pleasant Meadow Creek
Atchison Creek
Fourmile Creek Canal
Sixmile Cr
Pleasant Creek
North Santee R
Little Crow I
Big Duck Cr
Duck Cr
INTRACOASTAL WATERWAY (see notes)
St M 415
St M 420
Fl R 4s 16ft 3M "4" PA
Fl R 4s 12ft 3M "12"
Fl G 4s 16ft 4M "15"
Fl R 4s 12ft 3M "18"
Fl R 4s 12ft 3M "22"
G "19"
R "16"
R "24"
Nautical Miles
415
416
420

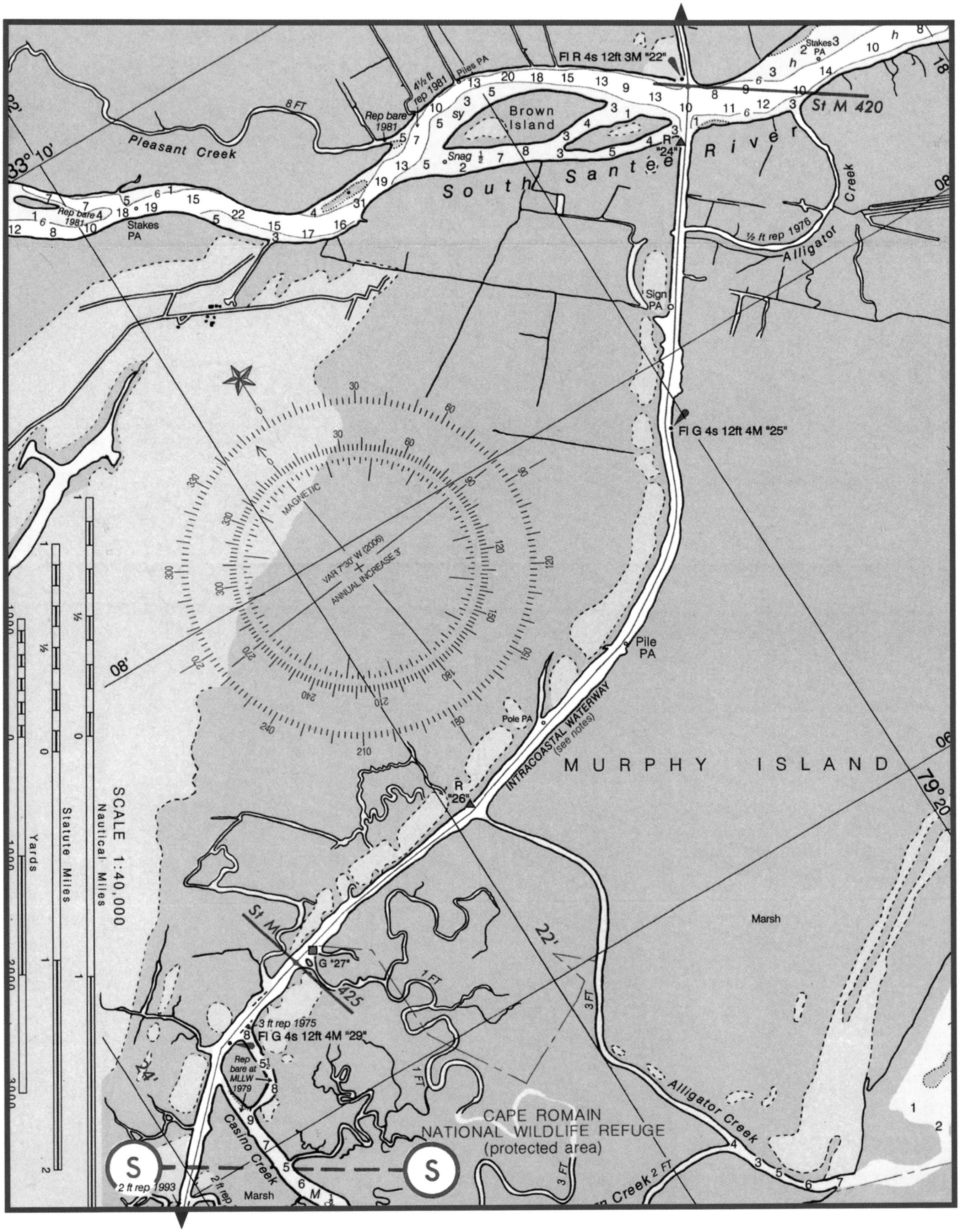

420

Fl R 4s 12ft 3M "22"

St M 420

Brown Island

R "24"

South Santee River

Pleasant Creek

Alligator Creek

Sign PA

Fl G 4s 12ft 4M "25"

VAR 7°30' W (2006)
ANNUAL INCREASE 3'

MAGNETIC

Pile PA

Pole PA

INTRACOASTAL WATERWAY
(see notes)

MURPHY ISLAND

R "26"

SCALE 1:40,000
Nautical Miles
Statute Miles
Yards

Marsh

425

St M 425

G "27"

3 ft rep 1975

Fl G 4s 12ft 4M "29"

Rep bare at MLLW 1979

CAPE ROMAIN
NATIONAL WILDLIFE REFUGE
(protected area)

Casino Creek

Alligator Creek

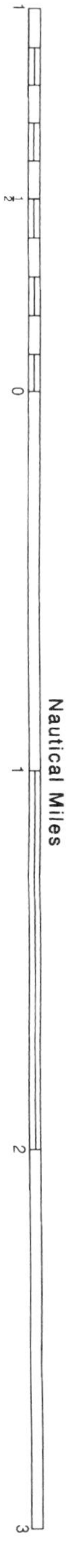

Nautical Miles

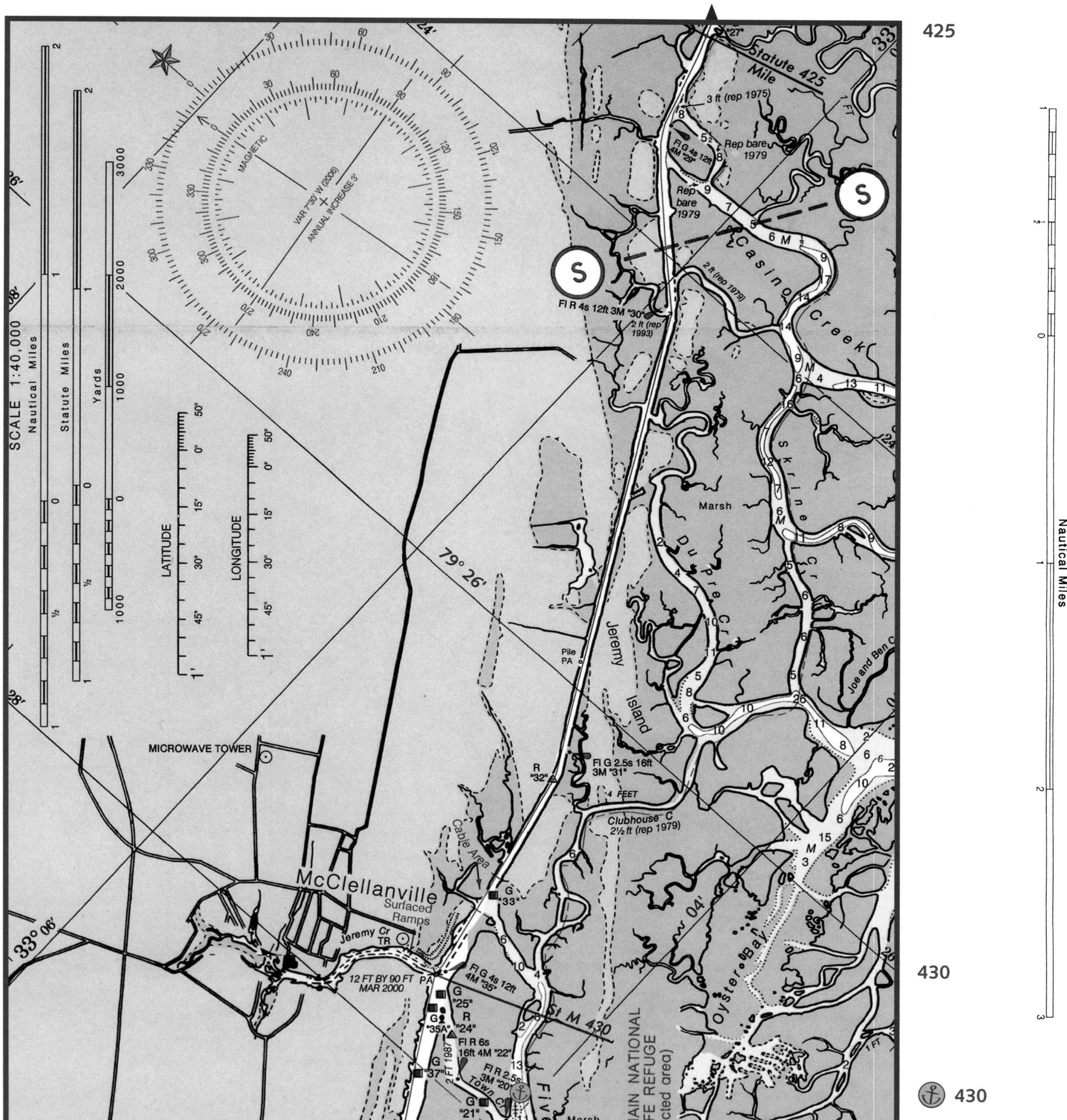
425
430
430
SCALE 1:40,000
Nautical Miles
Statute Miles
Yards
LATITUDE
LONGITUDE
MAGNETIC
VAR 7°30' W (2006)
ANNUAL INCREASE 3'
Statute 425
Mile
3 ft (rep 1975)
Rep bare
1979
Casino Creek
Skrine Cr
Du Pre Cr
Joe and Ben C
Marsh
Jeremy Island
Pile PA
Fl R 4s 12ft 3M "30"
Fl G 4s 12ft 4M "29"
Fl G 2.5s 16ft 3M "31"
4 FEET
Clubhouse C
2½ ft (rep 1979)
Cable Area
MICROWAVE TOWER
McClellanville
Surfaced Ramps
Jeremy Cr
12 FT BY 90 FT
MAR 2000
Fl G 4s 12ft 4M "35"
St M 430
Fl R 6s 16ft 4M "22"
Fl R 2.5s 3M "20"
Town C
Oyster Bay
Five
Marsh
NATIONAL
LIFE REFUGE
79° 26'
33° 06'
Nautical Miles

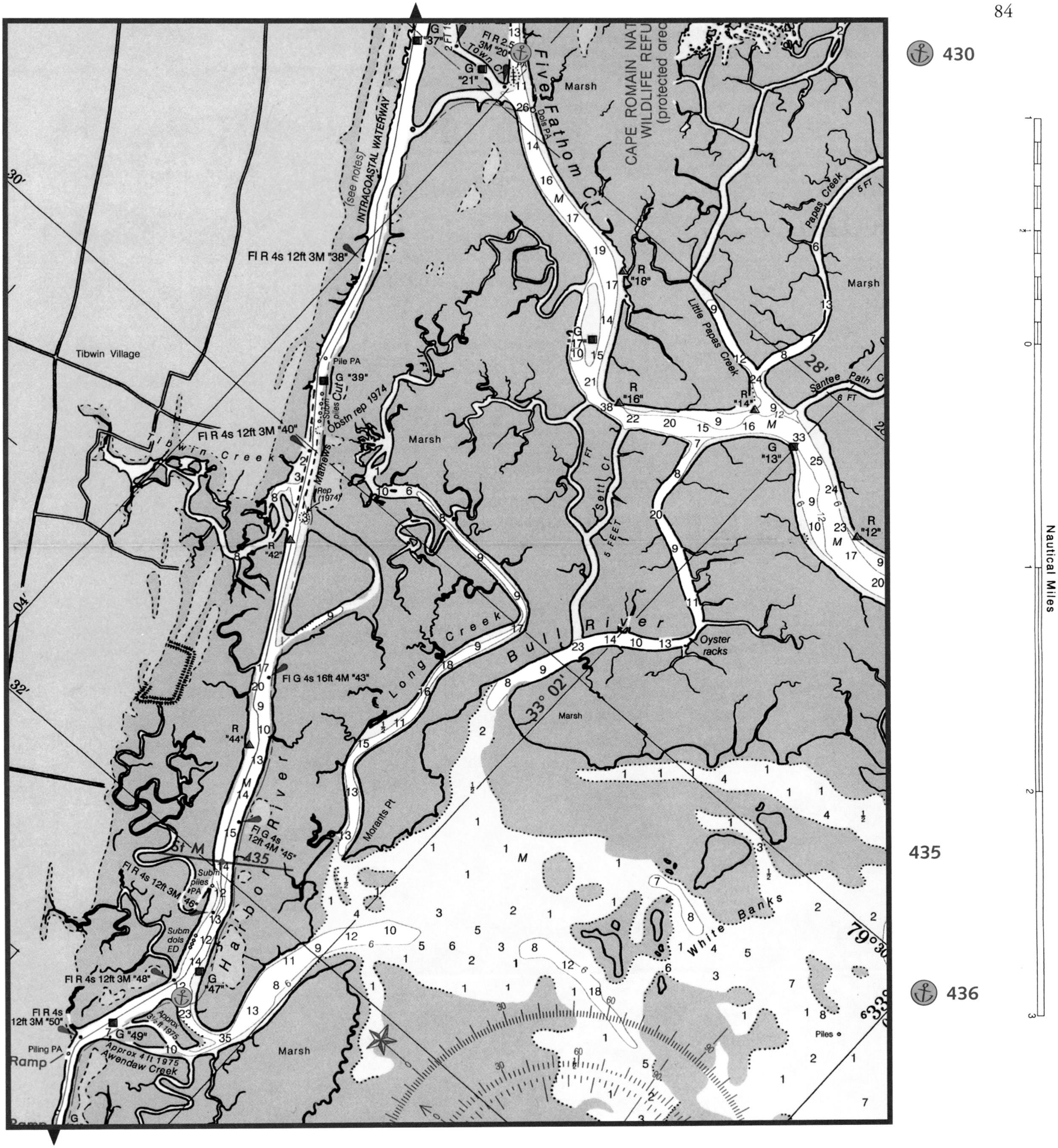

430
435
436
Nautical Miles
INTRACOASTAL WATERWAY
(see notes)
CAPE ROMAIN NAT
WILDLIFE REFU
(protected area
Five Fathom Cr
Town Cr
Marsh
Tibwin Village
Tibwin Creek
Fl R 4s 12ft 3M "38"
Fl R 4s 12ft 3M "40"
Fl G 4s 16ft 4M "43"
Fl G 4s 12ft 4M "45"
Fl R 4s 12ft 3M "46"
Fl R 4s 12ft 3M "48"
Fl R 4s 12ft 3M "50"
G "39"
Pile PA
Obstn rep 1974
Rep (1974)
Mathews Cut
Long Creek
Bull River
Oyster racks
Sett Cr
5 FEET
Little Papas Creek
Papas Creek
Santee Path
Harbor River
Morants Pt
White Banks
Piles
Piling PA
Ramp
Awendaw Creek
Approx 4 ft 1975
Subm piles
Subm dols ED
33° 02'
79° 30'
28'
30'
32'
04'

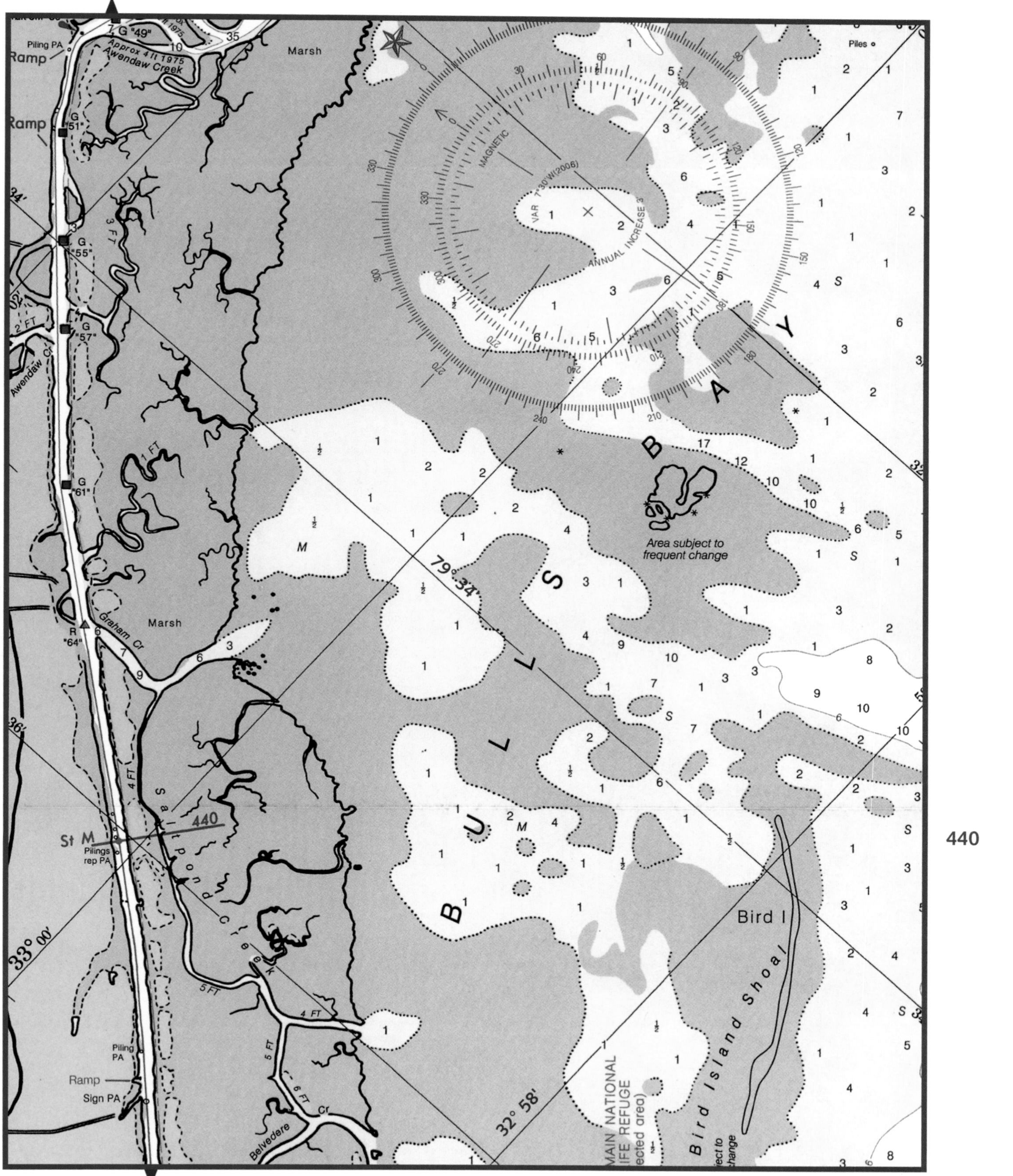
Marsh
Piling PA
Ramp
Awendaw Creek
Area subject to frequent change
BULLS BAY
Graham Cr
Salt Pond Creek
Bird I
Bird Island Shoal
Belvedere Cr
Pilings rep PA
Piling PA
Ramp
Sign PA
Nautical Miles
440

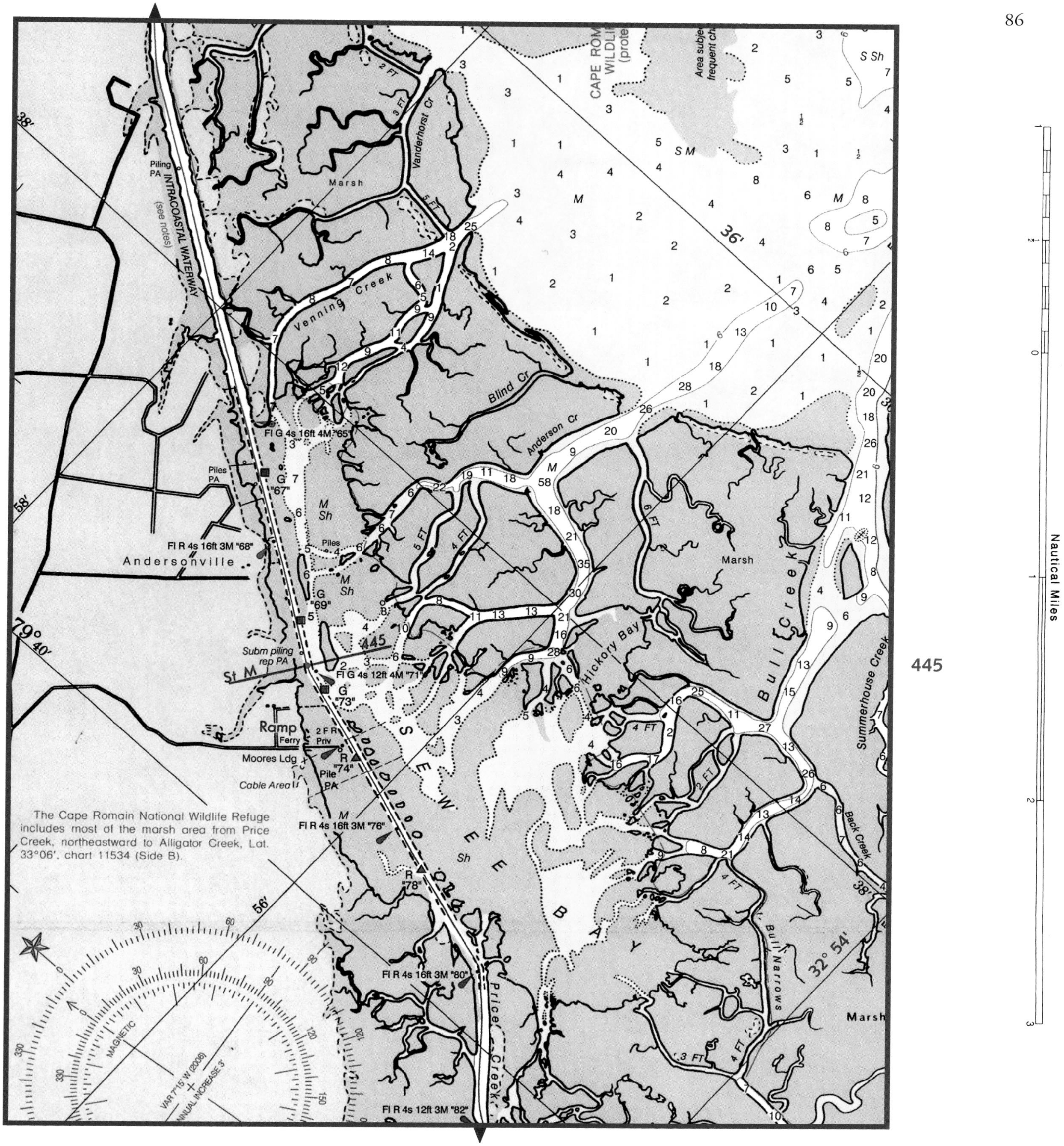

The Cape Romain National Wildlife Refuge includes most of the marsh area from Price Creek, northeastward to Alligator Creek, Lat. 33°06', chart 11534 (Side B).

CAPE ROMAIN WILDLIFE (prote

Area subject to frequent ch

INTRACOASTAL WATERWAY (see notes)

Piling PA

Marsh

Vanderhorst Cr

Venning Creek

Blind Cr

Anderson Cr

Fl G 4s 16ft 4M "65"

Piles PA

G "67"

M Sh

Piles

Fl R 4s 16ft 3M "68"

Andersonville

G "69"

445

Subm piling rep PA

St M

Fl G 4s 12ft 4M "71"

G "73"

Ramp

Ferry

2 F R Priv

Moores Ldg

R "74"

Pile PA

Cable Area

Fl R 4s 16ft 3M "76"

R "78"

S E W E E B A Y

Hickory Bay

Bull Creek

Summerhouse Creek

Back Creek

Bull Narrows

Marsh

Fl R 4s 16ft 3M "80"

Price Creek

Fl R 4s 12ft 3M "82"

MAGNETIC

VAR 7°15'W (2006)

ANNUAL INCREASE 3'

79° 40'

58'

56'

38'

36'

32° 54'

Nautical Miles

445

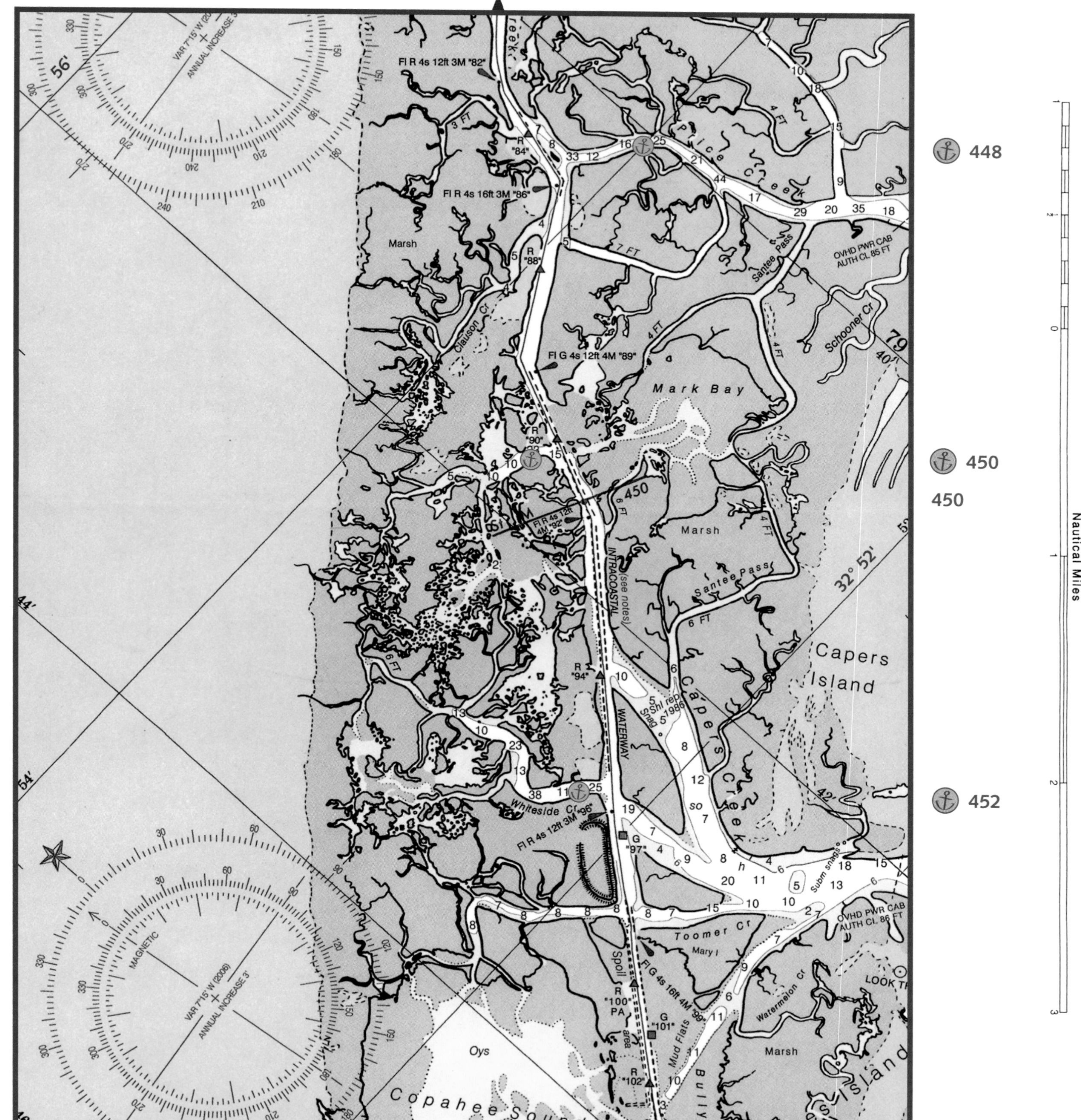
Fl R 4s 12ft 3M "82"
Fl R 4s 16ft 3M "86"
Fl G 4s 12ft 4M "89"
Fl R 4s 12ft 3M "96"
Fl G 4s 16ft 4M "99"
Price Creek
Santee Pass
Schooner Cr
Clauson Cr
Mark Bay
Marsh
INTRACOASTAL
WATERWAY
(see notes)
Capers Island
Capers Creek
Whiteside Cr
Toomer Cr
Mary I
Watermelon Cr
Mud Flats
Spoil
Oys
Copahee Sound
OVHD PWR CAB AUTH CL 85 FT
OVHD PWR CAB AUTH CL 86 FT
32° 52'
448
450
452
Nautical Miles

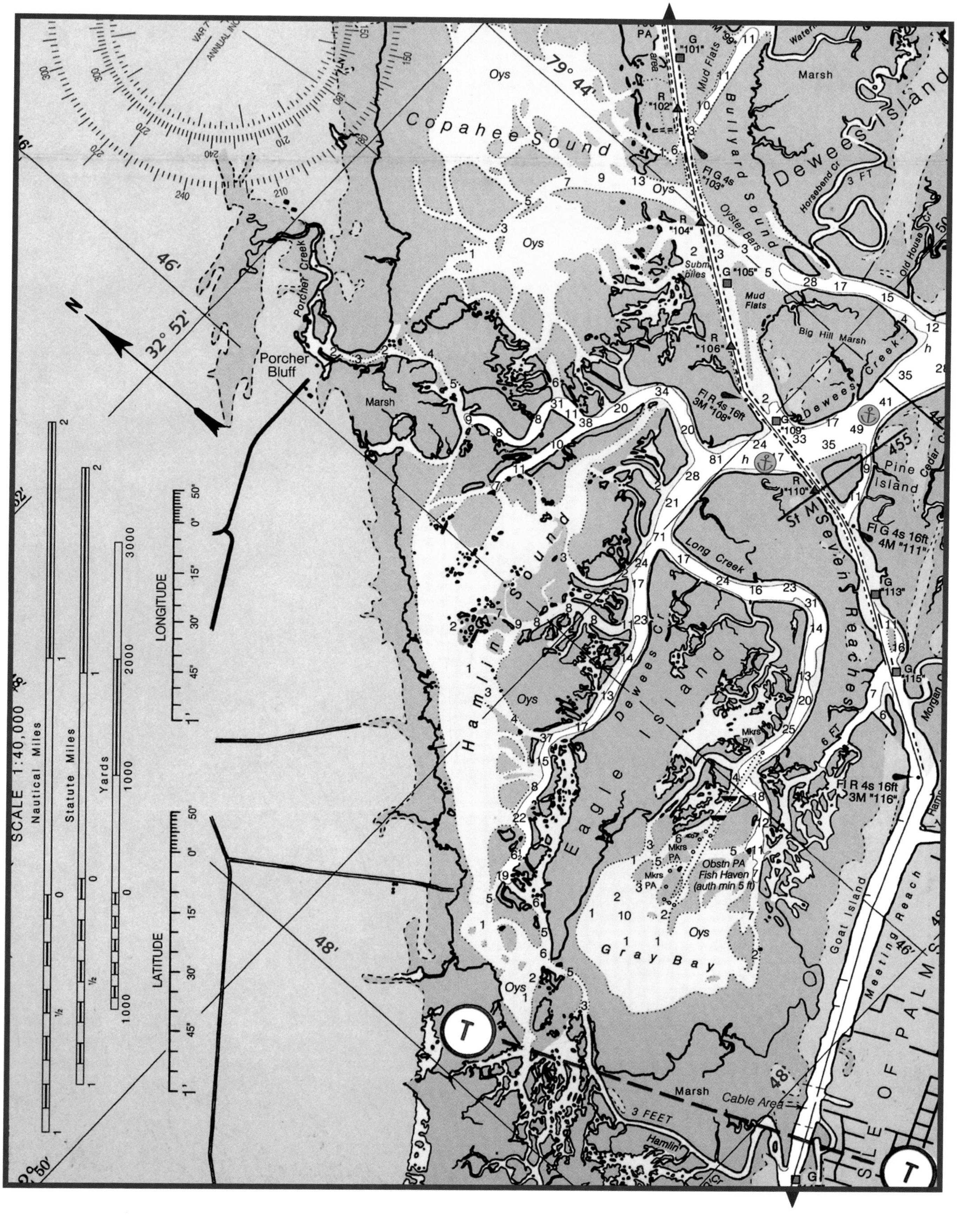

Copahee Sound
Bullyard Sound
Dewees Island
Horsebend Cr
Old House Cr
Porcher Creek
Porcher Bluff
Big Hill Marsh
Dewees Creek
Pine Island
Cedar Cr
St M Seven Reaches
Long Creek
Dewees Cr
Eagle Island
Hamlin Sound
Gray Bay
Goat Island
Meeting Reach
ISLE OF PALMS
Morgan Cr
Hamlin Cr
Marsh
Cable Area
3 FEET
Oys
Mud Flats
Oyster Bars
Subm piles
Obstn PA
Fish Haven
(auth min 5 ft)
Mkrs PA
Fl G 4s "103"
R "102"
R "104"
G "105"
R "106"
Fl R 4s 16ft 3M "108"
G "109"
R "110"
Fl G 4s 16ft 4M "111"
G "113"
G "115"
Fl R 4s 16ft 3M "116"
G "101"
M "99"
32° 52'
79° 44'
46'
48'

455

455

SCALE 1:40,000
Nautical Miles
Statute Miles
Yards
LATITUDE
LONGITUDE

Nautical Miles

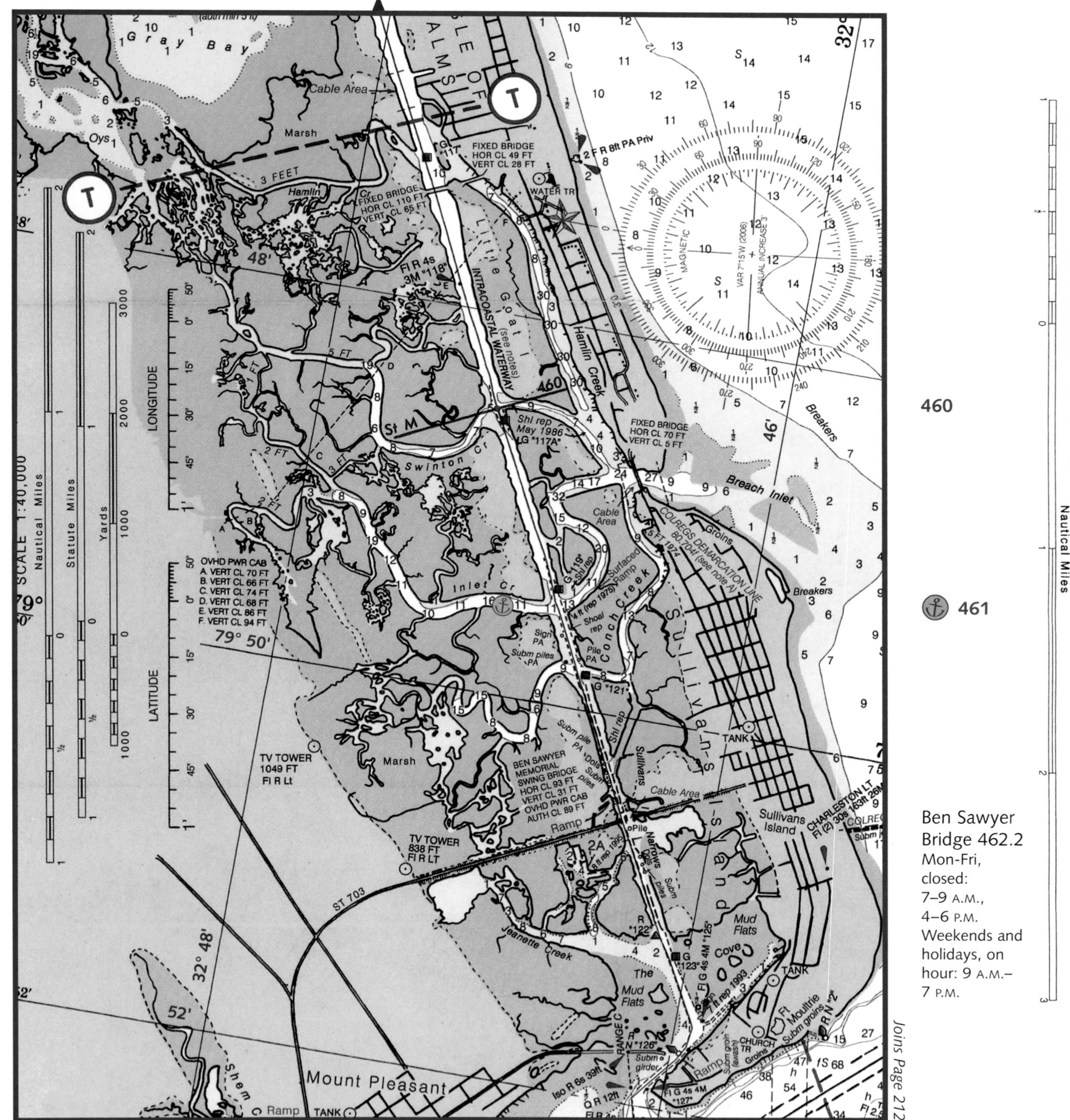

460

461

Ben Sawyer Bridge 462.2
Mon-Fri, closed:
7–9 A.M.,
4–6 P.M.
Weekends and holidays, on hour: 9 A.M.–7 P.M.

Nautical Miles

Joins Page 212

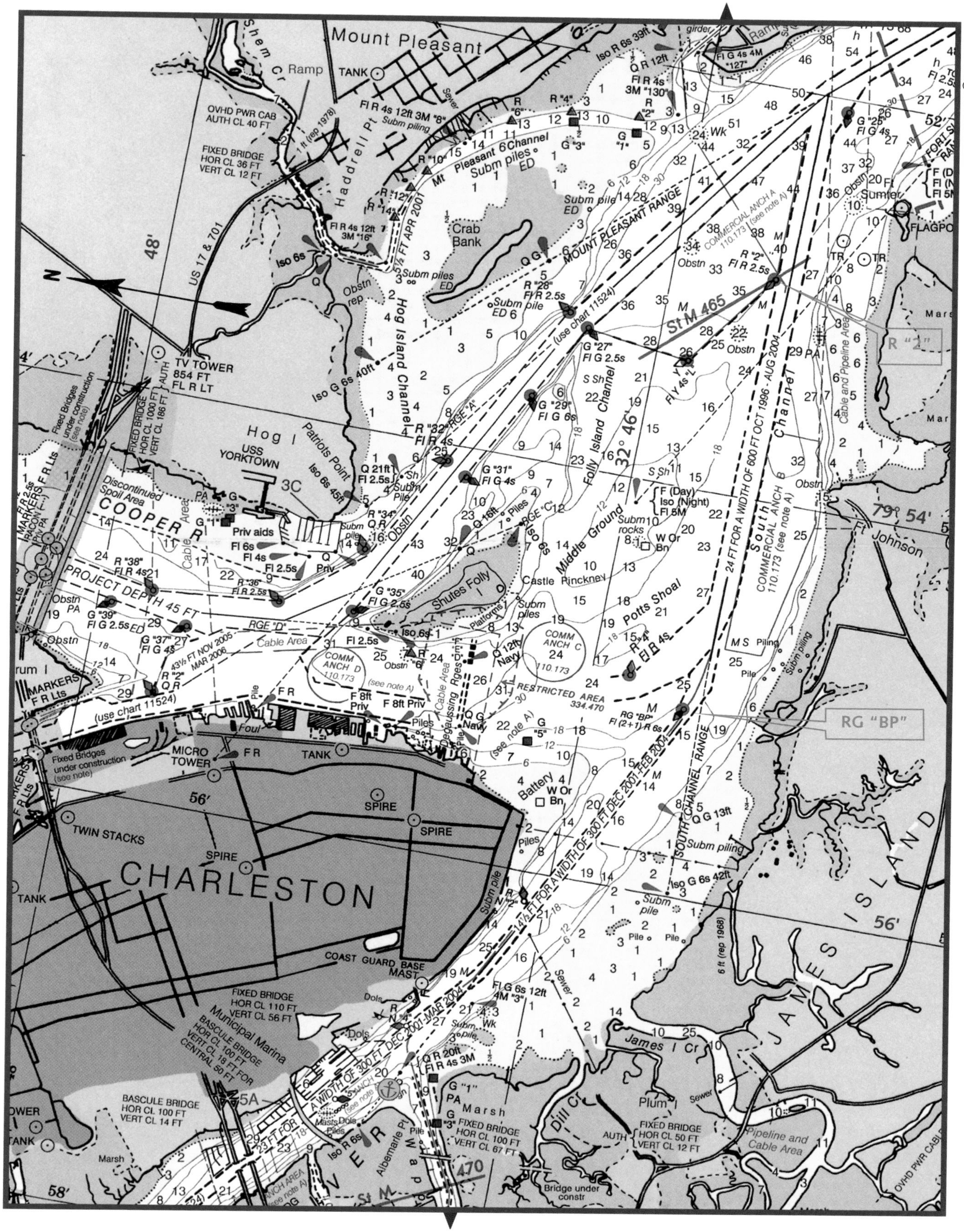

Joins Page 212

465

R "2"
32° 45.6'N
79° 52.9'W

RG "BP"
32° 45.6'N
79° 55.1'W

Ashley River Bridge (469)
(not on ICW)
56 feet

469

470

Nautical Miles
0 1 2 3

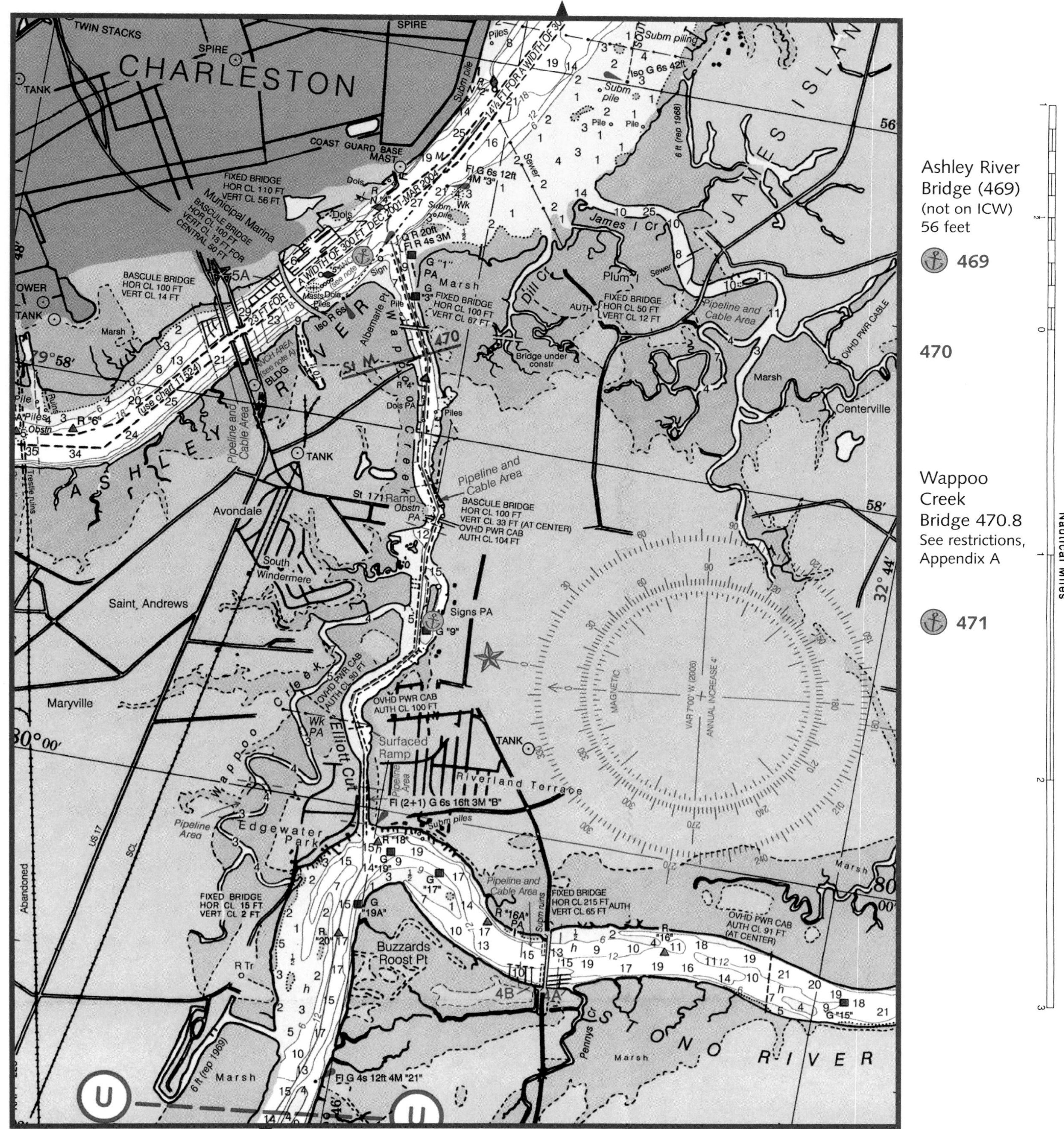
CHARLESTON
TWIN STACKS
SPIRE
TANK
COAST GUARD BASE
MAST
FIXED BRIDGE
HOR CL 110 FT
VERT CL 56 FT
Municipal Marina
BASCULE BRIDGE
HOR CL 100 FT
VERT CL 18 FT FOR
CENTRAL 50 FT
BASCULE BRIDGE
HOR CL 100 FT
VERT CL 14 FT
TOWER
Marsh
ASHLEY RIVER
Albemarle Pt
Pipeline and Cable Area
FIXED BRIDGE
HOR CL 100 FT
VERT CL 67 FT
FIXED BRIDGE
HOR CL 50 FT
VERT CL 12 FT
Bridge under constr
James I Cr
Plum I
Dill Cr
JAMES ISLAND
Centerville
OVHD PWR CABLE
Avondale
South Windermere
Saint Andrews
Maryville
Wappoo Creek
BASCULE BRIDGE
HOR CL 100 FT
VERT CL 33 FT (AT CENTER)
OVHD PWR CAB
AUTH CL 104 FT
Signs PA
OVHD PWR CAB
AUTH CL 100 FT
Surfaced Ramp
Elliott Cut
Riverland Terrace
Fl (2+1) G 6s 16ft 3M "B"
Edgewater Park
FIXED BRIDGE
HOR CL 15 FT
VERT CL 2 FT
FIXED BRIDGE
HOR CL 215 FT
VERT CL 65 FT
OVHD PWR CAB
AUTH CL 91 FT
(AT CENTER)
Buzzards Roost Pt
STONO RIVER
Pennys Cr
Marsh
Fl G 4s 12ft 4M "21"
VAR 7°00' W (2006)
ANNUAL INCREASE 4'
MAGNETIC
Abandoned
US 17
SCL
Nautical Miles
Ashley River Bridge (469)
(not on ICW)
56 feet
469
470
Wappoo Creek Bridge 470.8
See restrictions, Appendix A
471

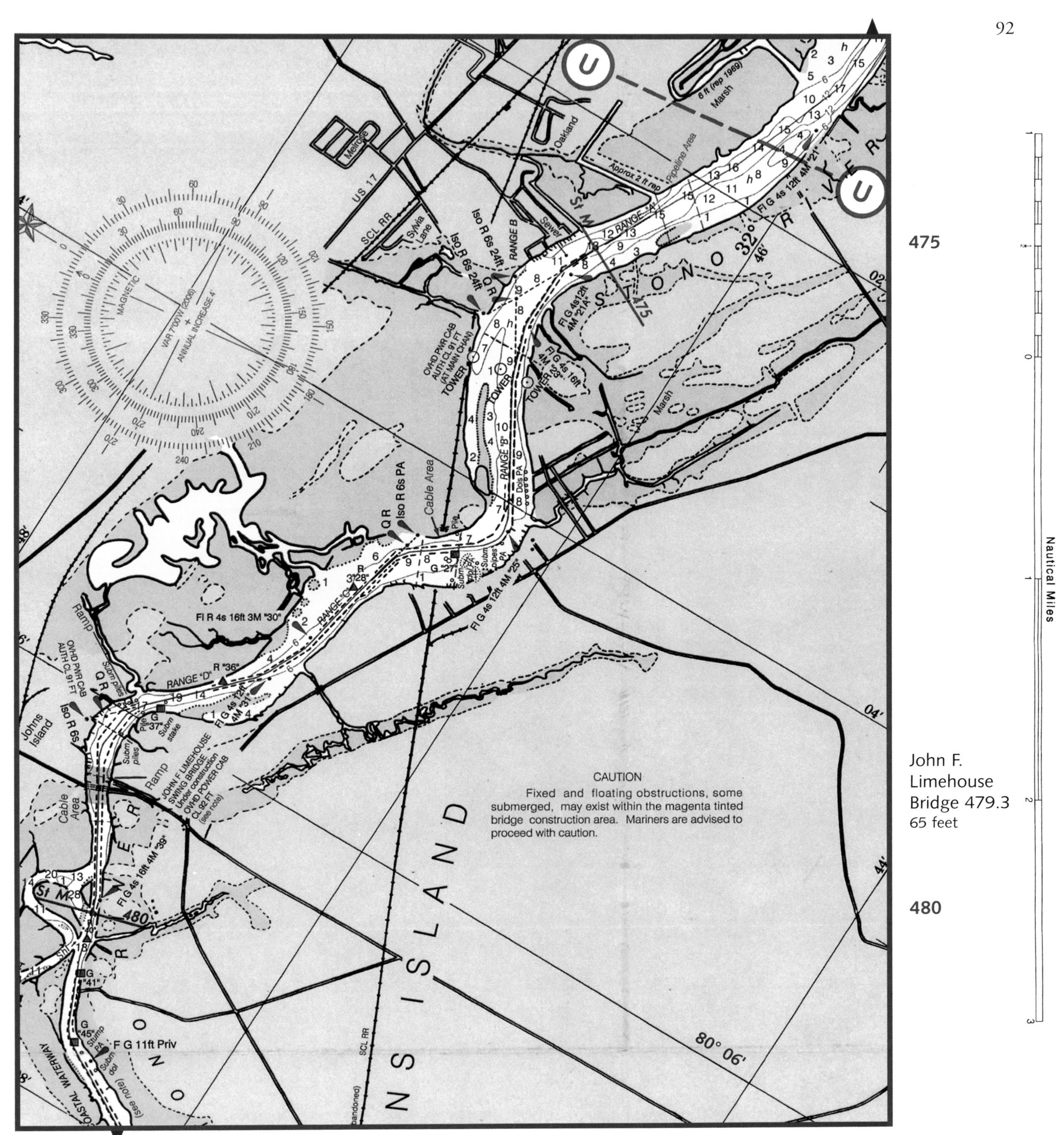

475

John F.
Limehouse
Bridge 479.3
65 feet

480

Nautical Miles

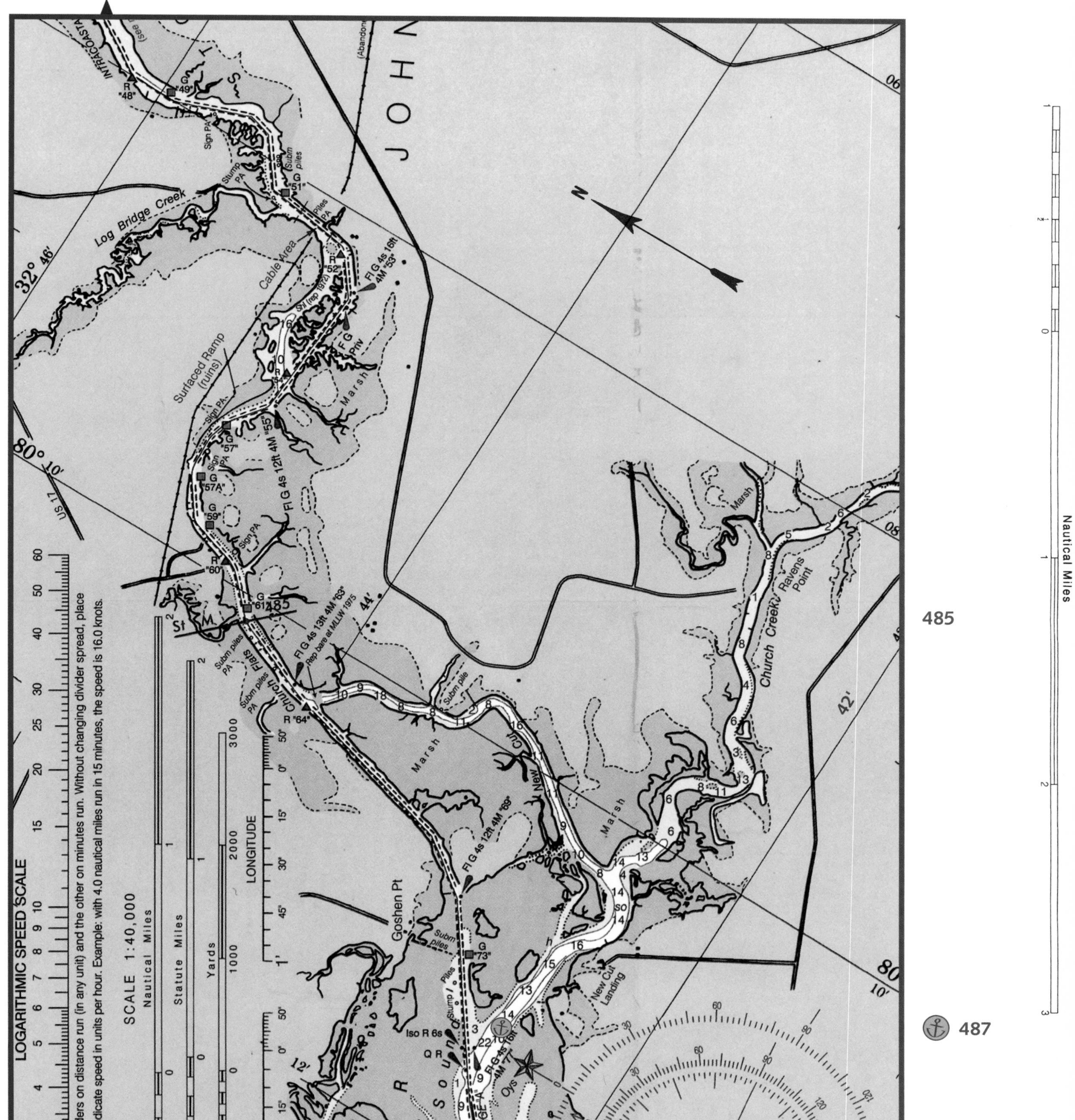

LOGARITHMIC SPEED SCALE
...viders on distance run (in any unit) and the other on minutes run. Without changing divider spread, place indicate speed in units per hour. Example: with 4.0 nautical miles run in 15 minutes, the speed is 16.0 knots.
SCALE 1:40,000
Nautical Miles
Statute Miles
Yards
LONGITUDE
Log Bridge Creek
Cable Area
Surfaced Ramp (ruins)
Marsh
Church Flats
Church Creek
Ravens Point
New Cut
New Cut Landing
Goshen Pt
Subm piles
Fl G 4s 16ft 4M "53"
Fl G 4s 12ft 4M "55"
Fl G 4s 13ft 4M "63"
Rep bare at MLLW 1975
Fl G 4s 12ft 4M "69"
Iso R 6s
Q R
32° 46'
80° 10'
44'
42'
Nautical Miles

485

487

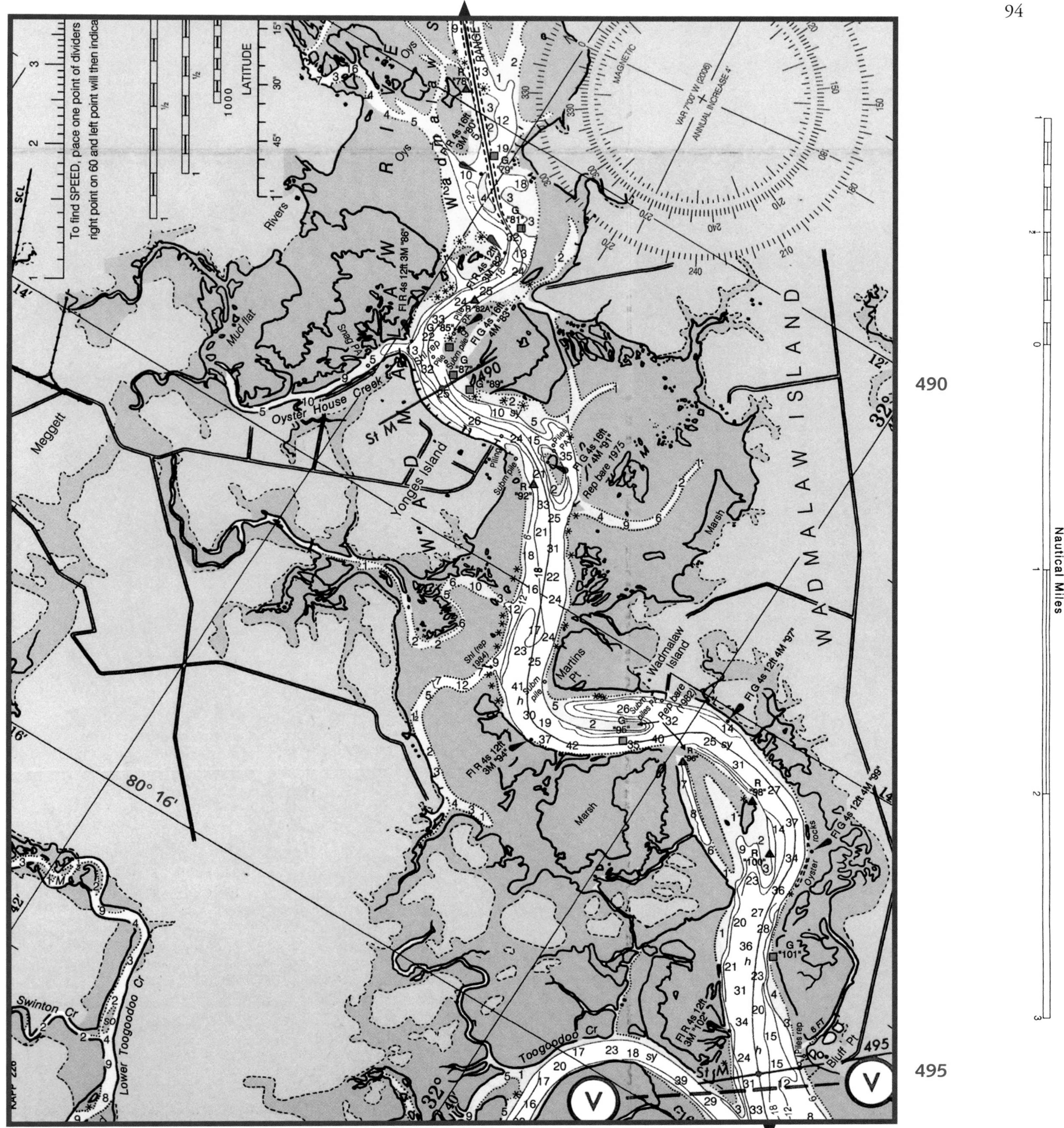
To find SPEED, pace one point of dividers right point on 60 and left point will then indica
LATITUDE
WADMALAW ISLAND
Wadmalaw Island
Martins Pt
Yonges Island
Oyster House Creek
Meggett
Mud flat
Toogoodoo Cr
Lower Toogoodoo Cr
Swinton Cr
Bluff Pt
Marsh
80° 16'
32°
MAGNETIC
VAR 7°00' W (2006)
ANNUAL INCREASE 4'
490
495
Nautical Miles

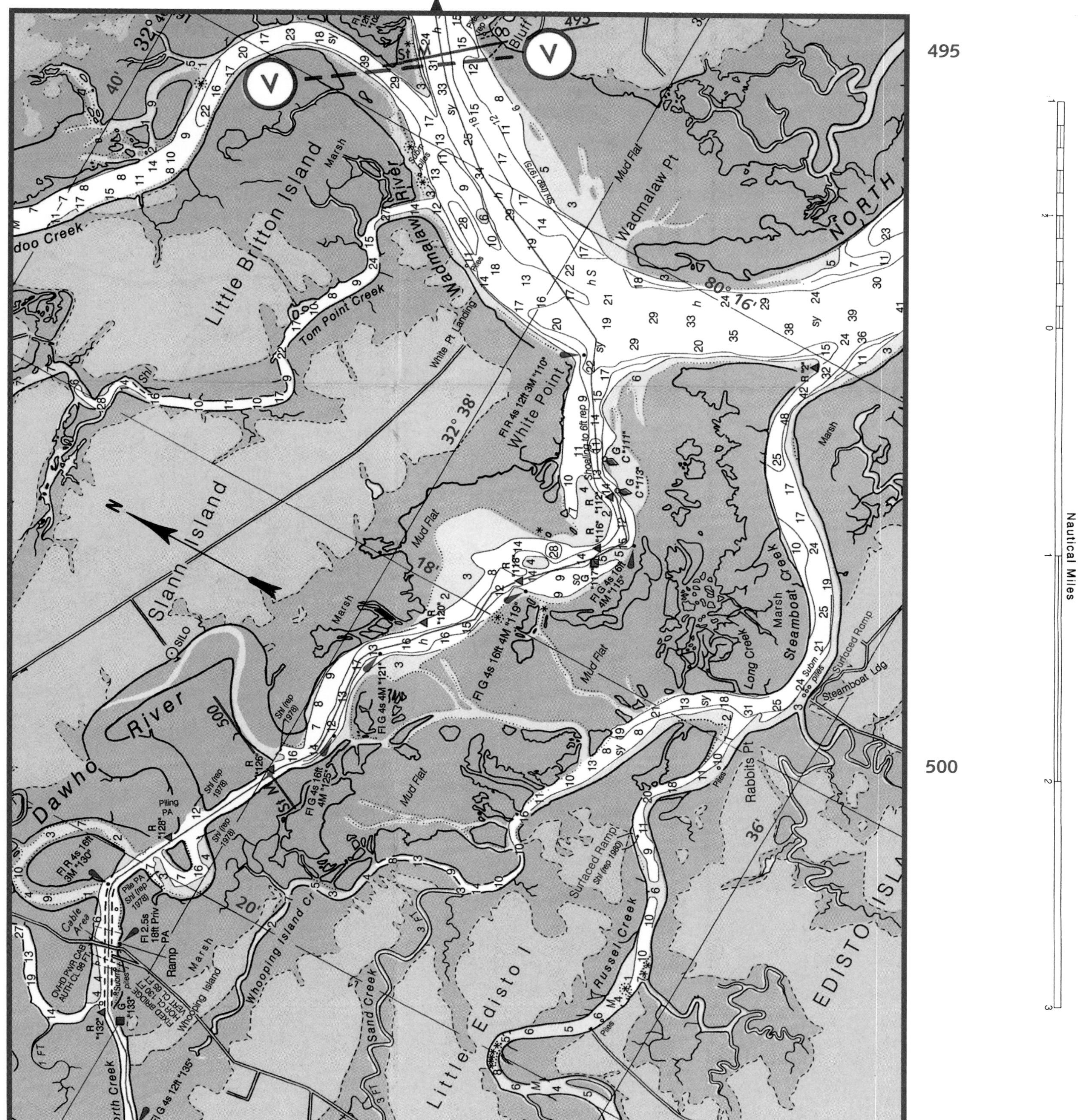

Little Britton Island
Tom Point Creek
Wadmalaw River
Wadmalaw Pt
White Pt Landing
White Point
Slann Island
Dawho River
Steamboat Creek
Long Creek
Whooping Island Cr
Whooping Island
Sand Creek
Little Edisto I
Russel Creek
Rabbits Pt
EDISTO ISLAND
NORTH
Mud Flat
Marsh
Nautical Miles
495
500

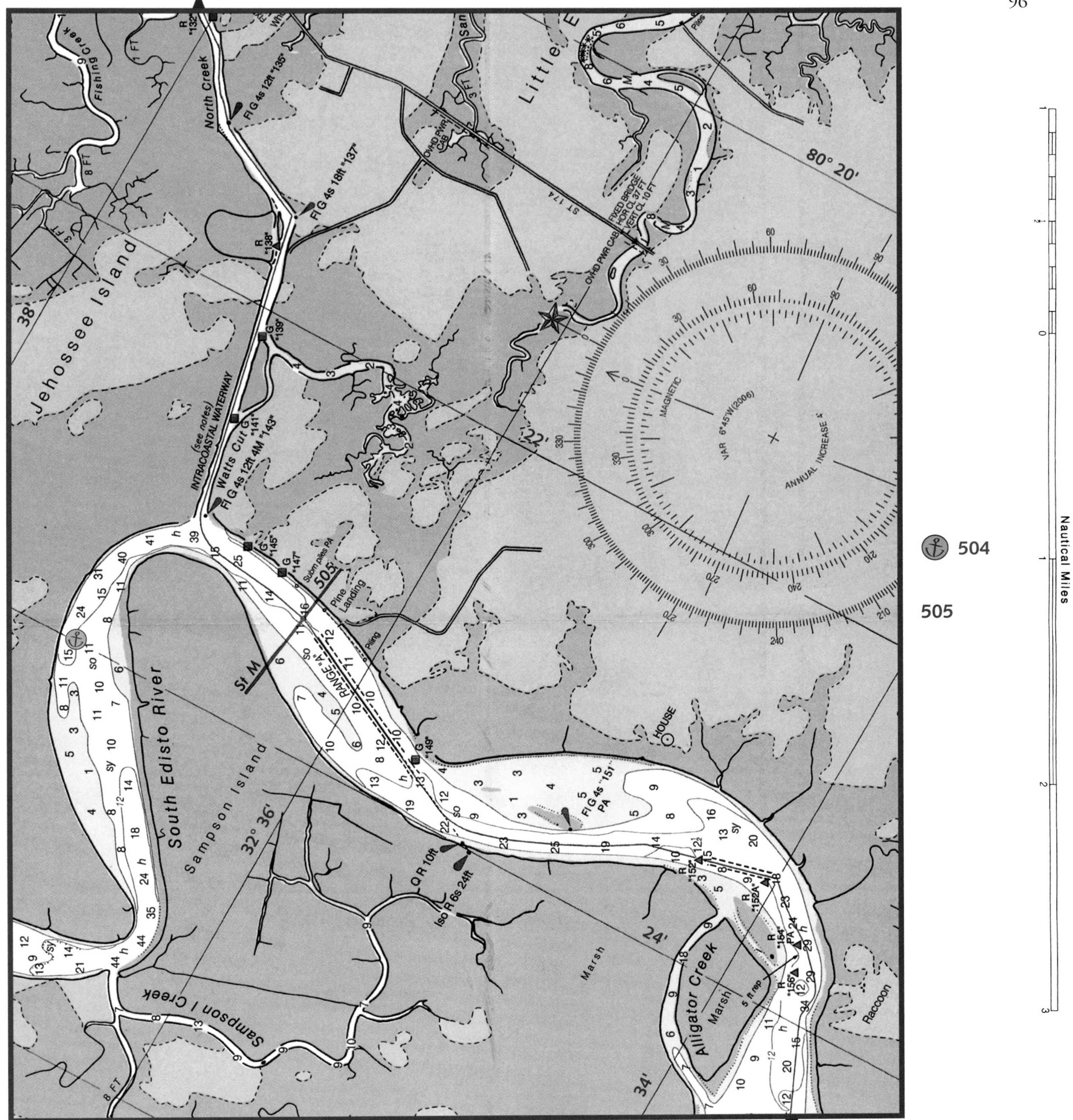
South Edisto River
Sampson Island
Jehossee Island
Sampson I Creek
Alligator Creek
North Creek
Fishing Creek
Watts Cut
INTRACOASTAL WATERWAY
(see notes)
Pine Landing
RANGE "A"
Marsh
Raccoon
HOUSE
32° 36'
80° 20'
FIXED BRIDGE
HOR CL 37 FT
VERT CL 10 FT
OVHD PWR CAB
ST 174
VAR 6°45'W(2006)
ANNUAL INCREASE 4'
MAGNETIC
504
505
Nautical Miles

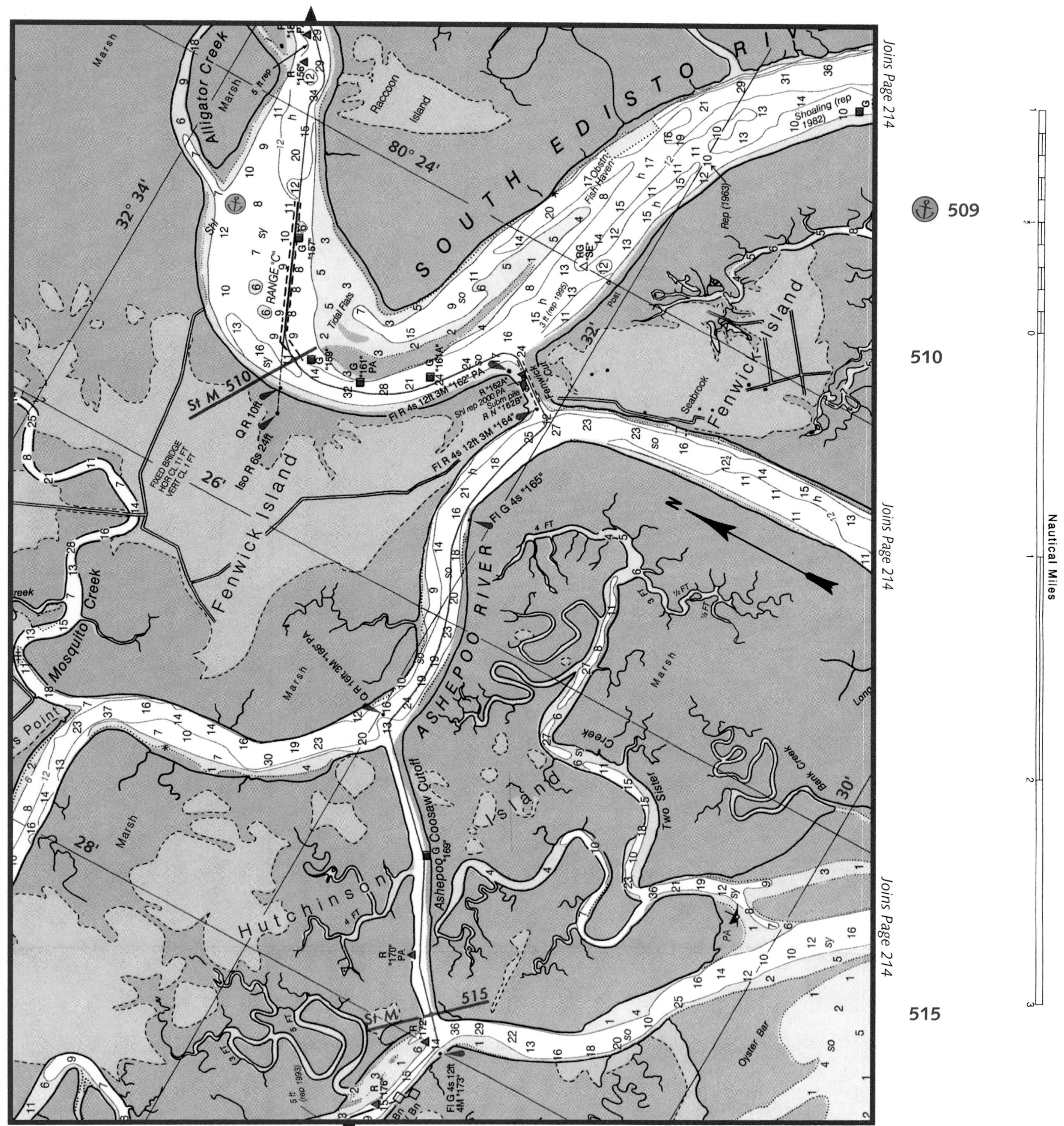

SOUTH EDISTO RIVER
ASHEPOO RIVER
Fenwick Island
Fenwick Island
Raccoon Island
Alligator Creek
Mosquito Creek
Hutchinson Island
Ashepoo Coosaw Cutoff
Fenwick Cut
Two Sister Creek
Bank Creek
Creek
Seabrook
Tidal Flats
Fish Haven
Oyster Bar
Marsh
St M 510
St M 515
FIXED BRIDGE HOR CL 11 FT VERT CL 11 FT
RANGE "C"
Q R 10ft
Iso R 6s 24ft
Fl R 4s 12ft 3M "162" PA
Fl R 4s 12ft 3M "164"
Fl G 4s "165"
Q R 16ft 3M "166" PA
Fl G 4s 12ft 4M "173"
Shoaling (rep 1982)
Rep (1963)
Shl rep 2000 PA
Subm pile
Joins Page 214
Joins Page 214
Joins Page 214
509
510
515
Nautical Miles
80° 24'
32° 34'
32'
30'
28'
26'

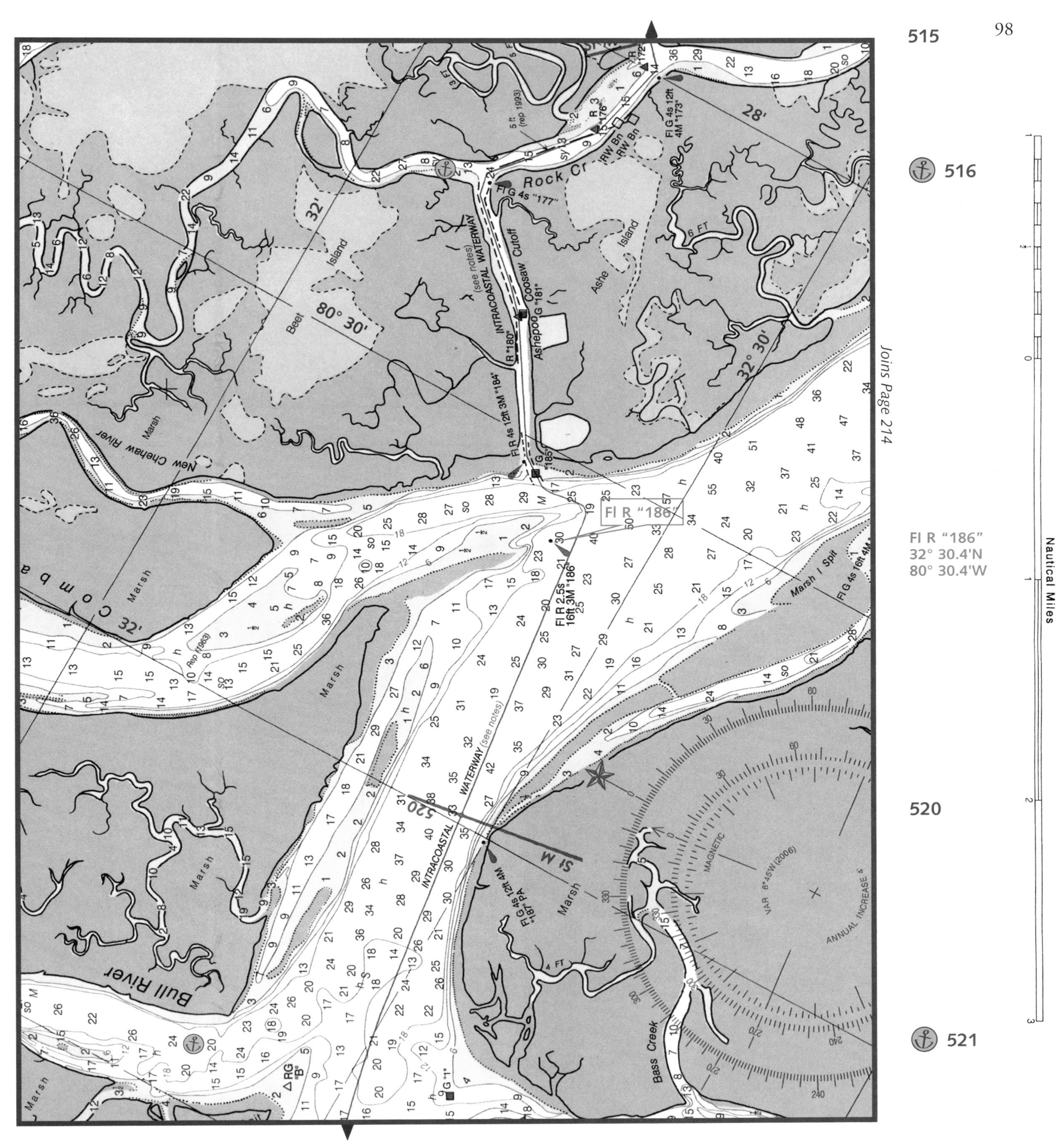

515
516
520
521
Joins Page 214
Fl R "186"
32° 30.4'N
80° 30.4'W
Nautical Miles
Bull River
New Chehaw River
Combahee
Rock Cr
Bass Creek
Beet Island
Ashe Island
Ashepoo Coosaw Cutoff
INTRACOASTAL WATERWAY (see notes)
Marsh I Spit
St M
80° 30'
32° 30'
32'
28'
VAR 6°45'W (2006)
ANNUAL INCREASE 4'
MAGNETIC

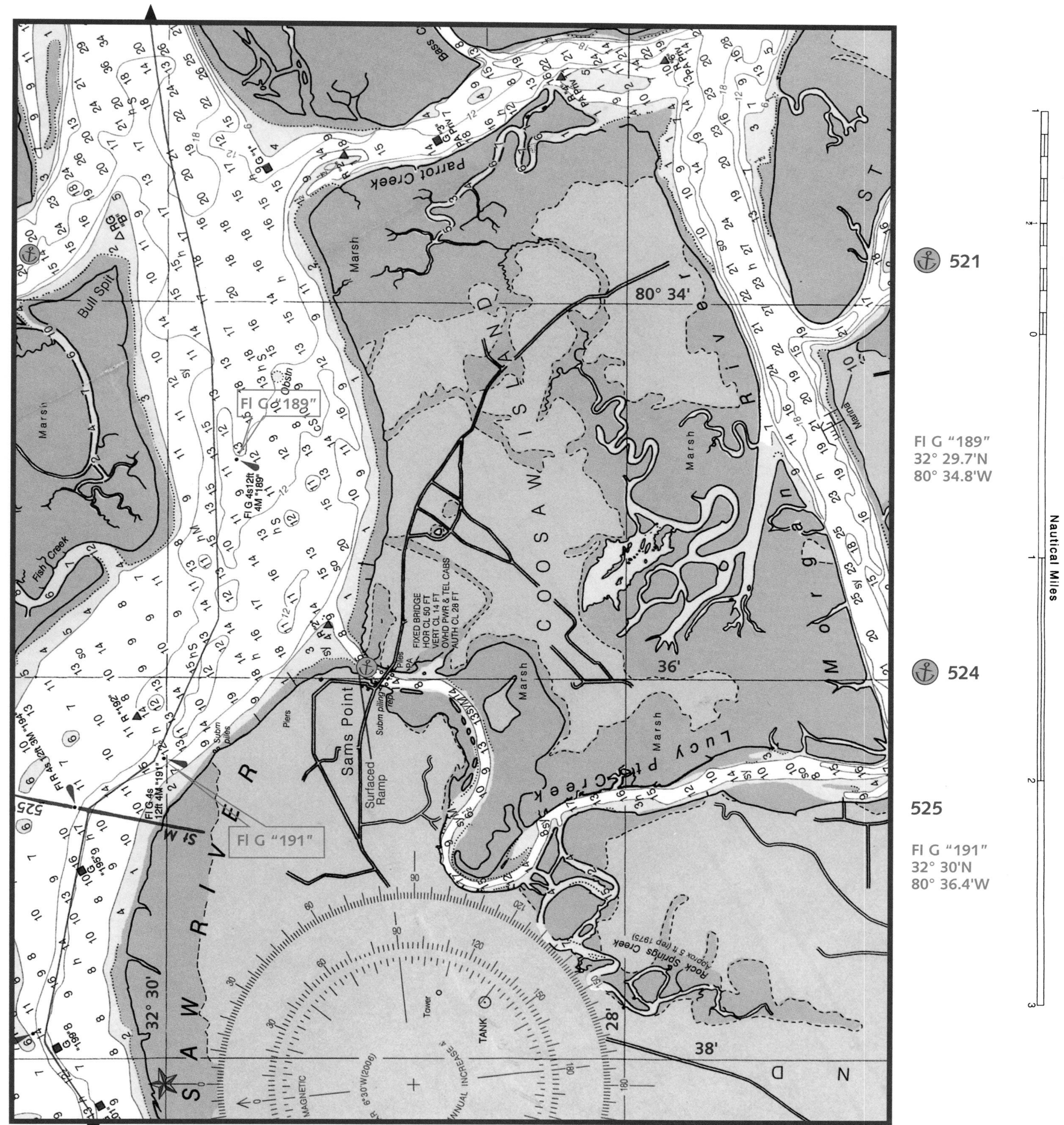
521
Fl G "189"
32° 29.7'N
80° 34.8'W
524
525
Fl G "191"
32° 30'N
80° 36.4'W
Nautical Miles
Parrot Creek
Bull Spit
Marsh
Fish Creek
Sams Point
Surfaced Ramp
Piers
COOSAW ISLAND
Morgan River
Lucy Point Creek
Rock Springs Creek
SAW RIVER
FIXED BRIDGE
HOR CL 50 FT
VERT CL 14 FT
OVHD PWR & TEL CABS
AUTH CL 28 FT
80° 34'
36'
38'
32° 30'
28'
Tower
TANK
MAGNETIC

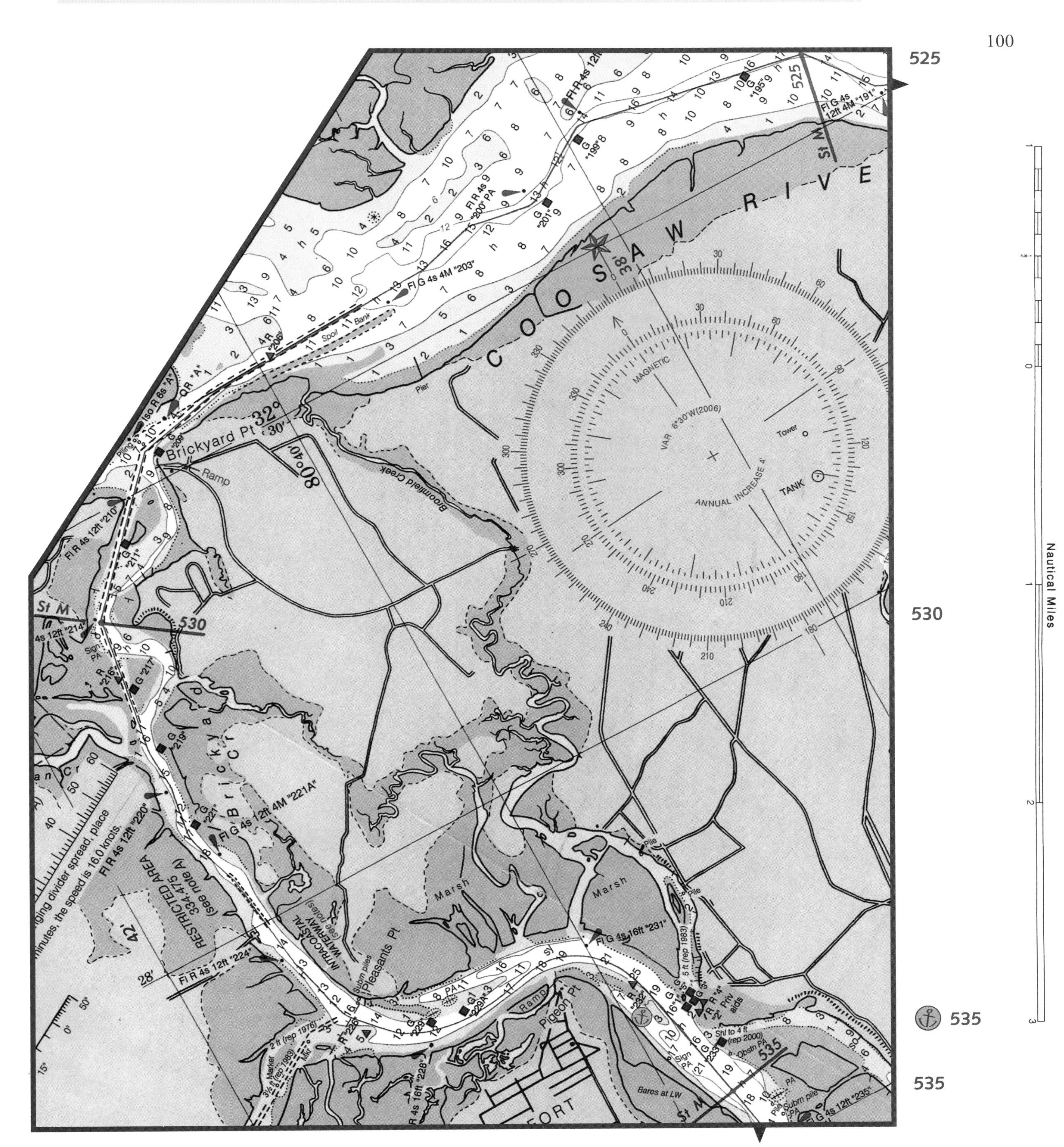
525
530
535
535
Nautical Miles
COOSAW RIVER
Brickyard Pt
Bloomfield Creek
Brickyard Cr
Pleasants Pt
Pigeon Pt
Marsh
INTRACOASTAL WATERWAY (see notes)
RESTRICTED AREA 334.475 (see note A)
VAR 6°30'W(2006)
ANNUAL INCREASE 4'
MAGNETIC
TANK
Tower
Ramp
Pier
FORT
Bares at LW
Fl G 4s 4M "203"
Fl R 4s 9 15 "200" PA
Fl G 4s 12ft 4M "221A"
Fl R 4s 12ft "220"
Fl R 4s 12ft "224"
Fl R 4s 12ft "210"
Fl G 4s 16ft "231"
Iso R 6s "A"
QR "A"
Fl G 4s 12ft 4M "191"
Fl G 4s 12ft "235"
...minutes, the speed is 16.0 knots.
...ging divider spread, place

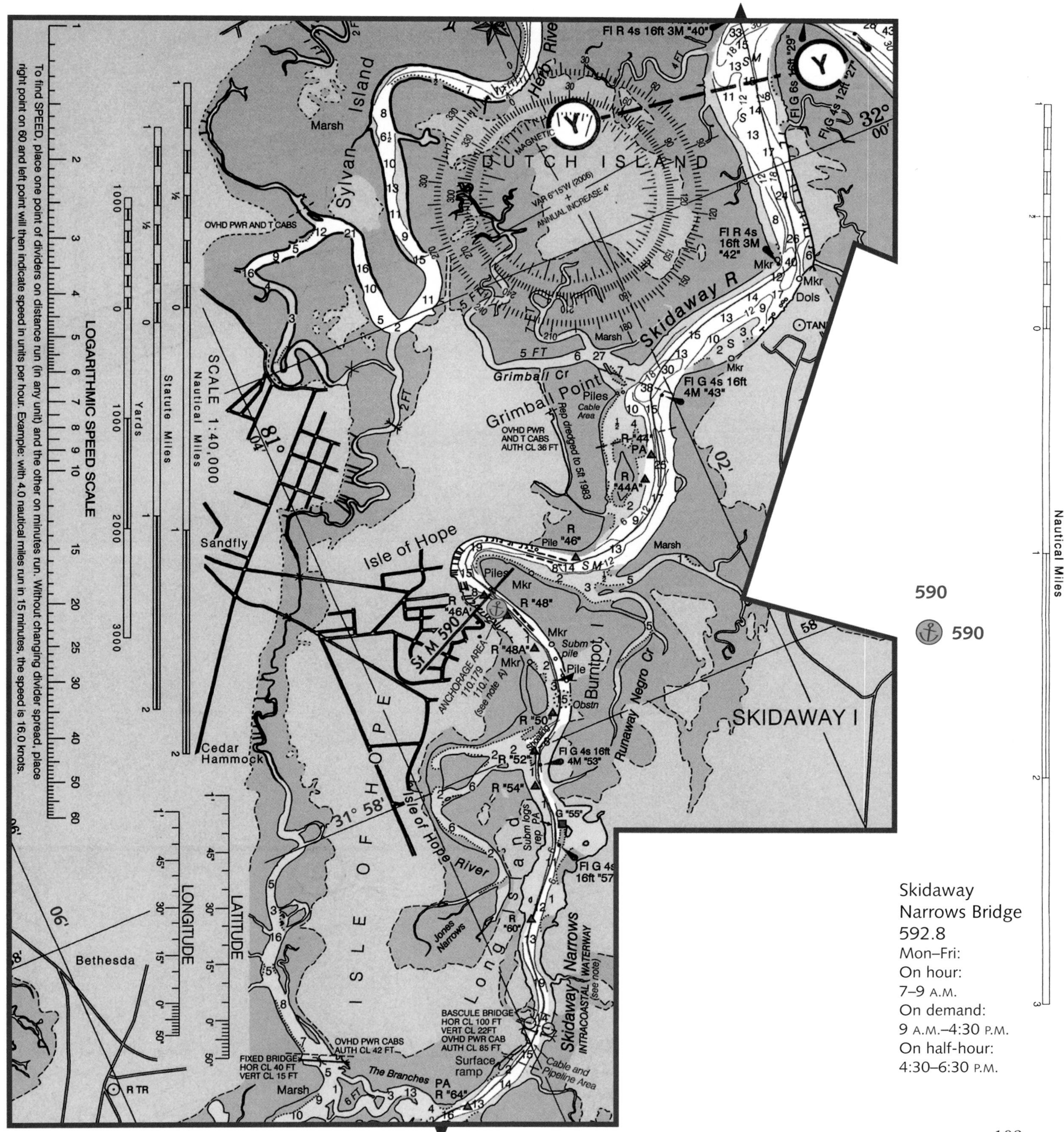

590

590

Skidaway Narrows Bridge 592.8
Mon–Fri:
On hour:
7–9 A.M.
On demand:
9 A.M.–4:30 P.M.
On half-hour:
4:30–6:30 P.M.

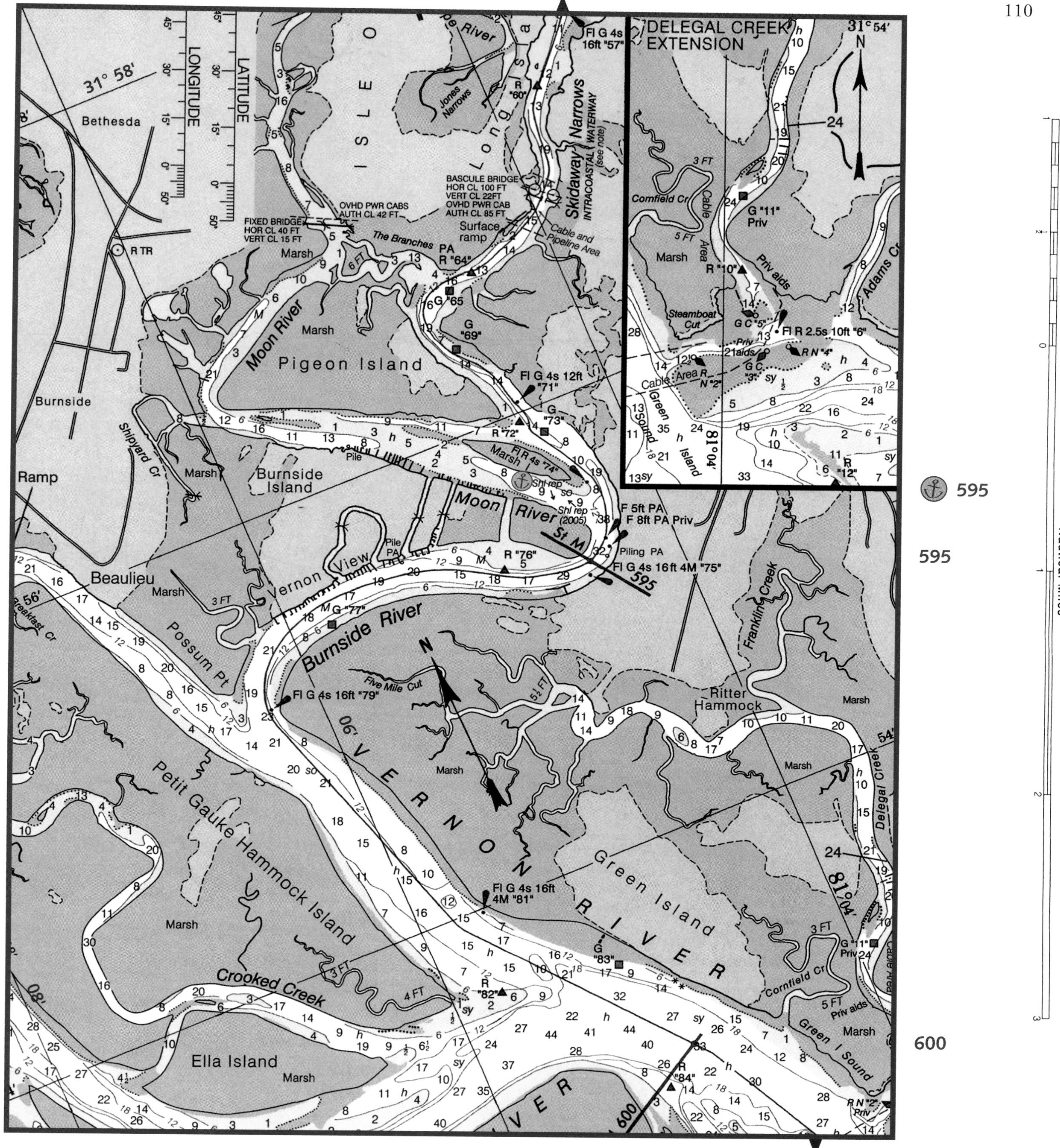

DELEGAL CREEK EXTENSION
Vernon River
Burnside River
Moon River
Skidaway Narrows
INTRACOASTAL WATERWAY (see note)
Pigeon Island
Burnside Island
Green Island
Petit Gauke Hammock Island
Ella Island
Crooked Creek
Possum Pt
Beaulieu
Burnside
Bethesda
Ritter Hammock
Franklin Creek
Delegal Creek
Five Mile Cut
Vernon View
Isle of Hope
Jones Narrows
The Branches
Cornfield Cr
Green I Sound
Adams Cr
Shipyard Cr
Steamboat Cut
Marsh
Ramp
R TR
BASCULE BRIDGE HOR CL 100 FT VERT CL 22FT
OVHD PWR CAB AUTH CL 85 FT
OVHD PWR CABS AUTH CL 42 FT
FIXED BRIDGE HOR CL 40 FT VERT CL 15 FT
Surface ramp
Cable and Pipeline Area
Fl G 4s 16ft "57"
Fl G 4s 12ft "71"
Fl R 4s "74"
Fl G 4s 16ft 4M "75"
Fl G 4s 16ft "79"
Fl G 4s 16ft 4M "81"
Fl R 2.5s 10ft "6"
F 5ft PA
F 8ft PA Priv
Piling PA
Shl rep (2005)
31° 58'
31° 54'
81°04'
LATITUDE
LONGITUDE
595
600
Nautical Miles

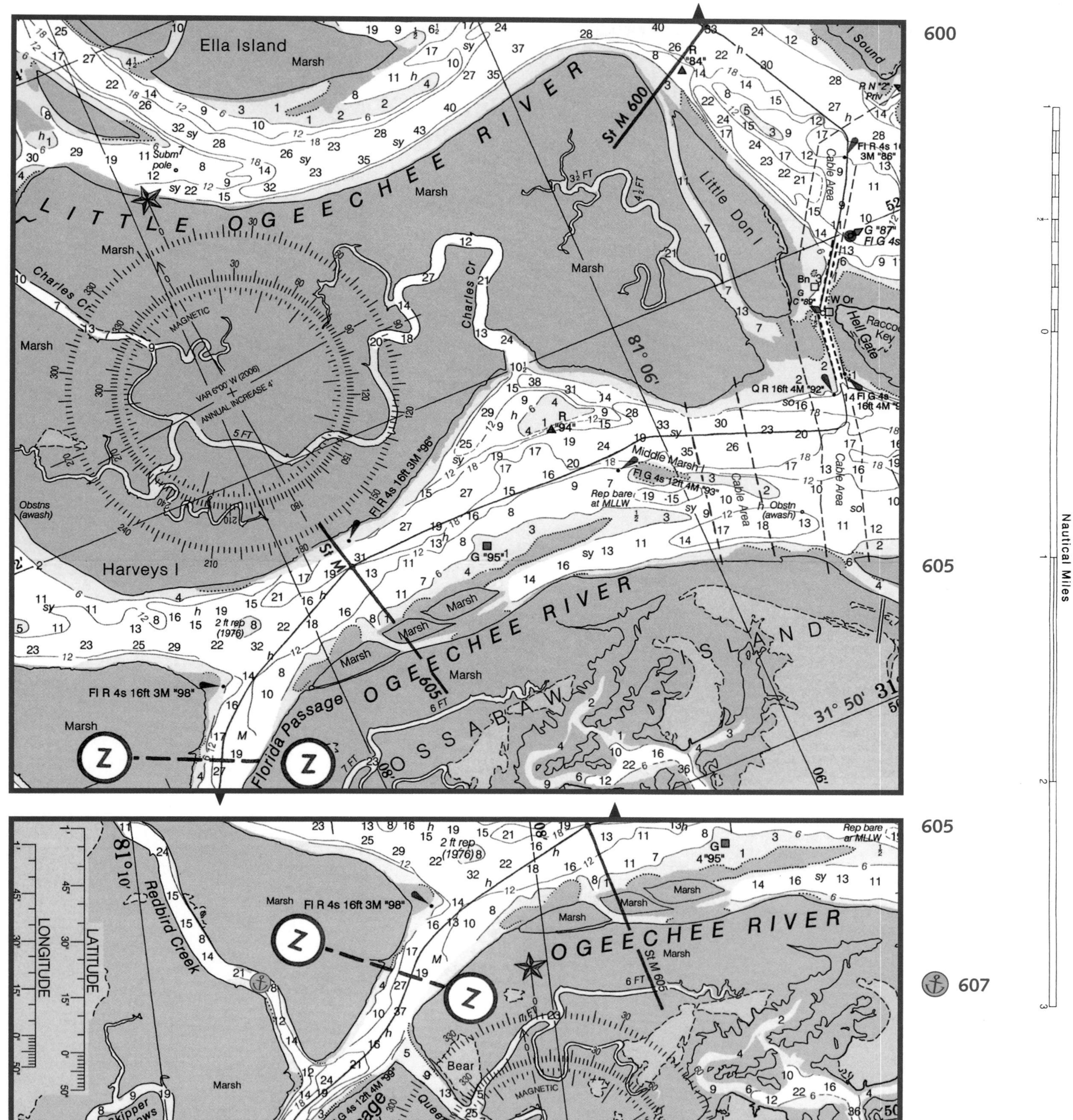

Ella Island
LITTLE OGEECHEE RIVER
St M 600
Little Don I
Charles Cr
Harveys I
Middle Marsh I
Raccoon Key
Hell Gate
Cable Area
VAR 6°00' W (2006)
ANNUAL INCREASE 4'
MAGNETIC
Fl R 4s 16ft 3M "96"
Fl G 4s 12ft 4M "93"
Fl R 4s 16ft 3M "98"
Q R 16ft 4M "92"
Fl G 4s
Fl R 4s
3M "86"
G "87"
G "95"
R "94"
R "84"
Rep bare at MLLW
Obstn (awash)
Obstns (awash)
2 ft rep (1976)
Subm pole
Florida Passage
OGEECHEE RIVER
OSSABAW ISLAND
St M 605
81° 06'
81° 08'
31° 50'
Marsh
600
605
Redbird Creek
Bear
LATITUDE
LONGITUDE
81° 10'
Nautical Miles
607

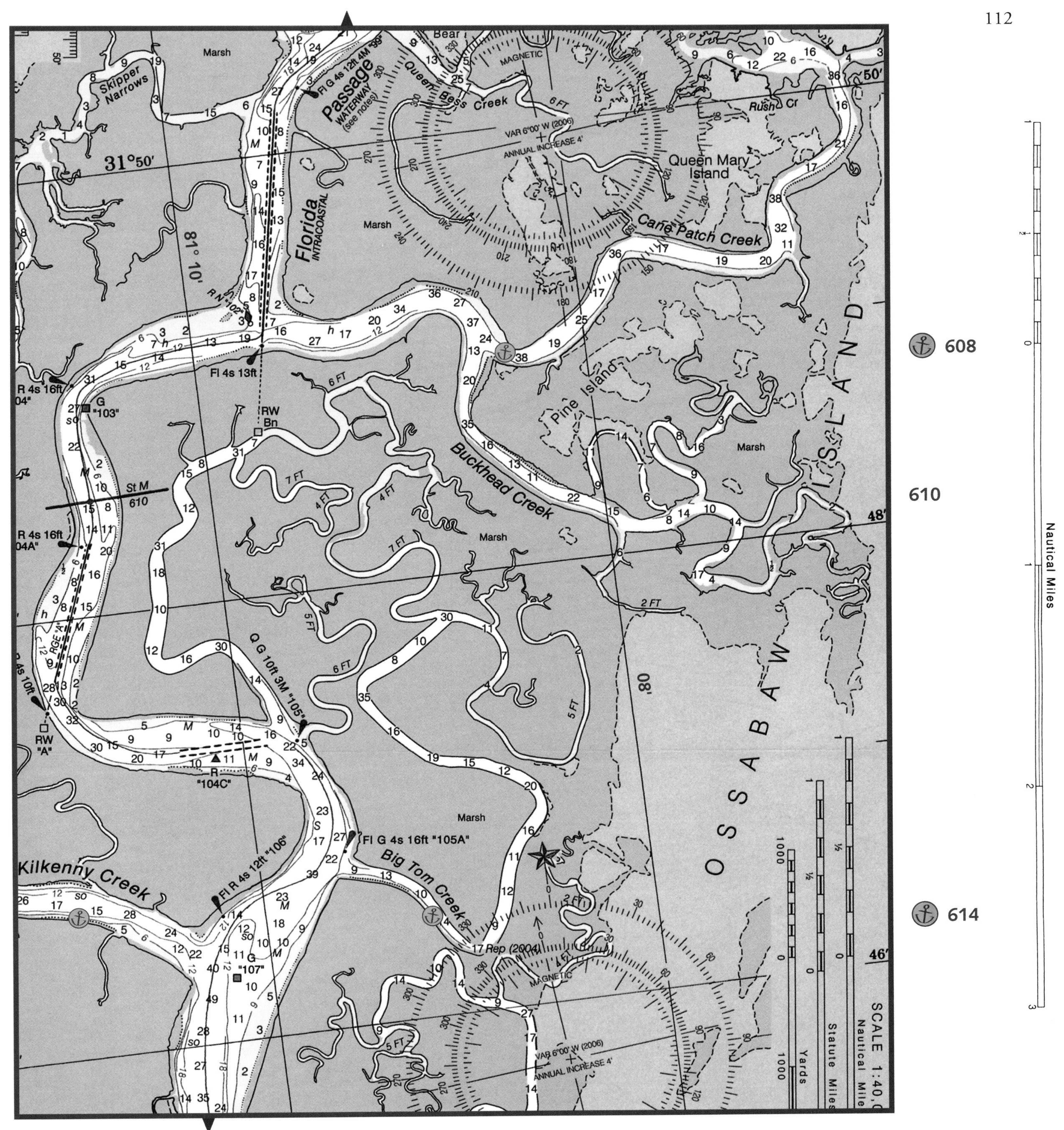
Skipper Narrows
Passage
WATERWAY
(see notes)
Florida
INTRACOASTAL
Queen Bess Creek
Queen Mary Island
Cane Patch Creek
Rush Cr
Pine Island
Buckhead Creek
Big Tom Creek
Kilkenny Creek
OSSABAW ISLAND
Marsh
31°50′
81° 10′
Fl 4s 13ft
RW Bn
St M 610
QG 10ft 3M "105"
Fl G 4s 16ft "105A"
Fl R 4s 12ft "106"
G "103"
R "104C"
G "107"
RW "A"
17 Rep (2004)
VAR 6°00′ W (2006)
ANNUAL INCREASE 4′
MAGNETIC
SCALE 1:40,0
Nautical Miles
Statute Miles
Yards
Nautical Miles
608
610
614

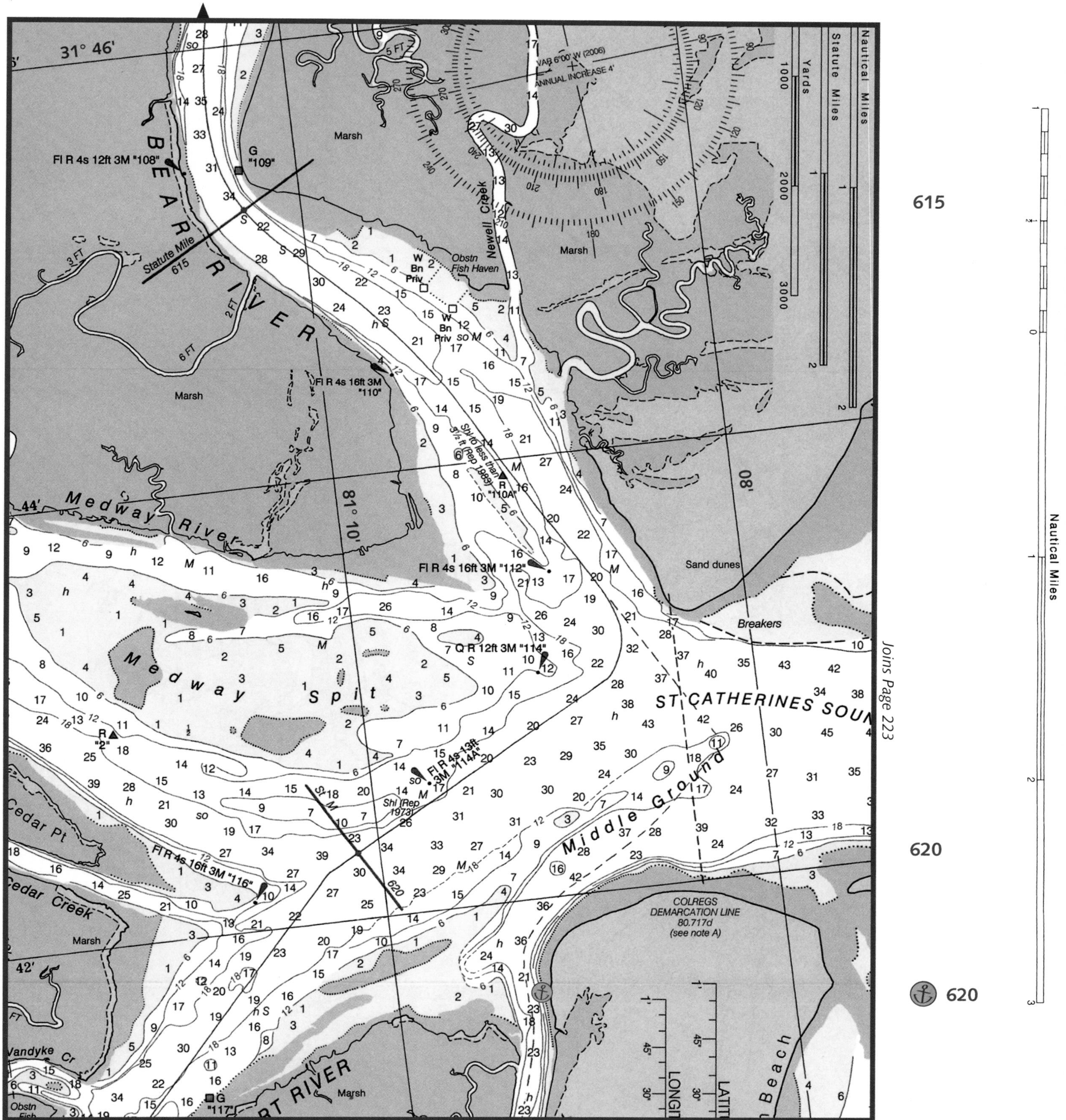

31° 46'
BEAR RIVER
Fl R 4s 12ft 3M "108"
G "109"
Marsh
Statute Mile 615
VAR 6°00' W (2006)
ANNUAL INCREASE 4'
Newell Creek
W Bn Priv
Obstn Fish Haven
Fl R 4s 16ft 3M "110"
Shl to less than 3½ ft (Rep 1989)
R "110A"
44'
Medway River
81° 10'
80'
Fl R 4s 16ft 3M "112"
Sand dunes
Breakers
Q R 12ft 3M "114"
Medway Spit
ST CATHERINES SOUND
R "2"
Fl R 4s 13ft 3M "114A"
Shl (Rep 1973)
Cedar Pt
Cedar Creek
Fl R 4s 16ft 3M "116"
Middle Ground
620
COLREGS DEMARCATION LINE 80.717d (see note A)
42'
Vandyke Cr
Obstn Fish
G "117"
RT RIVER
Marsh
LONGITUDE
LATITUDE
Beach
Yards
Statute Miles
Nautical Miles
615
620
620
Joins Page 223
Nautical Miles

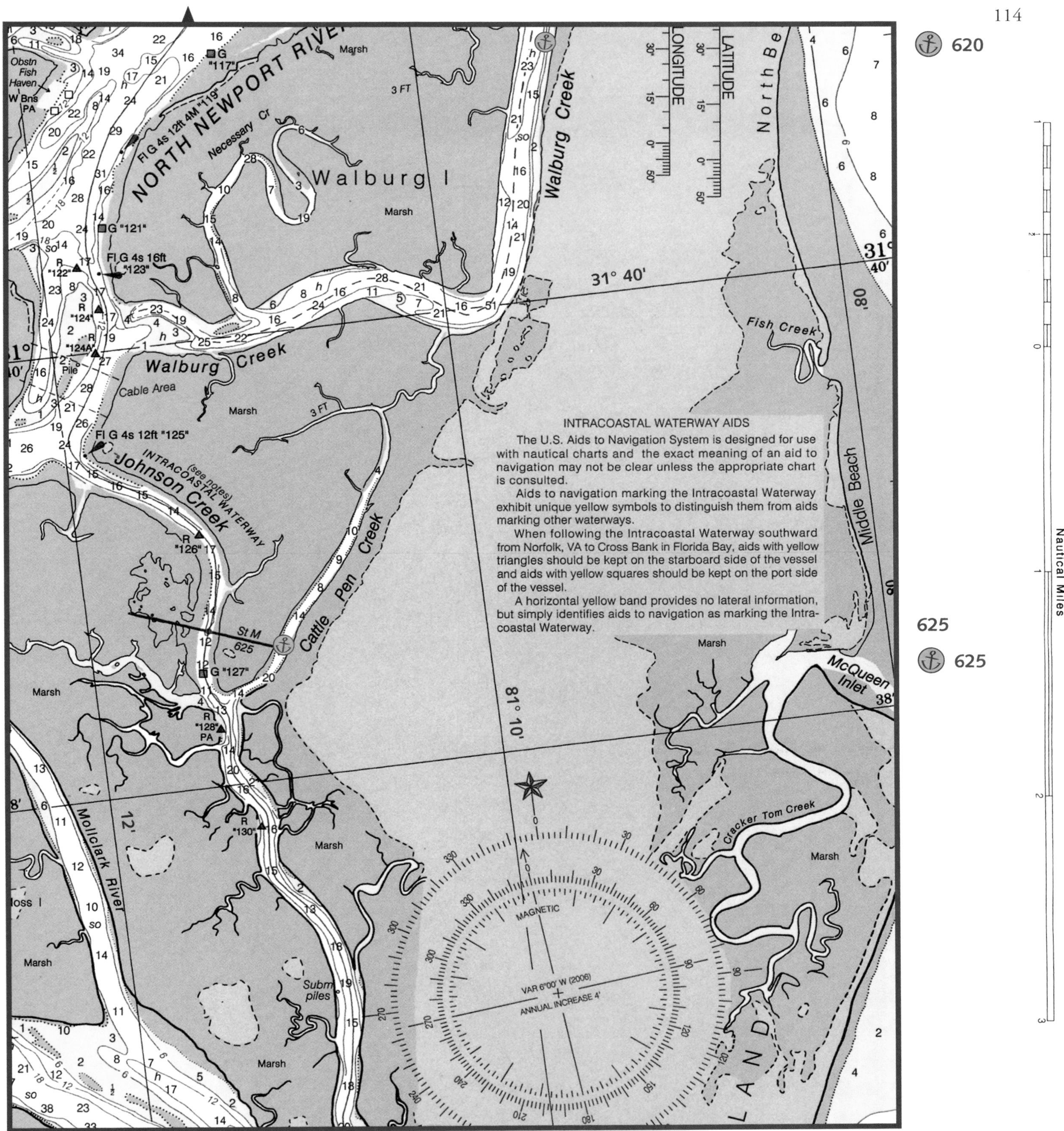

620
625
625
NORTH NEWPORT RIVER
Walburg I
Walburg Creek
Johnson Creek
INTRACOASTAL WATERWAY (see notes)
Cattle Pen Creek
Necessary Cr
Cable Area
Mollclark River
Fish Creek
Cracker Tom Creek
McQueen Inlet
Middle Beach
North Be
Marsh
31° 40'
81° 10'
LATITUDE
LONGITUDE
MAGNETIC
VAR 6°00' W (2006)
ANNUAL INCREASE 4'
Nautical Miles
INTRACOASTAL WATERWAY AIDS
The U.S. Aids to Navigation System is designed for use with nautical charts and the exact meaning of an aid to navigation may not be clear unless the appropriate chart is consulted.
Aids to navigation marking the Intracoastal Waterway exhibit unique yellow symbols to distinguish them from aids marking other waterways.
When following the Intracoastal Waterway southward from Norfolk, VA to Cross Bank in Florida Bay, aids with yellow triangles should be kept on the starboard side of the vessel and aids with yellow squares should be kept on the port side of the vessel.
A horizontal yellow band provides no lateral information, but simply identifies aids to navigation as marking the Intracoastal Waterway.

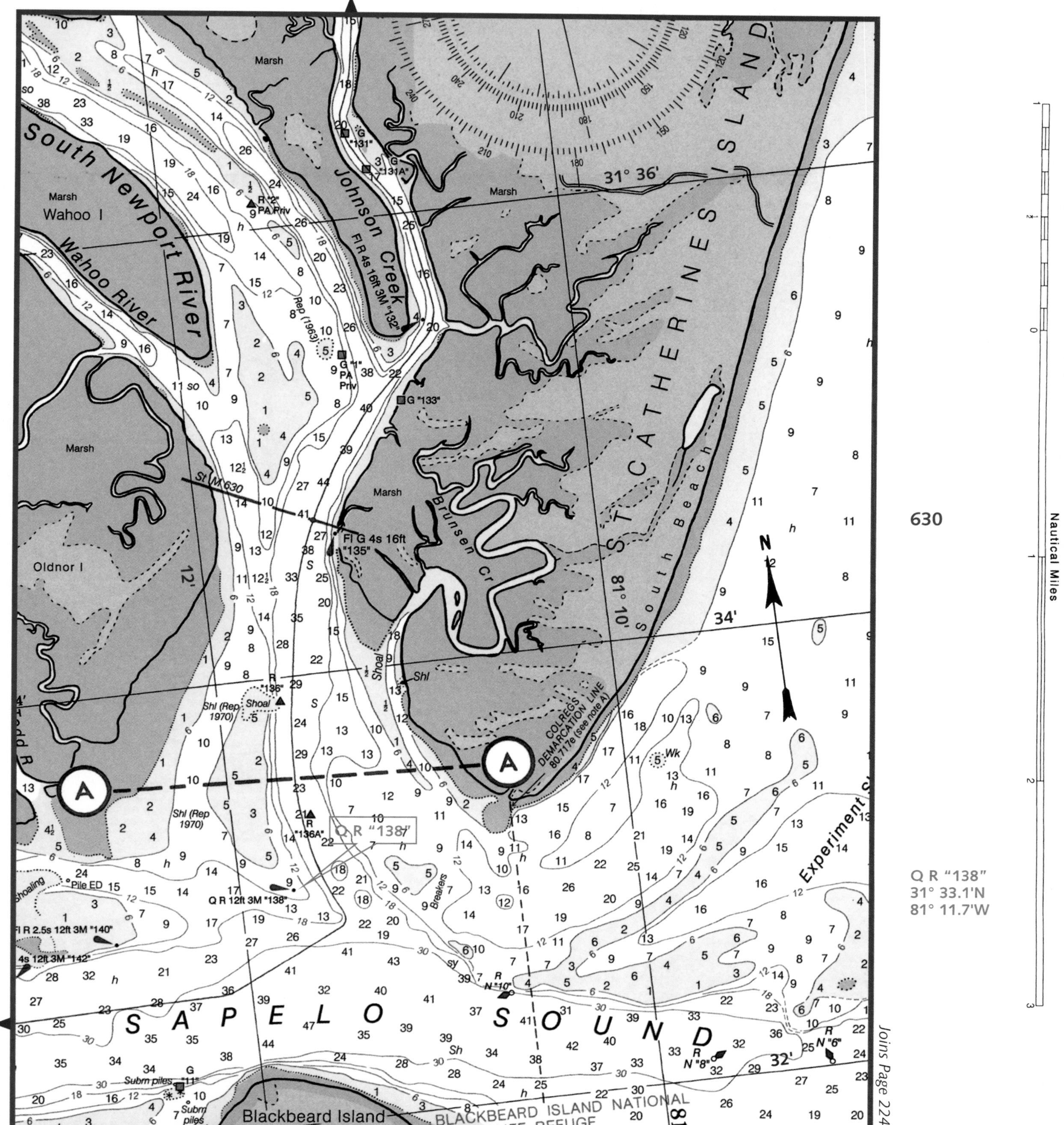

South Newport River
Wahoo I
Wahoo River
Johnson Creek
Marsh
Oldnor I
Brunsen Cr
ST CATHERINES ISLAND
South Beach
Fl R 4s 16ft 3M "132"
Fl G 4s 16ft "135"
St M 630
COLREGS DEMARCATION LINE 80.717e (see note A)
Experiment Sh
Q R 12ft 3M "138"
Fl R 2.5s 12ft 3M "140"
4s 12ft 3M "142"
SAPELO SOUND
Blackbeard Island
BLACKBEARD ISLAND NATIONAL WILDLIFE REFUGE
Joins Page 224
31° 36'
34'
32'
81° 10'
Nautical Miles
630
Q R "138"
31° 33.1'N
81° 11.7'W

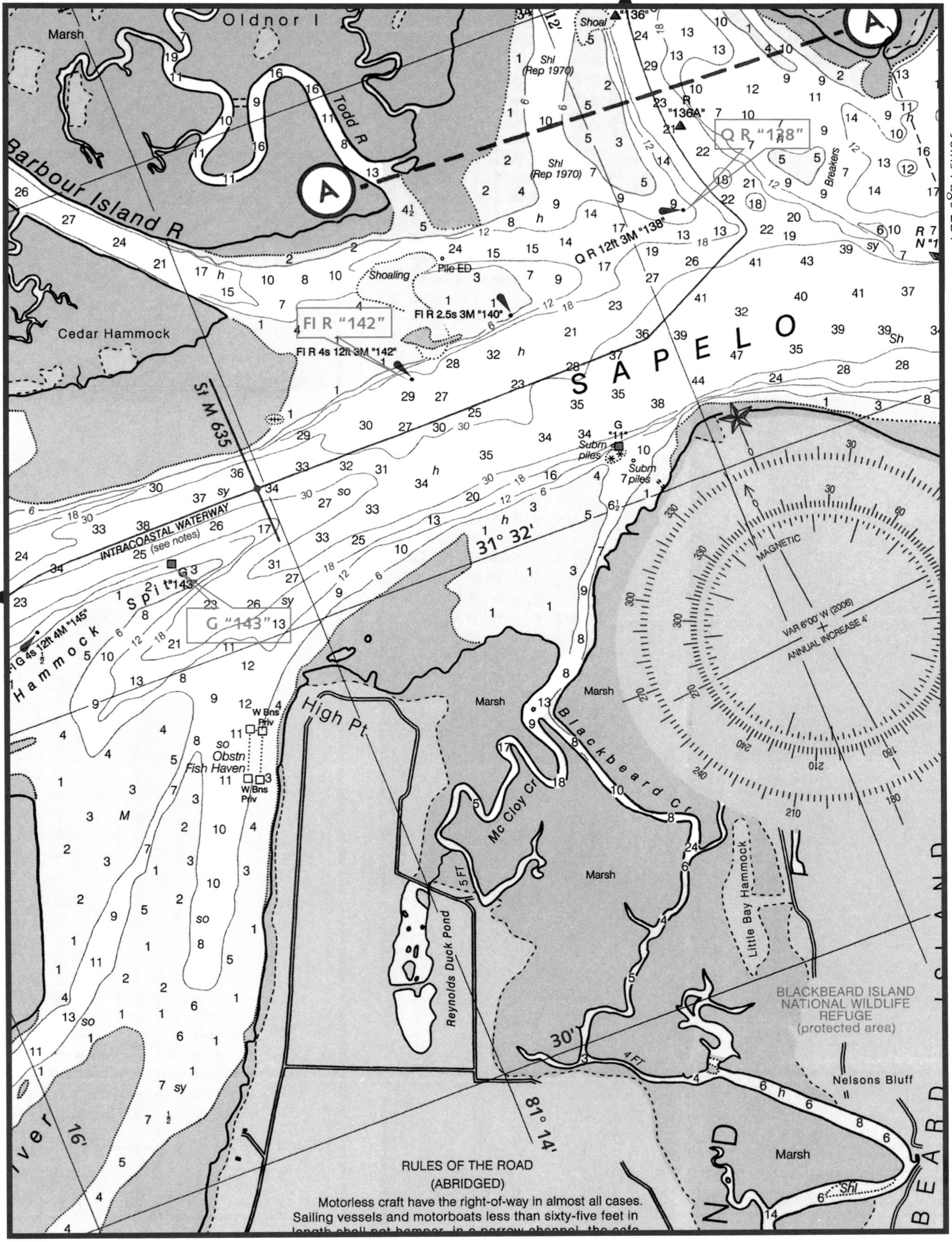

Joins Page 224

Q R "138"
31° 33.1'N
81° 11.7'W

F R "142"
31° 32.8'N
81° 13.2'W

635

G "143"
31° 32.6'N
81° 14.5'W

Nautical Miles

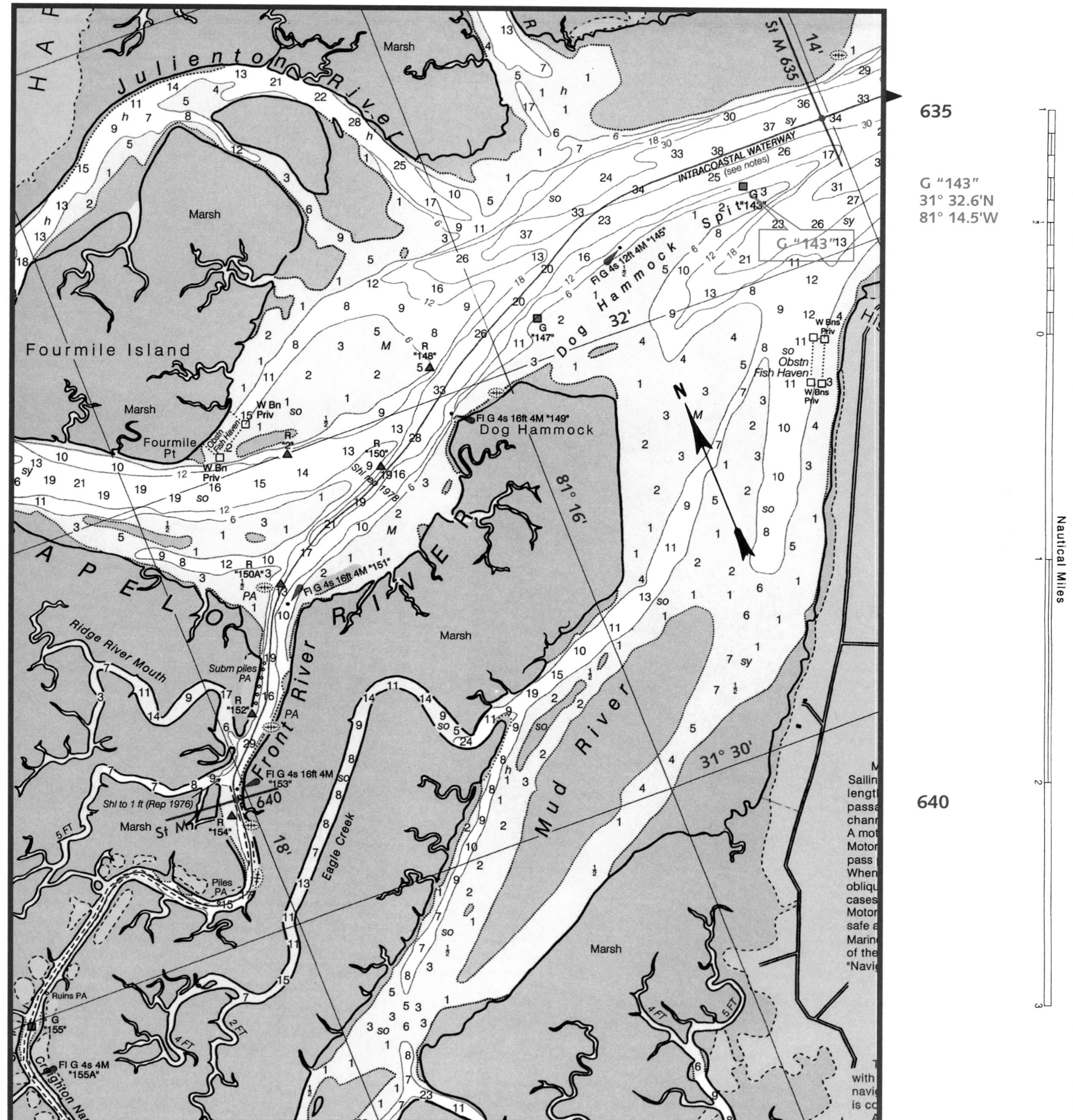
Julienton River
Marsh
Fourmile Island
Fourmile Pt
Dog Hammock Spit
Dog Hammock
INTRACOASTAL WATERWAY (see notes)
St M 635
635
G "143"
31° 32.6'N
81° 14.5'W
Fl G 4s 12ft 4M "145"
G "147"
R "148"
Fl G 4s 16ft 4M "149"
R "150"
R "150A"
Fl G 4s 16ft 4M "151"
R "152"
Fl G 4s 16ft 4M "153"
R "154"
G "155"
Fl G 4s 4M "155A"
Shl rep 1978
Shl to 1 ft (Rep 1976)
Obstn Fish Haven
W Bn Priv
W Bns Priv
Subm piles PA
Piles PA
Ruins PA
Ridge River Mouth
SAPELO RIVER
Front River
Eagle Creek
Mud River
81° 16'
31° 30'
32'
640
St M 640
Creighton Na
Nautical Miles
0
1
2
3

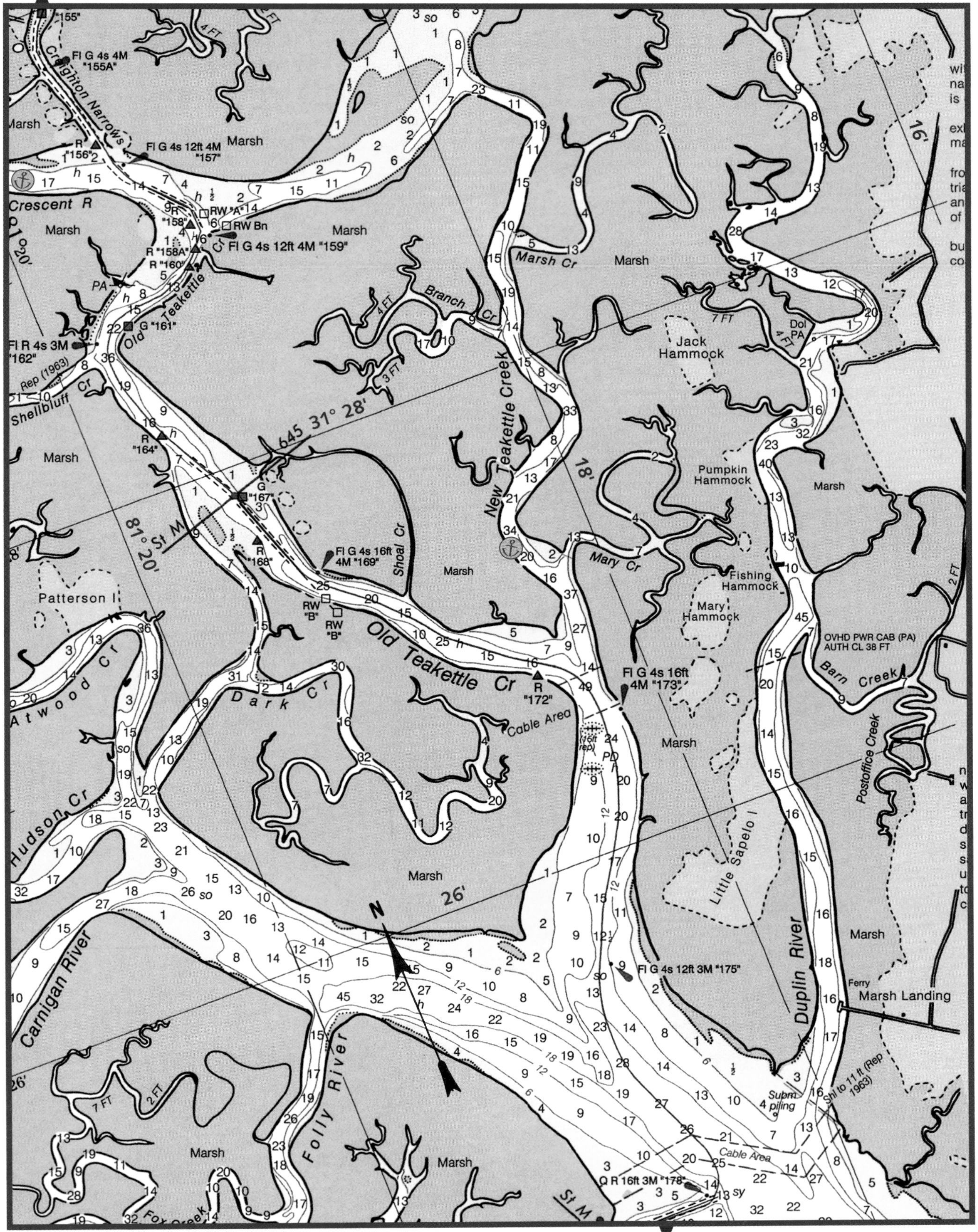
Creighton Narrows
Fl G 4s 4M "155A"
Fl G 4s 12ft 4M "157"
Crescent R
Fl G 4s 12ft 4M "159"
Old Teakettle Cr
Fl R 4s 3M "162"
Shellbluff Cr
Rep (1963)
645 31° 28'
81° 20'
St M
Patterson I
Atwood Cr
Hudson Cr
Carnigan River
Folly River
Fox Creek
Dark Cr
Shoal Cr
Fl G 4s 16ft 4M "169"
Old Teakettle Cr
Cable Area
New Teakettle Creek
Branch Cr
Marsh Cr
Mary Cr
Fl G 4s 16ft 4M "173"
Fl G 4s 12ft 3M "175"
Q R 16ft 3M "178"
Subm 4 piling
Shl to 11 ft (Rep 1963)
Little Sapelo I
Duplin River
Jack Hammock
Pumpkin Hammock
Fishing Hammock
Mary Hammock
OVHD PWR CAB (PA) AUTH CL 38 FT
Barn Creek
Postoffice Creek
Ferry
Marsh Landing
Marsh

643

645

646

Nautical Miles

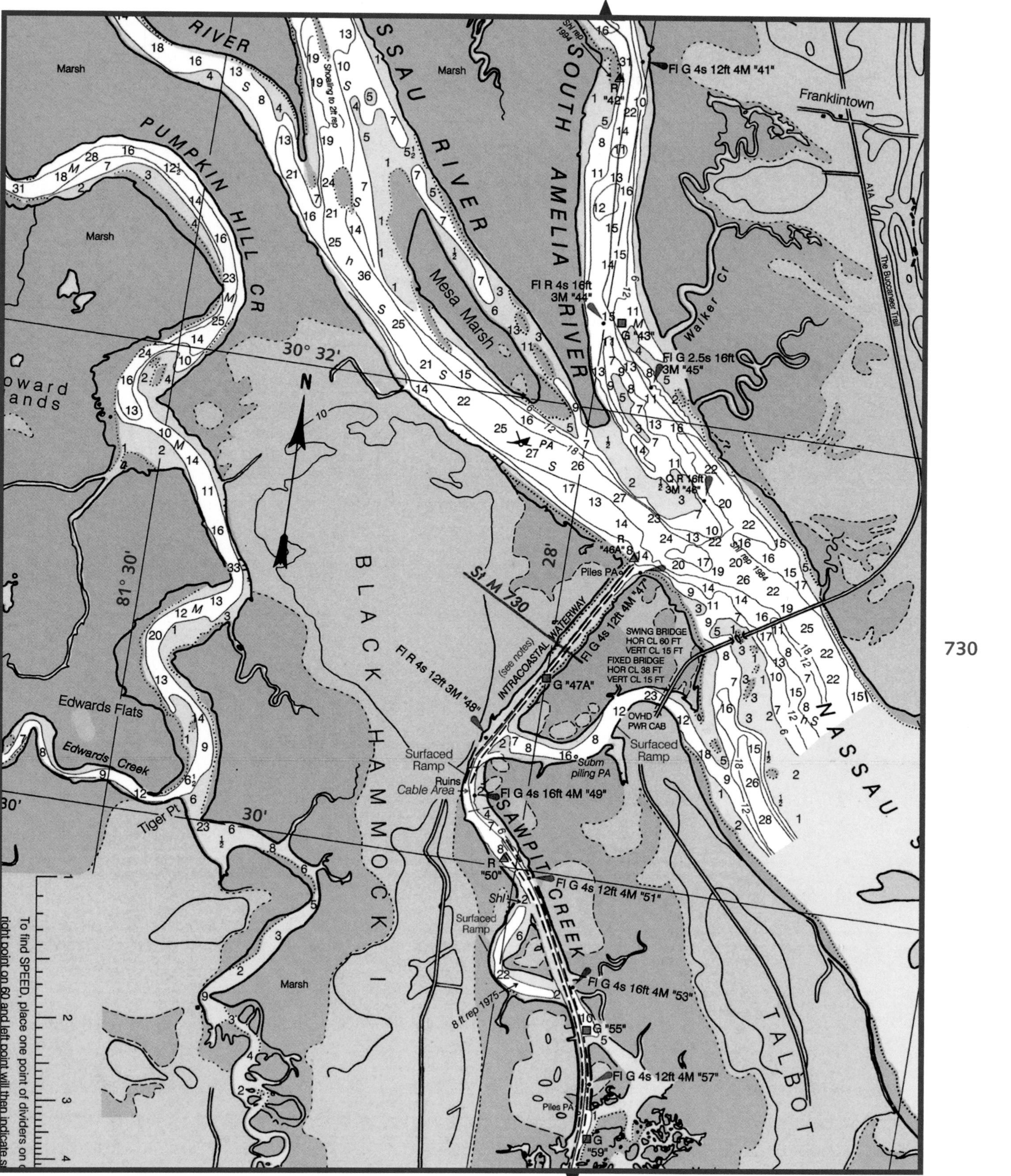

RIVER
Marsh
PUMPKIN HILL CR
SOUTH AMELIA RIVER
Fl G 4s 12ft 4M "41"
Franklintown
Walker Cr
Mesa Marsh
Fl R 4s 16ft 3M "44"
G "43"
Fl G 2.5s 16ft 3M "45"
30° 32'
Q R 16ft 3M "46"
BLACK HAMMOCK I
81° 30'
St M 730
INTRACOASTAL WATERWAY
Fl G 4s 12ft 4M "47"
SWING BRIDGE HOR CL 60 FT VERT CL 15 FT
FIXED BRIDGE HOR CL 38 FT VERT CL 15 FT
OVHD PWR CAB
Fl R 4s 12ft 3M "48"
G "47A"
NASSAU
Edwards Flats
Edwards Creek
Surfaced Ramp
Cable Area
Fl G 4s 16ft 4M "49"
Tiger Pt
SAWPIT CREEK
Fl G 4s 12ft 4M "51"
Fl G 4s 16ft 4M "53"
G "55"
Fl G 4s 12ft 4M "57"
G "59"
TALBOT
Nautical Miles
To find SPEED, place one point of dividers on right point on 60 and left point will then indicate

730

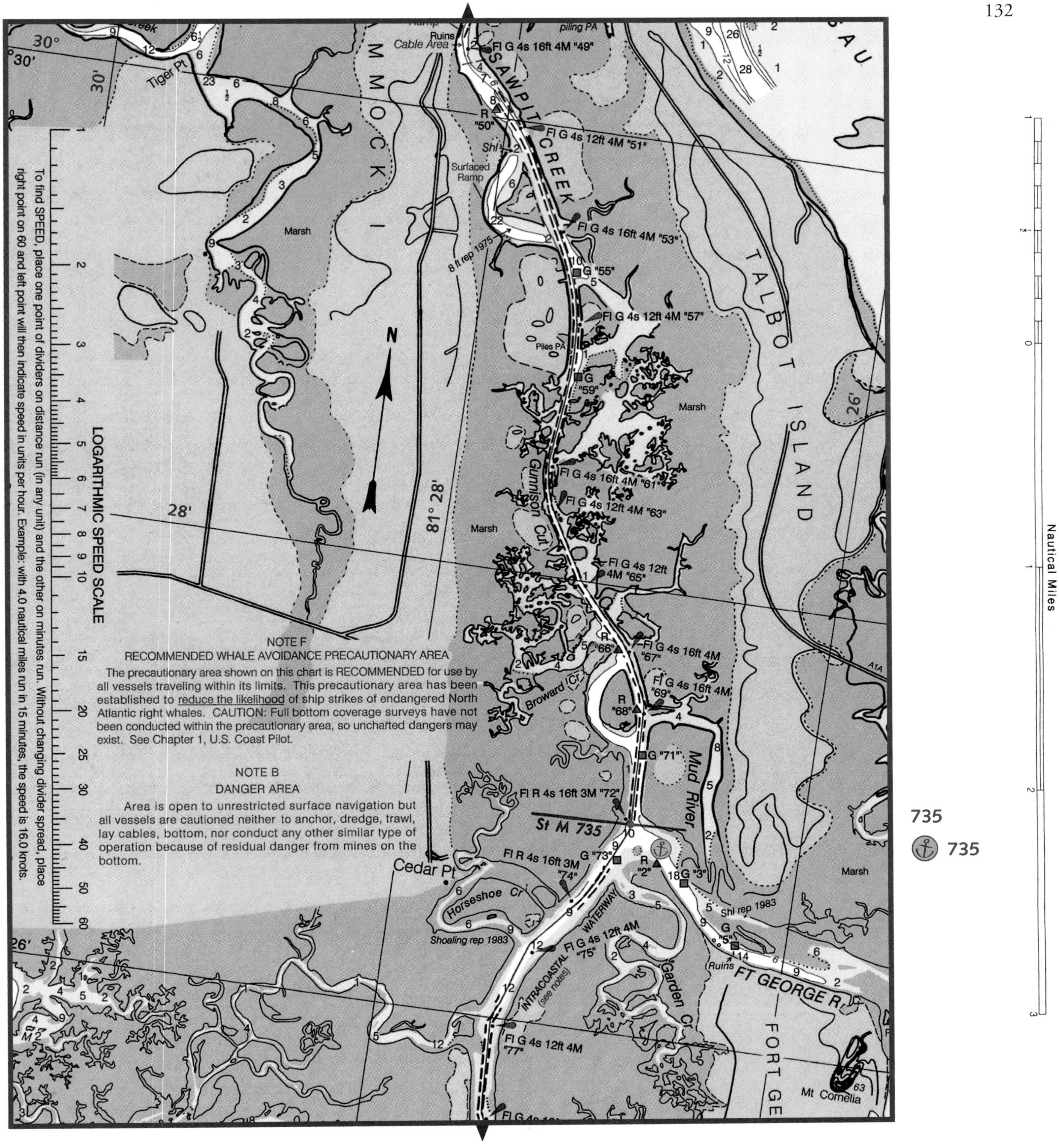

LOGARITHMIC SPEED SCALE

To find SPEED, place one point of dividers on distance run (in any unit) and the other on minutes run. Without changing divider spread, place right point on 60 and left point will then indicate speed in units per hour. Example: with 4.0 nautical miles run in 15 minutes, the speed is 16.0 knots.

NOTE F
RECOMMENDED WHALE AVOIDANCE PRECAUTIONARY AREA

The precautionary area shown on this chart is RECOMMENDED for use by all vessels traveling within its limits. This precautionary area has been established to reduce the likelihood of ship strikes of endangered North Atlantic right whales. CAUTION: Full bottom coverage surveys have not been conducted within the precautionary area, so uncharted dangers may exist. See Chapter 1, U.S. Coast Pilot.

NOTE B
DANGER AREA

Area is open to unrestricted surface navigation but all vessels are cautioned neither to anchor, dredge, trawl, lay cables, bottom, nor conduct any other similar type of operation because of residual danger from mines on the bottom.

SAWPIT CREEK
TALBOT ISLAND
Gunnison Cut
Mud River
Broward Cr
Horseshoe Cr
Garden Cr
FT GEORGE R.
FORT GE
INTRACOASTAL WATERWAY (see notes)
Cedar Pt
Tiger Pt
Mt Cornelia
Marsh
St M 735
Fl G 4s 16ft 4M "49"
Fl G 4s 12ft 4M "51"
Fl G 4s 16ft 4M "53"
Fl G 4s 12ft 4M "57"
Fl G 4s 16ft 4M "61"
Fl G 4s 12ft 4M "63"
Fl G 4s 12ft 4M "65"
Fl G 4s 16ft 4M "67"
Fl G 4s 16ft 4M "69"
Fl R 4s 16ft 3M "72"
Fl R 4s 16ft 3M "74"
Fl G 4s 12ft 4M "75"
Fl G 4s 12ft 4M "77"
81° 28'
30° 30'
Nautical Miles

735

735

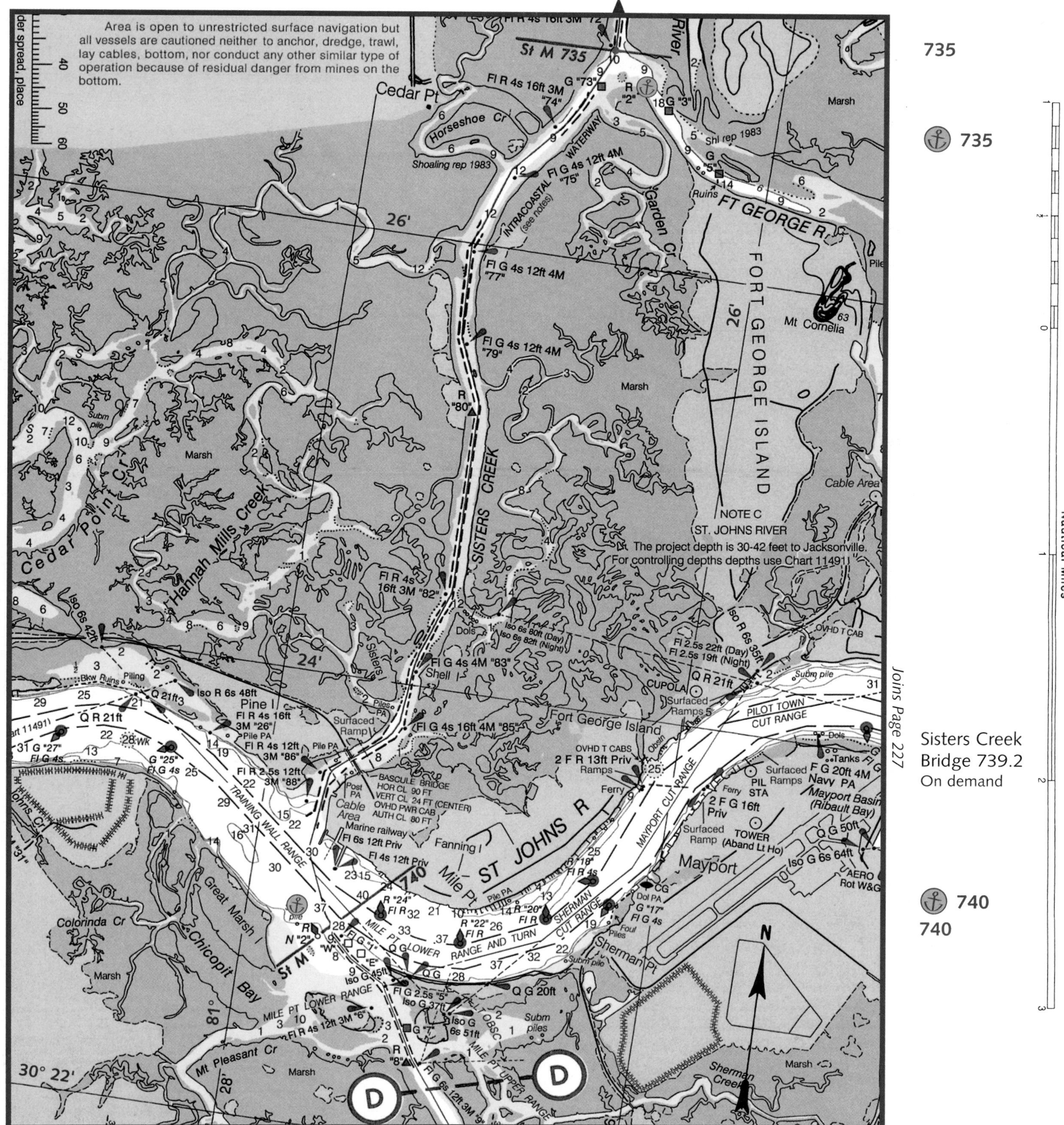

735

735

Sisters Creek Bridge 739.2
On demand

740

740

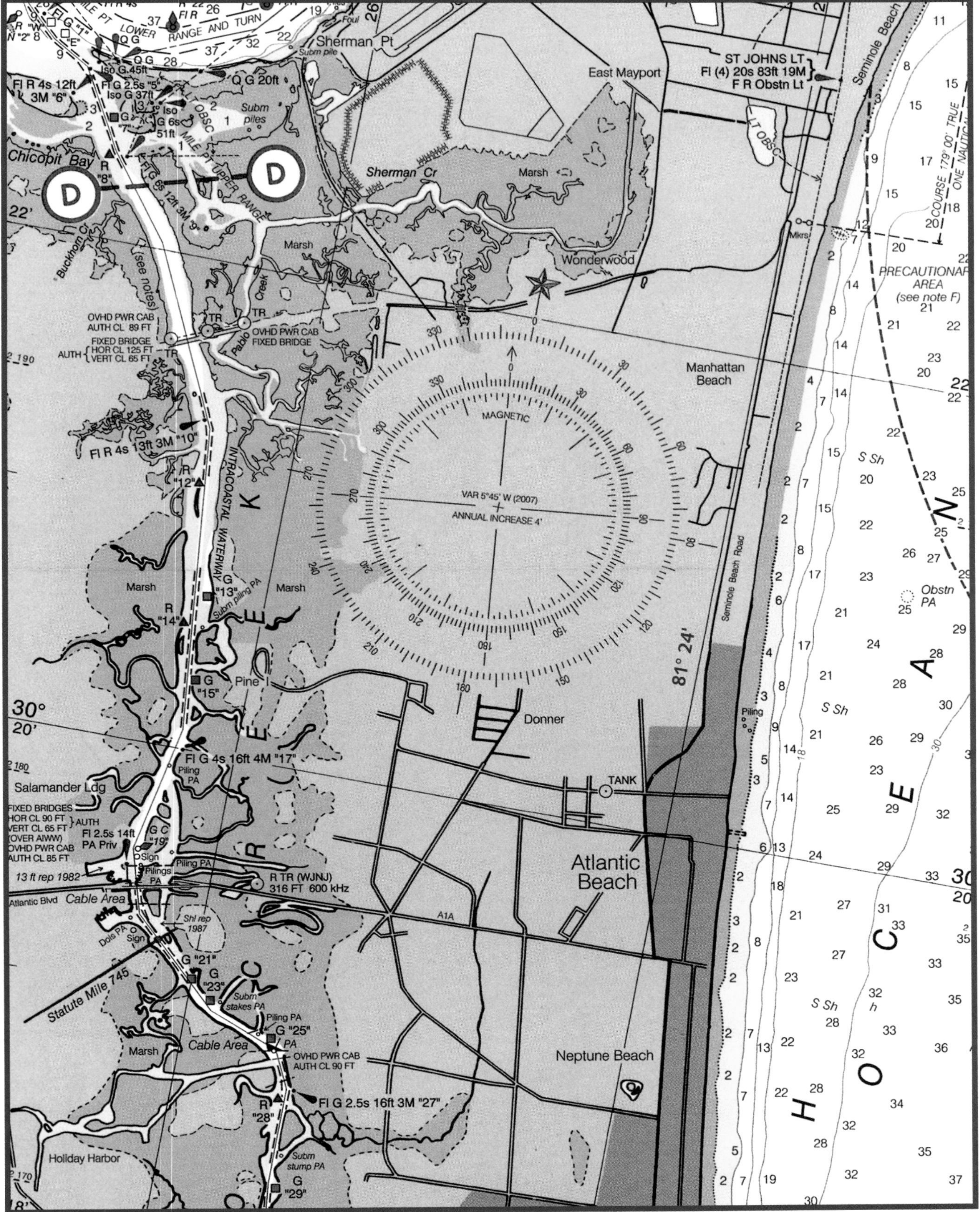

Sherman Pt
East Mayport
ST JOHNS LT
Fl (4) 20s 83ft 19M
F R Obstn Lt
Seminole Beach
LOWER RANGE AND TURN
Chicopit Bay
Sherman Cr
Marsh
Wonderwood
PRECAUTIONARY AREA
(see note F)
COURSE 179° 00' TRUE
Manhattan Beach
MAGNETIC
VAR 5°45' W (2007)
ANNUAL INCREASE 4'
INTRACOASTAL WATERWAY
Pablo Creek
OVHD PWR CAB
FIXED BRIDGE
Fl R 4s 13ft 3M "10"
Seminole Beach Road
81° 24'
Pine I
Donner
TANK
Salamander Ldg
Fl G 4s 16ft 4M "17"
Atlantic Beach
R TR (WJNJ)
316 FT 600 kHz
Atlantic Blvd
Cable Area
A1A
Statute Mile 745
Neptune Beach
Fl G 2.5s 16ft 3M "27"
Holiday Harbor
O C E A N
Nautical Miles

745

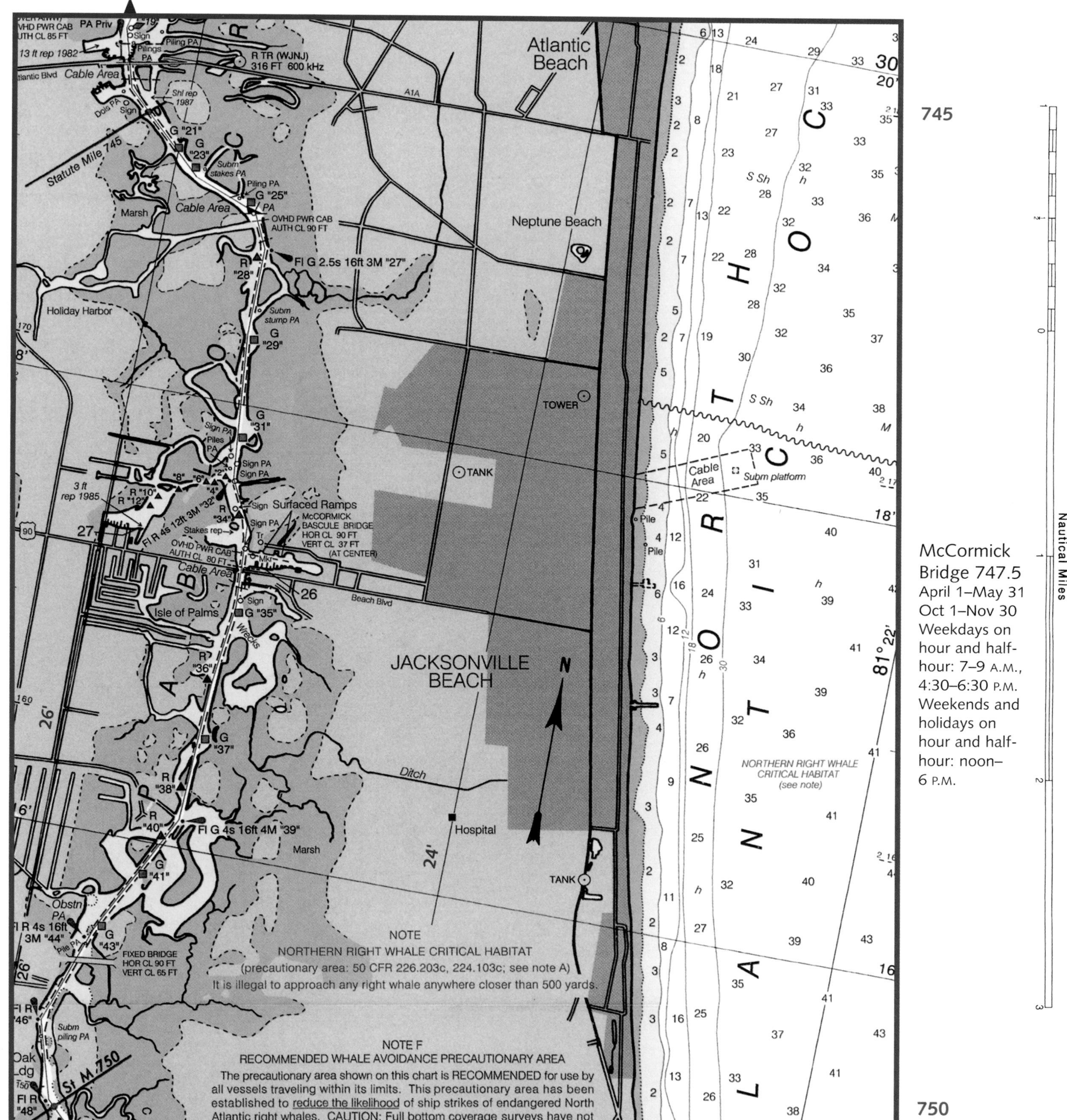

McCormick Bridge 747.5
April 1–May 31
Oct 1–Nov 30
Weekdays on hour and half-hour: 7–9 A.M., 4:30–6:30 P.M.
Weekends and holidays on hour and half-hour: noon–6 P.M.

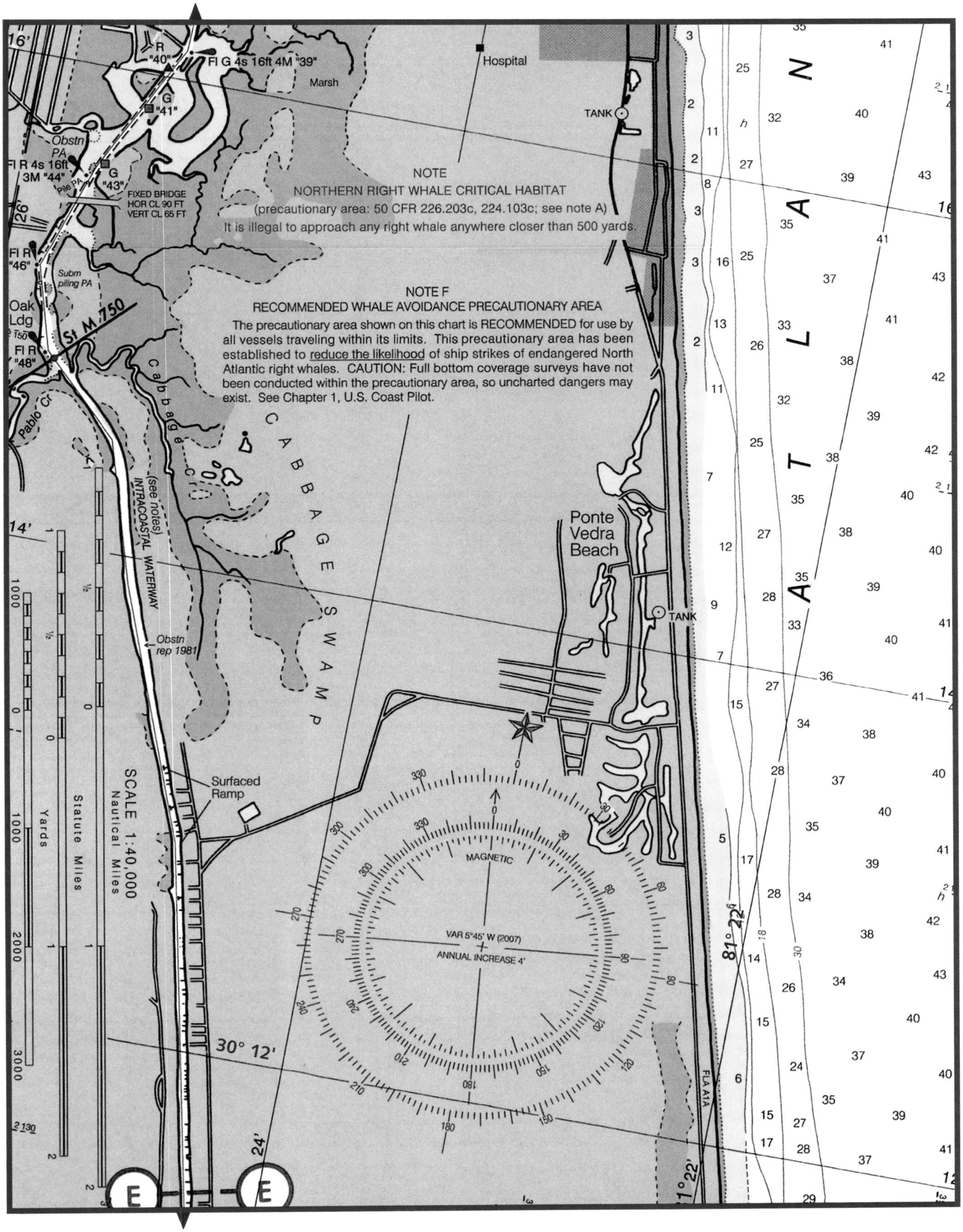

750

NOTE
NORTHERN RIGHT WHALE CRITICAL HABITAT
(precautionary area: 50 CFR 226.203c, 224.103c; see note A)
It is illegal to approach any right whale anywhere closer than 500 yards.

NOTE F
RECOMMENDED WHALE AVOIDANCE PRECAUTIONARY AREA
The precautionary area shown on this chart is RECOMMENDED for use by all vessels traveling within its limits. This precautionary area has been established to reduce the likelihood of ship strikes of endangered North Atlantic right whales. CAUTION: Full bottom coverage surveys have not been conducted within the precautionary area, so uncharted dangers may exist. See Chapter 1, U.S. Coast Pilot.

Hospital
Marsh
Fl G 4s 16ft 4M "39"
R "40"
G "41"
Obstn PA
Fl R 4s 16ft 3M "44"
G "43"
Pile PA
FIXED BRIDGE
HOR CL 90 FT
VERT CL 65 FT
Fl R "46"
Subm piling PA
Oak Ldg
Fl R "48"
St M 750
Pablo Cr
Cabbage Cr
CABBAGE SWAMP
(see notes)
INTRACOASTAL WATERWAY
Obstn rep 1981
Surfaced Ramp
TANK
Ponte Vedra Beach
FLA A1A
ATLANTIC
MAGNETIC
VAR 5°45' W (2007)
ANNUAL INCREASE 4'
30° 12'
81° 22'
24'
16'
14'
SCALE 1:40,000
Nautical Miles
Statute Miles
Yards
Nautical Miles

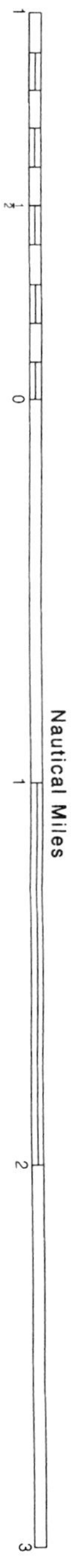

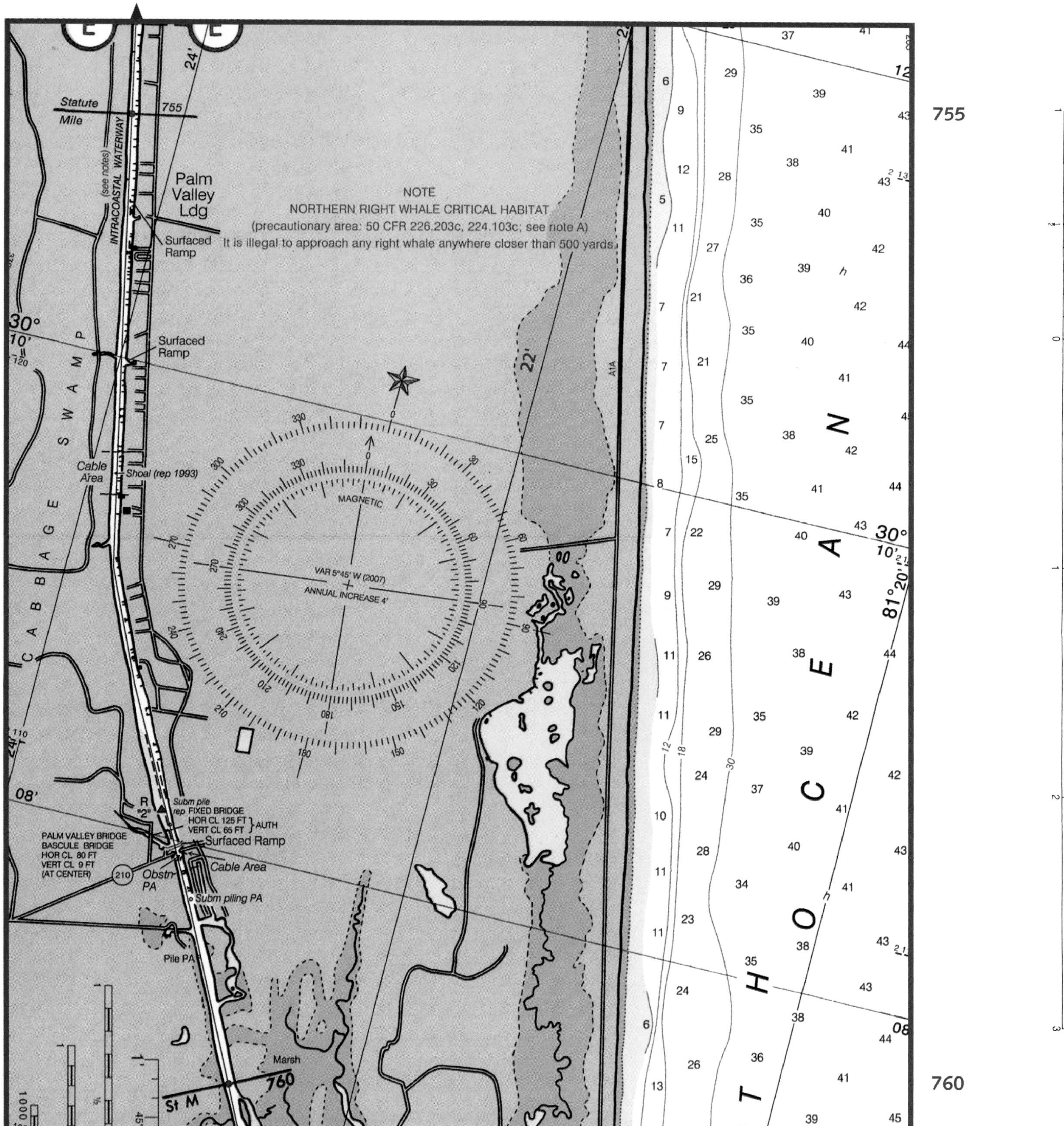
Statute
Mile
755
Palm
Valley
Ldg
INTRACOASTAL WATERWAY
(see notes)
Surfaced
Ramp
NOTE
NORTHERN RIGHT WHALE CRITICAL HABITAT
(precautionary area: 50 CFR 226.203c, 224.103c; see note A)
It is illegal to approach any right whale anywhere closer than 500 yards.
Surfaced
Ramp
CABBAGE SWAMP
Cable
Area
Shoal (rep 1993)
MAGNETIC
VAR 5°45' W (2007)
ANNUAL INCREASE 4'
A1A
THE OCEAN
Subm pile
rep
FIXED BRIDGE
HOR CL 125 FT
VERT CL 65 FT
AUTH
PALM VALLEY BRIDGE
BASCULE BRIDGE
HOR CL 80 FT
VERT CL 9 FT
(AT CENTER)
Surfaced Ramp
Cable Area
Obstn
PA
Subm piling PA
Pile PA
Marsh
St M
760
Nautical Miles
755
760

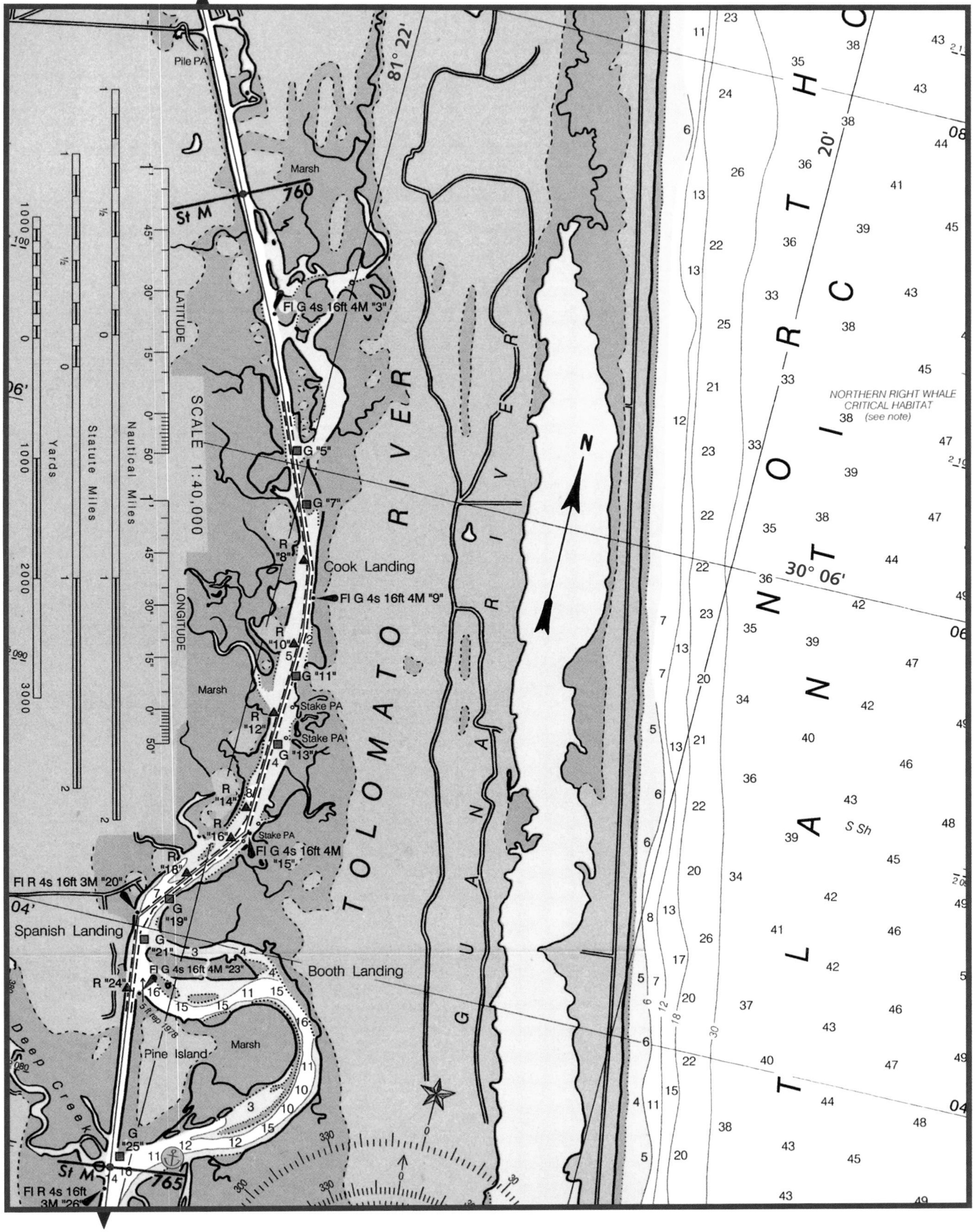

TOLOMATO RIVER
GUANA RIVER
ATLANTIC OCEAN
NORTHERN RIGHT WHALE CRITICAL HABITAT (see note)
Cook Landing
Booth Landing
Spanish Landing
Pine Island
Deep Creek
Marsh
Pile PA
Stake PA
Fl G 4s 16ft 4M "3"
Fl G 4s 16ft 4M "9"
Fl G 4s 16ft 4M "15"
Fl G 4s 16ft 4M "23"
Fl R 4s 16ft 3M "20"
Fl R 4s 16ft 3M "26"
SCALE 1:40,000
LATITUDE
LONGITUDE
Nautical Miles
Statute Miles
Yards
St M 760
St M 765
30° 06'
81° 22'
760
765
765

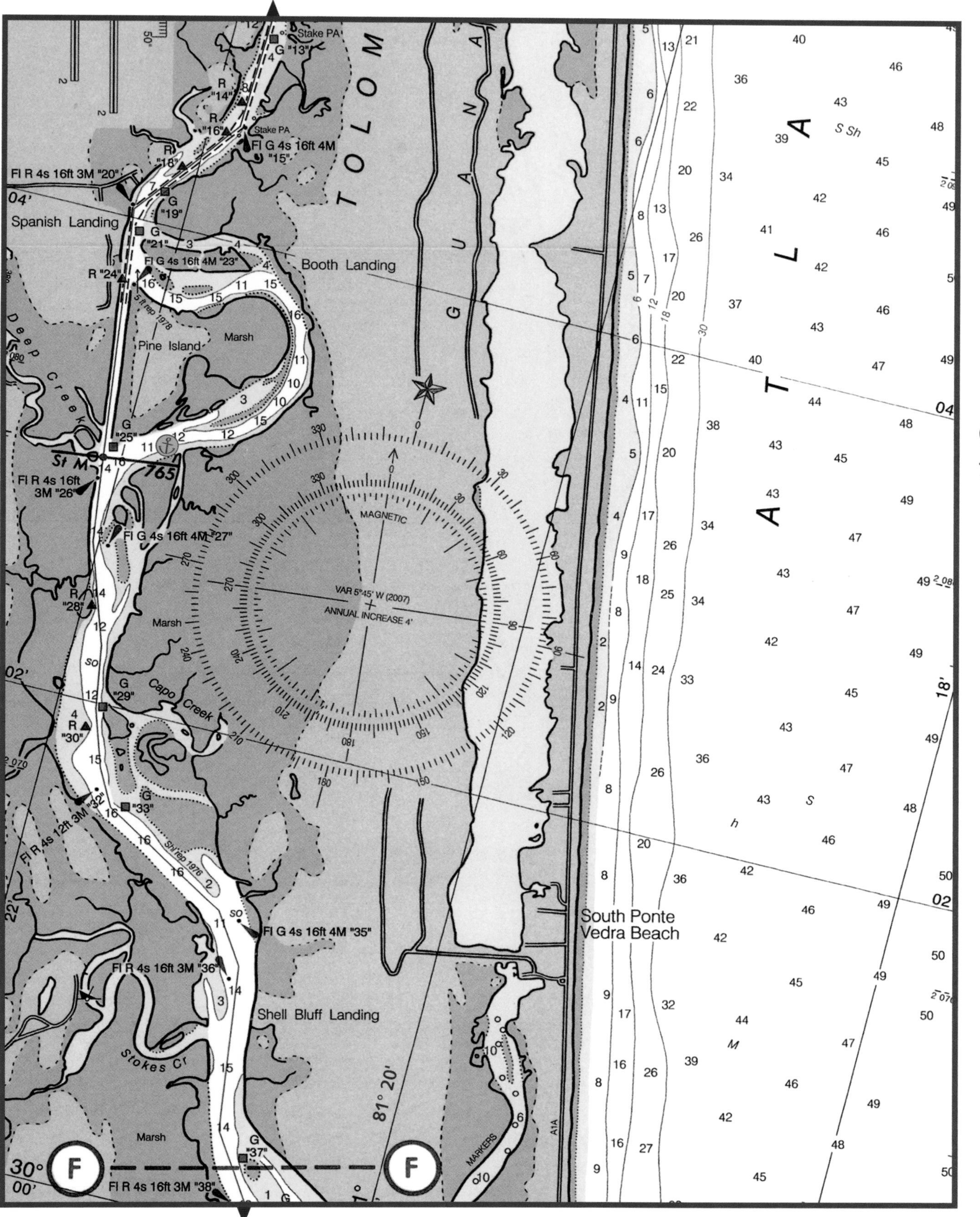
TOLOMATO
ATLANTIC
Spanish Landing
Booth Landing
Pine Island
Marsh
Deep Creek
Capo Creek
Shell Bluff Landing
Stokes Cr
South Ponte Vedra Beach
MAGNETIC
VAR 5°45' W (2007)
ANNUAL INCREASE 4'
Fl R 4s 16ft 3M "20"
Fl G 4s 16ft 4M "15"
Fl G 4s 16ft 4M "23"
Fl R 4s 16ft 3M "26"
Fl G 4s 16ft 4M "27"
Fl R 4s 12ft 3M "32"
Fl G 4s 16ft 4M "35"
Fl R 4s 16ft 3M "36"
Fl R 4s 16ft 3M "38"
Stake PA
765
81° 20'
30° 00'
A1A
MARKERS
Nautical Miles

765

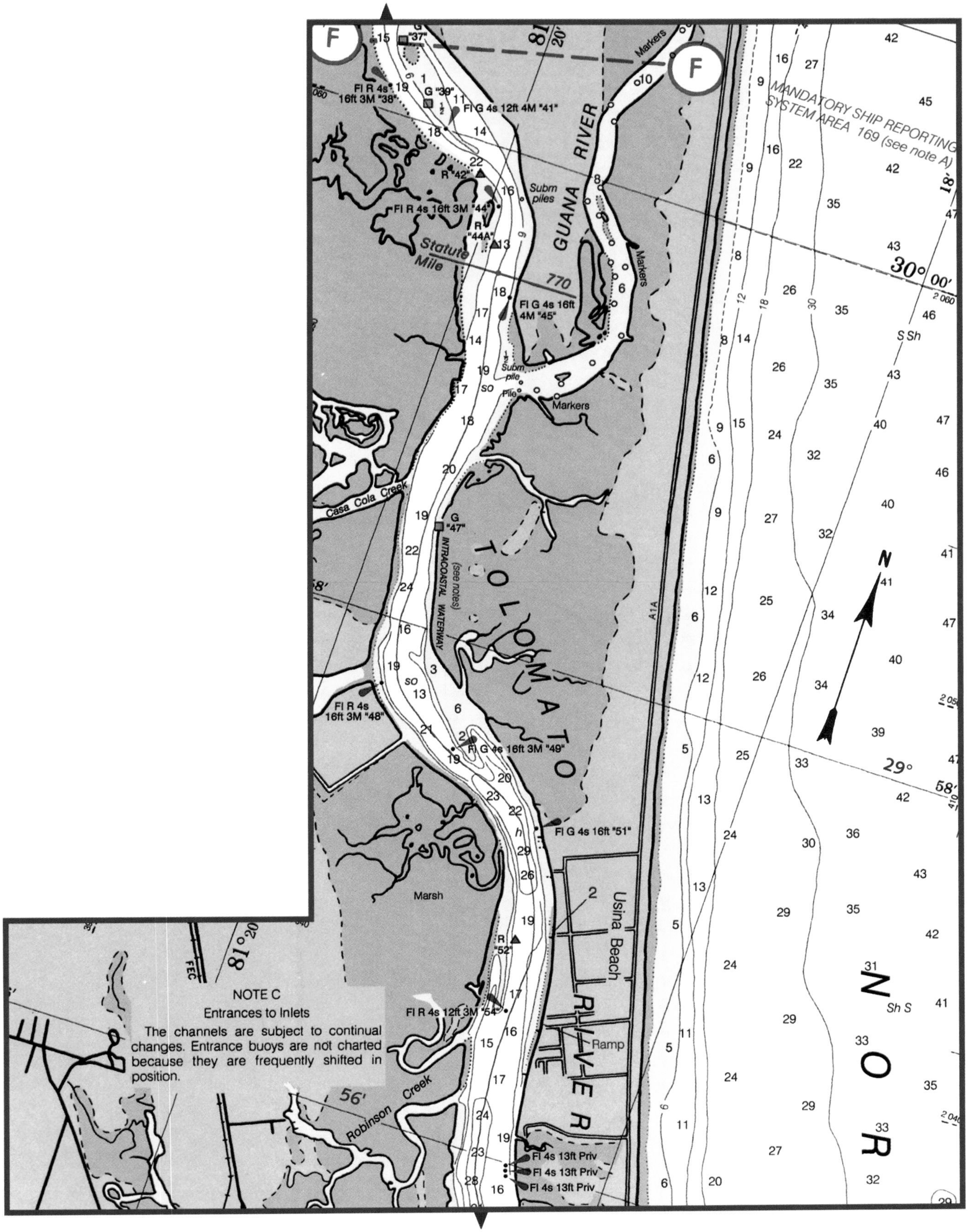
MANDATORY SHIP REPORTING SYSTEM AREA 169 (see note A)
GUANA RIVER
Markers
Statute Mile
770
Subm piles
Fl R 4s 19 16ft 3M "38"
G "39"
Fl G 4s 12ft 4M "41"
R "42"
Fl R 4s 16ft 3M "44"
R "44A"
Fl G 4s 16ft 4M "45"
Subm pile
Pile
Casa Cola Creek
G "47"
INTRACOASTAL WATERWAY
(see notes)
TOLOMATO
Fl R 4s 16ft 3M "48"
Fl G 4s 16ft 3M "49"
Fl G 4s 16ft "51"
Marsh
R "52"
Fl R 4s 12ft 3M "54"
Usina Beach
Ramp
RIVER
A1A
Robinson Creek
Fl 4s 13ft Priv
Fl 4s 13ft Priv
Fl 4s 13ft Priv
30° 00′
29° 58′
18′
56′
81° 20′
FEC
N
NOR
S Sh
Sh S
NOTE C
Entrances to Inlets
The channels are subject to continual changes. Entrance buoys are not charted because they are frequently shifted in position.

770

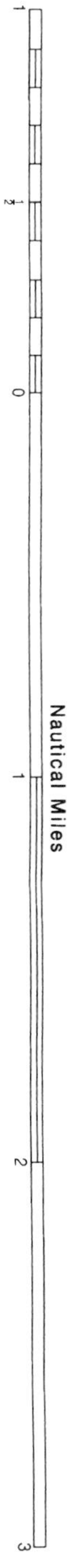
Nautical Miles
1
0
1
2
3

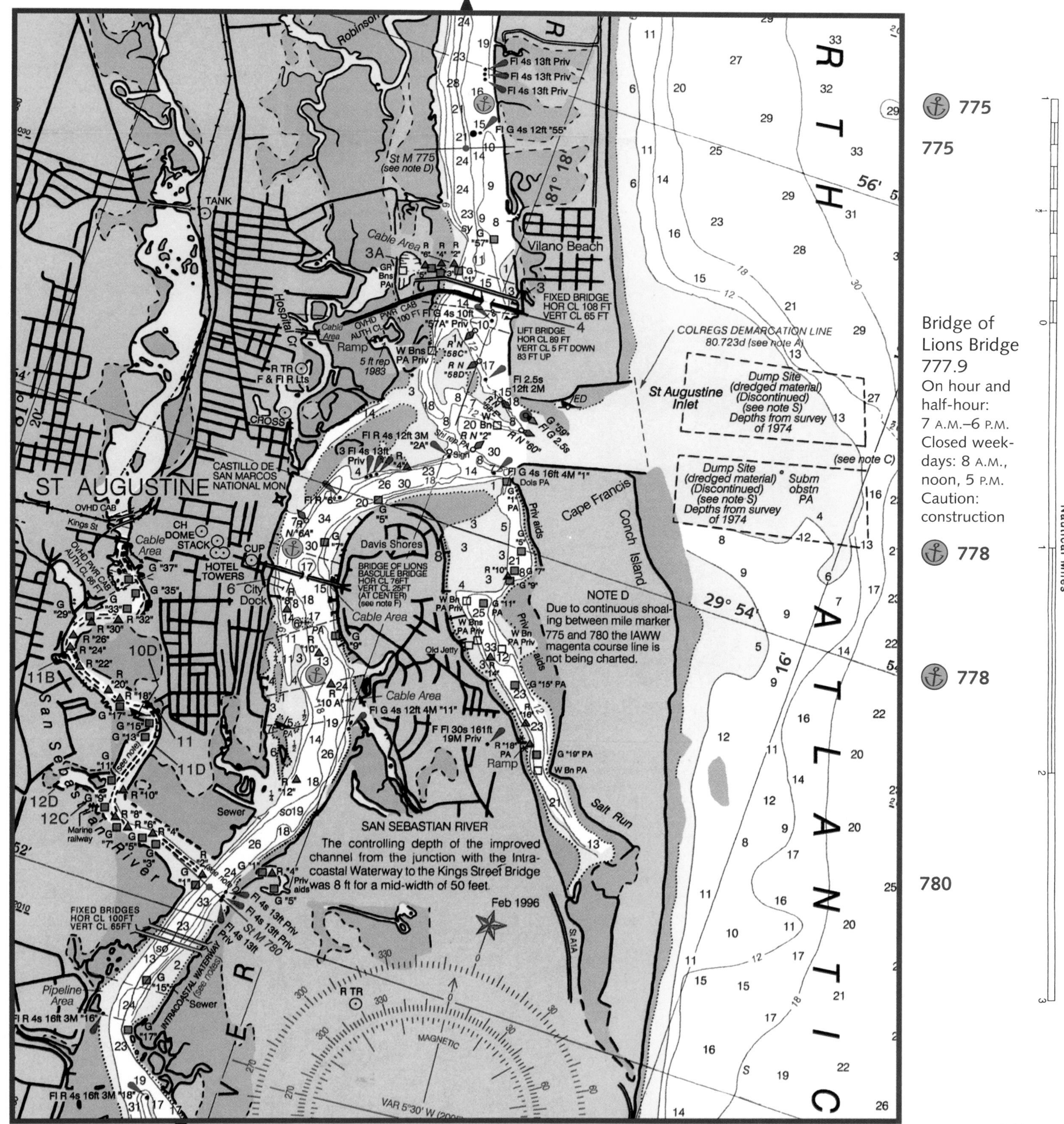

775

775

Bridge of Lions Bridge 777.9
On hour and half-hour: 7 A.M.–6 P.M. Closed weekdays: 8 A.M., noon, 5 P.M. Caution: construction

778

778

780

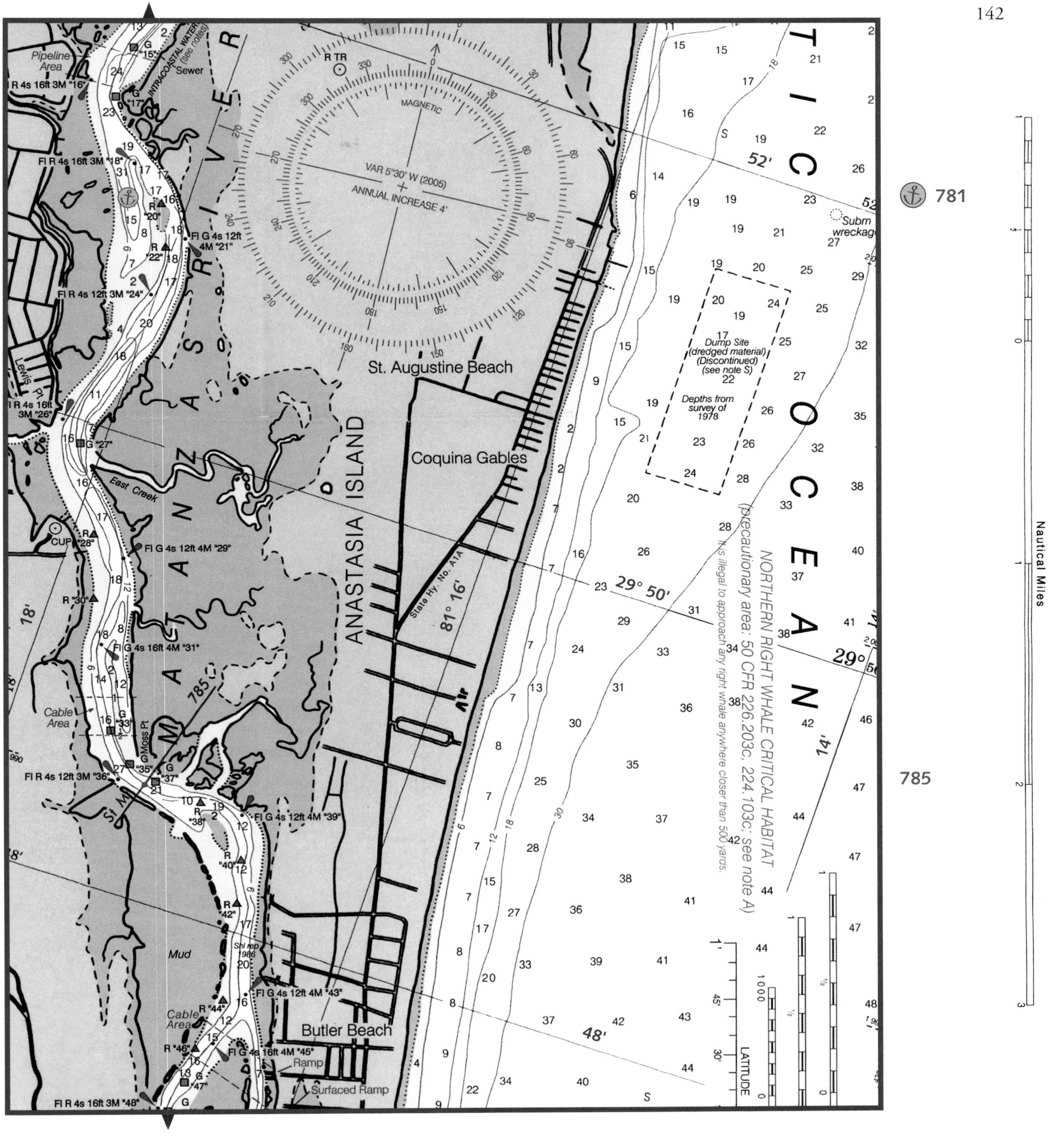

ATLANTIC OCEAN

NORTHERN RIGHT WHALE CRITICAL HABITAT
(precautionary area: 50 CFR 226.203c, 224.103c; see note A)
It is illegal to approach any right whale anywhere closer than 500 yards.

Dump Site
(dredged material)
(Discontinued)
(see note S)

Depths from
survey of
1978

ANASTASIA ISLAND

MATANZAS RIVER

St. Augustine Beach

Coquina Gables

Butler Beach

State Hy. No. A1A

East Creek

Moss Pt

Lewis Pt

Mud

Cable Area

Pipeline Area

INTRACOASTAL WATERWAY (see notes)

Sewer

Ramp

Surfaced Ramp

Subm wreckage

VAR 5°30' W (2005)
ANNUAL INCREASE 4'

MAGNETIC

R TR

CUP

Fl R 4s 16ft 3M "16"

Fl R 4s 16ft 3M "18"

Fl G 4s 12ft 4M "21"

Fl R 4s 12ft 3M "24"

Fl R 4s 16ft 3M "26"

Fl G 4s 12ft 4M "29"

Fl G 4s 16ft 4M "31"

Fl R 4s 12ft 3M "36"

Fl G 4s 12ft 4M "39"

Fl G 4s 12ft 4M "43"

Fl G 4s 16ft 4M "45"

Fl R 4s 16ft 3M "48"

29° 52'

29° 50'

29° 48'

81° 16'

781

785

LATITUDE

Nautical Miles

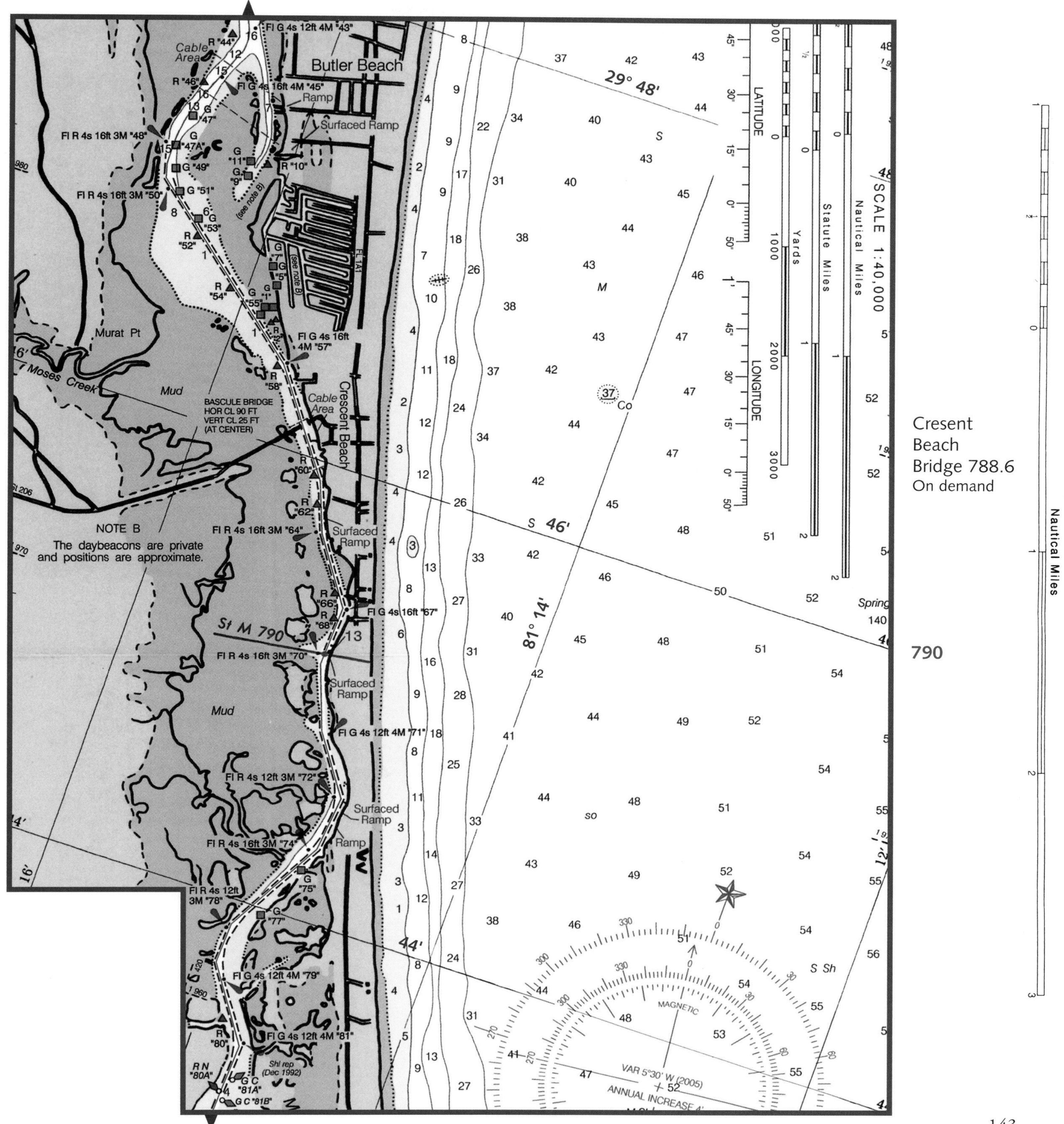

Butler Beach
Crescent Beach
Murat Pt
Moses Creek
Mud
Cable Area
Ramp
Surfaced Ramp
BASCULE BRIDGE
HOR CL 90 FT
VERT CL 25 FT
(AT CENTER)
NOTE B
The daybeacons are private
and positions are approximate.
St M 790
FI G 4s 12ft 4M "43"
FI G 4s 16ft 4M "45"
FI R 4s 16ft 3M "48"
FI R 4s 16ft 3M "50"
FI G 4s 16ft 4M "57"
FI R 4s 16ft 3M "64"
FI G 4s 16ft "67"
FI R 4s 16ft 3M "70"
FI G 4s 12ft 4M "71"
FI R 4s 12ft 3M "72"
FI R 4s 16ft 3M "74"
FI R 4s 12ft 3M "78"
FI G 4s 12ft 4M "79"
FI G 4s 12ft 4M "81"
Shl rep (Dec 1992)
29° 48'
81° 14'
LATITUDE
LONGITUDE
SCALE 1:40,000
Yards
Statute Miles
Nautical Miles
MAGNETIC
VAR 5°30' W (2005)
ANNUAL INCREASE
Spring
Cresent Beach
Bridge 788.6
On demand
790

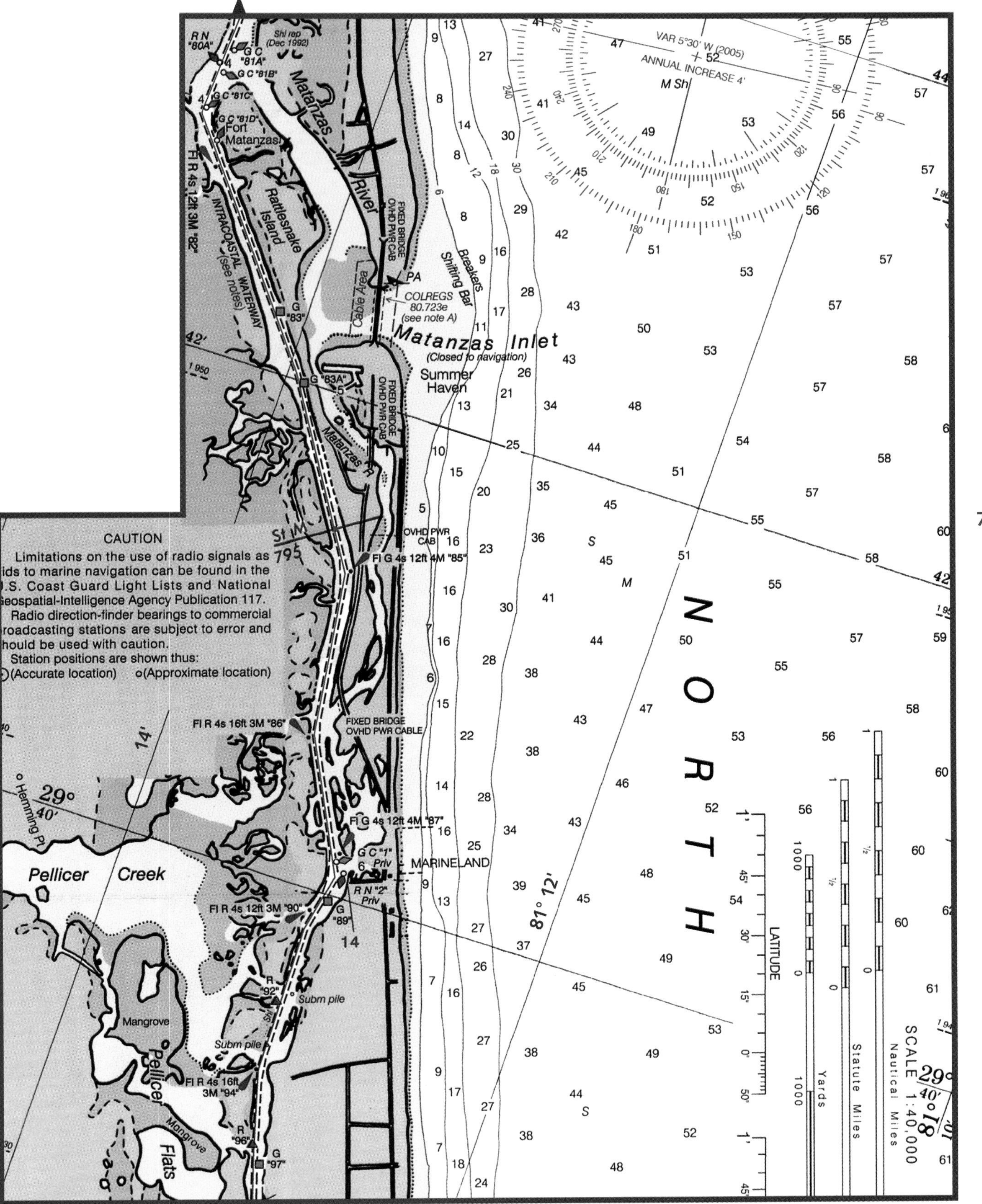
CAUTION
Limitations on the use of radio signals as aids to marine navigation can be found in the U.S. Coast Guard Light Lists and National Geospatial-Intelligence Agency Publication 117.
Radio direction-finder bearings to commercial broadcasting stations are subject to error and should be used with caution.
Station positions are shown thus:
(Accurate location) o(Approximate location)
Matanzas Inlet
(Closed to navigation)
Summer Haven
MARINELAND
Pellicer Creek
Pellicer Flats
Mangrove
Rattlesnake Island
Fort Matanzas
Matanzas River
INTRACOASTAL WATERWAY (see notes)
COLREGS 80.723e (see note A)
Cable Area
Breakers
Shifting Bar
FIXED BRIDGE OVHD PWR CAB
FIXED BRIDGE OVHD PWR CABLE
OVHD PWR CAB
Fl R 4s 12ft 3M "82"
Fl G 4s 12ft 4M "85"
Fl R 4s 16ft 3M "86"
Fl G 4s 12ft 4M "87"
Fl R 4s 12ft 3M "90"
Fl R 4s 16ft 3M "94"
Subm pile
Shl rep (Dec 1992)
Hemming Pt
VAR 5°30' W (2005)
ANNUAL INCREASE 4'
NORTH
81° 12'
29° 40'
29° 40' 18
SCALE 1:40,000
Nautical Miles
Statute Miles
Yards
LATITUDE
Nautical Miles
795

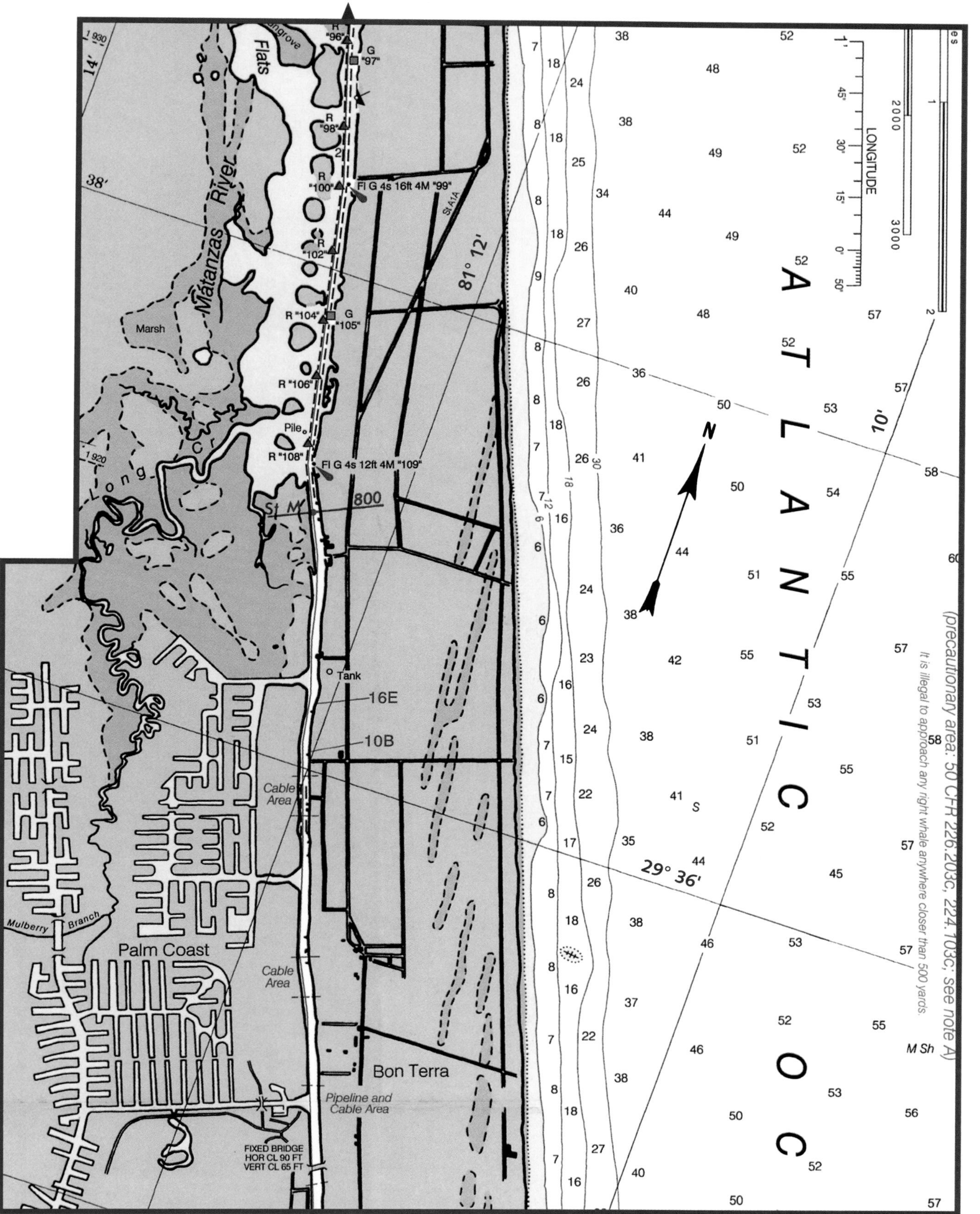
Flats
Matanzas River
Marsh
Long Cr
Palm Coast
Mulberry Branch
Bon Terra
Tank
16E
10B
Cable Area
Cable Area
Pipeline and Cable Area
FIXED BRIDGE HOR CL 90 FT VERT CL 65 FT
Fl G 4s 16ft 4M "99"
Fl G 4s 12ft 4M "109"
800
81° 12′
29° 36′
38′
10′
A T L A N T I C O C
(precautionary area: 50 CFR 226.203c, 224.103c; see note A)
It is illegal to approach any right whale anywhere closer than 500 yards.
LONGITUDE
Nautical Miles

800

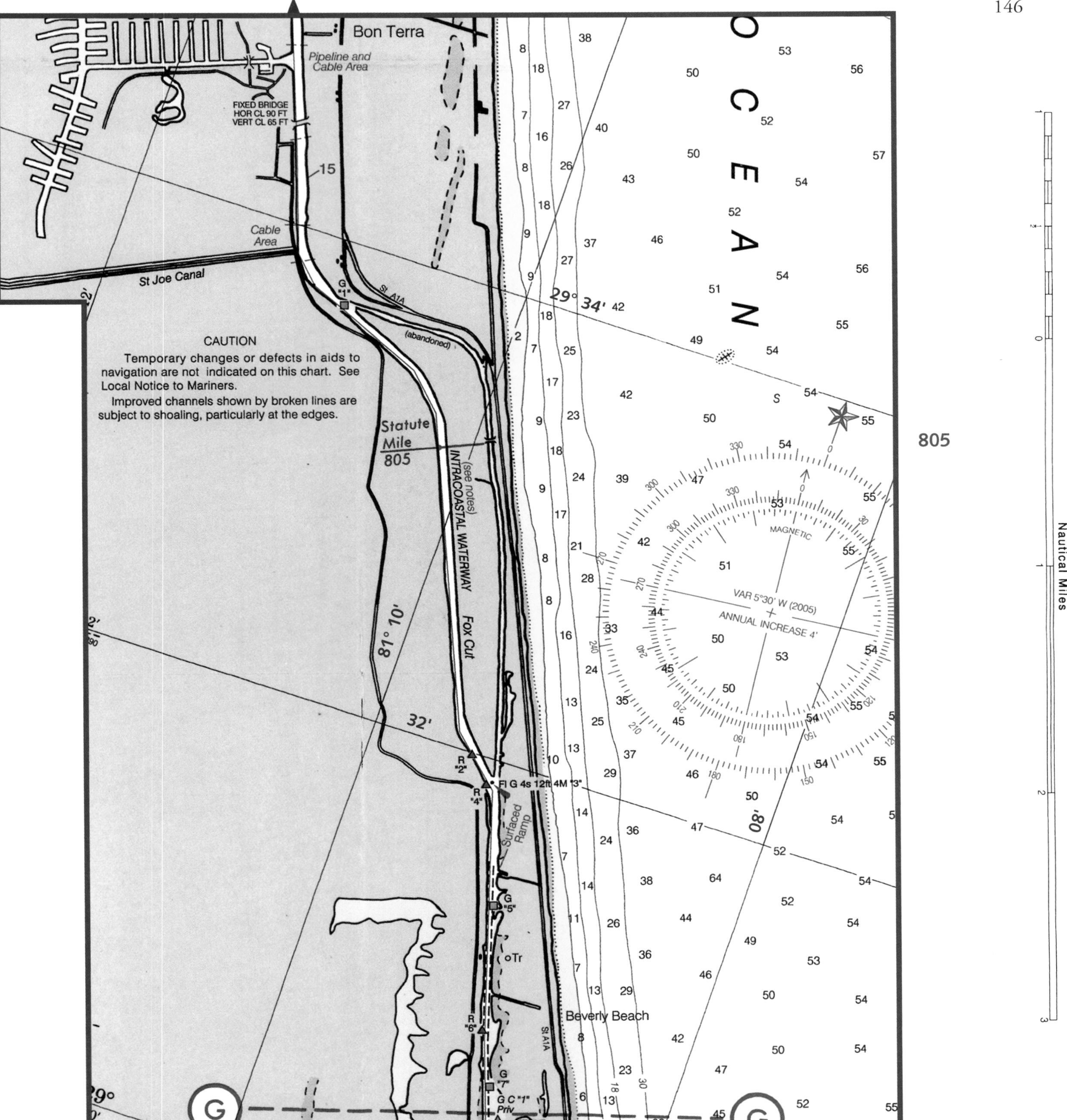

Bon Terra
Pipeline and Cable Area
FIXED BRIDGE
HOR CL 90 FT
VERT CL 65 FT
Cable Area
St Joe Canal
St A1A
(abandoned)
CAUTION
Temporary changes or defects in aids to navigation are not indicated on this chart. See Local Notice to Mariners.
Improved channels shown by broken lines are subject to shoaling, particularly at the edges.
Statute Mile 805
(see notes)
INTRACOASTAL WATERWAY
Fox Cut
81° 10'
32'
29° 34'
FI G 4s 12ft 4M "3"
Surfaced Ramp
Beverly Beach
O C E A N
VAR 5°30' W (2005)
ANNUAL INCREASE 4'
MAGNETIC
'80
805
Nautical Miles

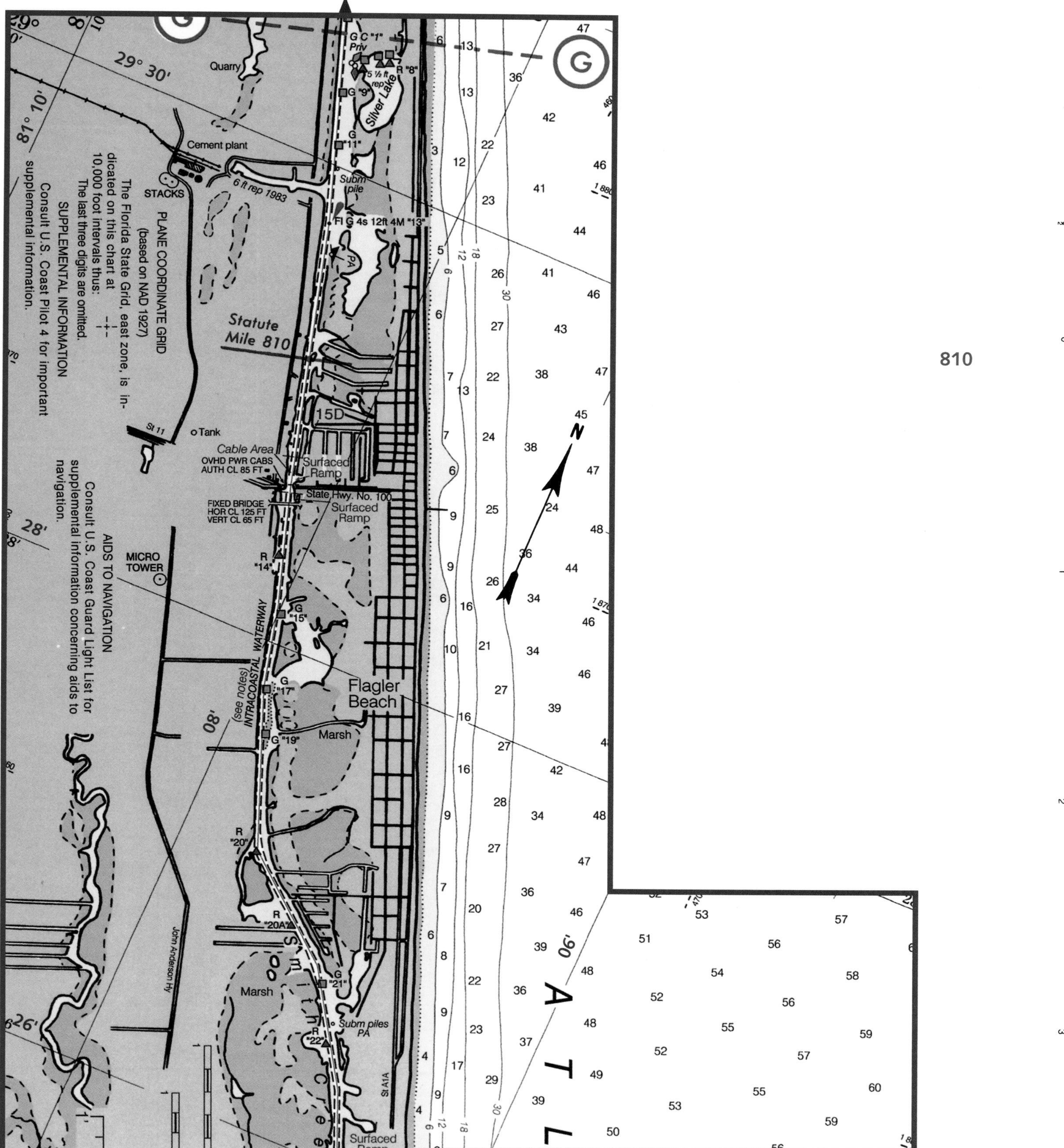

29° 30'
81° 10'
Quarry
Cement plant
STACKS
6 ft rep 1983
G C "1" Priv
R "8"
G "9"
5 ½ ft rep
Silver Lake
G "11"
Subm pile
Fl G 4s 12ft 4M "13"
PA
PLANE COORDINATE GRID
(based on NAD 1927)
The Florida State Grid, east zone, is indicated on this chart at 10,000 foot intervals thus:
The last three digits are omitted.
SUPPLEMENTAL INFORMATION
Consult U.S. Coast Pilot 4 for important supplemental information.
Statute Mile 810
15D
St 11
Tank
Cable Area
OVHD PWR CABS AUTH CL 85 FT
Surfaced Ramp
State Hwy. No. 100
FIXED BRIDGE HOR CL 125 FT VERT CL 65 FT
Surfaced Ramp
28'
MICRO TOWER
R "14"
AIDS TO NAVIGATION
Consult U.S. Coast Guard Light List for supplemental information concerning aids to navigation.
G "15"
INTRACOASTAL WATERWAY
(see notes)
G "17"
Flagler Beach
08'
G "19"
Marsh
R "20"
R "20A"
John Anderson Hy
G "21"
Marsh
Subm piles PA
R "22"
26'
St A1A
Surfaced Ramp
06'
A T L
810
Nautical Miles

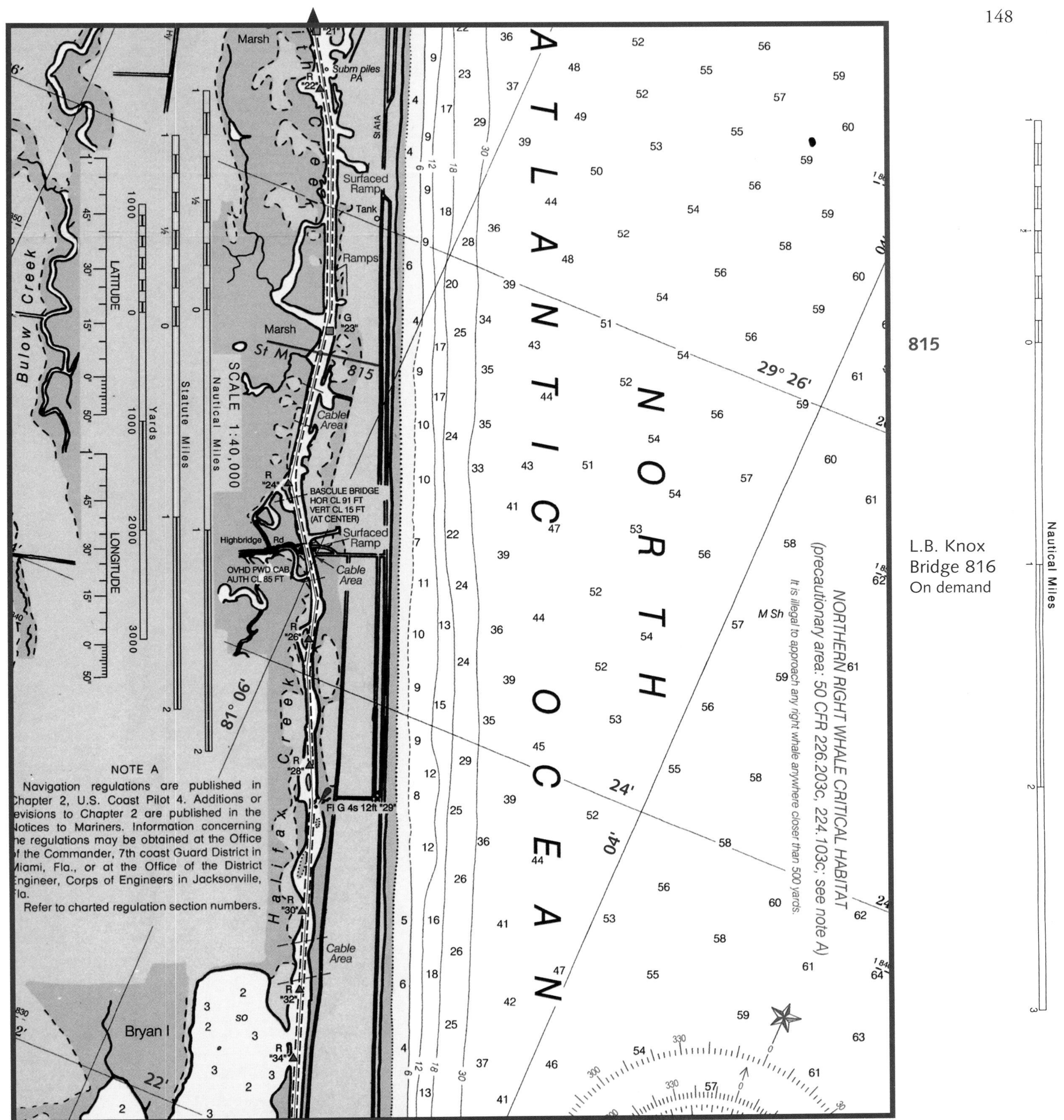

815

L.B. Knox
Bridge 816
On demand

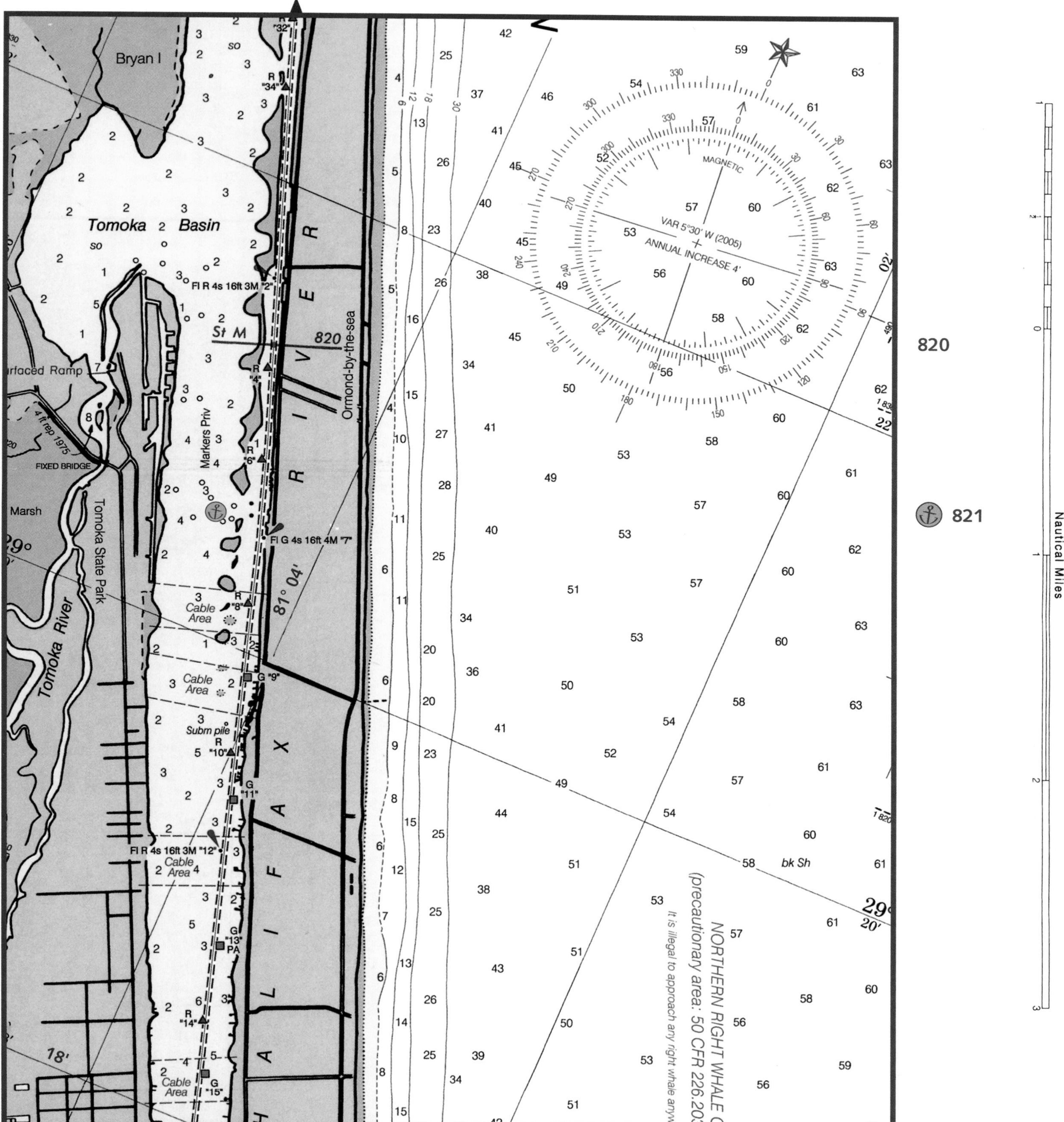
Bryan I
Tomoka Basin
St M
820
Ormond-by-the-sea
HALIFAX RIVER
Fl R 4s 16ft 3M "2"
Fl G 4s 16ft 4M "7"
Fl R 4s 16ft 3M "12"
Markers Priv
Cable Area
Subm pile
FIXED BRIDGE
Marsh
Tomoka State Park
Tomoka River
81° 04′
VAR 5°30′ W (2005)
ANNUAL INCREASE 4′
MAGNETIC
NORTHERN RIGHT WHALE C
(precautionary area: 50 CFR 226.203
It is illegal to approach any right whale anyw
bk Sh
820
821
Nautical Miles

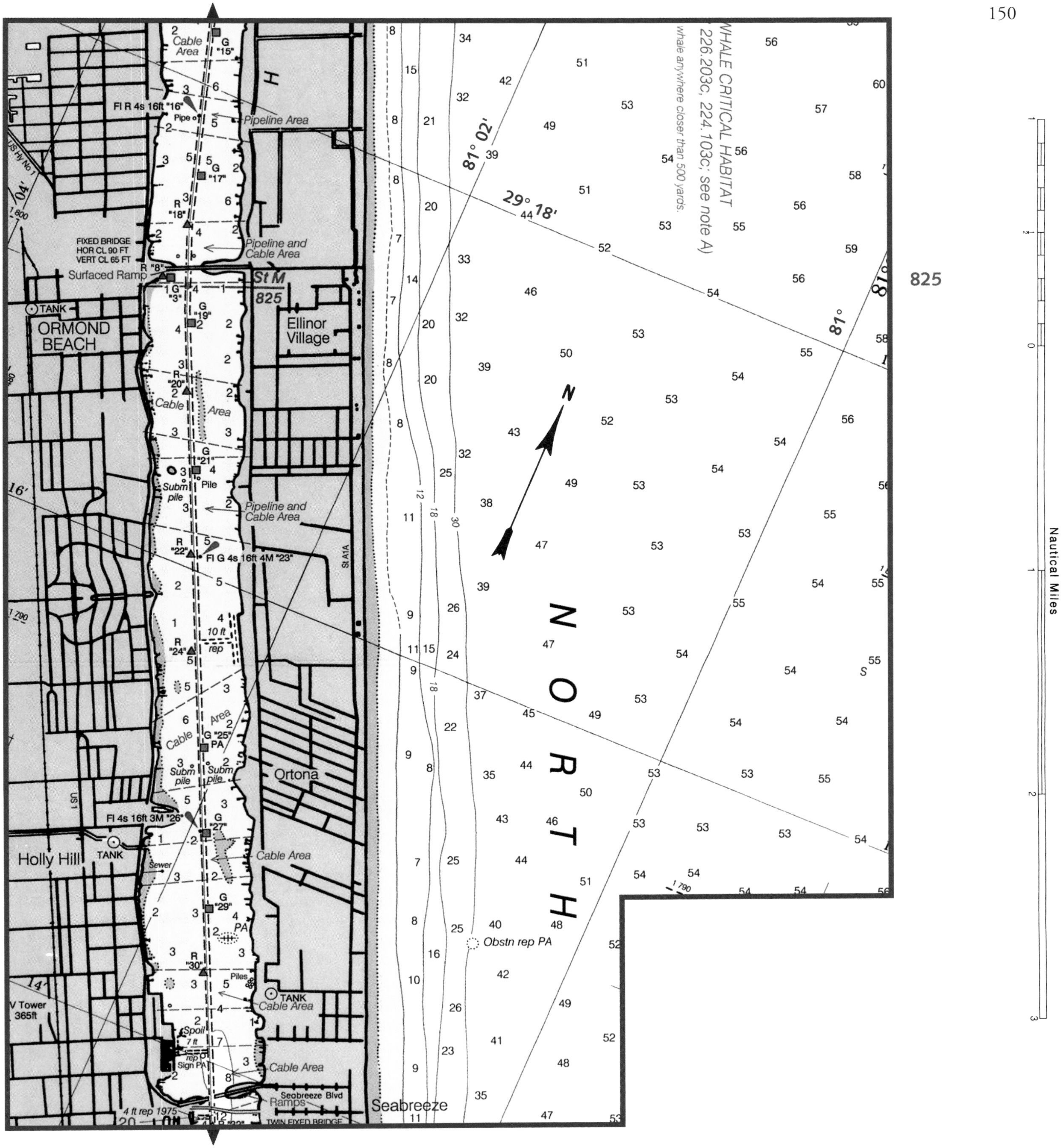
825
Nautical Miles
0
1
2
3
NORTH
N
WHALE CRITICAL HABITAT
226.203c, 224.103c; see note A)
whale anywhere closer than 500 yards.
81° 02′
81°
29° 18′
Obstn rep PA
Seabreeze
Seabreeze Blvd
Ramps
TWIN FIXED BRIDGE
4 ft rep 1975
Cable Area
Sign PA
rep
7 ft
Spoil
V Tower
365ft
TANK
Piles
Holly Hill
Sewer
Fl 4s 16ft 3M "26"
US 1
Ortona
Subm pile
Pipeline and
Cable Area
St A1A
Fl G 4s 16ft 4M "23"
10 ft
rep
Pile
ORMOND
BEACH
Ellinor
Village
St M
825
Surfaced Ramp
FIXED BRIDGE
HOR CL 90 FT
VERT CL 65 FT
Pipeline Area
Fl R 4s 16ft "16"
Pipe
US Hy No 1

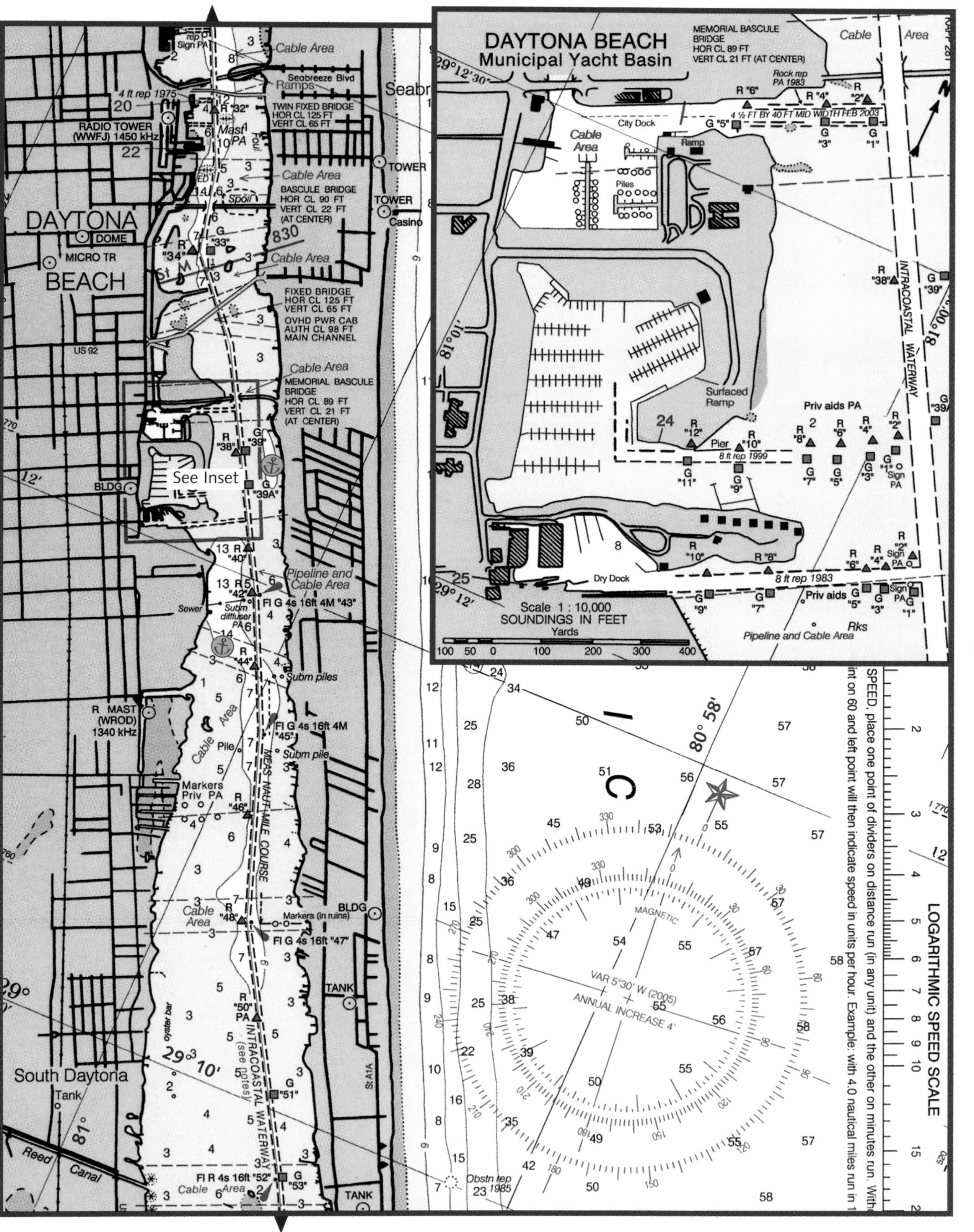

Main Street Bridge 829.7 (far map)
On demand

830 (far map)

Memorial Bridge 830.6 (far map)
Mon–Sat, from 7:45 A.M.–8:45 A.M.
On demand: 8:45 A.M.–4:45 P.M.
From 4:45 P.M.–5:45 P.M., only at 5:15 A.M.

831

832 (far map)

Nautical Miles

OCEAN
Port Orange
Allandale
Halifax Estates
Wilbur-by-the-Sea
HALIFAX RIVER
Rose Bay
Wilbur Bay
Daggett I
Pelican I
Live Oak Pt
Inlet Harbor
Mill Cr
Tenmile Cr
Fozzard Cr
Dead End Cr
Lost Cr
Spruce Cr
Marsh
Cable Area
Pipeline Area
Spoil Area
Ramps
TV TOWER
SPIRE
TANK
St M 835
St M 840
FIXED BRIDGE
HOR CL 90 FT
VERT CL 65 FT
Shoaling rep 1992
Subm steel pile PA
Obstn rep 1985
NORTHERN RIGHT WHALE CRITICAL HABITAT
(precautionary area: 50 CFR 226.203c, 224.103c; see note A)
It is illegal to approach any right whale anywhere closer than 500 yards.
Dump Site
(dredged material)
(Discontinued)
(see note S)
Depths from surveys
of 1973-1974
n. Without changing divider spread, place
run in 15 minutes, the speed is 16.0 knots.
Nautical Miles
835
840

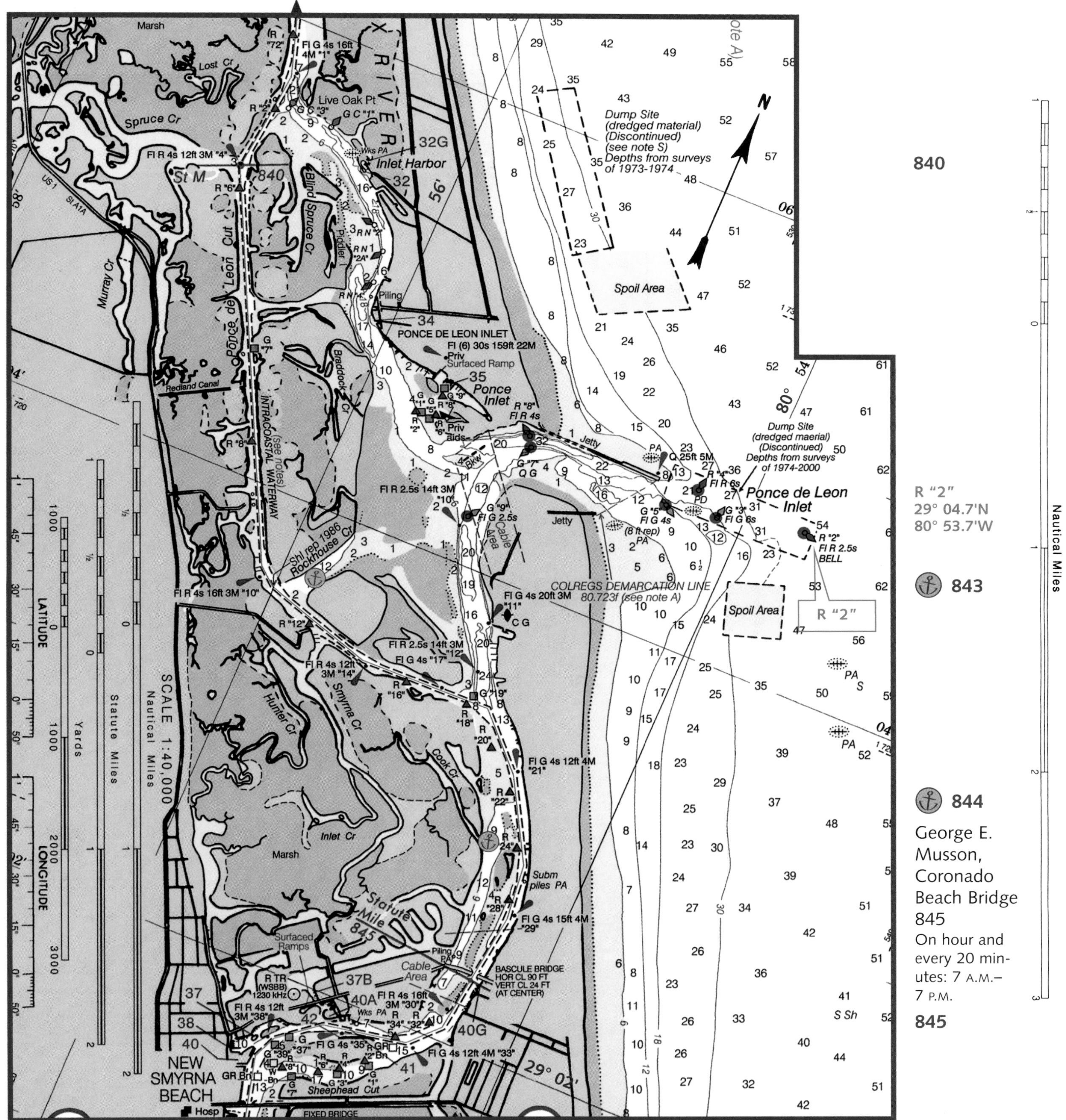

Ponce de Leon Inlet
Ponce Inlet
PONCE DE LEON INLET
Inlet Harbor
Live Oak Pt
Spruce Cr
Lost Cr
Murray Cr
Ponce de Leon Cut
Blind Spruce Cr
Bradock Cr
Rockhouse Cr
Hunter Cr
Smyrna Cr
Cook Cr
Inlet Cr
Sheephead Cut
Redland Canal
INTRACOASTAL WATERWAY
Marsh
NEW SMYRNA BEACH
Hosp
Dump Site (dredged material) (Discontinued) (see note S) Depths from surveys of 1973-1974
Dump Site (dredged maerial) (Discontinued) Depths from surveys of 1974-2000
Spoil Area
COLREGS DEMARCATION LINE 80.723f (see note A)
BASCULE BRIDGE HOR CL 90 FT VERT CL 24 FT (AT CENTER)
FIXED BRIDGE
Surfaced Ramp
Surfaced Ramps
Cable Area
Subm piles PA
Statute Mile 845
SCALE 1:40,000
LATITUDE
LONGITUDE
Yards
Statute Miles
Nautical Miles
840
R "2"
29° 04.7'N
80° 53.7'W
843
844
George E. Musson, Coronado Beach Bridge 845
On hour and every 20 minutes: 7 A.M.–7 P.M.
845

850

FIXED BRIDGE
HOR CL 90 FT
VERT CL 65 FT
OVERHEAD POWER CABLE
AUTHORIZED CL 85 FT

Cable Area

Fl R 4s 16ft 3M "42"

G "43"

NEW
SMYRNA
BEACH

Subm pile

R "46"

Fl G 4s16ft 4M "45"

Callalisa Creek

Mangrove

G "5" PA

Priv aids

G "47"

Fl G 4s 12ft 4M "49"

R "48"

Surfaced Ramp

Browns Bay

TANK

R "50"

G "51"

Ramps

Pile

Shoaling rep 1993

Edgewater

Fl G 4s 16ft 4M "53"

R "52"

Marsh

US Hy No 1

G "55"

Statute Mile 850

28° 58'

80° 54'

29° 00'

R "56"

Fl G 4s 16ft 4M "57"

G "59"

Fl R 4s 12ft 3M "60"

R "62"

Fl G 4s 16ft 4M "63"

INDIAN

NORTH

VAR 5°30' W (2005)
ANNUAL INCREASE 4'

MAGNETIC

80° 50'

52'

02'

Nautical Miles

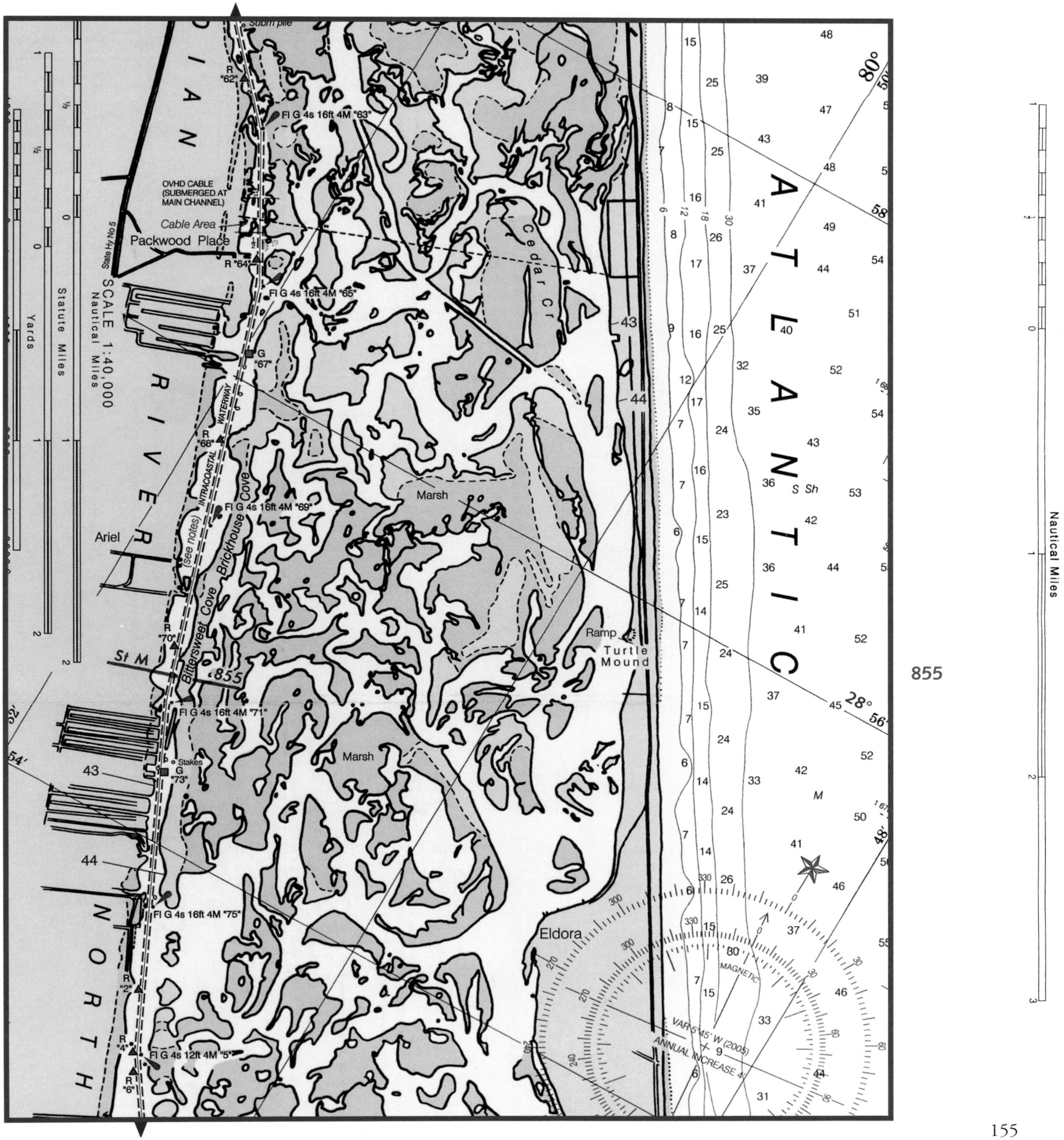
OVHD CABLE (SUBMERGED AT MAIN CHANNEL)
Cable Area
Packwood Place
State Hy No 5
SCALE 1:40,000
Nautical Miles
Statute Miles
Yards
R "62"
Fl G 4s 16ft 4M "63"
R "64"
Fl G 4s 16ft 4M "65"
G "67"
R "68"
Fl G 4s 16ft 4M "69"
R "70"
Fl G 4s 16ft 4M "71"
Stakes
G "73"
Fl G 4s 16ft 4M "75"
R "2"
R "4"
Fl G 4s 12ft 4M "5"
R "6"
INTRACOASTAL WATERWAY
(See notes)
Brickhouse Cove
Bittersweet Cove
St M
855
Ariel
RIVER
NORTH
Cedar Cr
Marsh
Marsh
Ramp
Turtle Mound
Eldora
ATLANTIC
S Sh
M
MAGNETIC
VAR 5°45' W (2005)
ANNUAL INCREASE 4'
28°
56'
54'
52'
80°
Nautical Miles
855

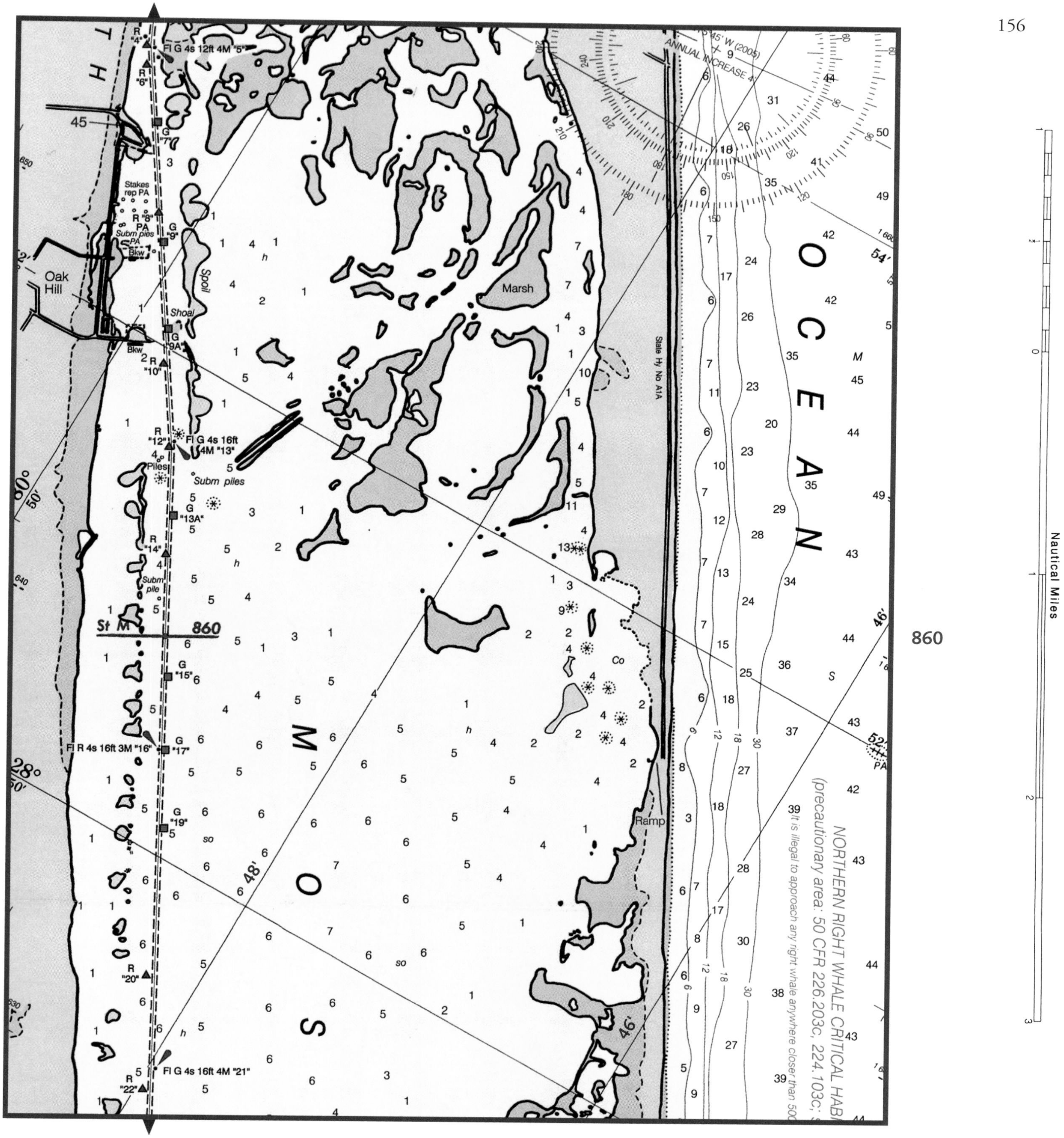

OCEAN
MOSQUITO
Oak Hill
Marsh
Spoil
Shoal
Ramp
State Hy No A1A
Stakes rep PA
Subm piles
Piles
Subm pile
St M 860
Fl G 4s 12ft 4M "5"
Fl G 4s 16ft 4M "13"
Fl R 4s 16ft 3M "16"
Fl G 4s 16ft 4M "21"
NORTHERN RIGHT WHALE CRITICAL HAB
(precautionary area: 50 CFR 226.203c, 224.103c;
It is illegal to approach any right whale anywhere closer than 500
ANNUAL INCREASE 4'
Nautical Miles
860

Nautical Miles

1 ½ 0 1 2 3

865

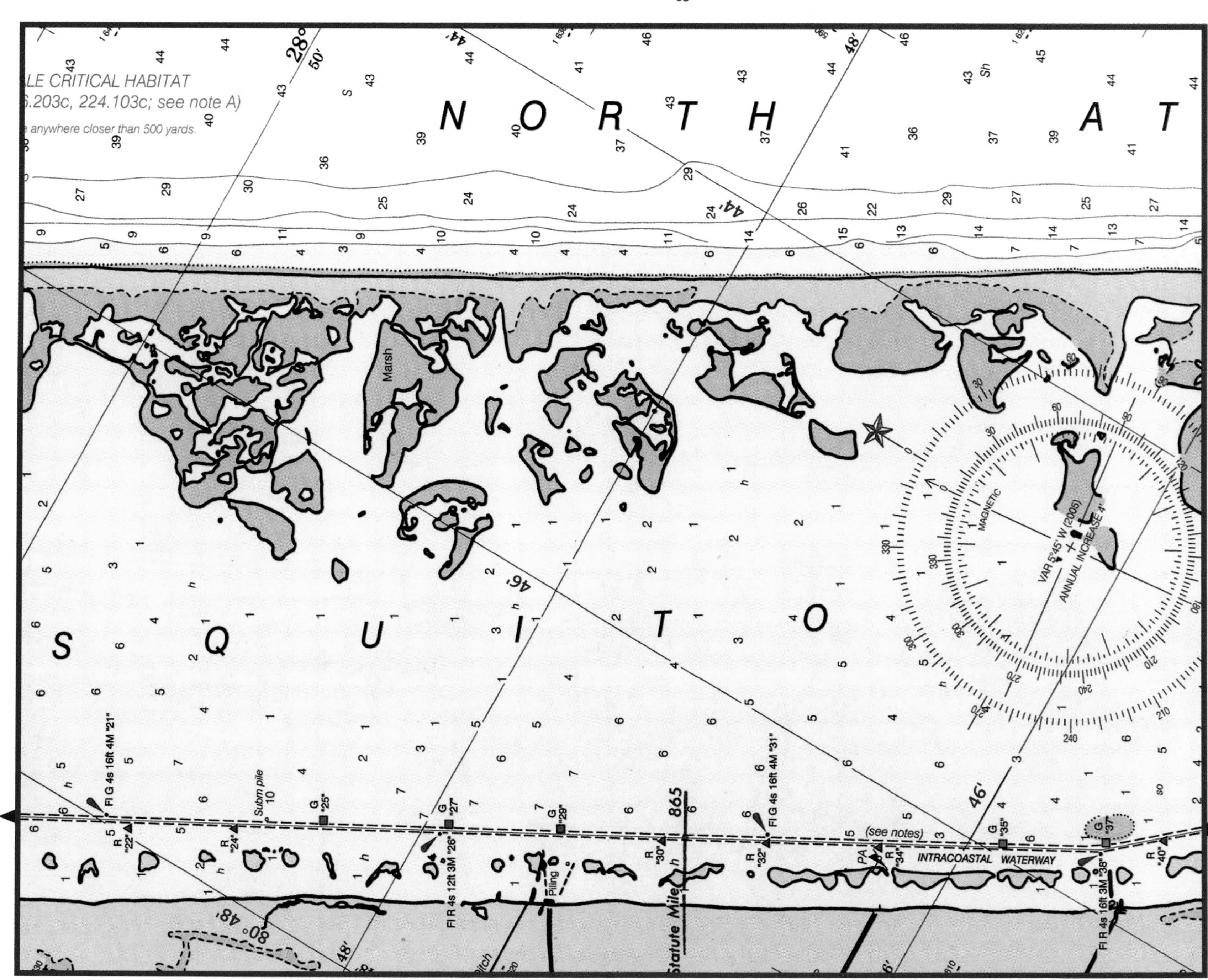

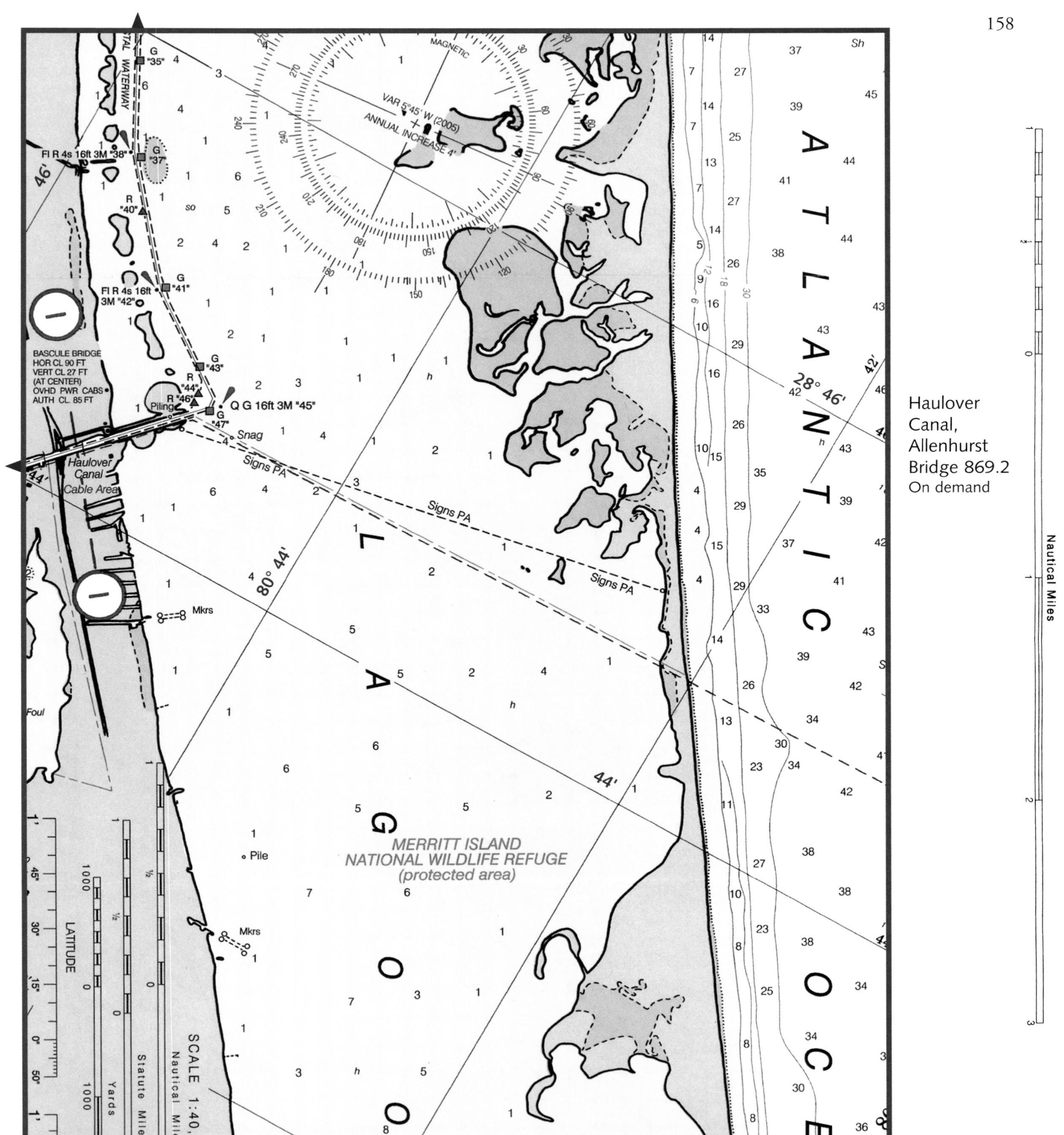

Haulover Canal, Allenhurst Bridge 869.2
On demand

Nautical Miles

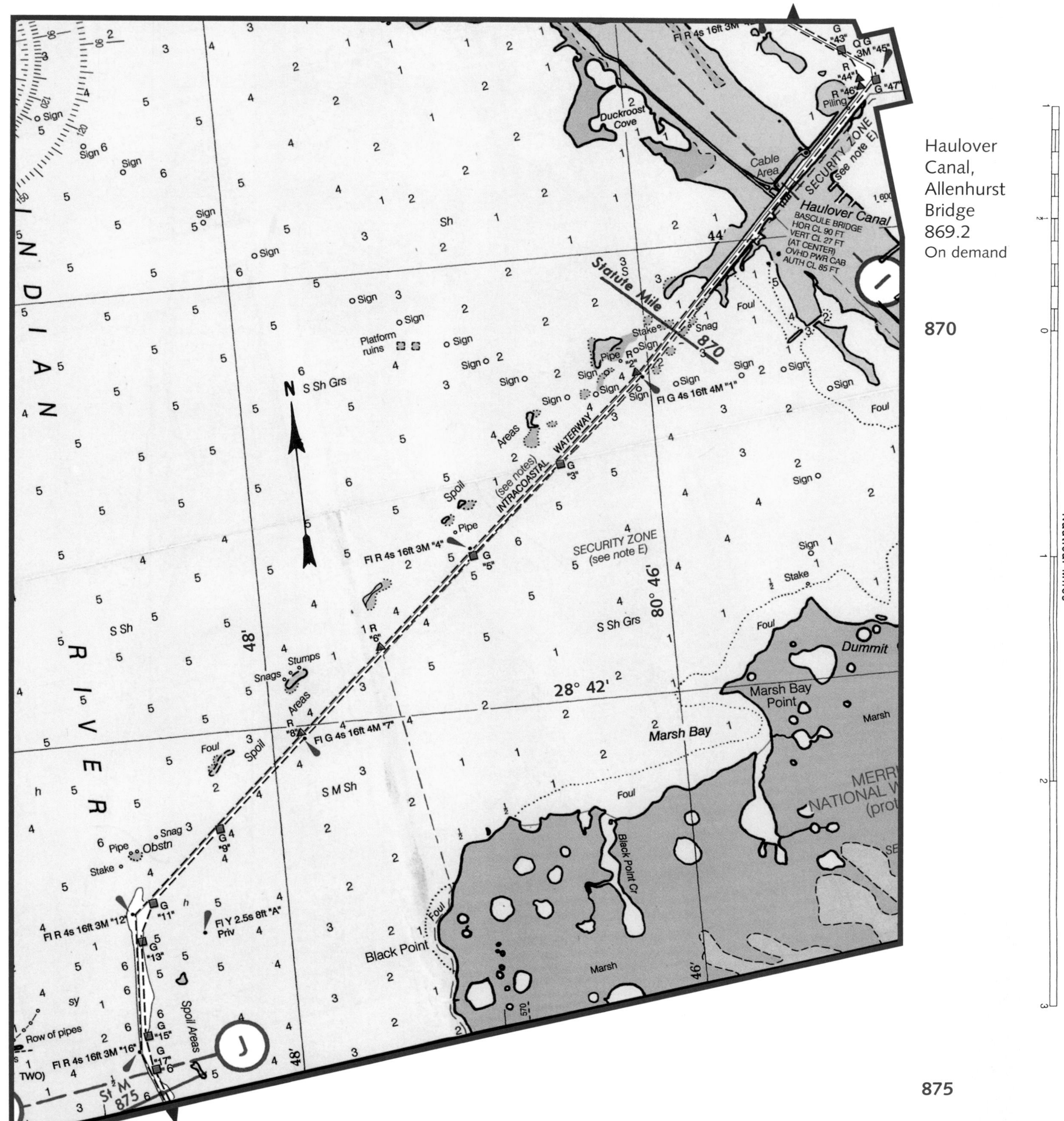

Haulover Canal, Allenhurst Bridge
869.2
On demand
870
875
Nautical Miles
INDIAN RIVER
Haulover Canal
BASCULE BRIDGE
HOR CL 90 FT
VERT CL 27 FT
(AT CENTER)
OVHD PWR CAB
AUTH CL 85 FT
SECURITY ZONE (see note E)
Cable Area
Duckroost Cove
Statute Mile 870
INTRACOASTAL WATERWAY
Spoil Areas (see notes)
Platform ruins
Dummit
Marsh Bay Point
Marsh Bay
Black Point
Black Point Cr
Marsh
28° 42'
80° 46'
48'
44'
Fl R 4s 16ft 3M "4"
Fl G 4s 16ft 4M "1"
Fl G 4s 16ft 4M "7"
Fl R 4s 16ft 3M "12"
Fl Y 2.5s 8ft "A" Priv
Fl R 4s 16ft 3M "16"
Row of pipes

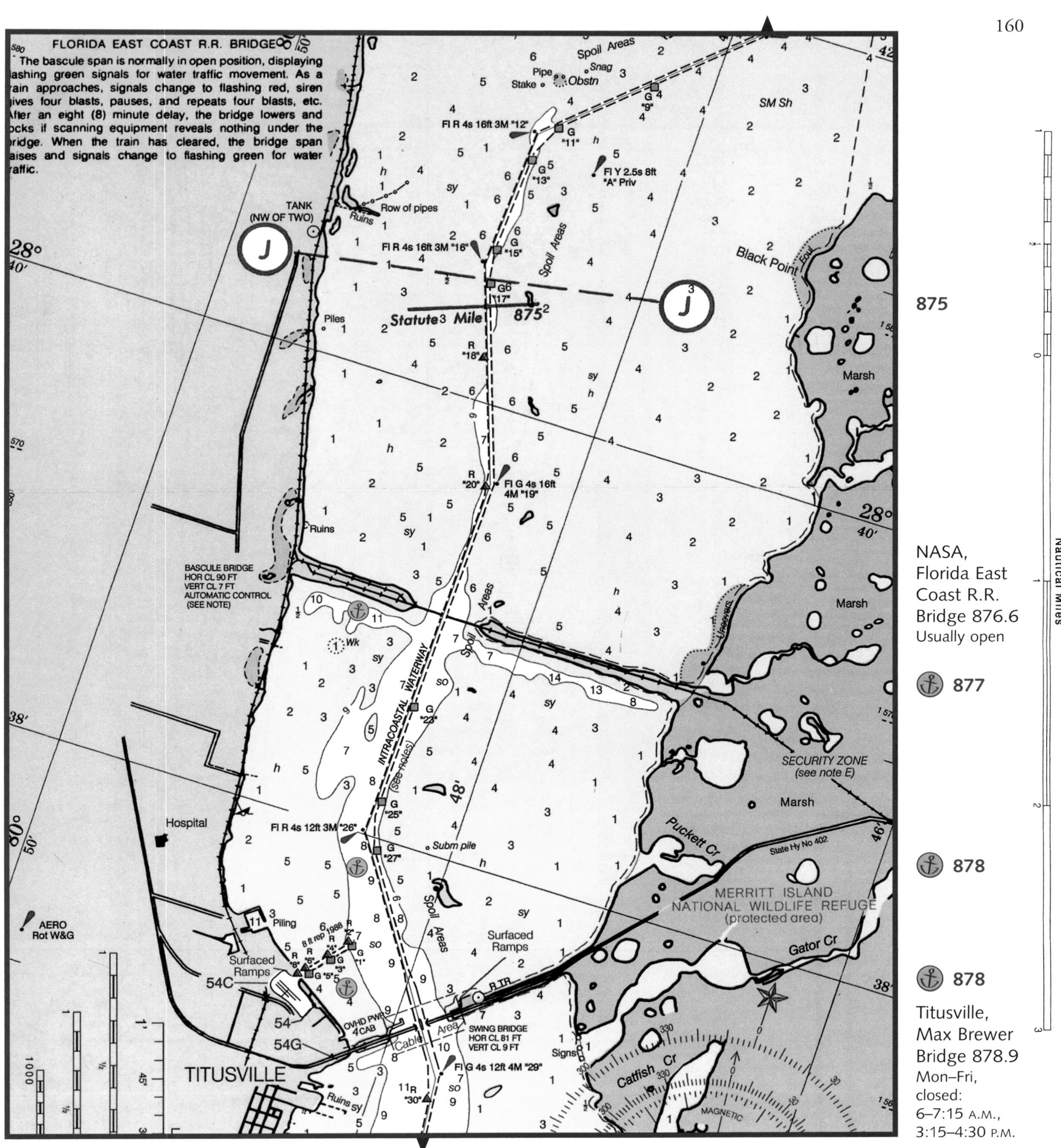
FLORIDA EAST COAST R.R. BRIDGE
The bascule span is normally in open position, displaying flashing green signals for water traffic movement. As a train approaches, signals change to flashing red, siren gives four blasts, pauses, and repeats four blasts, etc. After an eight (8) minute delay, the bridge lowers and locks if scanning equipment reveals nothing under the bridge. When the train has cleared, the bridge span raises and signals change to flashing green for water traffic.
TANK (NW OF TWO)
Row of pipes
Ruins
Spoil Areas
Pipe
Snag
Stake
Obstn
SM Sh
Fl R 4s 16ft 3M "12"
Fl Y 2.5s 8ft "A" Priv
Fl R 4s 16ft 3M "16"
Black Point
Statute Mile 875
Piles
Marsh
Fl G 4s 16ft 4M "19"
BASCULE BRIDGE HOR CL 90 FT VERT CL 7 FT AUTOMATIC CONTROL (SEE NOTE)
INTRACOASTAL WATERWAY
(See notes)
SECURITY ZONE (see note E)
Hospital
Fl R 4s 12ft 3M "26"
Subm pile
Puckett Cr
State Hy No 402
MERRITT ISLAND NATIONAL WILDLIFE REFUGE (protected area)
AERO Rot W&G
Piling
Surfaced Ramps
Gator Cr
OVHD PWR 4 CAB
Cable Area
SWING BRIDGE HOR CL 81 FT VERT CL 9 FT
Signs
TITUSVILLE
Fl G 4s 12ft 4M "29"
Catfish Cr
MAGNETIC
Nautical Miles
875
NASA, Florida East Coast R.R. Bridge 876.6
Usually open
877
878
878
Titusville, Max Brewer Bridge 878.9
Mon–Fri, closed: 6–7:15 A.M., 3:15–4:30 P.M.

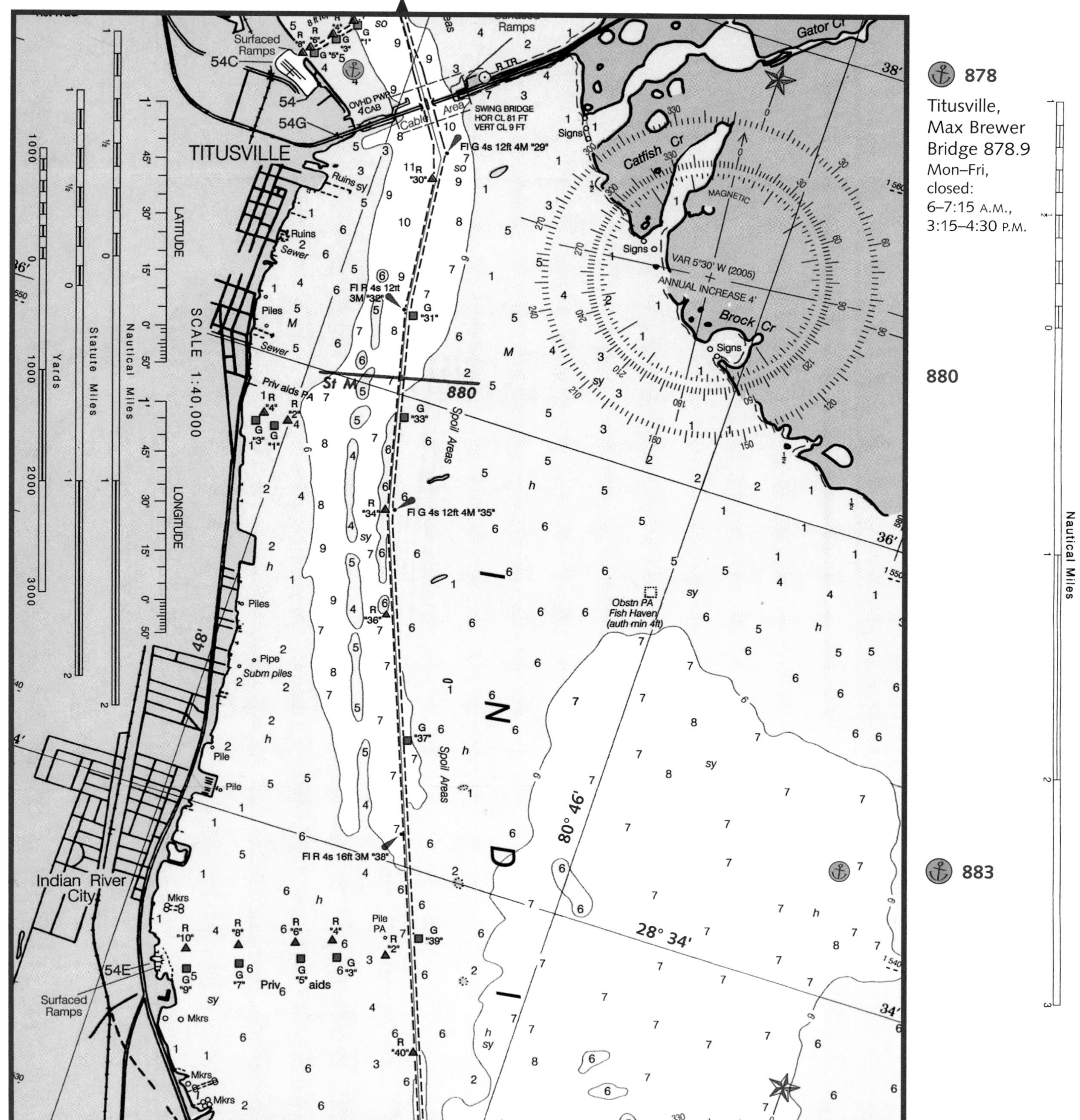
878
Titusville,
Max Brewer
Bridge 878.9
Mon–Fri,
closed:
6–7:15 A.M.,
3:15–4:30 P.M.
880
883
TITUSVILLE
Surfaced Ramps
54C
54
54G
OVHD PWR
4 CAB
Cable Area
SWING BRIDGE
HOR CL 81 FT
VERT CL 9 FT
Gator Cr
Catfish Cr
Brock Cr
Signs
MAGNETIC
VAR 5°30' W (2005)
ANNUAL INCREASE 4'
Fl G 4s 12ft 4M "29"
Fl R 4s 12ft 3M "32"
Fl G 4s 12ft 4M "35"
Fl R 4s 16ft 3M "38"
Ruins
Sewer
Piles
Priv aids PA
St M
Spoil Areas
Obstn PA
Fish Haven
(auth min 4ft)
Pipe
Subm piles
Pile
Indian River City
Mkrs
54E
Priv "5" aids
SCALE 1:40,000
LATITUDE
LONGITUDE
Nautical Miles
Statute Miles
Yards
80° 46'
28° 34'
INDIAN

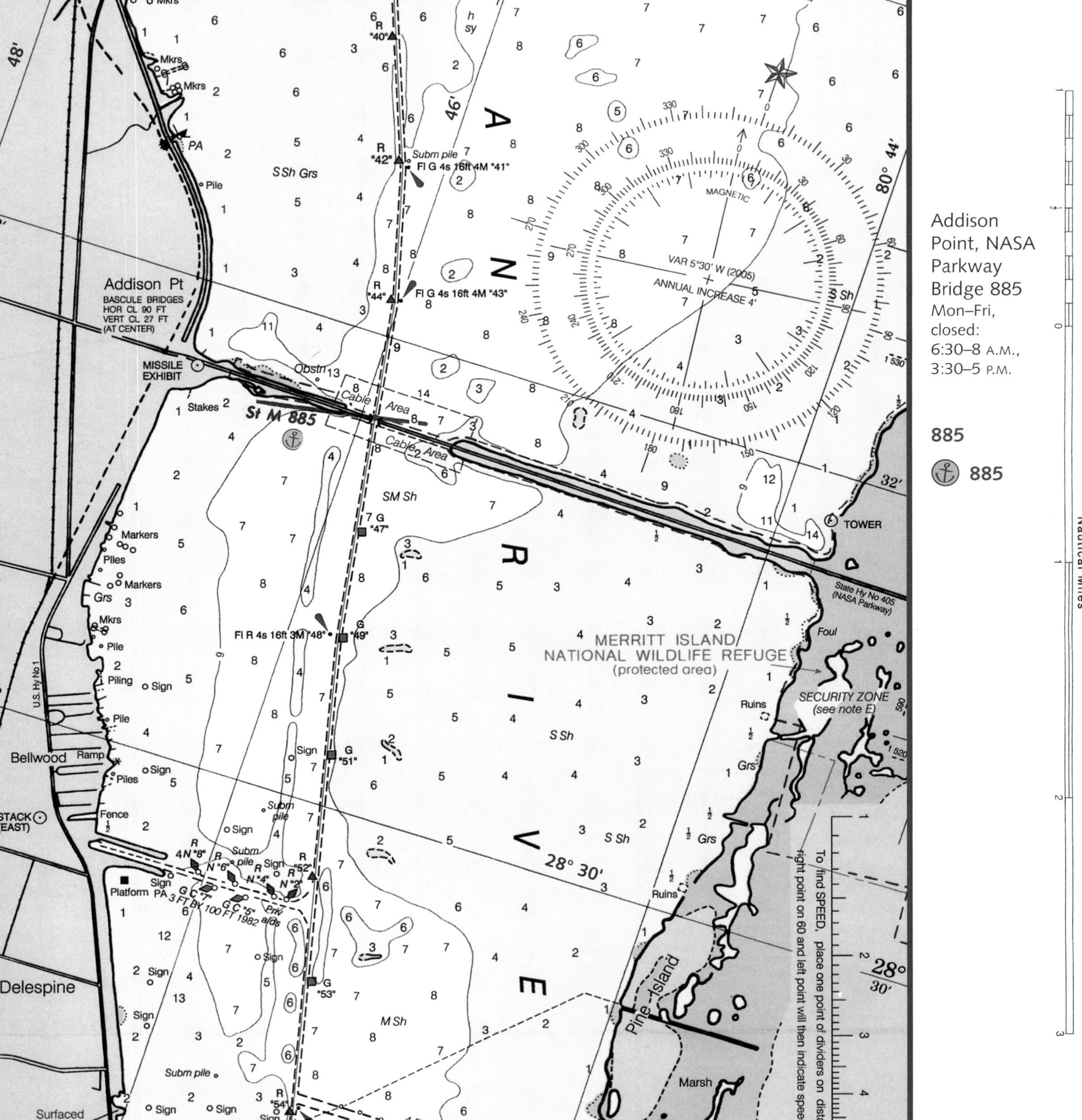

Addison Point, NASA Parkway Bridge 885

Mon–Fri, closed: 6:30–8 A.M., 3:30–5 P.M.

885

885

See Page 228 For Barge Canal

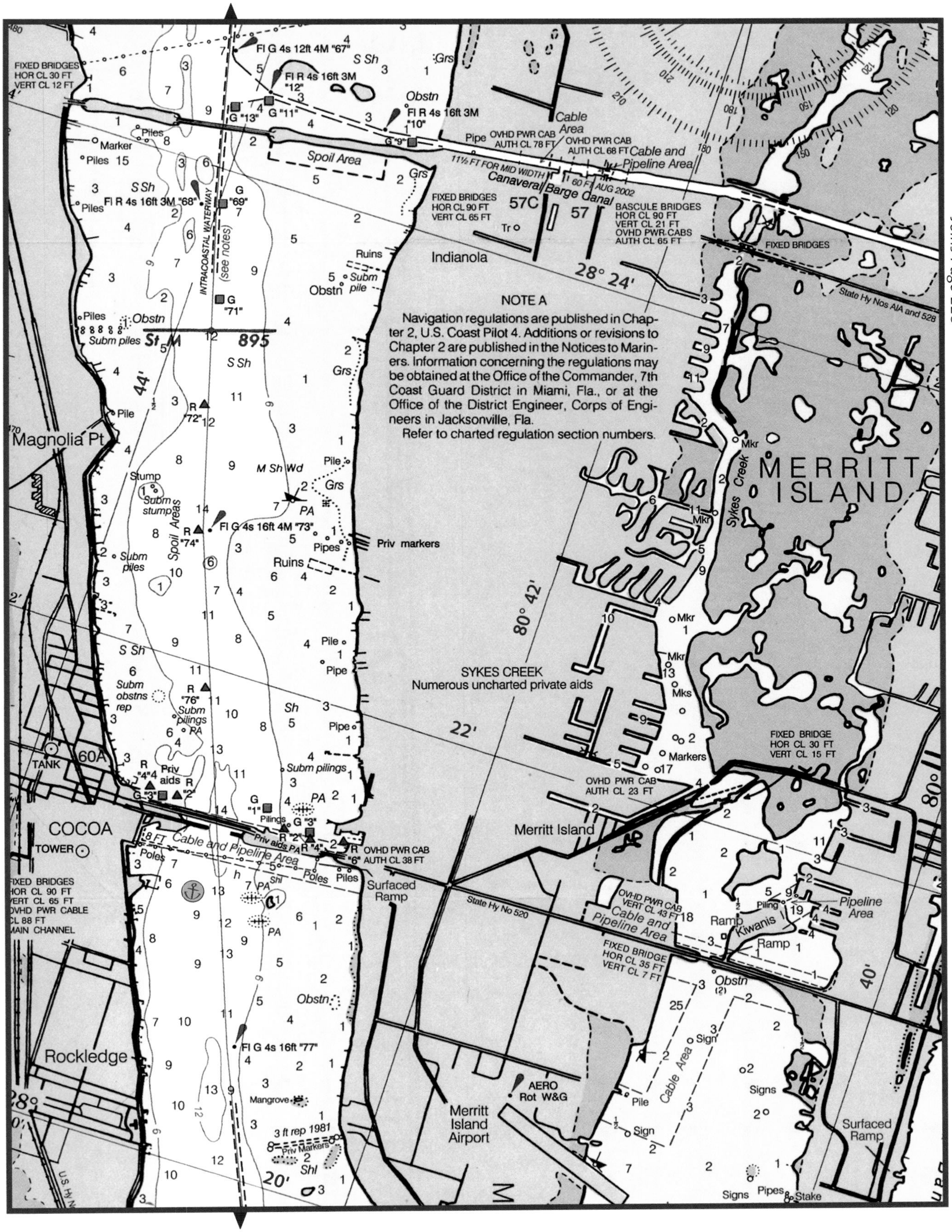

See page 228 for Barge Canal bridge information

Joins Page 228

895

897

NOTE A

Navigation regulations are published in Chapter 2, U.S. Coast Pilot 4. Additions or revisions to Chapter 2 are published in the Notices to Mariners. Information concerning the regulations may be obtained at the Office of the Commander, 7th Coast Guard District in Miami, Fla., or at the Office of the District Engineer, Corps of Engineers in Jacksonville, Fla.

Refer to charted regulation section numbers.

SYKES CREEK
Numerous uncharted private aids

MERRITT ISLAND

Nautical Miles

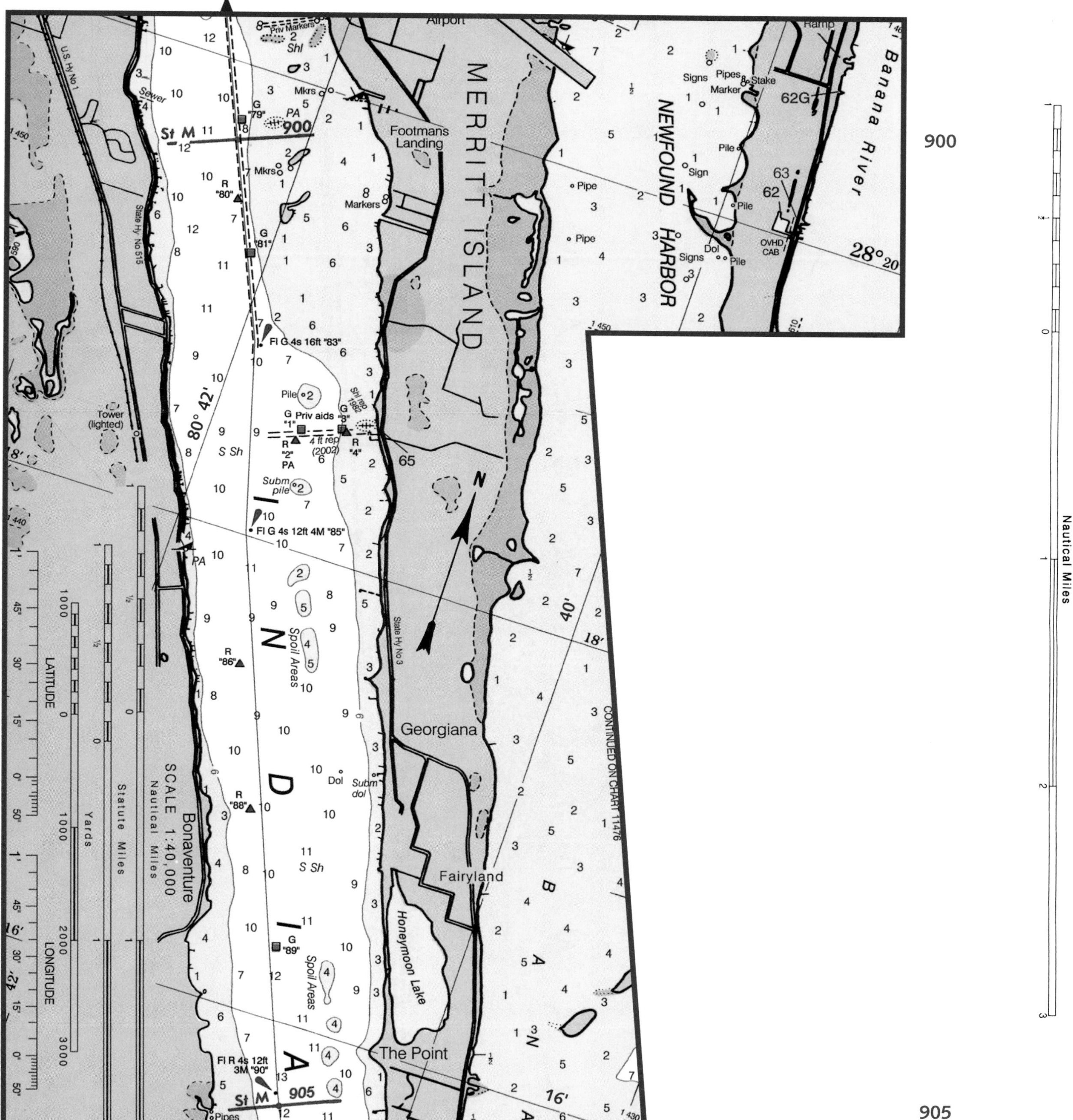
MERRITT ISLAND
NEWFOUND HARBOR
Banana River
Footmans Landing
Georgiana
Fairyland
Honeymoon Lake
The Point
Bonaventure
SCALE 1:40,000
Nautical Miles
Statute Miles
Yards
LATITUDE
LONGITUDE
CONTINUED ON CHART 11476
Nautical Miles

900

905

905

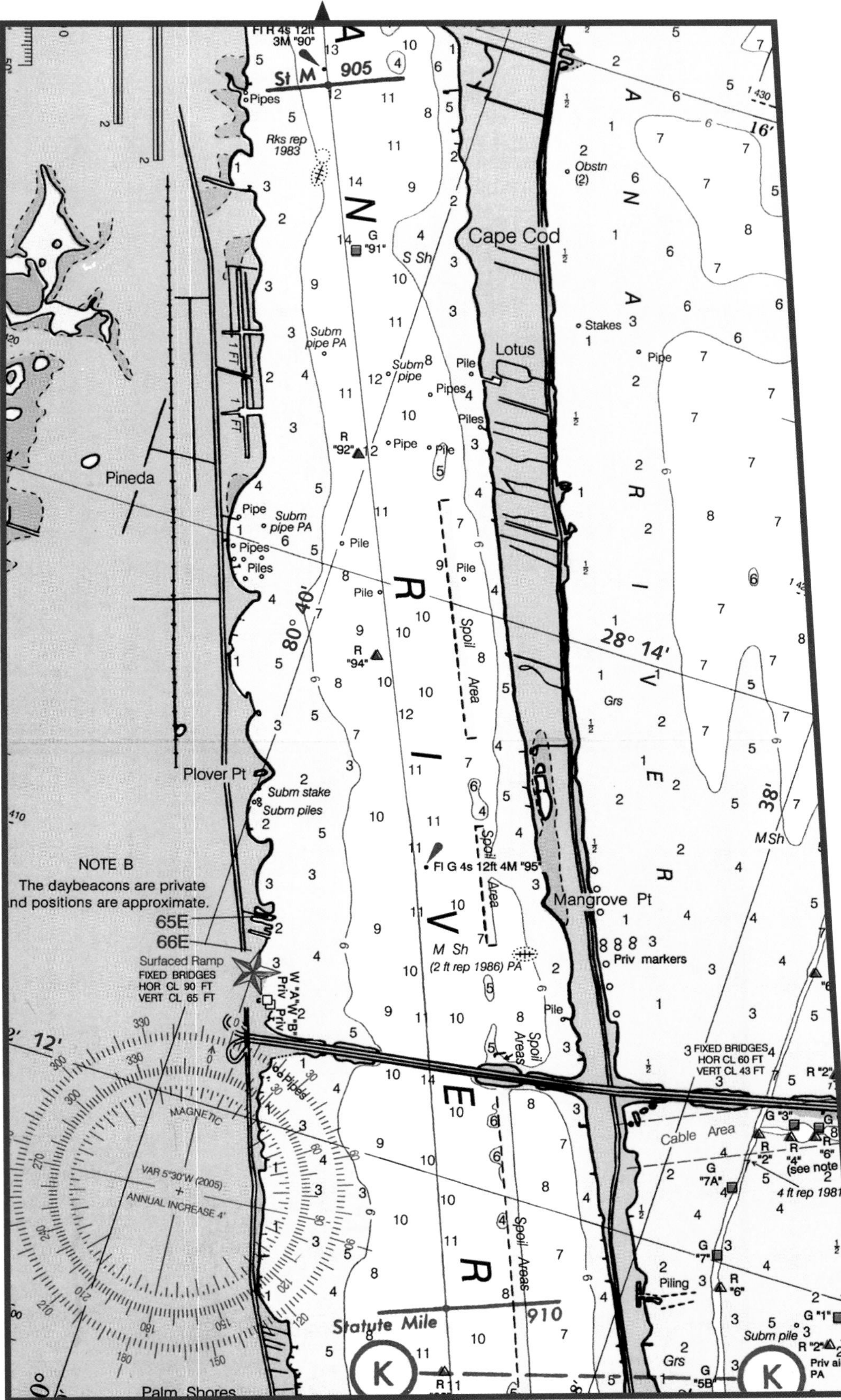
Fl R 4s 12ft 3M "90"
St M 905
Rks rep 1983
Cape Cod
Lotus
Obstn (2)
Stakes
Pineda
Plover Pt
Mangrove Pt
Priv markers
M Sh
(2 ft rep 1986) PA
Fl G 4s 12ft 4M "95"
Spoil Area
Spoil Areas
28° 14'
80° 40'
NOTE B
The daybeacons are private
and positions are approximate.
65E
66E
Surfaced Ramp
FIXED BRIDGES
HOR CL 90 FT
VERT CL 65 FT
3 FIXED BRIDGES
HOR CL 60 FT
VERT CL 43 FT
Cable Area
(see note
4 ft rep 1981
Piling
MAGNETIC
VAR 5°30'W (2005)
ANNUAL INCREASE 4'
Statute Mile
910
Subm pile
Priv aids PA
Palm Shores
Nautical Miles

910

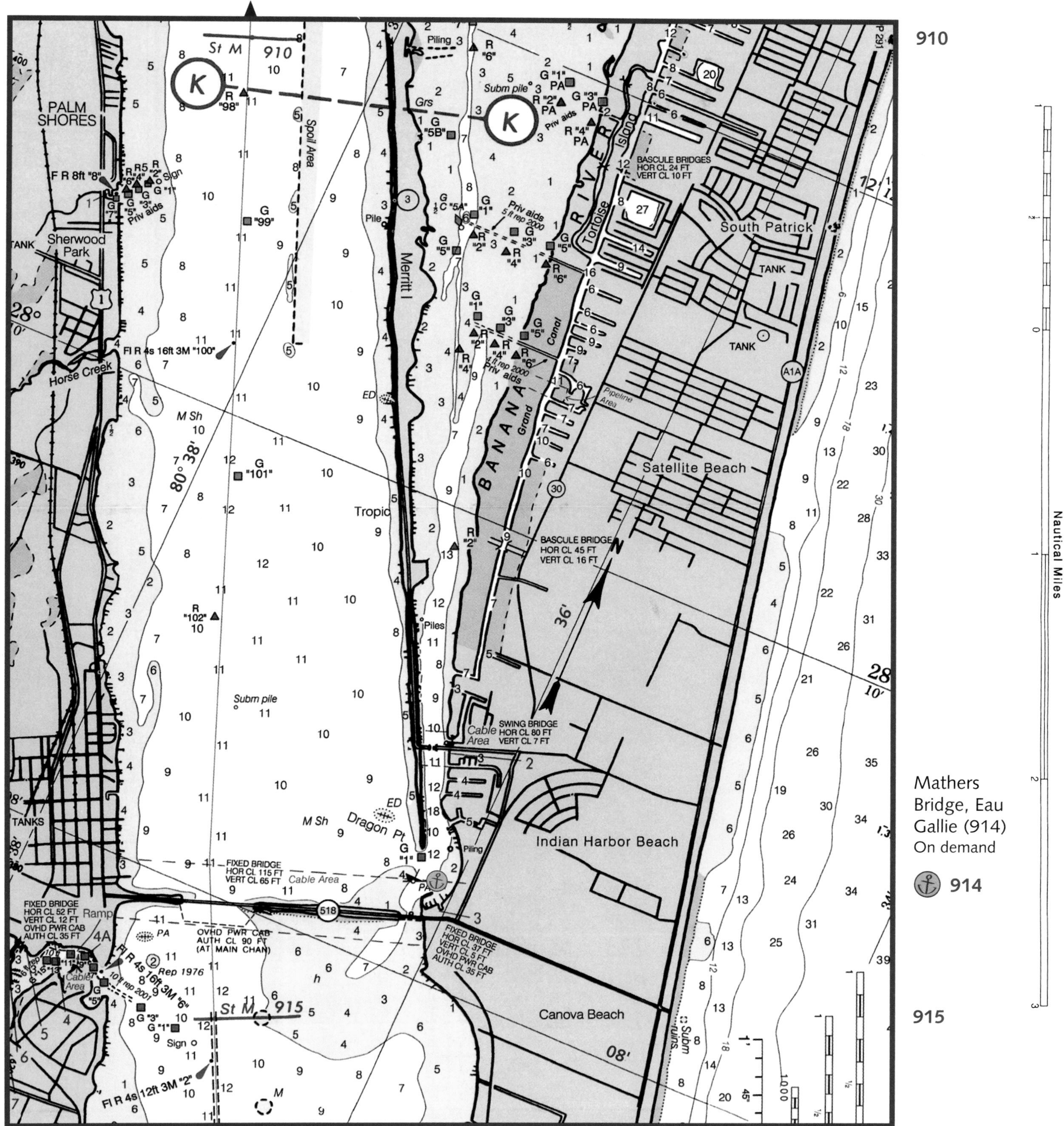

910

Mathers Bridge, Eau Gallie (914)
On demand

914

915

915

St M 915

Canova Beach

Subm ruins

Fl R 4s 12ft 3M "2"

80° 36'

G "3"

Pipeline Area

Priv aids

6 ft rep 1999

Spoil Area

VAR 5°45' W (2005)
ANNUAL INCREASE 4'

MAGNETIC

Wells Pt

Fl G 2.5s 12ft 3M "5" PA

34'

SCALE 1:40,000
Nautical Miles
Statute Miles
Yards

LATITUDE

LONGITUDE

FIXED BRIDGE
HOR CL 10 FT
VERT CL 2 FT

FIXED BRIDGE
HOR CL 80 FT
VERT CL 65 FT

FIXED BRIDGE
HOR CL 30 FT
VERT CL 6 FT

FIXED BRIDGE
HOR CL 117 FT
VERT CL 65 FT

Melbourne

Surfaced Ramp

Cable Area

Ramps

516

Indialantic

Stakes

TANK

(see note B)
4½ ft rep (1975)

WIDTH 100 FT 1992

Subm pile

G 12ft 3M "7"

Piles

Fisherman Pt

Markers

Breakers

Fl G 4s 12ft 4M "7"

Obstn rep PA 1983

Obstn rep PA 1972

Melbourne Beach

St M 10 920

Obstn PA

Crab Pt

Mkrs rep 1982

LT OBSC

28° 04'

N O R T H

920

Nautical Miles

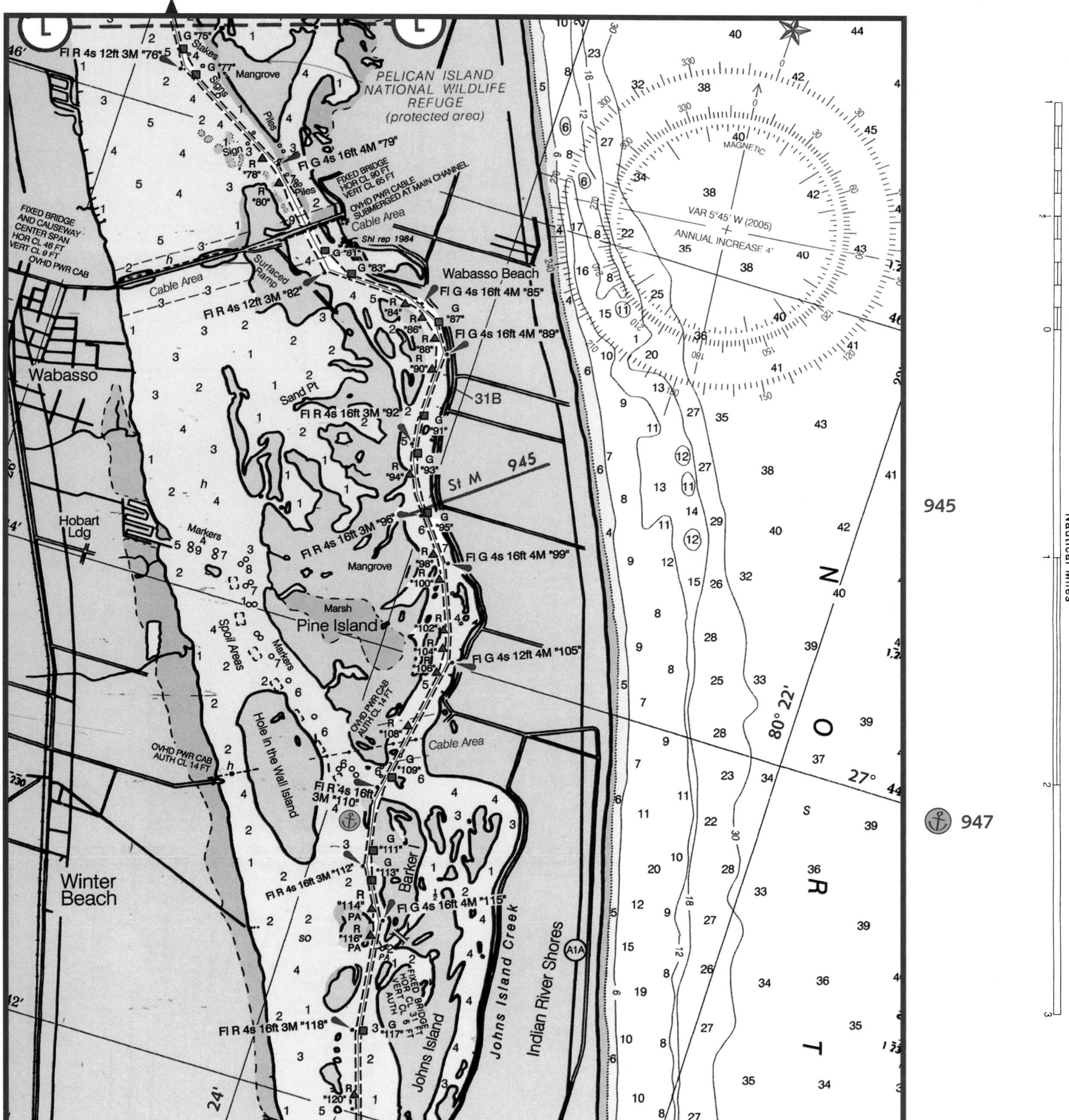
PELICAN ISLAND
NATIONAL WILDLIFE
REFUGE
(protected area)
Mangrove
Stakes
Signs
Piles
Sign
FI R 4s 12ft 3M "76"
FI G 4s 16ft 4M "79"
FIXED BRIDGE
HOR CL 90 FT
VERT CL 65 FT
OVHD PWR CABLE
SUBMERGED AT MAIN CHANNEL
Cable Area
Shl rep 1984
FIXED BRIDGE
AND CAUSEWAY
CENTER SPAN
HOR CL 46 FT
VERT CL 9 FT
OVHD PWR CAB
Surfaced Ramp
Wabasso Beach
FI R 4s 12ft 3M "82"
FI G 4s 16ft 4M "85"
FI G 4s 16ft 4M "89"
Wabasso
Sand Pt
FI R 4s 16ft 3M "92"
31B
St M 945
Hobart
Ldg
Markers
FI R 4s 16ft 3M "96"
FI G 4s 16ft 4M "99"
Mangrove
Marsh
Pine Island
Spoil Areas
FI G 4s 12ft 4M "105"
OVHD PWR CAB
AUTH CL 14 FT
Cable Area
Hole in the Wall Island
OVHD PWR CAB
AUTH CL 14 FT
FI R 4s 16ft
3M "110"
Winter
Beach
Barker
FI R 4s 16ft 3M "112"
FI G 4s 16ft 4M "115"
Johns Island Creek
Indian River Shores
A1A
FIXED BRIDGE
HOR CL 35 FT
VERT CL 6 FT
AUTH
Johns Island
FI R 4s 16ft 3M "118"
VAR 5°45' W (2005)
ANNUAL INCREASE 4'
MAGNETIC
80° 22'
27°
NORTH
945
947
Nautical Miles

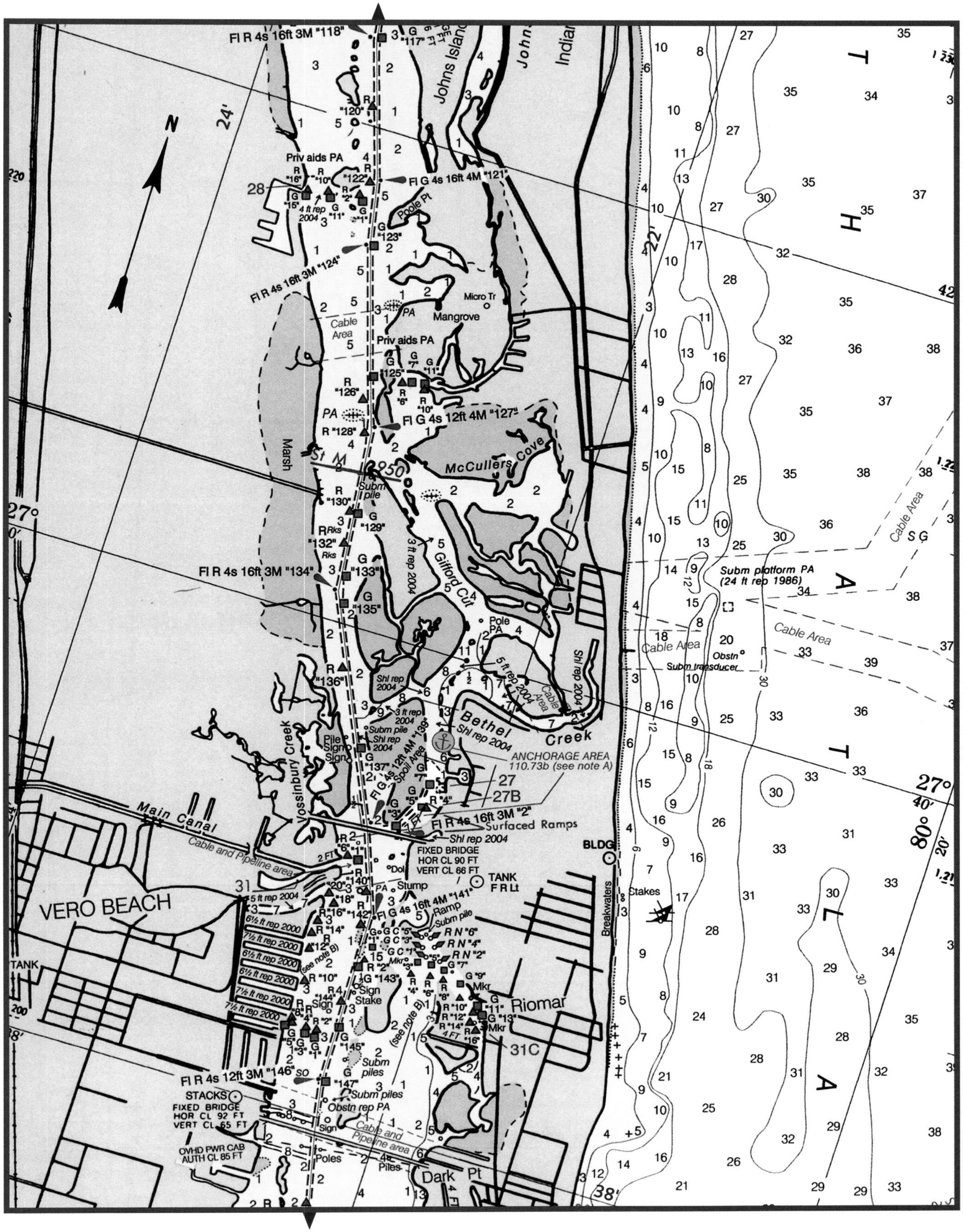
VERO BEACH
Riomar
Main Canal
Vossinbury Creek
Bethel Creek
Gifford Cut
McCullers Cove
Poole Pt
Dark Pt
Johns Island
Marsh
Mangrove
ANCHORAGE AREA
110.73b (see note A)
FIXED BRIDGE
HOR CL 90 FT
VERT CL 66 FT
FIXED BRIDGE
HOR CL 92 FT
VERT CL 65 FT
OVHD PWR CAB
AUTH CL 85 FT
Cable and Pipeline area
Subm platform PA
(24 ft rep 1986)
Breakwaters
Stakes
BLDG
TANK
STACKS
Surfaced Ramps
Cable Area
Fl R 4s 16ft 3M "118"
Fl G 4s 16ft 4M "121"
Fl R 4s 16ft 3M "124"
Fl G 4s 12ft 4M "127"
Fl R 4s 16ft 3M "134"
Fl R 4s 16ft 3M "2"
Fl G 4s 16ft 4M "141"
Fl R 4s 12ft 3M "146"
Priv aids PA

950

951.9

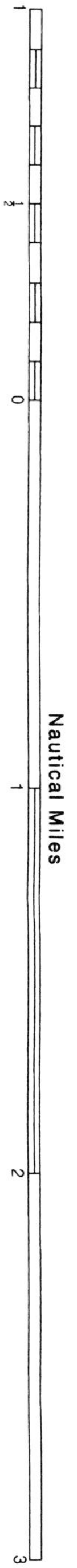
Nautical Miles
1
0
1
2
3

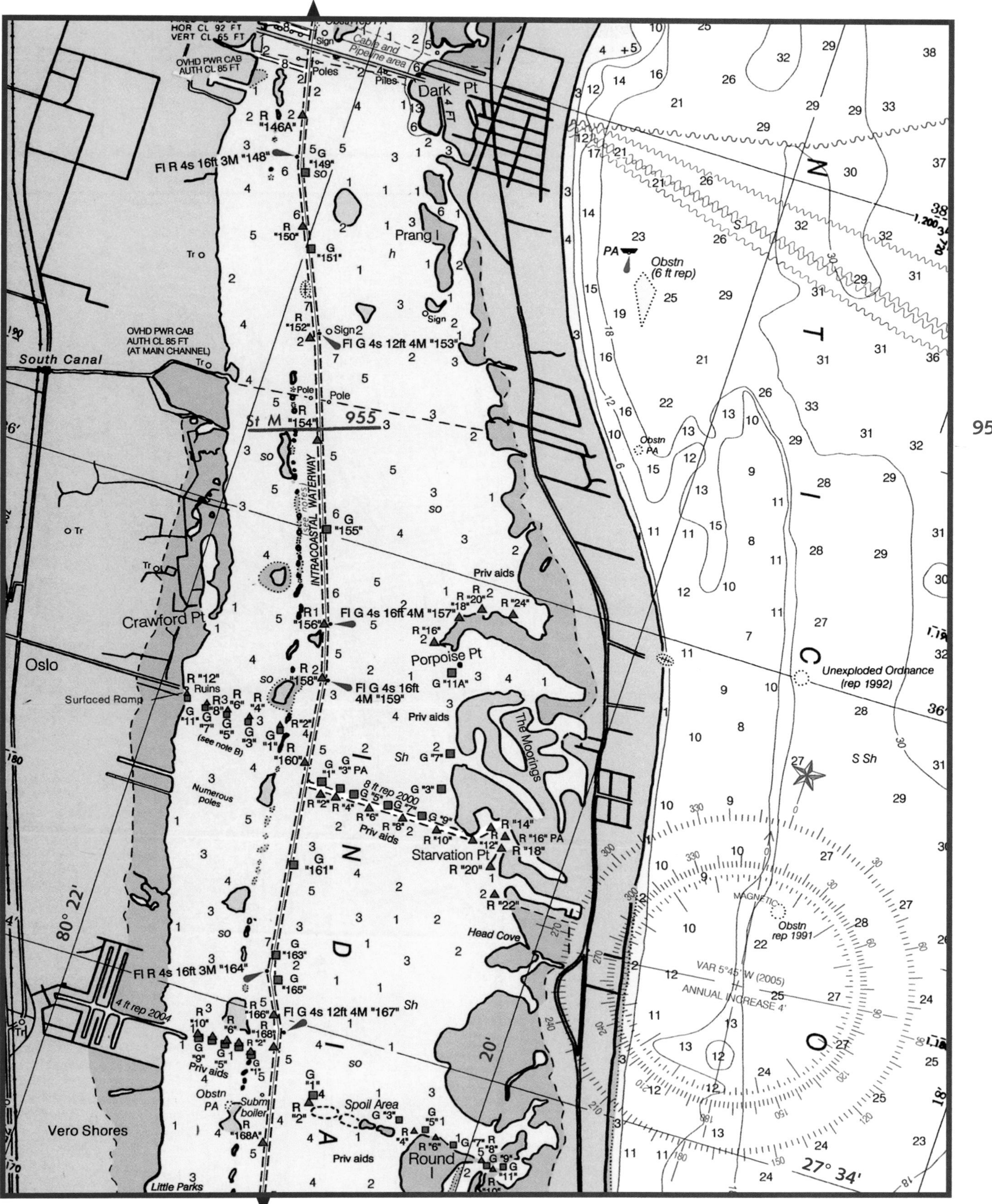

HOR CL 92 FT
VERT CL 65 FT
OVHD PWR CAB AUTH CL 85 FT
Cable and Pipeline area
Poles
Piles
Dark Pt
R "146A"
Fl R 4s 16ft 3M "148"
G "149"
Prang I
R "150"
G "151"
OVHD PWR CAB AUTH CL 85 FT (AT MAIN CHANNEL)
South Canal
R "152"
Fl G 4s 12ft 4M "153"
Sign
Pole
St M 955
R "154"
INTRACOASTAL WATERWAY
G "155"
Priv aids
Crawford Pt
Fl G 4s 16ft 4M "157"
Porpoise Pt
Oslo
Surfaced Ramp
Ruins
Fl G 4s 16ft 4M "159"
The Moorings
(see note B)
Numerous poles
8 ft rep 2000
Starvation Pt
Head Cove
Fl R 4s 16ft 3M "164"
Fl G 4s 12ft 4M "167"
4 ft rep 2004
Obstn PA
Subm boiler
Spoil Area
Vero Shores
Round I
Little Parks
80° 22′
20′
PA
Obstn (6 ft rep)
Obstn PA
N
T
I
C
O
Unexploded Ordnance (rep 1992)
S Sh
MAGNETIC
Obstn rep 1991
VAR 5°45′ W (2005)
ANNUAL INCREASE 4′
27° 34′
Nautical Miles

955

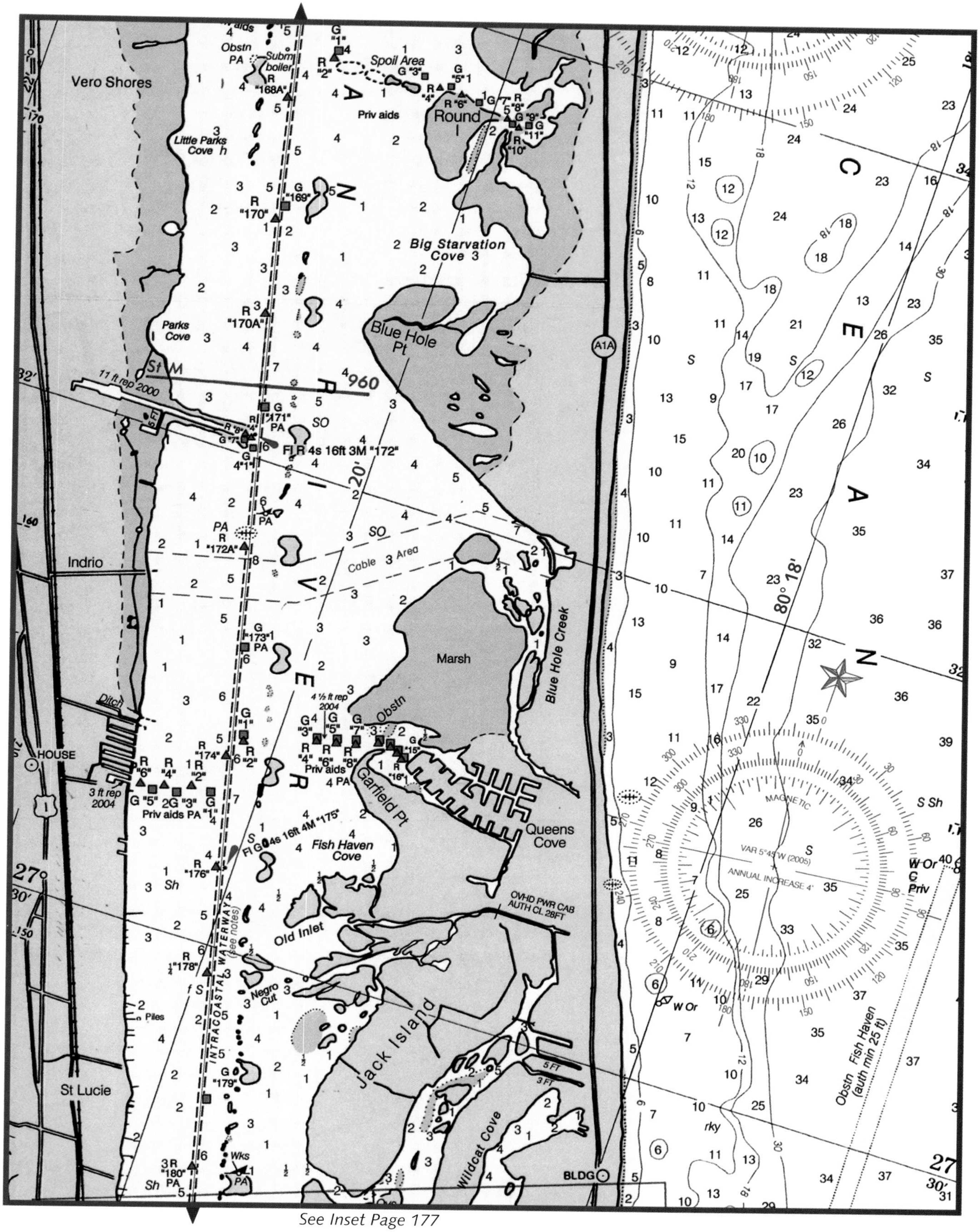

960

Vero Shores

Little Parks Cove

Parks Cove

Spoil Area

Priv aids

Round I

Big Starvation Cove

Blue Hole Pt

A1A

St M

11 ft rep 2000

Fl R 4s 16ft 3M "172"

Cable Area

Indrio

Marsh

Blue Hole Creek

4 ½ ft rep 2004

Obstn

Garfield Pt

Queens Cove

Fish Haven Cove

Fl G 4s 16ft 4M "175"

3 ft rep 2004

Priv aids PA

HOUSE

Ditch

INTRACOASTAL WATERWAY (see notes)

Old Inlet

OVHD PWR CAB AUTH CL 28FT

Negro Cut

Jack Island

Wildcat Cove

Piles

St Lucie

Wks

BLDG

OCEAN

VAR 5°45'W (2005)

ANNUAL INCREASE 4'

MAGNETIC

Obstn Fish Haven (auth min 25 ft)

W Or C Priv

S Sh

W Or

rky

80°18'

27° 30'

Nautical Miles

See Inset Page 177

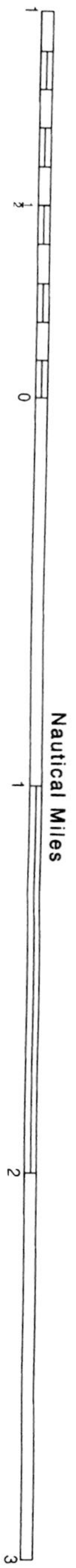

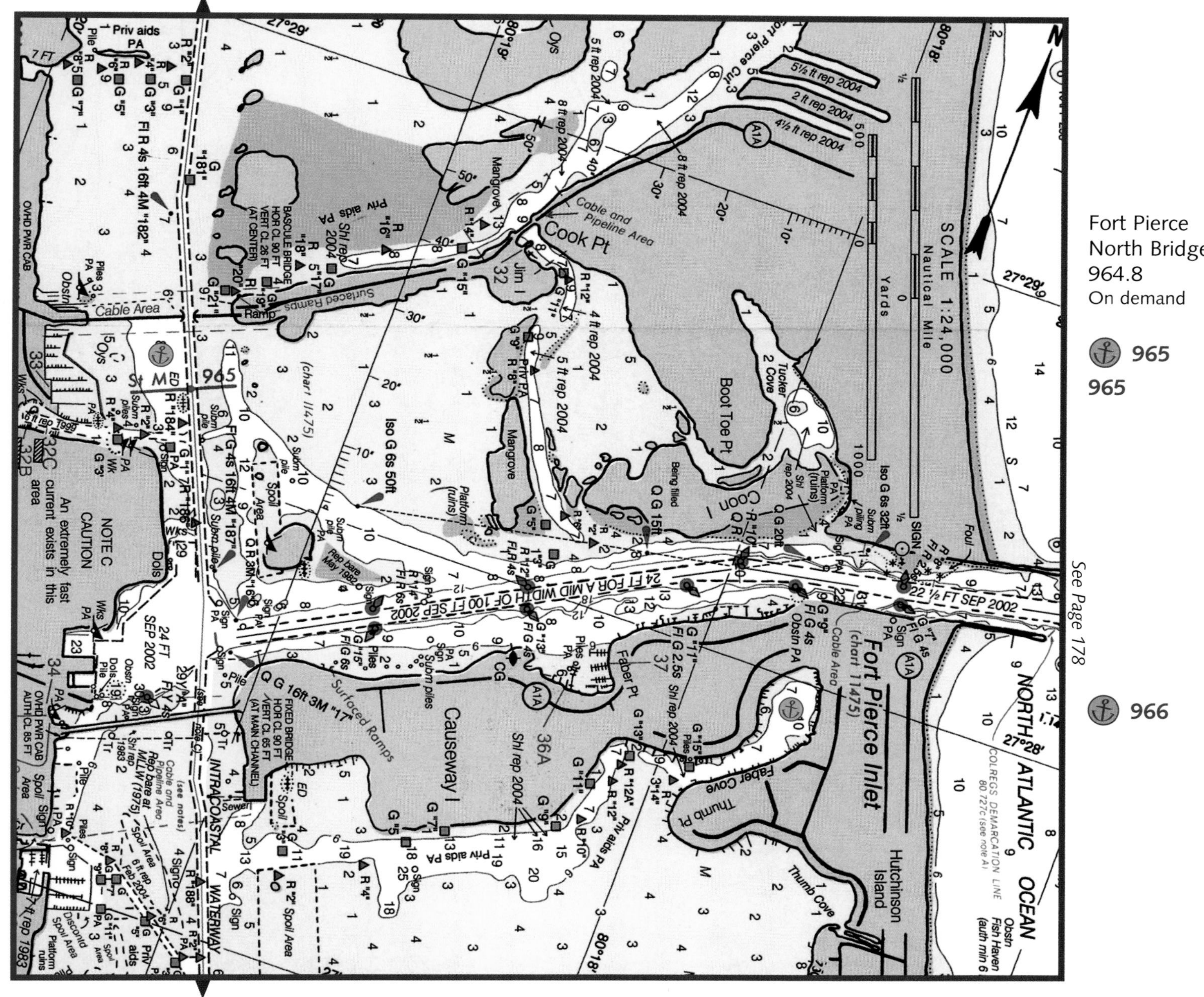

Fort Pierce
North Bridge
964.8
On demand

965

965

966

See Page 178

Fort Pierce
North Bridge
964.8
On demand

965

965

R "4"
27° 28.5'N
80° 16.2'W

966

970

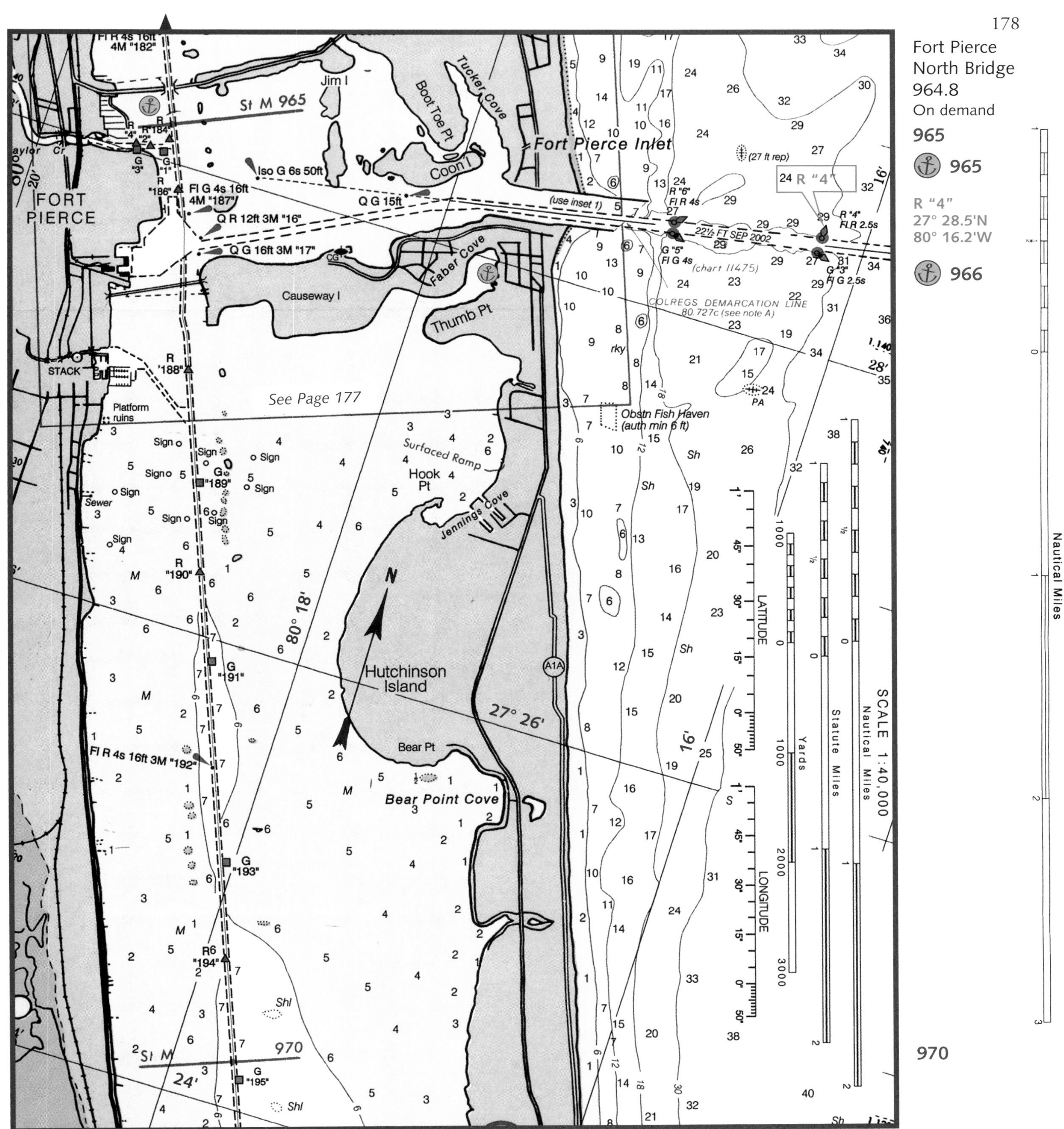

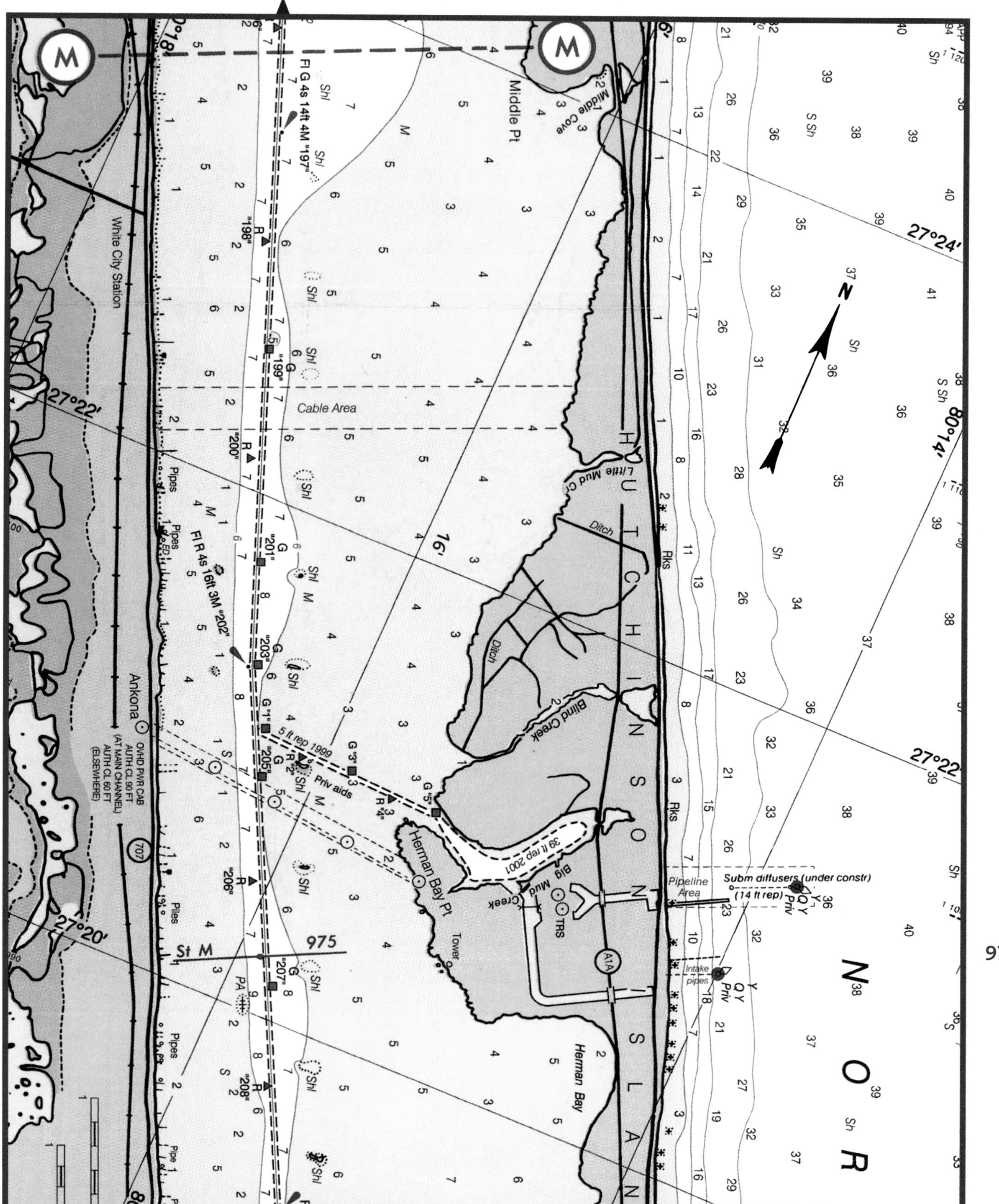

Middle Pt
Middle Cove
White City Station
Cable Area
Fl G 4s 14ft 4M "197"
Fl R 4s 16ft 3M "202"
Little Mud Cr
Ditch
Blind Creek
5 ft rep 1999
Priv aids
39 ft rep 2001
Herman Bay Pt
Big Mud Creek
Herman Bay
Tower
TRS
Ankona
OVHD PWR CAB
AUTH CL 80 FT
(AT MAIN CHANNEL)
AUTH CL 60 FT
(ELSEWHERE)
Pipes
St M
975
HUTCHINSON ISLAND
Rks
Pipeline Area
Subm diffusers (under constr)
(14 ft rep)
Intake pipes
Q Y Priv
N O R
27°24'
27°22'
27°20'
80°14'
16'
A1A
707
Nautical Miles

975

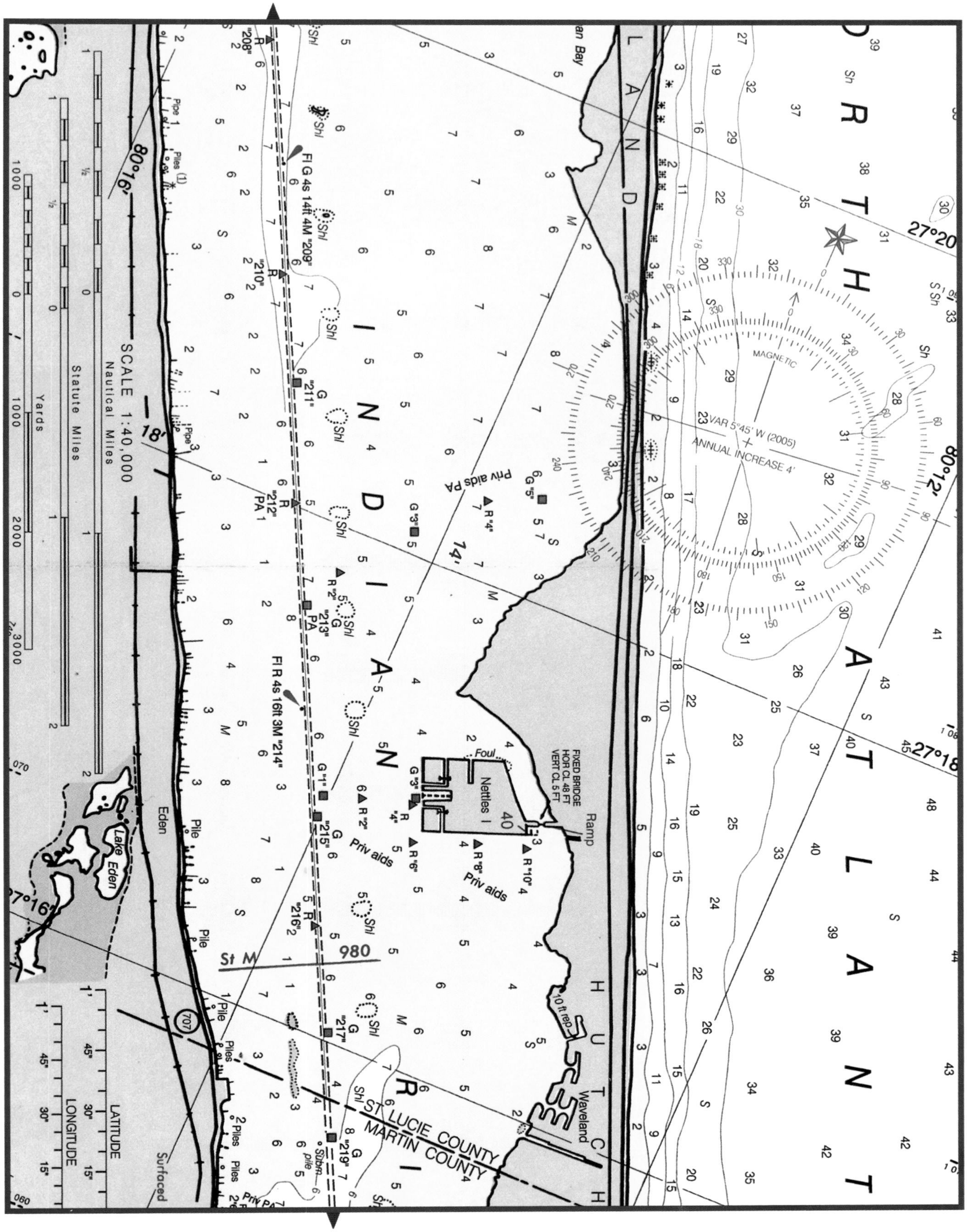

NORTH ATLANTIC

INDIAN RIVER

LAND

HUTCHINSON ISLAND

Waveland

Nettles I

Eden

Lake Eden

ST LUCIE COUNTY

MARTIN COUNTY

FIXED BRIDGE
HOR CL 48 FT
VERT CL 5 FT

Ramp

Foul

10 ft rep

Priv aids

Priv aids PA

Fl G 4s 14ft 4M "209"

Fl R 4s 16ft 3M "214"

VAR 5°45' W (2005)
ANNUAL INCREASE 4'

MAGNETIC

St M 980

980

27°20'

27°18'

27°16'

80°12'

80°16'

Surfaced

SCALE 1:40,000

Nautical Miles

Statute Miles

Yards

LATITUDE

LONGITUDE

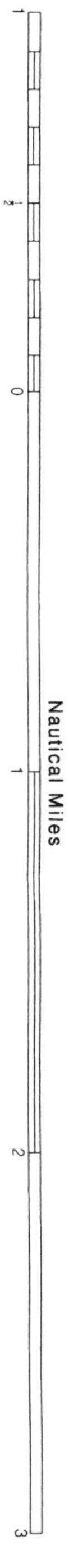

Nautical Miles

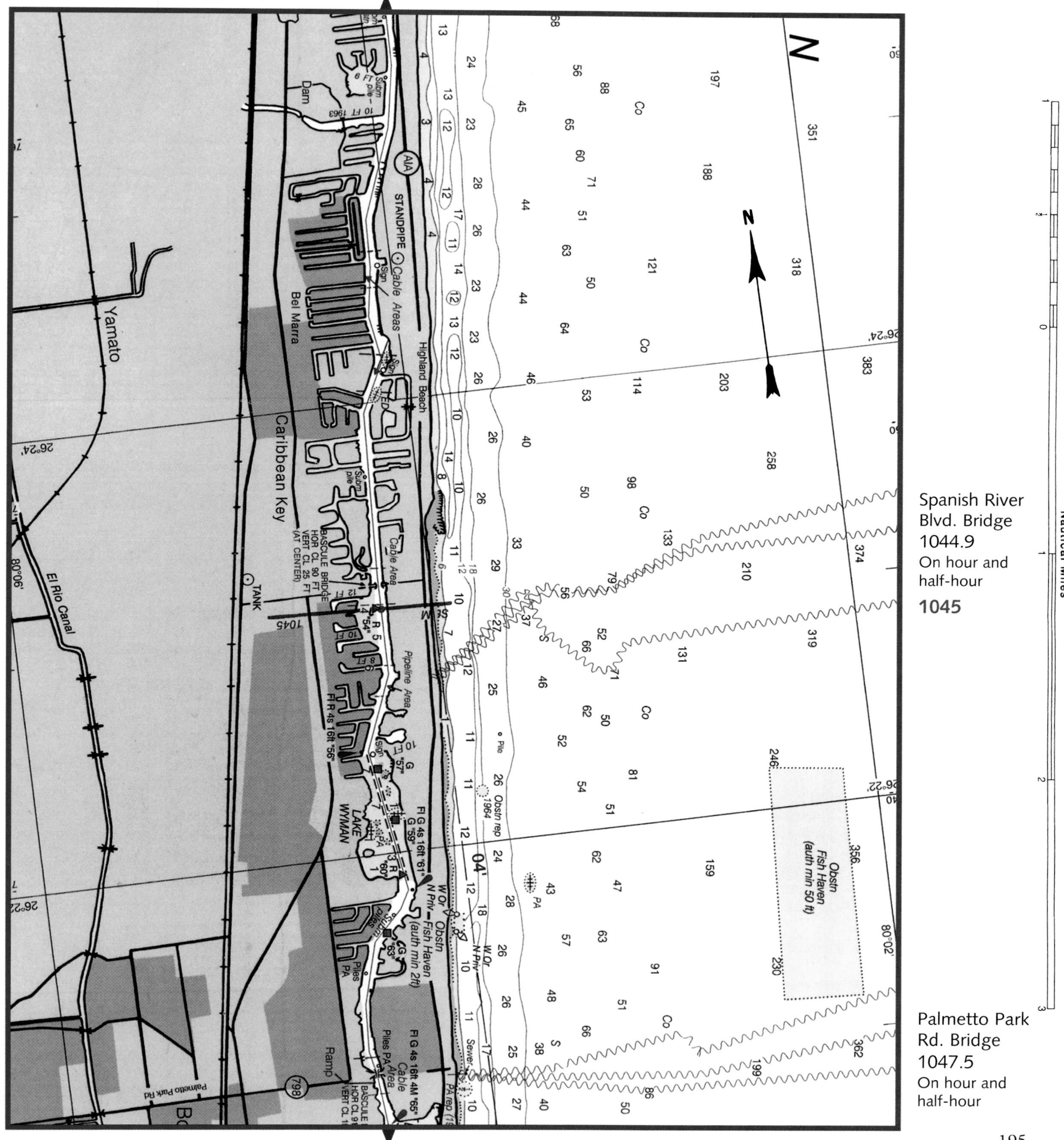

Spanish River Blvd. Bridge 1044.9
On hour and half-hour
1045
Palmetto Park Rd. Bridge 1047.5
On hour and half-hour
Nautical Miles
Highland Beach
Yamato
Bel Marra
Caribbean Key
El Rio Canal
LAKE WYMAN
STANDPIPE
TANK
Cable Areas
Pipeline Area
Obstn Fish Haven (auth min 50 ft)
BASCULE BRIDGE HOR CL 90 FT VERT CL 25 FT (AT CENTER)
Palmetto Park Rd

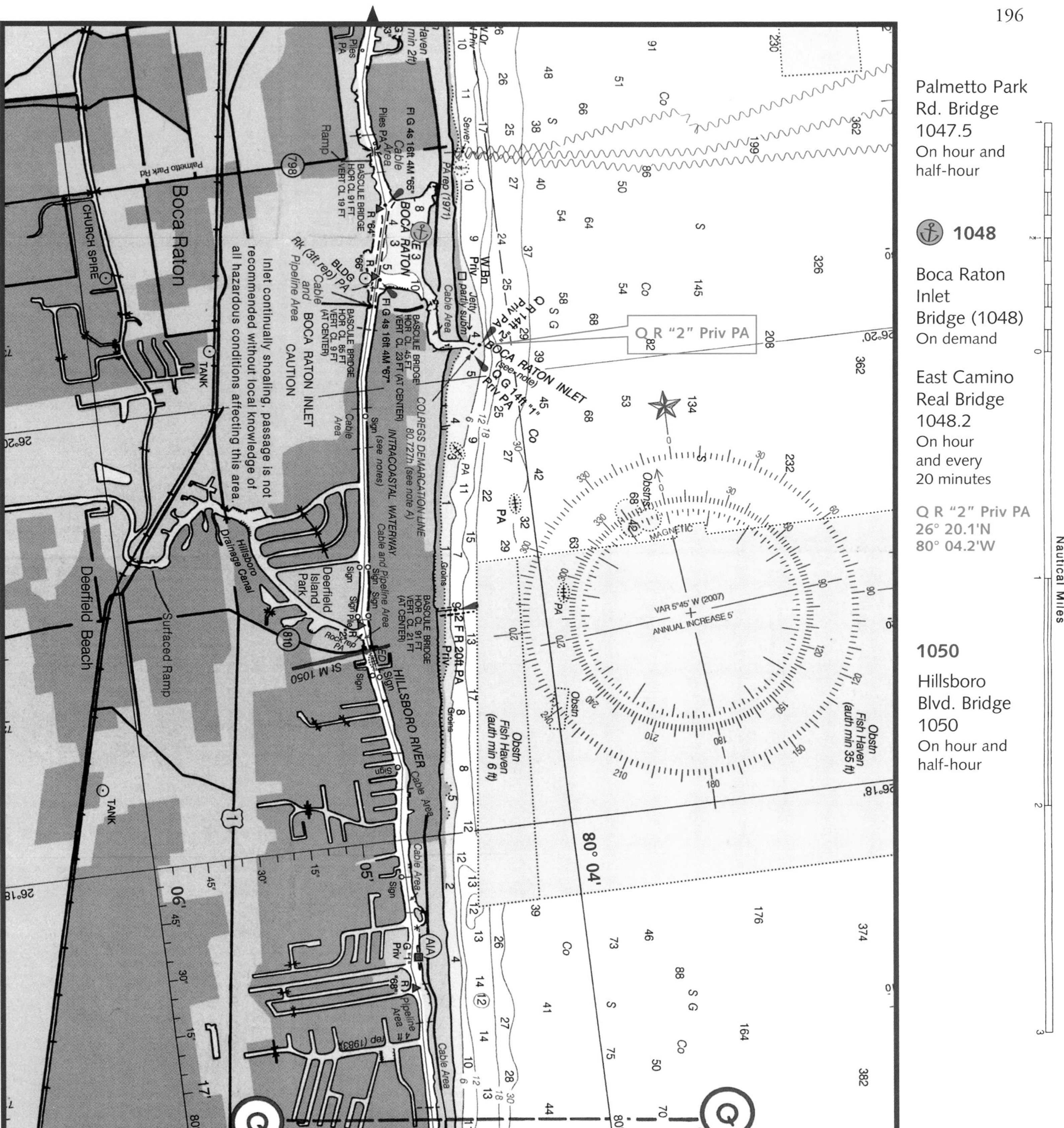

Palmetto Park Rd. Bridge 1047.5
On hour and half-hour

1048

Boca Raton Inlet Bridge (1048)
On demand

East Camino Real Bridge 1048.2
On hour and every 20 minutes

Q R "2" Priv PA
26° 20.1'N
80° 04.2'W

1050

Hillsboro Blvd. Bridge 1050
On hour and half-hour

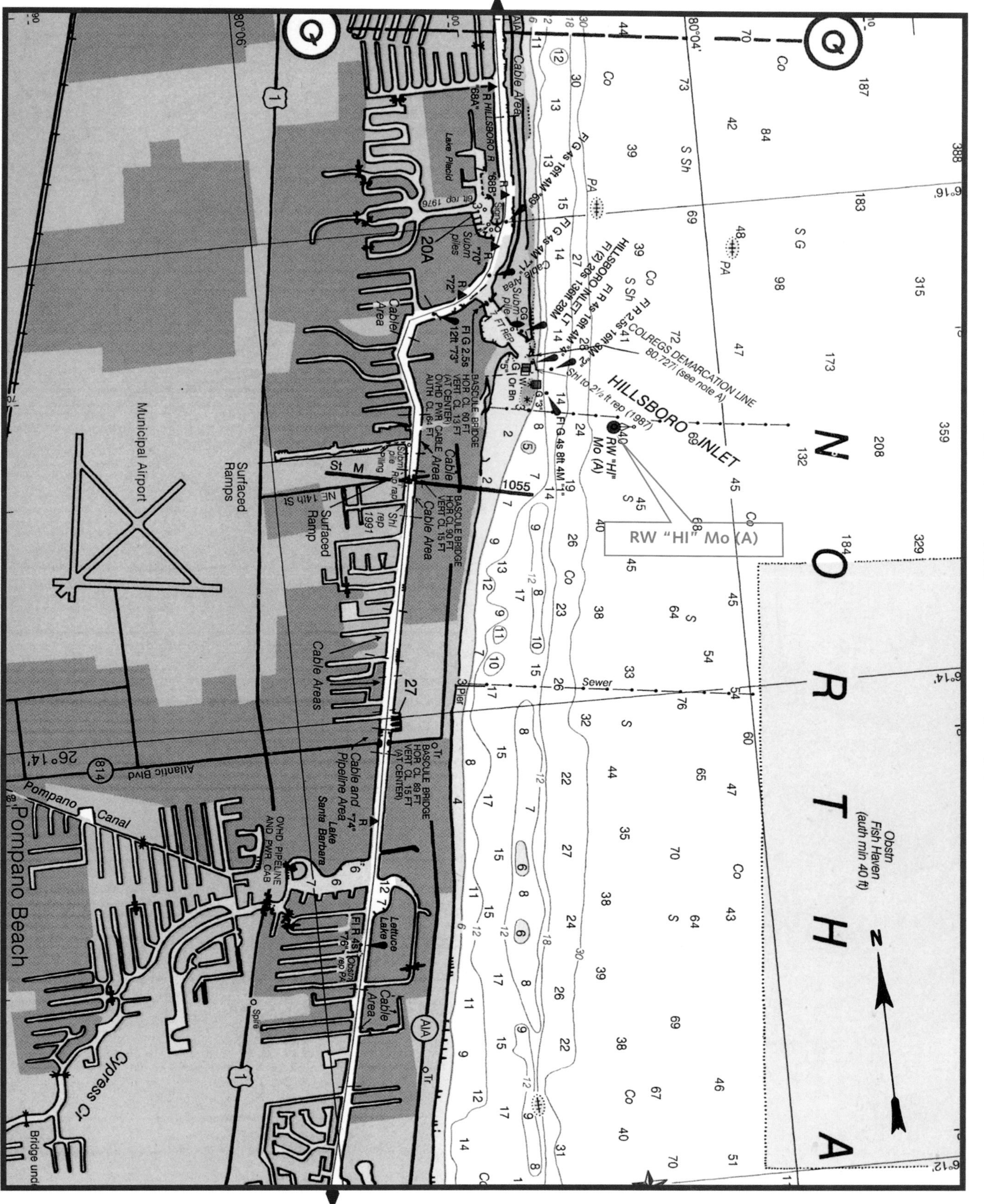

Hillsboro Inlet Bridge (1054)
On hour and every 15 minutes

Northeast 14th Street Bridge 1055
On quarter and three-quarter hour

1055

RW "HI" Mo (A)
26° 15.1'N
80° 04.5'W

Atlantic Blvd. Bridge 1056
On hour and half-hour

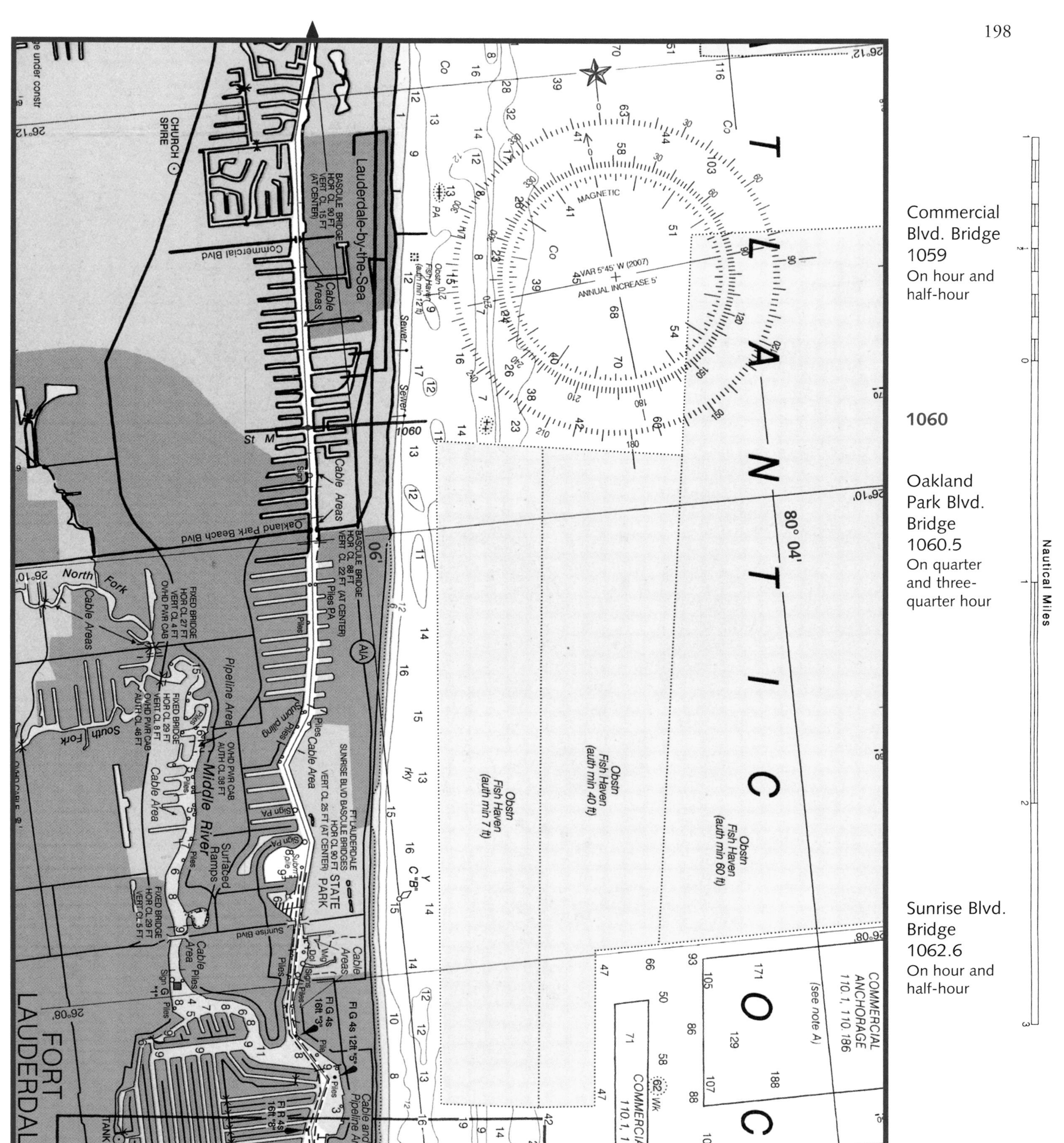

Commercial Blvd. Bridge
1059
On hour and half-hour

1060

Oakland Park Blvd. Bridge
1060.5
On quarter and three-quarter hour

Sunrise Blvd. Bridge
1062.6
On hour and half-hour

Joins Page 233

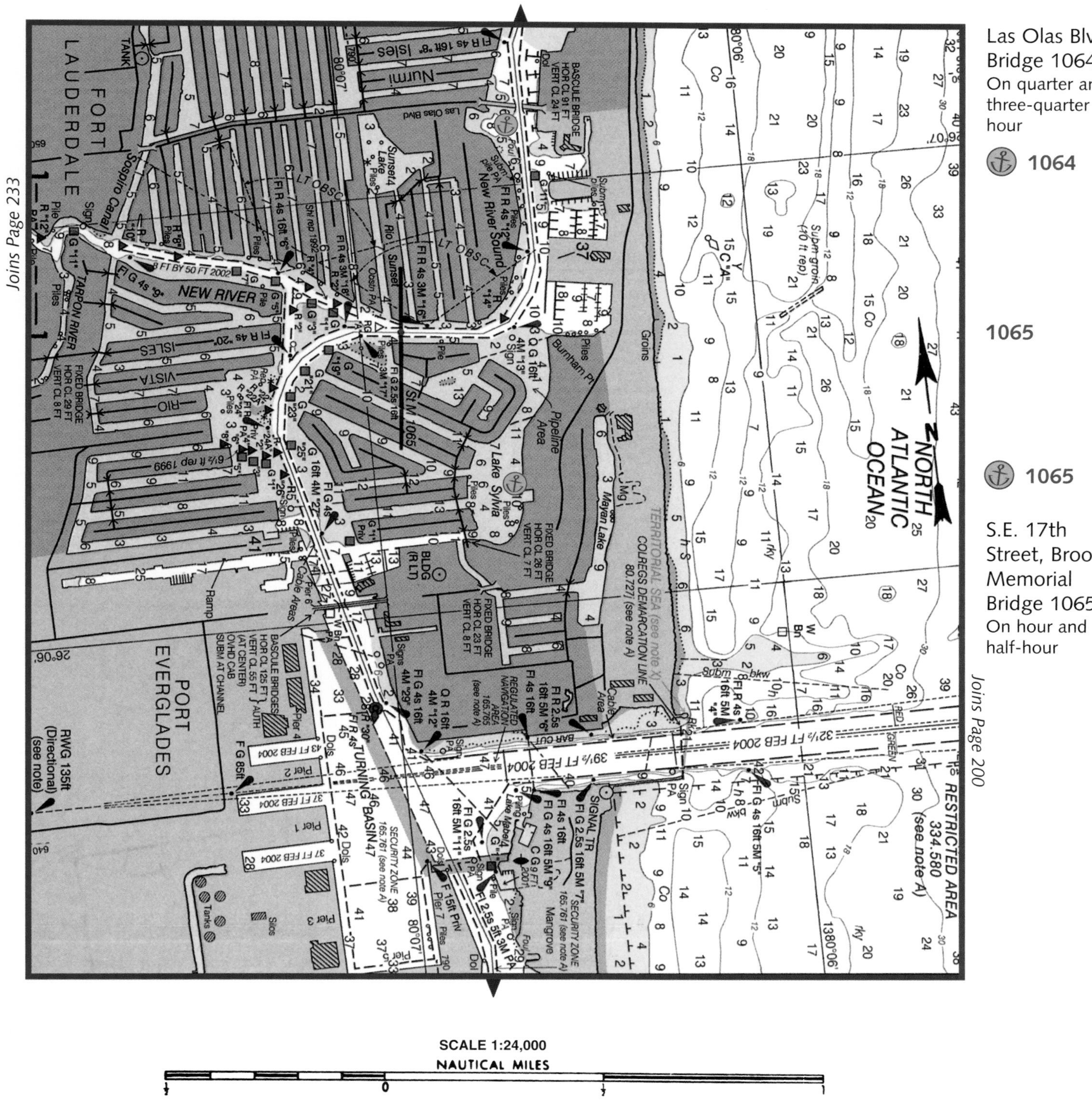

Joins Page 200

Las Olas Blvd. Bridge 1064.0
On quarter and three-quarter hour

1064

1065

1065

S.E. 17th Street, Brooks Memorial Bridge 1065.9
On hour and half-hour

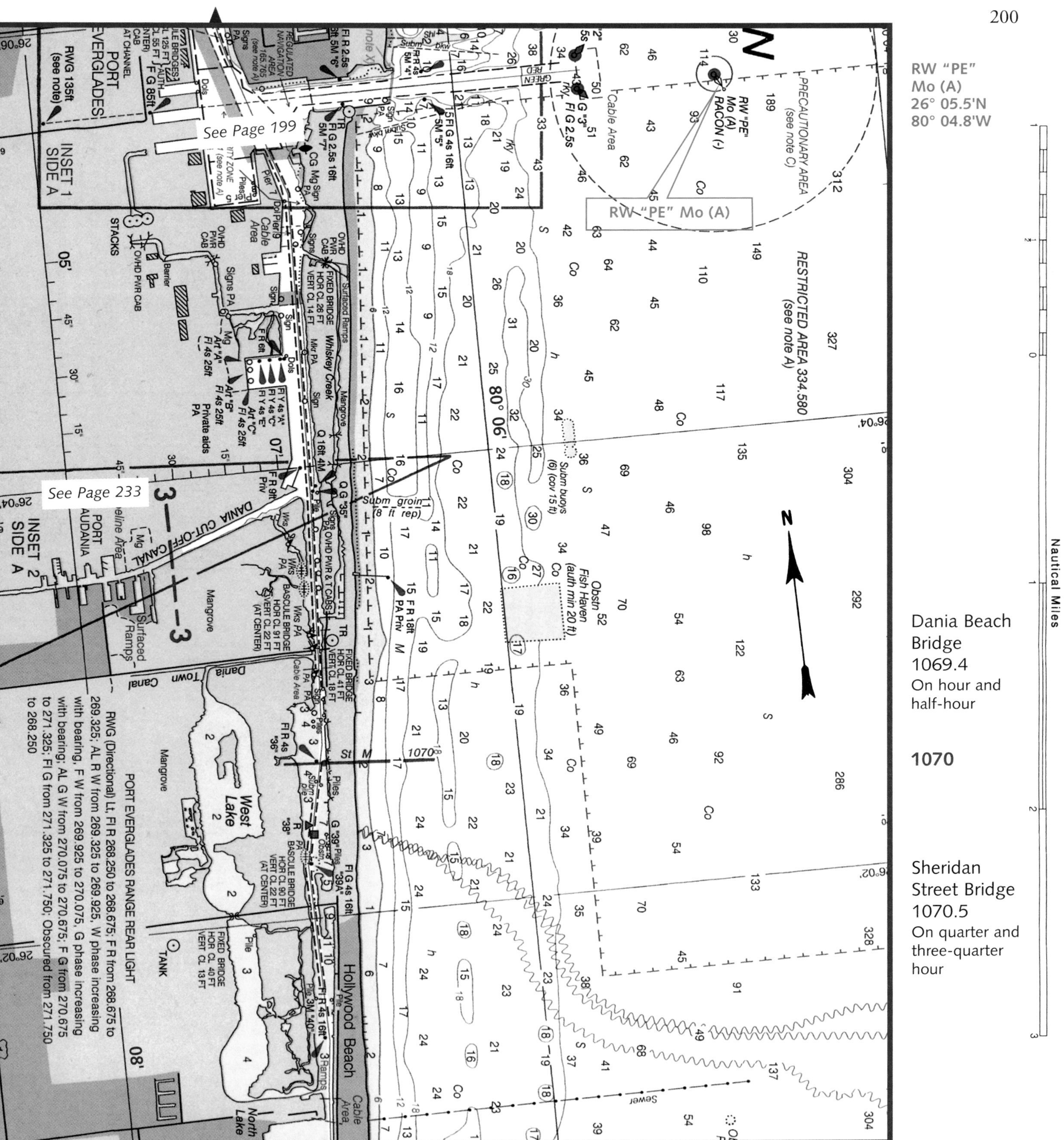
RW "PE"
Mo (A)
26° 05.5'N
80° 04.8'W
Dania Beach
Bridge
1069.4
On hour and
half-hour
1070
Sheridan
Street Bridge
1070.5
On quarter and
three-quarter
hour
Nautical Miles
RW "PE" Mo (A)
RESTRICTED AREA 334.580
(see note A)
PRECAUTIONARY AREA
(see note C)
See Page 199
See Page 233
INSET 1
SIDE A
INSET 2
SIDE A
PORT
EVERGLADES
PORT
LAUDANIA
DANIA CUT-OFF CANAL
Dania Town Canal
West
Lake
North
Lake
Hollywood Beach
Whiskey Creek
Mangrove
STACKS
TANK
Obstn
Fish Haven
(auth min 20 ft)
Subm buoys
(6) (cov 15 ft)
Subm groin
(8 ft rep)
Cable Area
Sewer
80° 06'
PORT EVERGLADES RANGE REAR LIGHT
RWG (Directional) Lt, Fl R 268.250 to 268.675; F R from 268.675 to
269.325; AL R W from 269.325 to 269.925, W phase increasing
with bearing, F W from 269.925 to 270.075, G phase increasing
with bearing; AL G W from 270.075 to 270.675; F G from 270.675
to 271.325; Fl G from 271.325 to 271.750; Obscured from 271.750
to 268.250

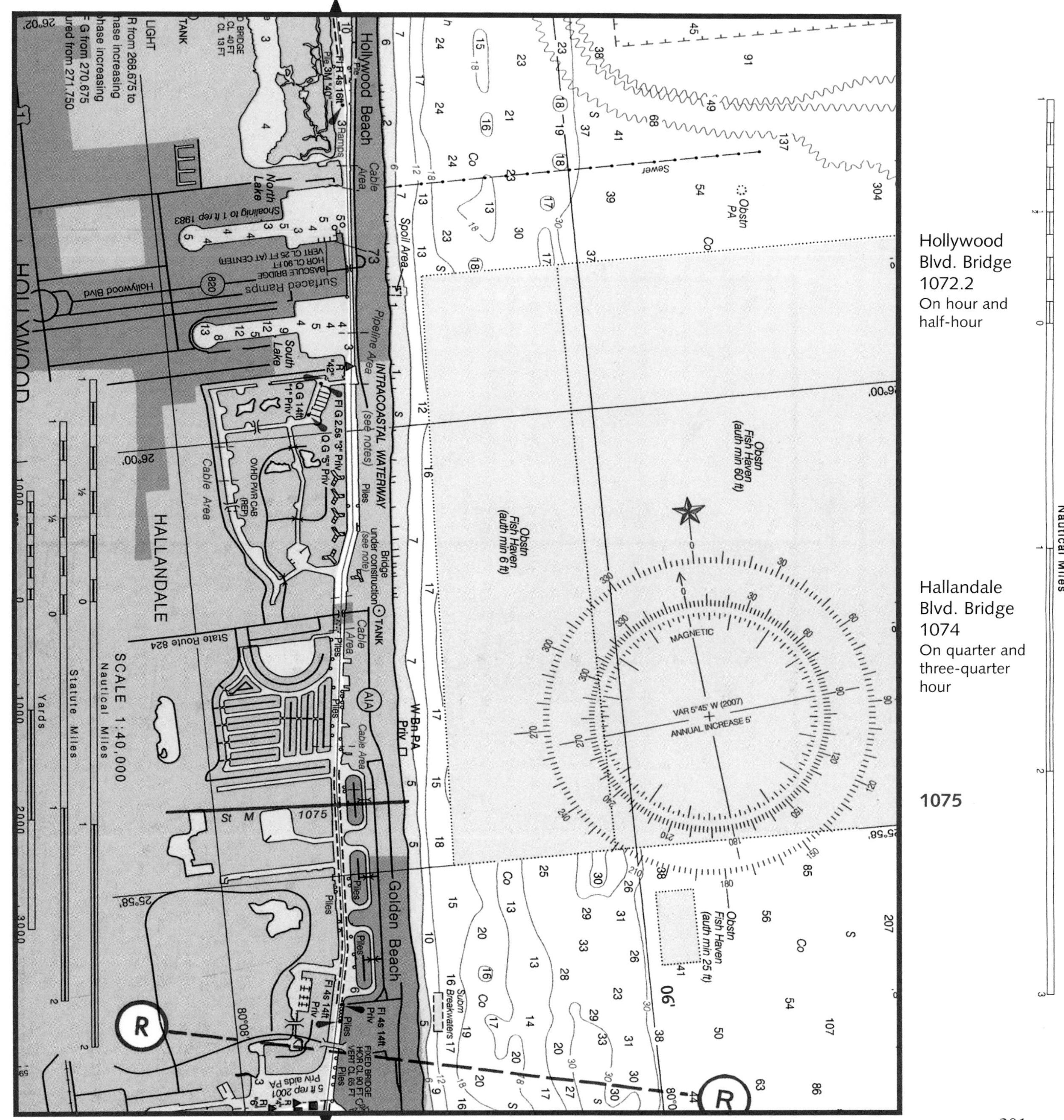

Hollywood Blvd. Bridge 1072.2
On hour and half-hour

Hallandale Blvd. Bridge 1074
On quarter and three-quarter hour

1075

Nautical Miles

1077

Sunny Isles
Bridge 1078
Weekdays on quarter and three-quarter hour: 7 A.M.–6 P.M. Weekends and holidays on quarter and three-quarter hour: 10 A.M.–6 P.M.

1080

1080

Q PA Priv
25° 53.9'N
80° 07.2'W

Broad
Causeway
Bridge
1081.4
On quarter and three-quarter hour: 8 A.M.–6 P.M.

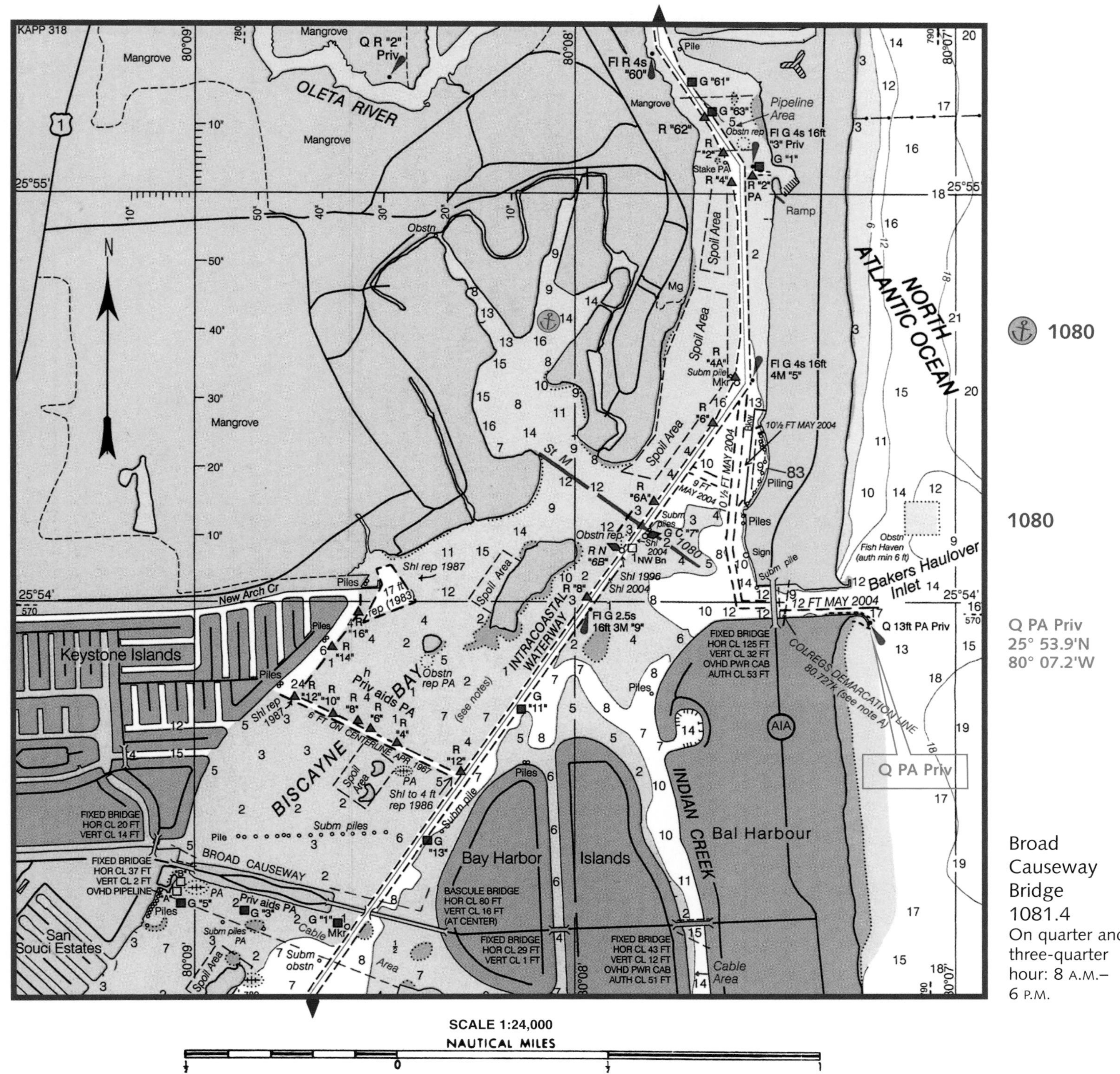

KAPP 318
OLETA RIVER
Mangrove
NORTH ATLANTIC OCEAN
Bakers Haulover Inlet
INTRACOASTAL WATERWAY
BISCAYNE BAY
Keystone Islands
New Arch Cr
BROAD CAUSEWAY
Bay Harbor Islands
Bal Harbour
INDIAN CREEK
San Souci Estates
Pipeline Area
Spoil Area
FIXED BRIDGE HOR CL 125 FT VERT CL 32 FT OVHD PWR CAB AUTH CL 53 FT
FIXED BRIDGE HOR CL 20 FT VERT CL 14 FT
FIXED BRIDGE HOR CL 37 FT VERT CL 2 FT OVHD PIPELINE
BASCULE BRIDGE HOR CL 80 FT VERT CL 16 FT (AT CENTER)
FIXED BRIDGE HOR CL 29 FT VERT CL 1 FT
FIXED BRIDGE HOR CL 43 FT VERT CL 12 FT OVHD PWR CAB AUTH CL 51 FT
COLREGS DEMARCATION LINE 80.727k (see note A)
Q 13ft PA Priv
Q PA Priv
SCALE 1:24,000
NAUTICAL MILES
1080
1080
Q PA Priv
25° 53.9'N
80° 07.2'W
Broad
Causeway
Bridge
1081.4
On quarter and
three-quarter
hour: 8 A.M.–
6 P.M.

79th St. Causeway Bridge 1084.6
On demand

1085

Julia Tuttle Bridge 1087.1
56 feet

Nautical Miles

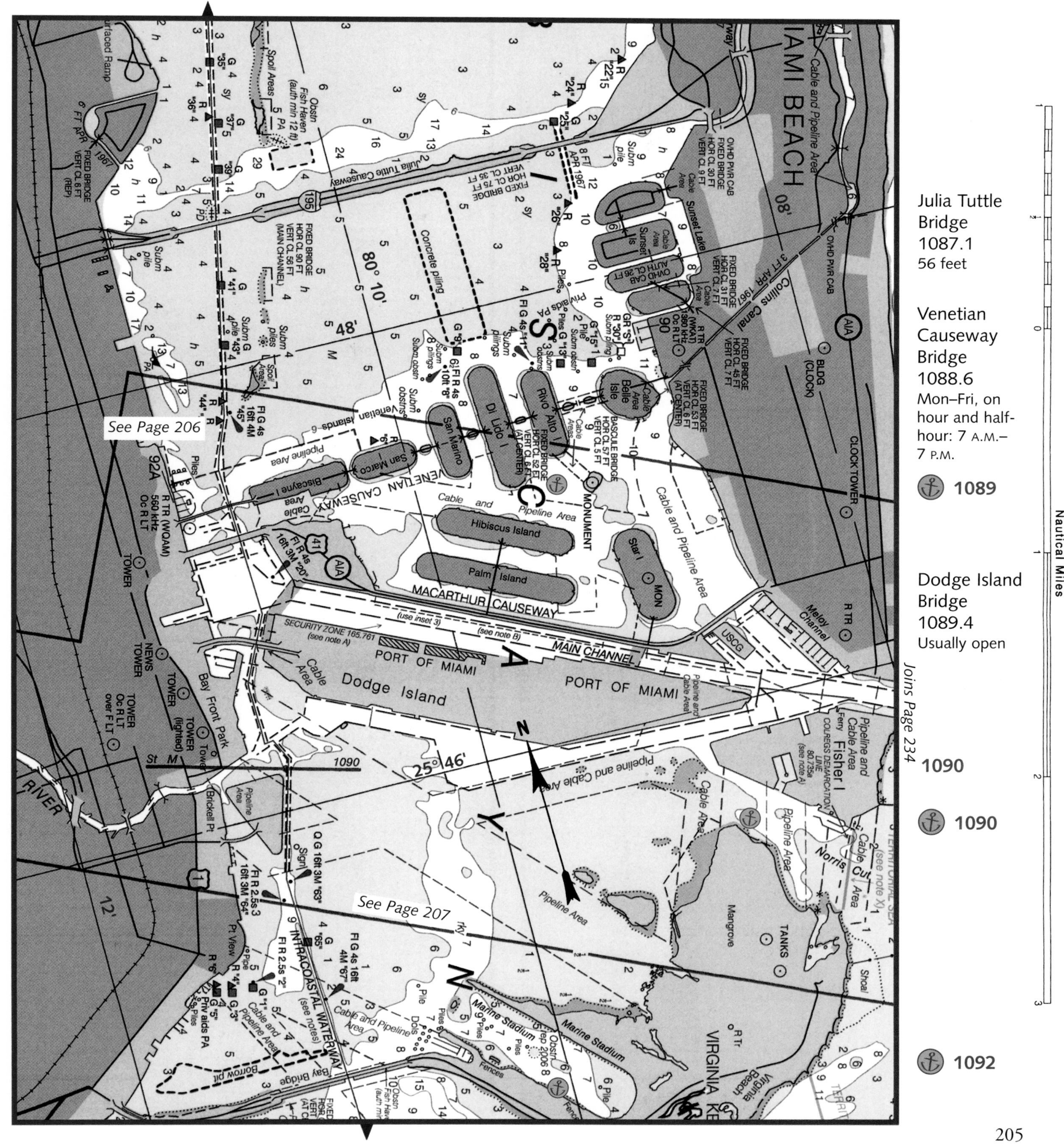

See Page 206
See Page 207
Joins Page 234

Joins Page 205

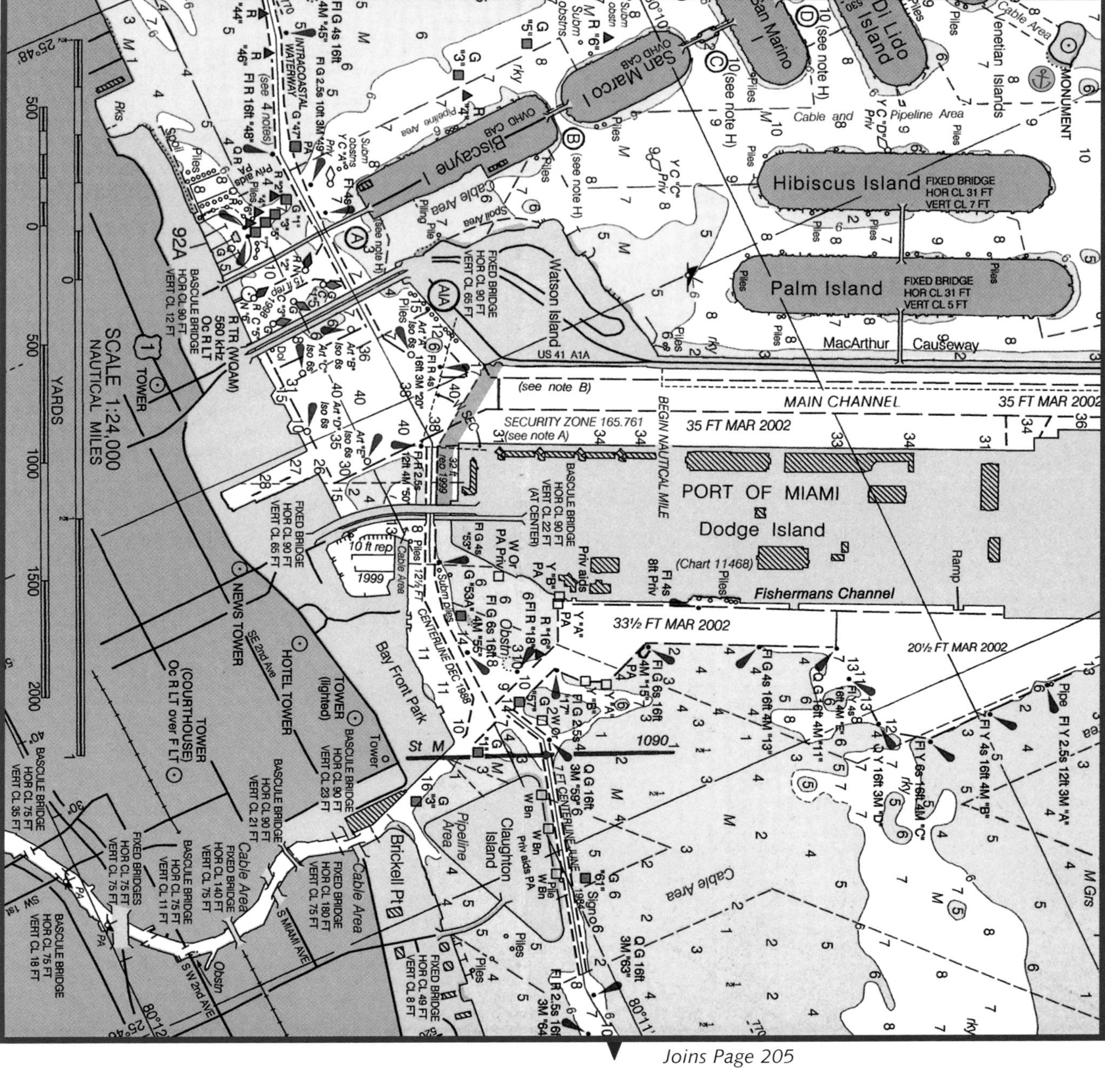

Joins Page 234

Joins Page 205

1089

Venetian Causeway Bridge 1088.6
Mon–Fri, on hour and half-hour: 7 A.M.–7 P.M.

Dodge Island Bridge 1089.4
Usually open

1090

Joins Page 205

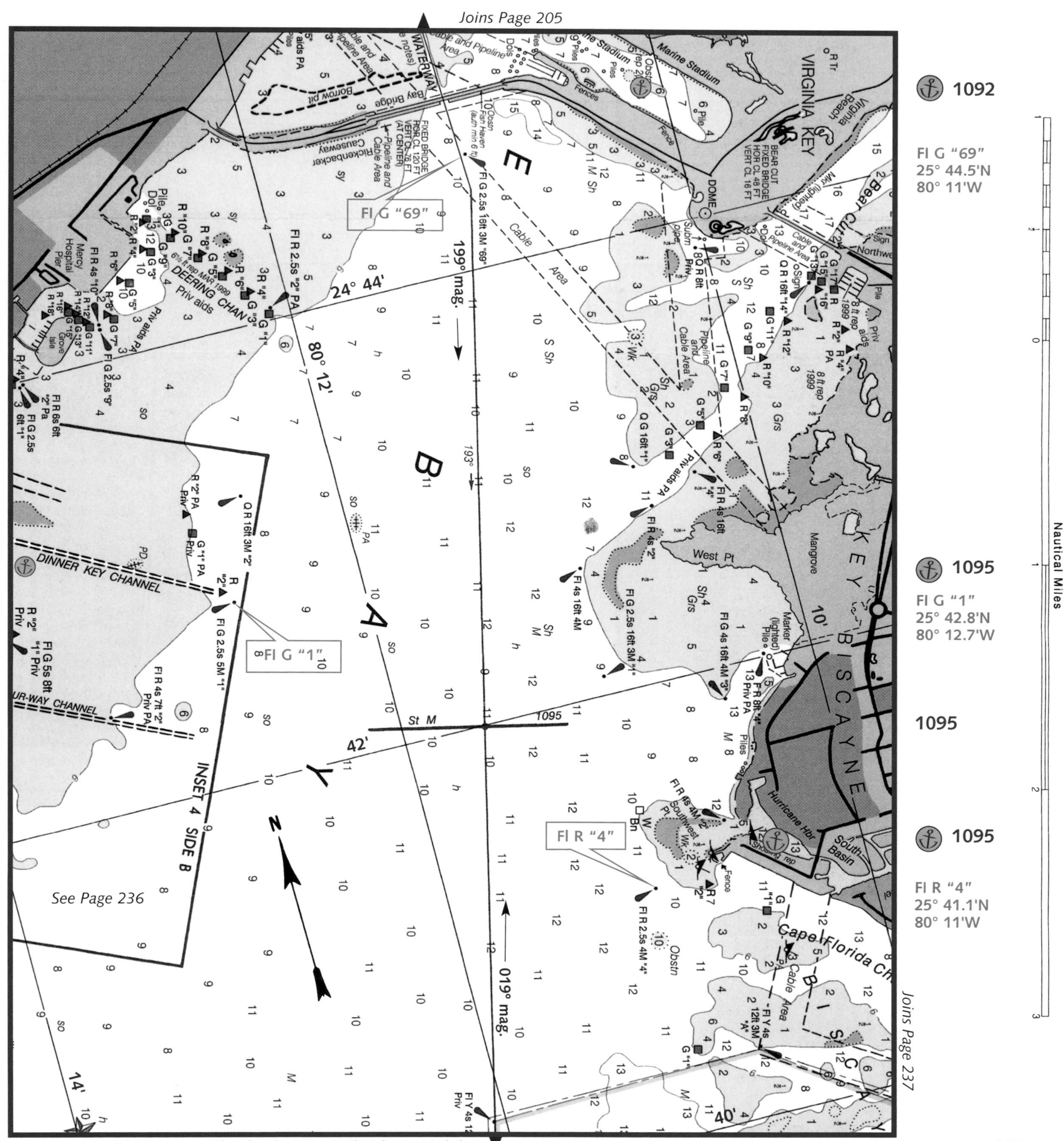

Joins Page 237

Joins Intracoastal Waterway Chartbook: Miami, Florida, to Mobile, Alabama

Joins Page 60

Joins Page 61

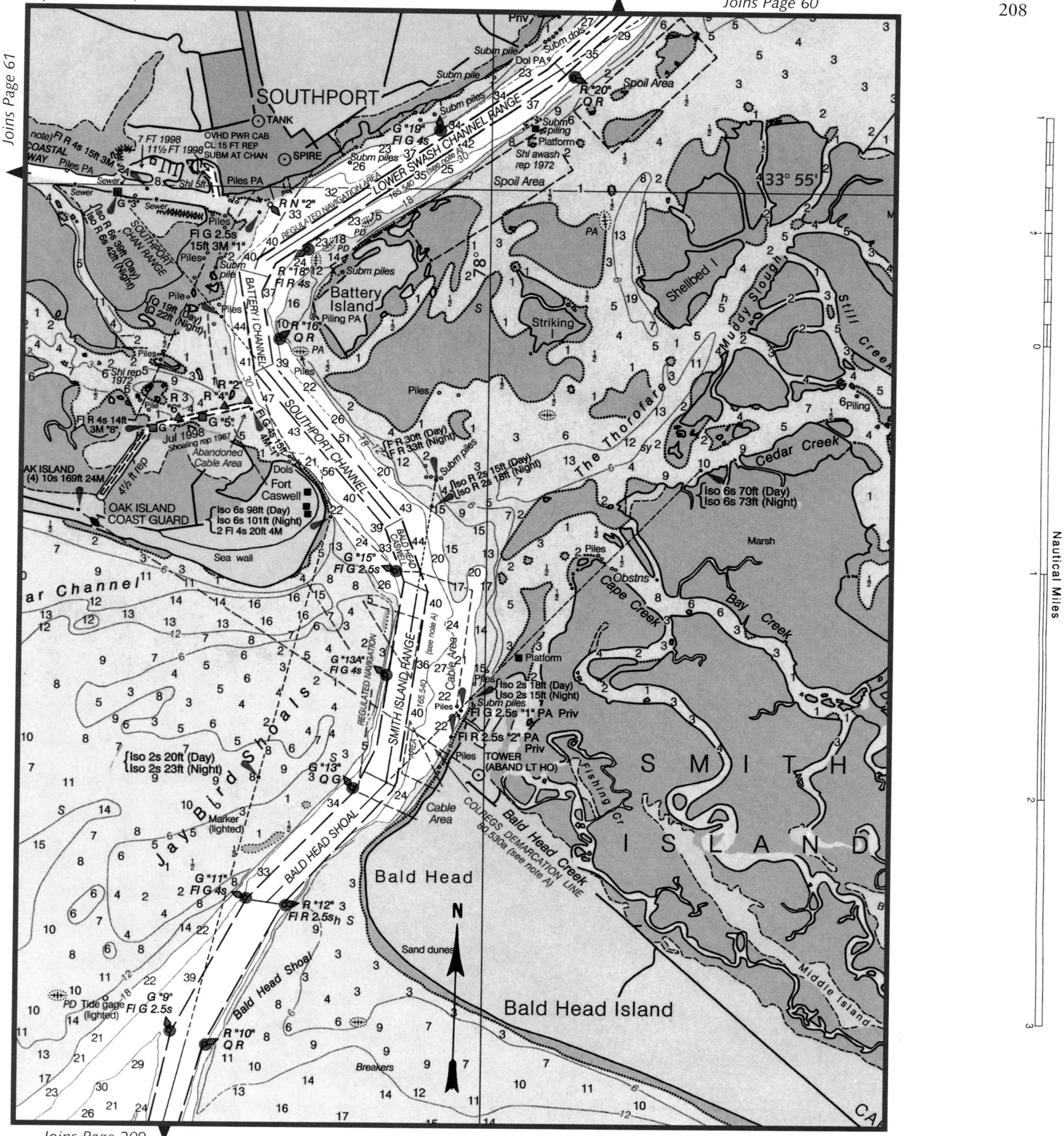

SOUTHPORT
TANK
SPIRE
OVHD PWR CAB
CL 15 FT REP
SUBM AT CHAN
7 FT 1998
11½ FT 1998
COASTAL
WAY
Piles PA
Sewer
Shl 5ft
R N "2"
G "3"
Fl G 2.5s
15ft 3M "1"
SOUTHPORT CHAN RANGE
Iso R 6s 39ft (Day)
Iso R 6s 42ft (Night)
Q 19ft (Day)
Q 22ft (Night)
Shl rep 1972
Fl R 4s 14ft 3M "8"
Jul 1998
Shoaling rep 1987
Abandoned Cable Area
OAK ISLAND
(4) 10s 169ft 24M
4½ ft rep
OAK ISLAND COAST GUARD
Iso 6s 98ft (Day)
Iso 6s 101ft (Night)
2 Fl 4s 20ft 4M
Fort Caswell
Dols
Sea wall
LOWER SWASH CHANNEL RANGE
REGULATED NAVIGATION AREA
G "19"
Fl G 4s
R "20"
Q R
Spoil Area
Shl awash 2
rep 1972
Platform
Subm piling
Subm piles
Subm pile
Subm dols
Dol PA
BATTERY I CHANNEL
R "18" Fl R 4s
R "16" Q R
Battery Island
Piling PA
SOUTHPORT CHANNEL
Fl G 4s 15ft 4M
F R 30ft (Day)
F R 33ft (Night)
Iso R 2s 15ft (Day)
Iso R 2s 18ft (Night)
BALD HEAD CASWELL
Striking I
Shellbed I
Muddy Slough
Still Creek
The Thorofare
Cedar Creek
Iso 6s 70ft (Day)
Iso 6s 73ft (Night)
Marsh
Obstns
Cape Creek
Bay Creek
33° 55'
78°
ar Channel
G "15"
Fl G 2.5s
G "13A"
Fl G 4s
SMITH ISLAND RANGE
Cable Area
Platform
Iso 2s 18ft (Day)
Iso 2s 15ft (Night)
Fl G 2.5s "1" PA Priv
Fl R 2.5s "2" PA Priv
TOWER (ABAND LT HO)
Fishing Cr
S M I T H
I S L A N D
Jay Bird Shoals
Iso 2s 20ft (Day)
Iso 2s 23ft (Night)
G "13"
Q G
Marker (lighted)
BALD HEAD SHOAL
Cable Area
COLREGS DEMARCATION LINE 80.530a (see note A)
Bald Head Creek
Bald Head
G "11"
Fl G 4s
R "12"
Fl R 2.5s
Sand dunes
Bald Head Shoal
Bald Head Island
Middle Island
G "9"
Fl G 2.5s
Tide gage (lighted)
R "10"
Q R
Breakers
Nautical Miles

Joins Page 209

Joins Page 208

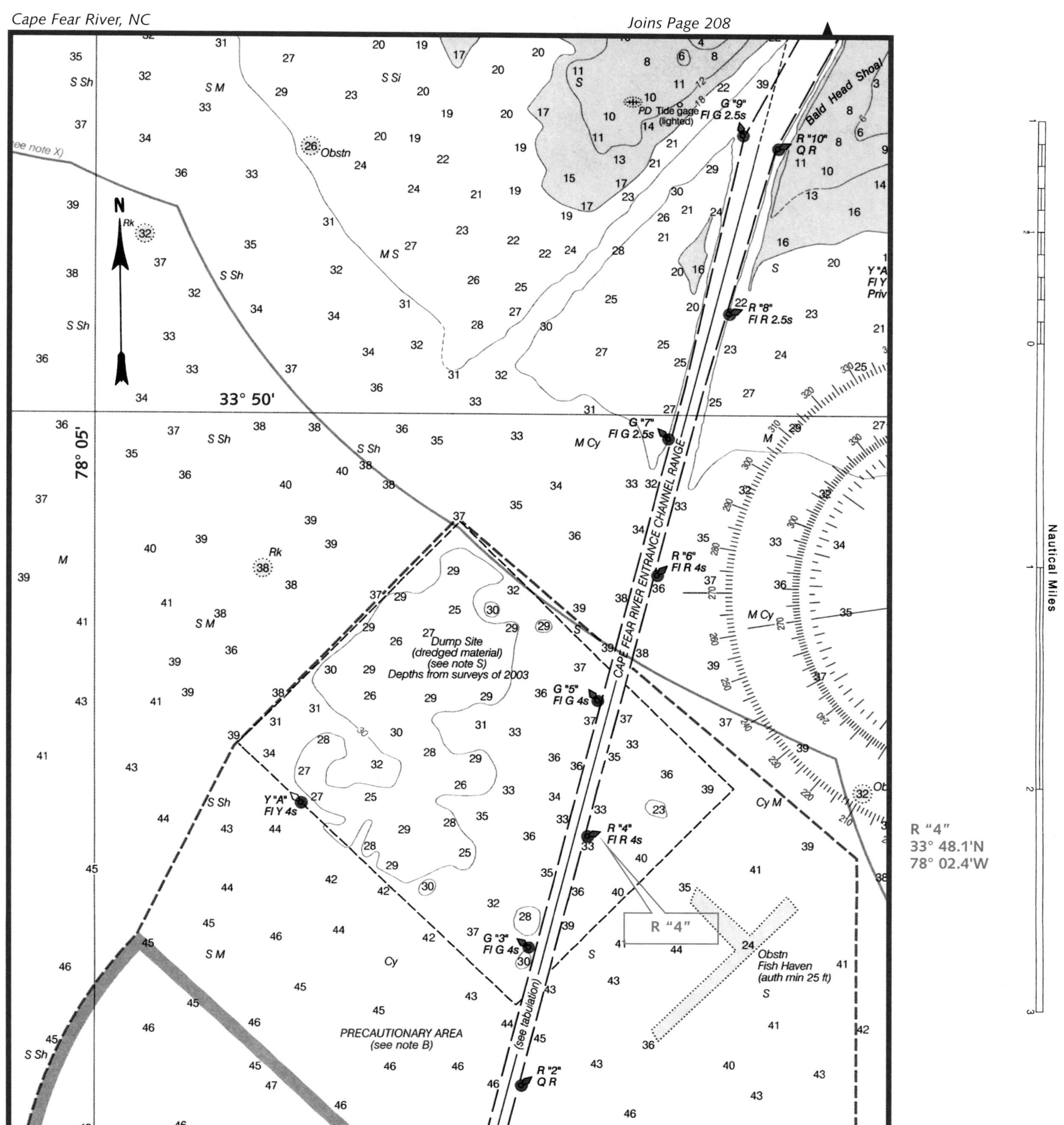

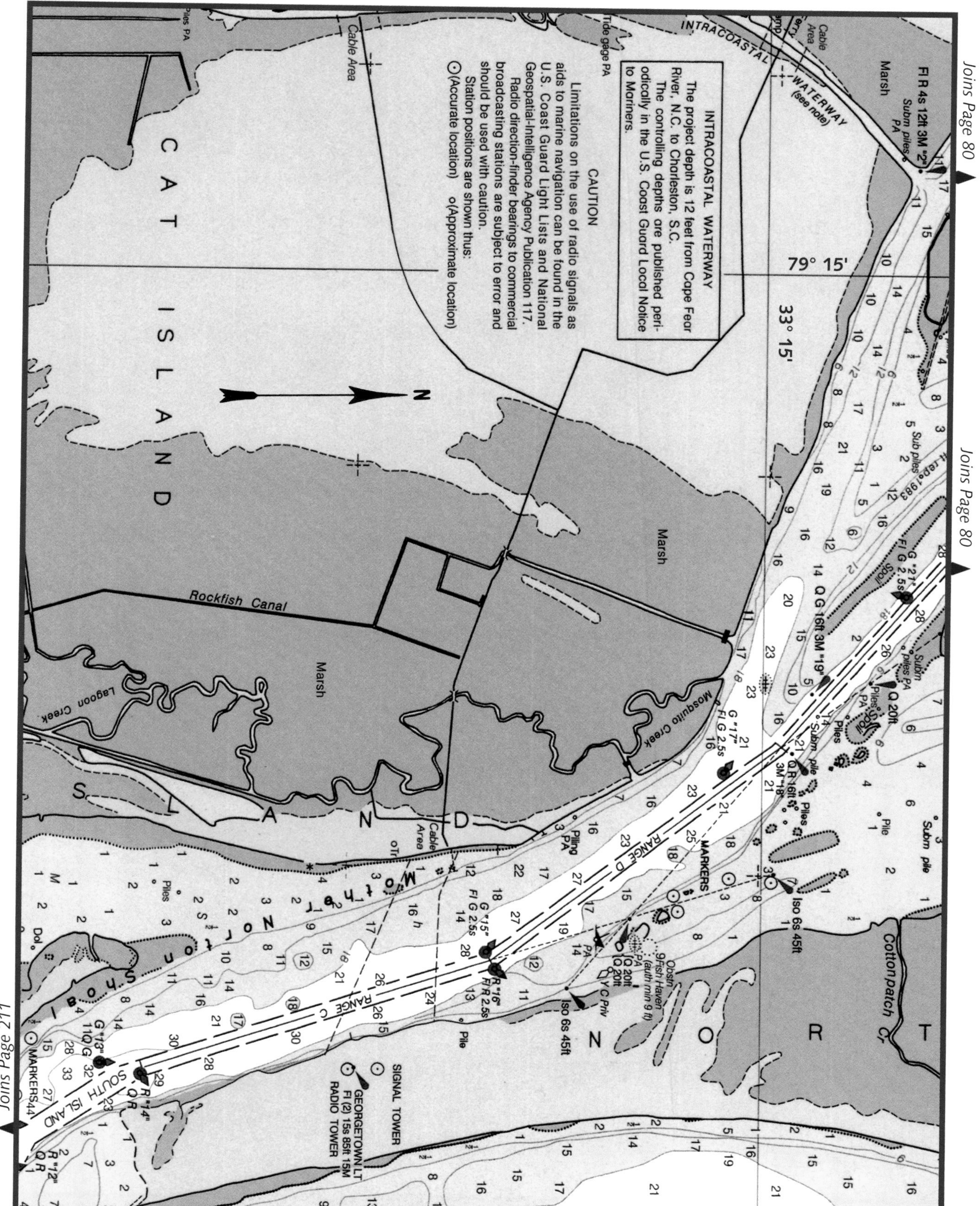
INTRACOASTAL WATERWAY
The project depth is 12 feet from Cape Fear River, N.C. to Charleston, S.C.
The controlling depths are published periodically in the U.S. Coast Guard Local Notice to Mariners.
CAUTION
Limitations on the use of radio signals as aids to marine navigation can be found in the U.S. Coast Guard Light Lists and National Geospatial-Intelligence Agency Publication 117.
Radio direction-finder bearings to commercial broadcasting stations are subject to error and should be used with caution.
Station positions are shown thus:
⊙(Accurate location) o(Approximate location)
CAT ISLAND
Marsh
Rockfish Canal
Lagoon Creek
Mosquito Creek
Cottonpatch Cr
Mother Norton Shoal
SOUTH ISLAND
RANGE C
RANGE D
GEORGETOWN LT
Fl (2) 15s 85ft 15M
RADIO TOWER
SIGNAL TOWER
MARKERS
Iso 6s 45ft
Q G 16ft 3M "19"
Q R 16ft 3M "18"
Fl R 4s 12ft 3M "2"
G "21" Fl G 2.5s
G "17" Fl G 2.5s
G "15" Fl G 2.5s
R "16" Fl R 2.5s
G "13" 11Q G
R "14" Q R
R "12" Q R
Q 20ft
Obstn
Fish Haven (auth min 9 ft)
Y C Priv
Cable Area
Tide gage PA
INTRACOASTAL WATERWAY (see note)
79° 15'
33° 15'
Joins Page 80
Joins Page 211
Nautical Miles

Joins Page 210

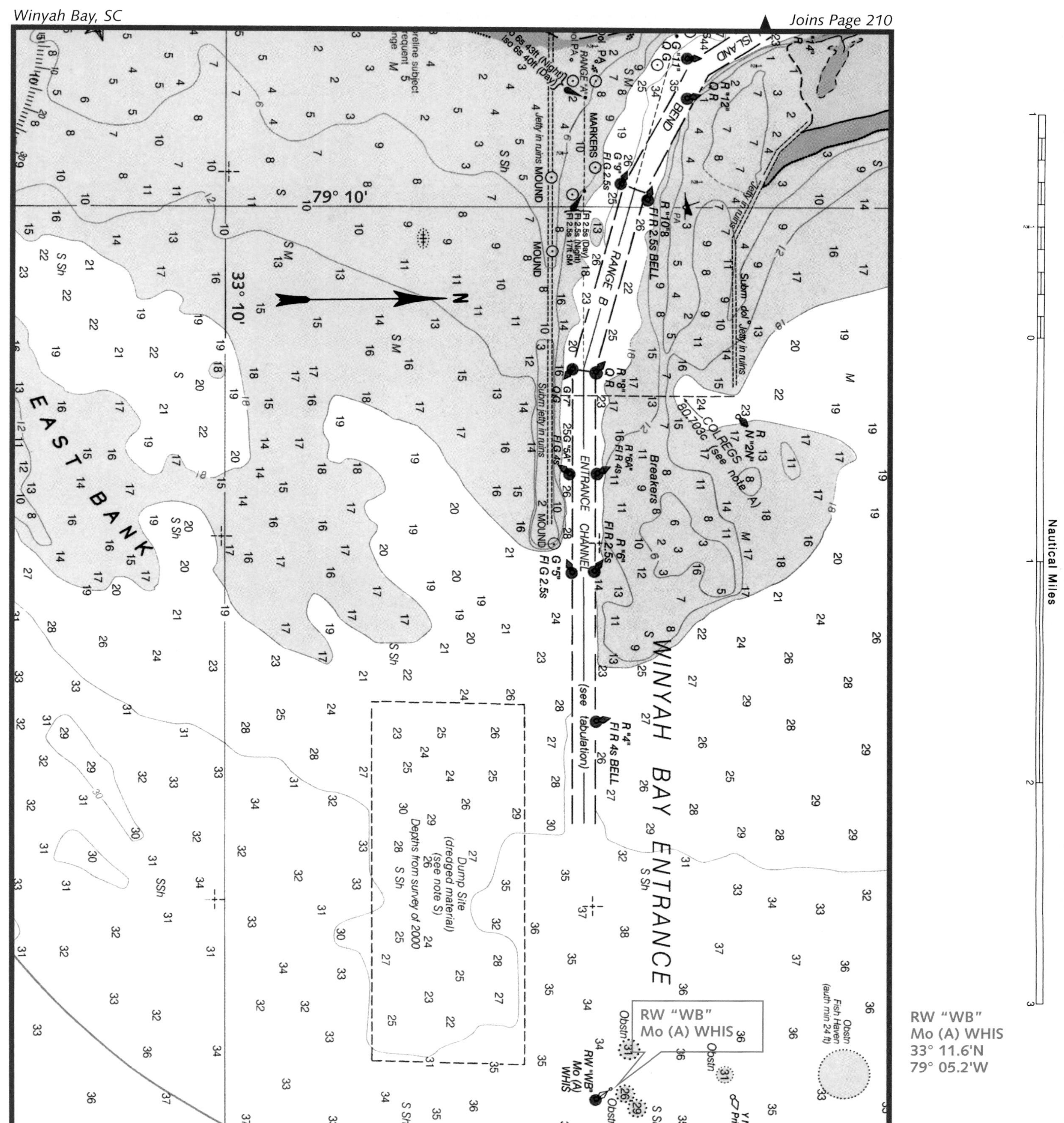

Charleston Entrance, SC

Joins Page 90

Joins Page 90

Joins Page 213

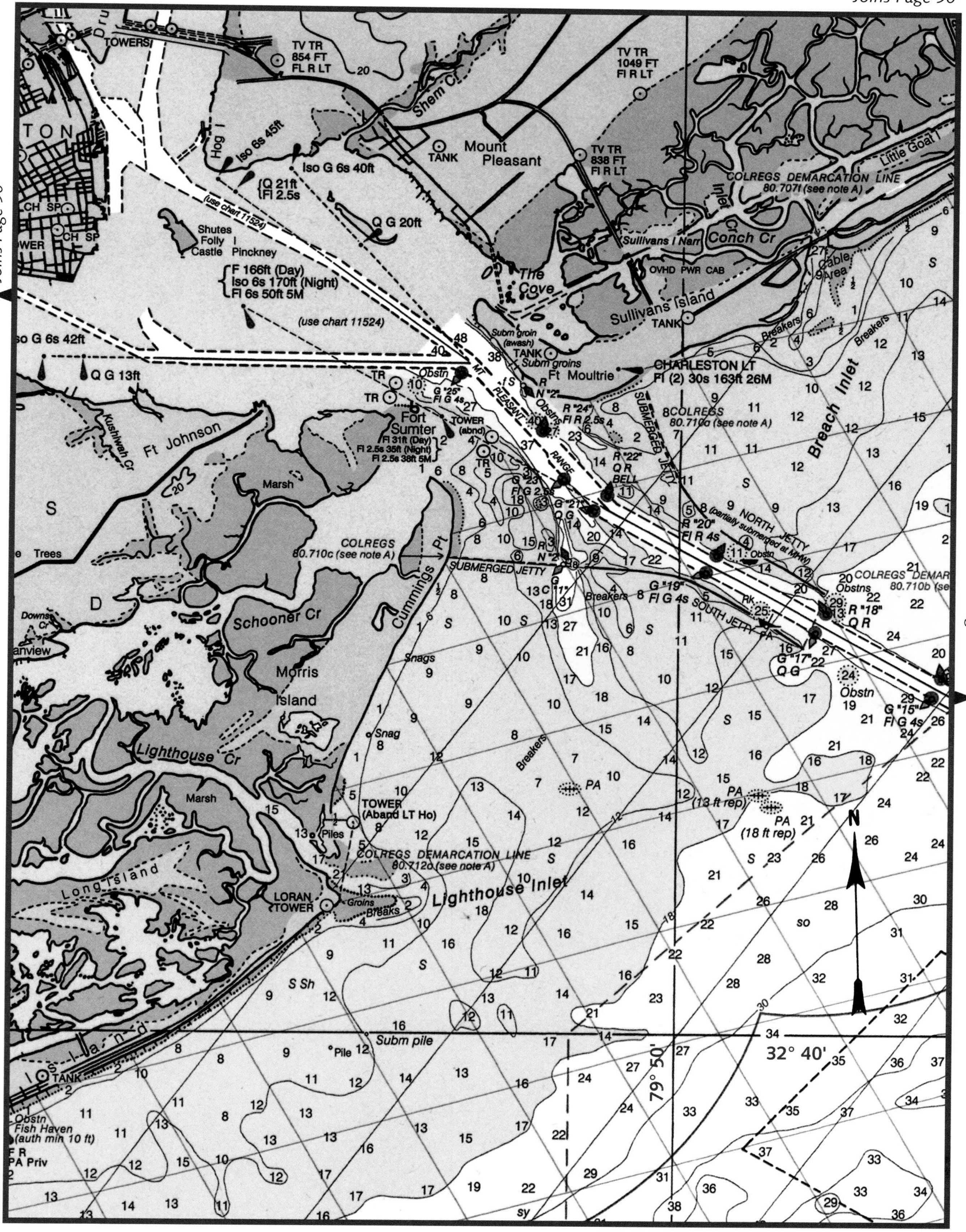

Nautical Miles

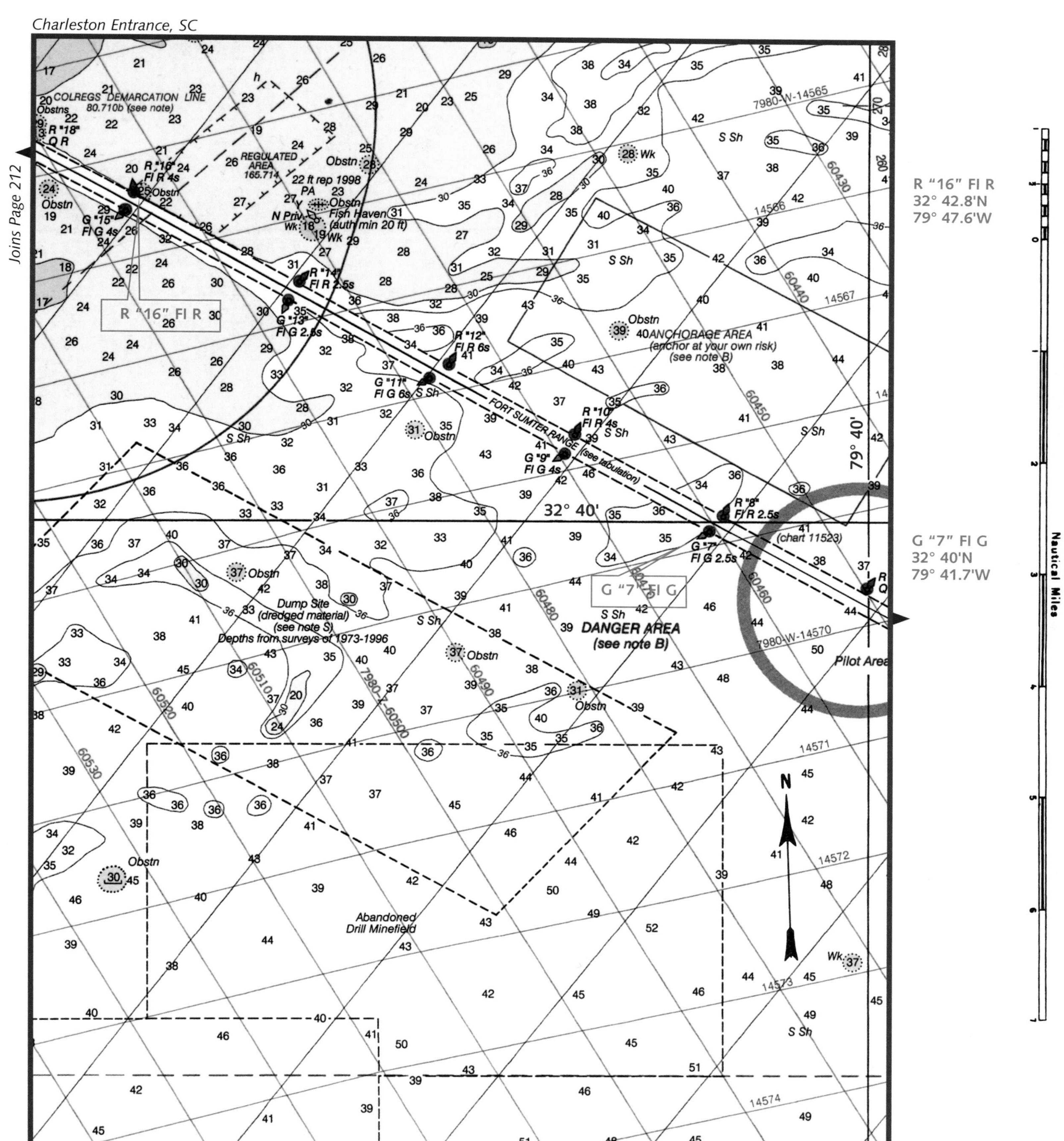

Joins Page 212
COLREGS DEMARCATION LINE
80.710b (see note)
R "18"
Q R
R "16"
Fl R 4s
G "15"
Fl G 4s
REGULATED AREA
165.714
Obstn
22 ft rep 1998
PA
N Priv
Fish Haven
(auth min 20 ft)
Wk
R "16" Fl R
R "14"
Fl R 2.5s
G "13"
Fl G 2.5s
R "12"
Fl R 6s
G "11"
Fl G 6s
S Sh
FORT SUMTER RANGE
(see tabulation)
R "10"
Fl R 4s
G "9"
Fl G 4s
Obstn
ANCHORAGE AREA
(anchor at your own risk)
(see note B)
32° 40'
79° 40'
R "8"
Fl R 2.5s
G "7"
Fl G 2.5s
(chart 11523)
G "7" Fl G
Dump Site
(dredged material)
(see note S)
Depths from surveys of 1973-1996
DANGER AREA
(see note B)
7980-W-14565
7980-W-14570
7980-Z-60500
Pilot Area
Abandoned
Drill Minefield
N
Nautical Miles
R "16" Fl R
32° 42.8'N
79° 47.6'W
G "7" Fl G
32° 40'N
79° 41.7'W

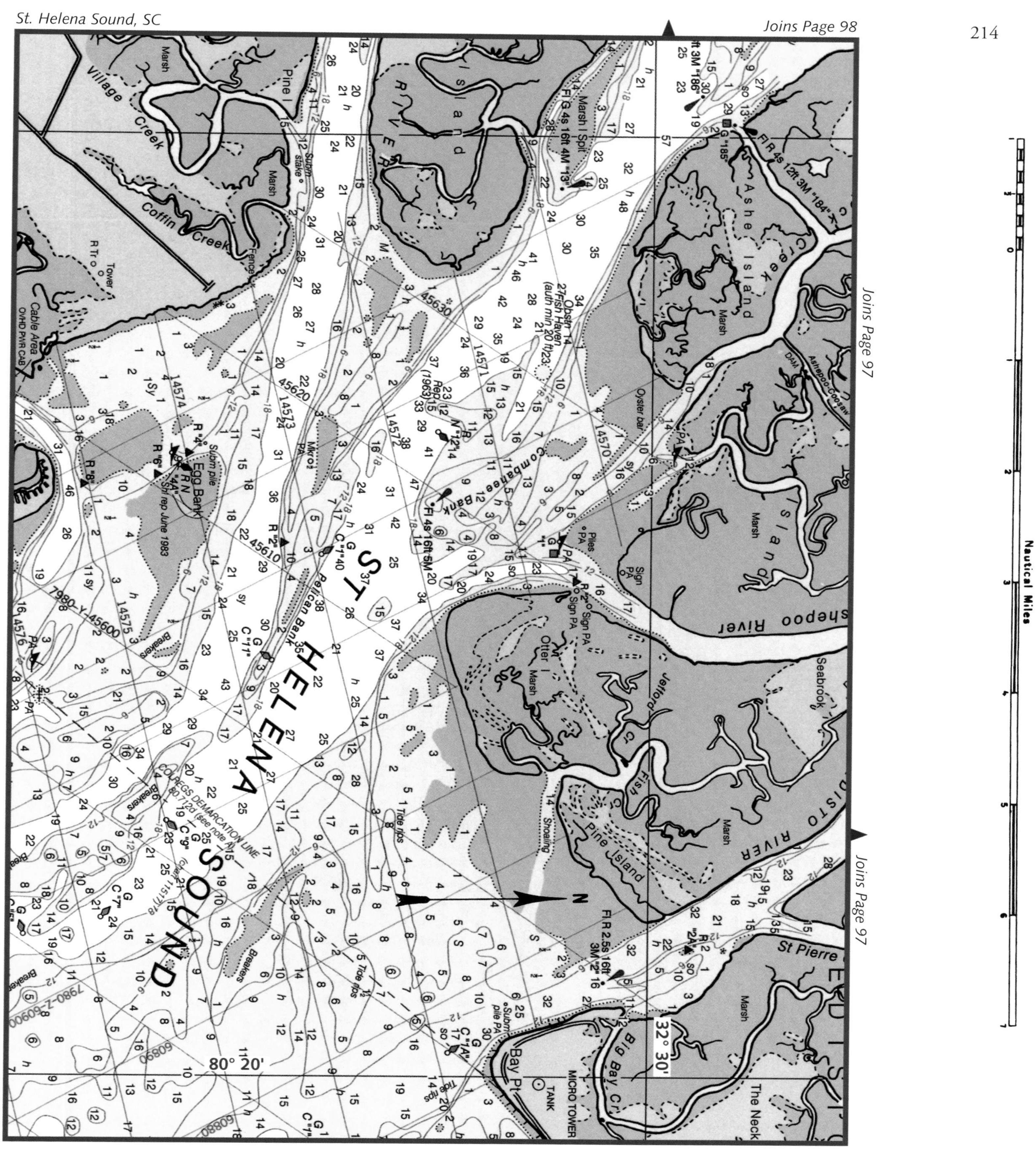

St. Helena Sound, SC

Joins Page 98

Joins Page 97

Joins Page 97

Joins Page 215

ST HELENA SOUND

Ashepoo River

EDISTO RIVER

St Pierre

Pine Island

Fish Cr

Jefford Cr

Otter I

Seabrook

Ashe Island

Combahee Bank

Pelican Bank

Egg Bank

Bay Pt

Big Bay Cr

The Neck

Coffin Creek

Village Creek

COLREGS DEMARCATION LINE

32° 30'

80° 20'

Nautical Miles

Joins Page 108

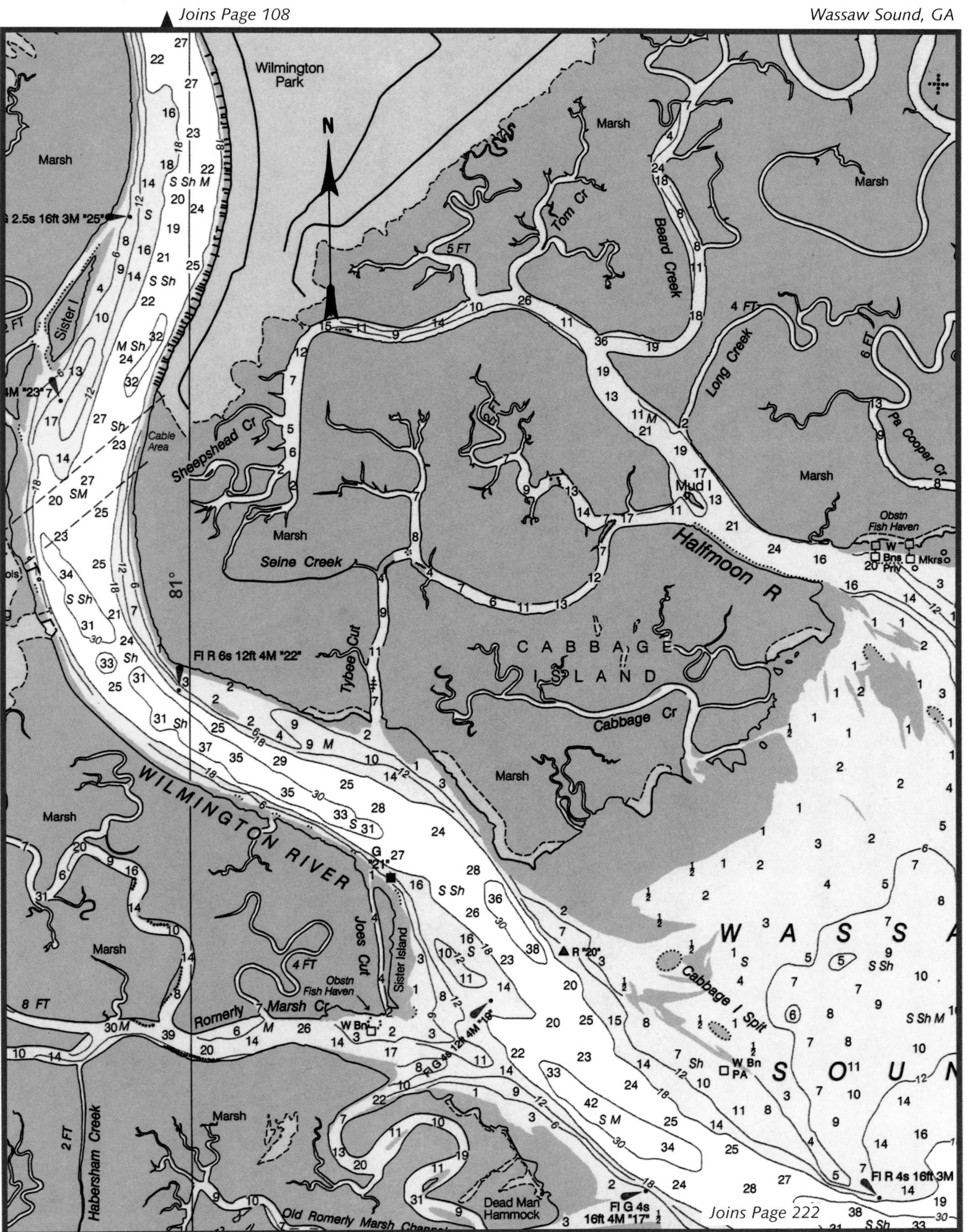

Joins Page 222

Inlets and Side Channels, Wassaw Sound, GA

Wassaw Sound, GA

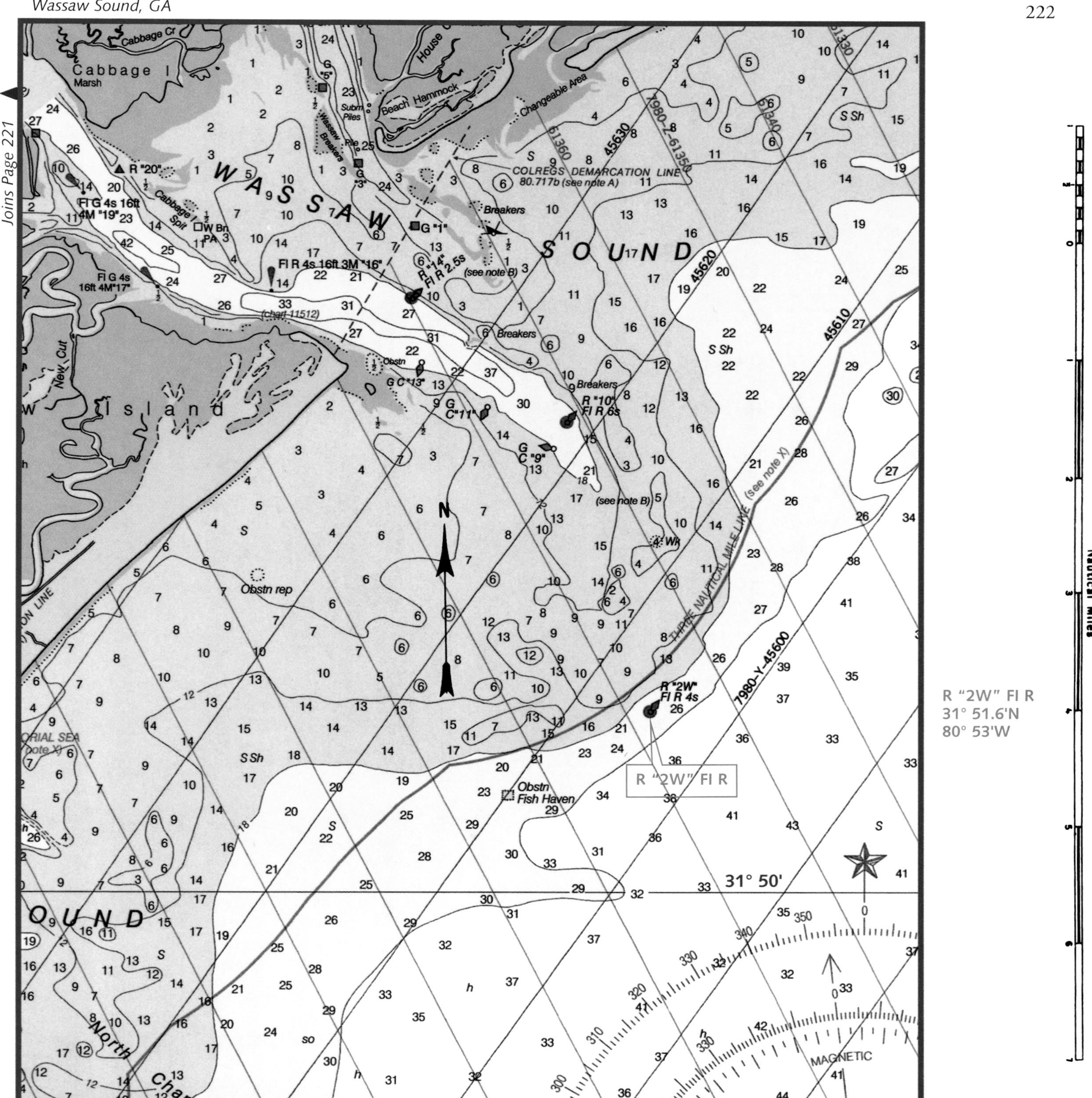

Joins Page 113

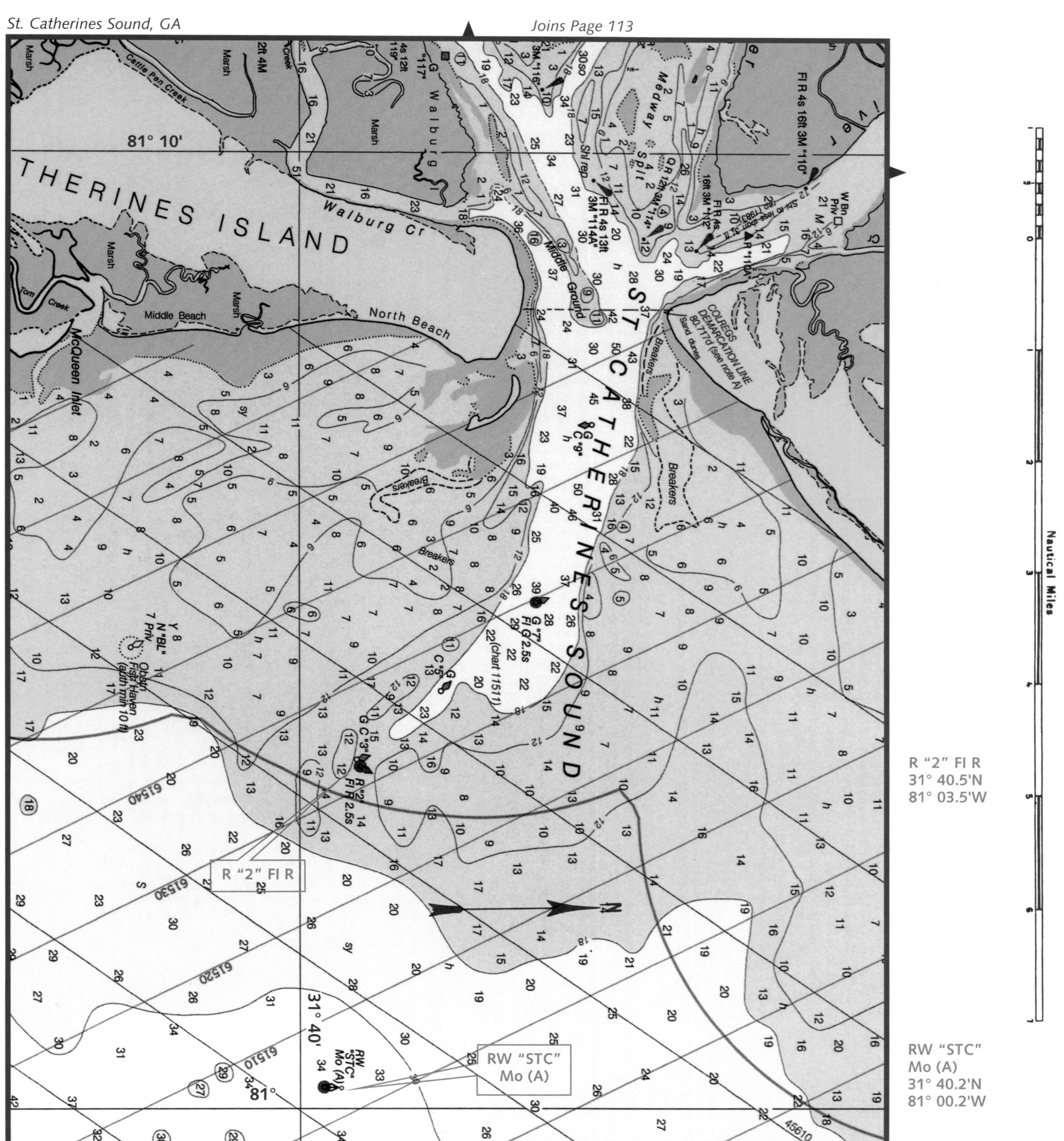

R "2" Fl R
31° 40.5'N
81° 03.5'W

RW "STC"
Mo (A)
31° 40.2'N
81° 00.2'W

Joins Page 115

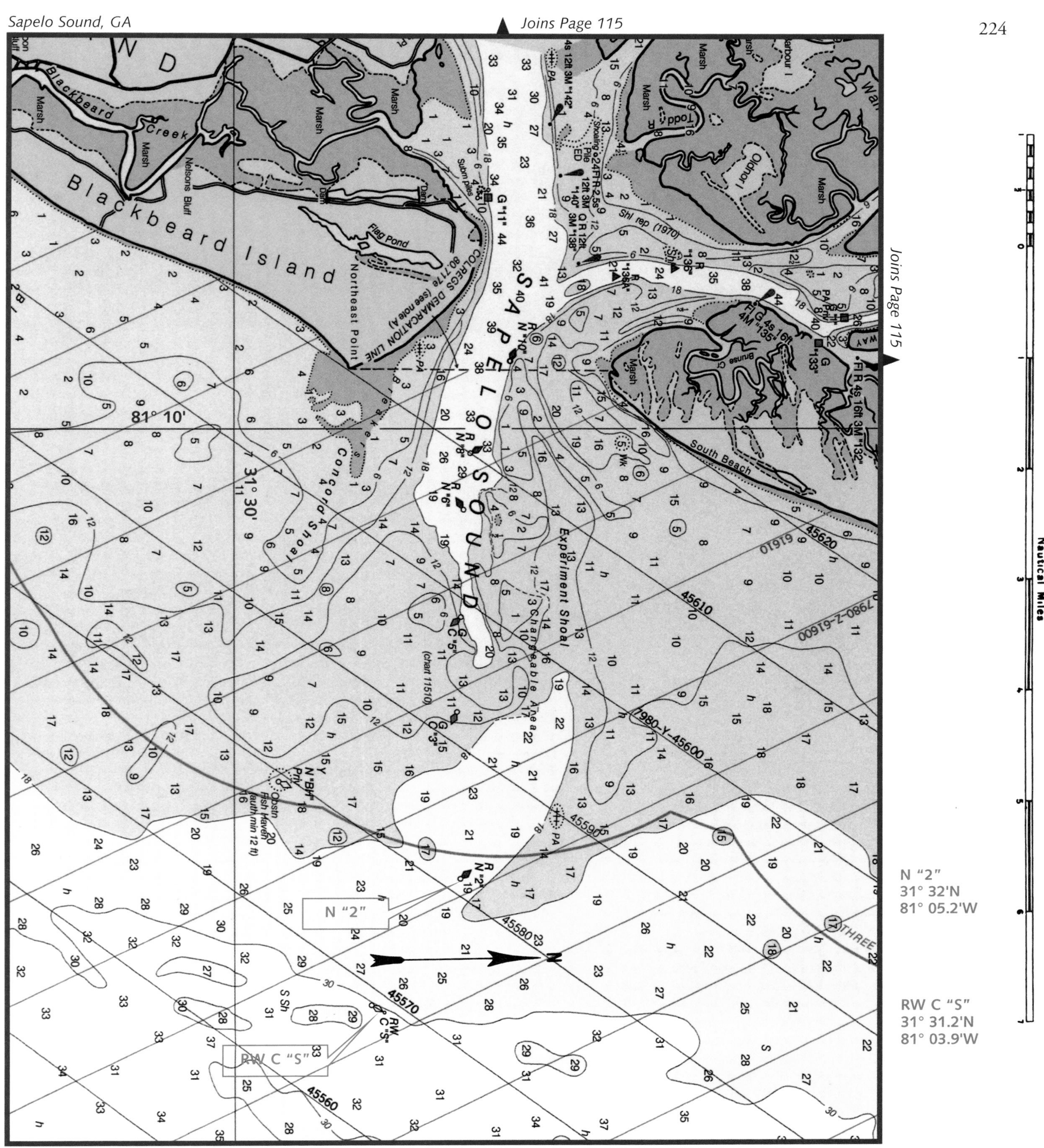

Joins Page 123

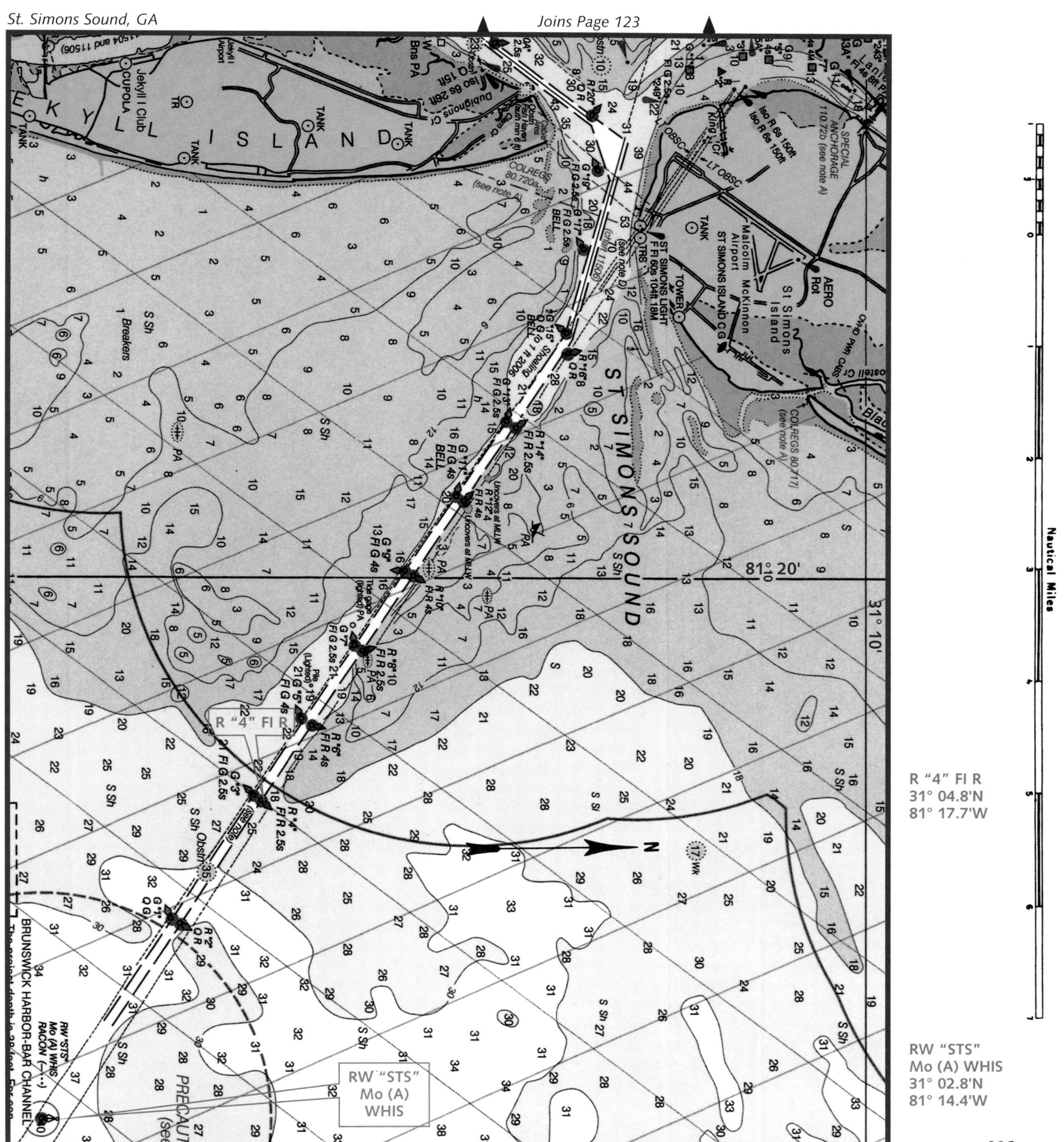

St. Marys River, GA/FL
Joins Page 128

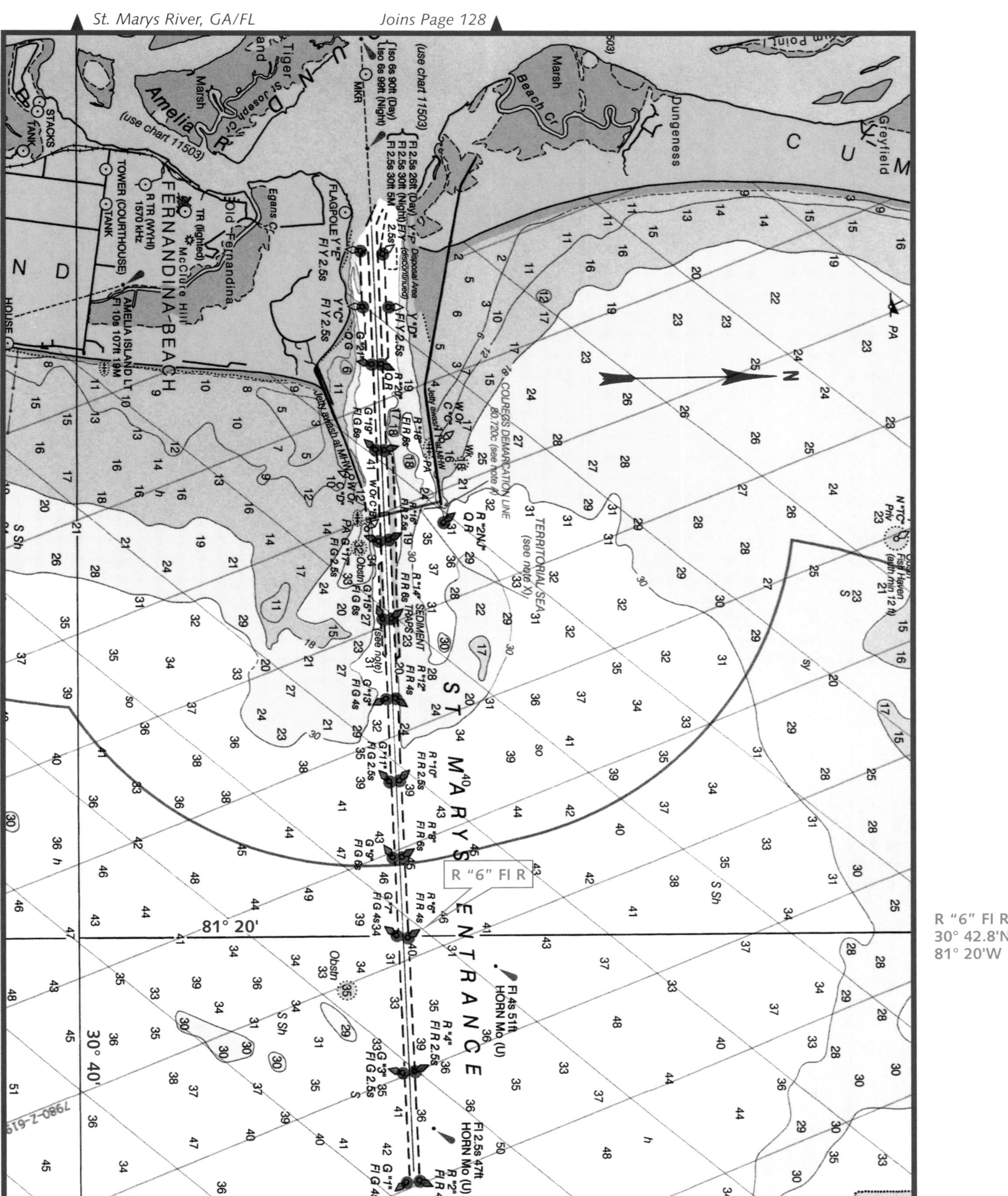

Nautical Miles

Joins Page 133

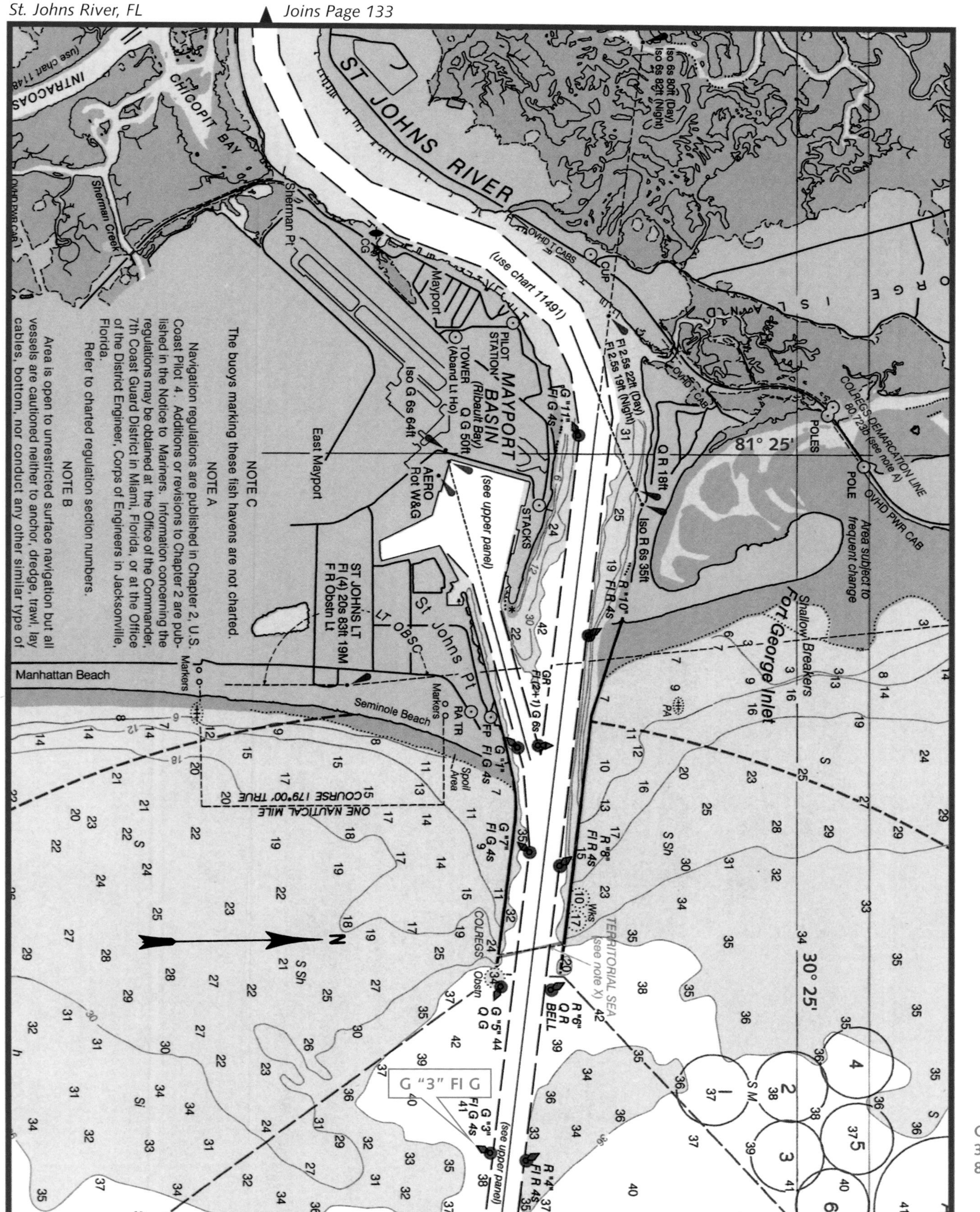

G "3" Fl G
30° 23.7'N
81° 21.7'W

Inlets and Side Channels, St. Johns River, FL

Christa McAuliffe Bridge (1.8)
Mon–Fri,
closed:
6:15–7:45 A.M.,
3:30–5:15 P.M.

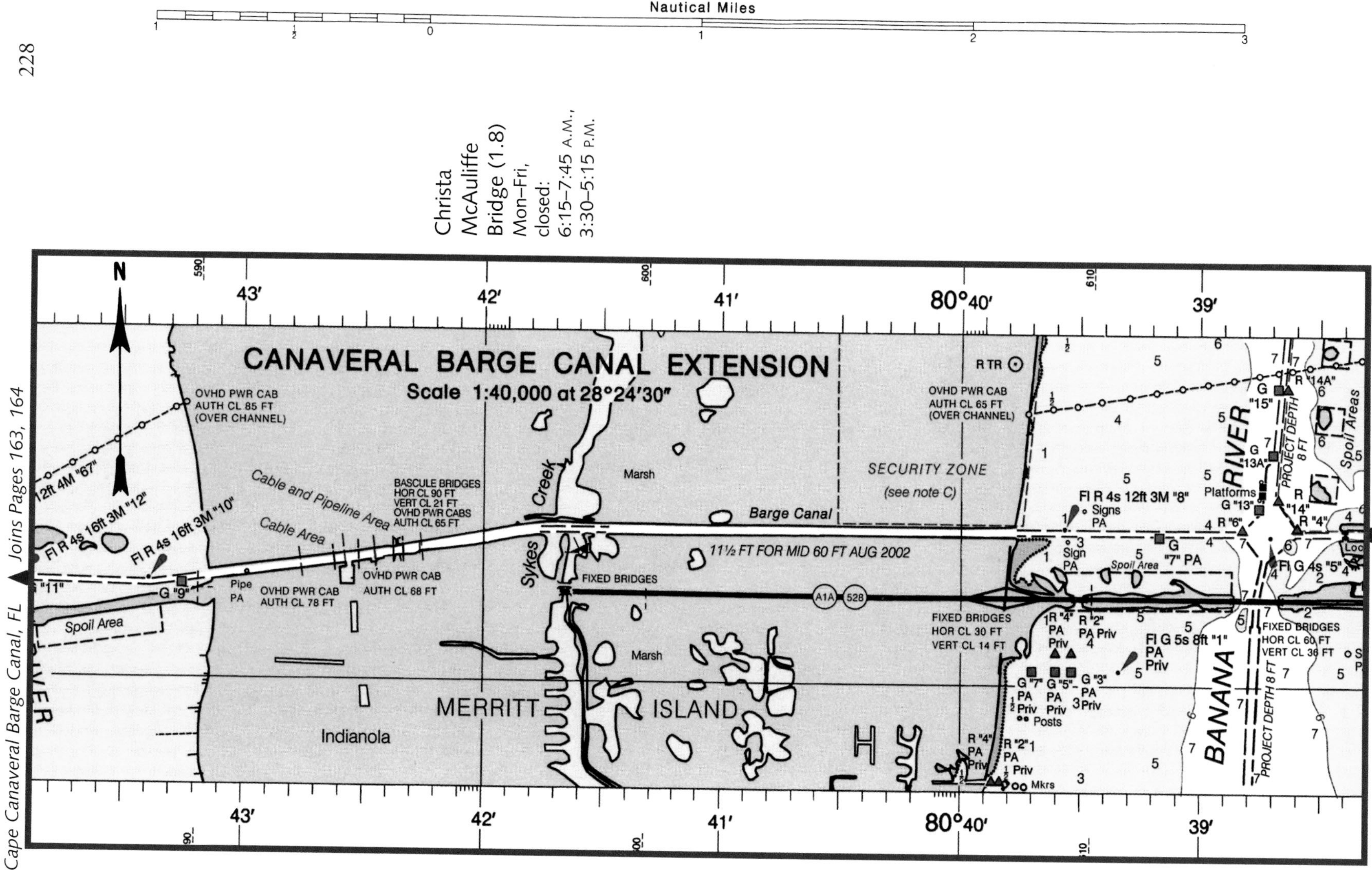

CANAVERAL BARGE CANAL

Call Florida bridges on VHF channel 09. The Canaveral Lock monitors VHF channel 13.

Mile	Bridge or Lock Name	Type	Clearance	Restricted Period	Regulated Hours
1.8	Christa McAuliffe Bridge (Rt. 3)	Bascule	25′	Monday–Friday	Closed: 6:15–7:45 A.M., 3:30–5:15 P.M.
6.2	Canaveral Barge Canal Lock	Lock	4′ lift	Daily	Open: 6 A.M.–9:30 P.M. CAUTION: Await signal before entering lock.
6.6	Canaveral Barge Canal Bridge (Rt. 401)	Bascule	25′	Monday–Friday	Closed: 6:30–8 A.M., 3:30–5:15 P.M.

Joins Page 207

Joins Page 235

1095

Nautical Miles

Inlets and Side Channels, Cape Florida Channel, FL

Great Dismal Swamp Canal (Route 2)

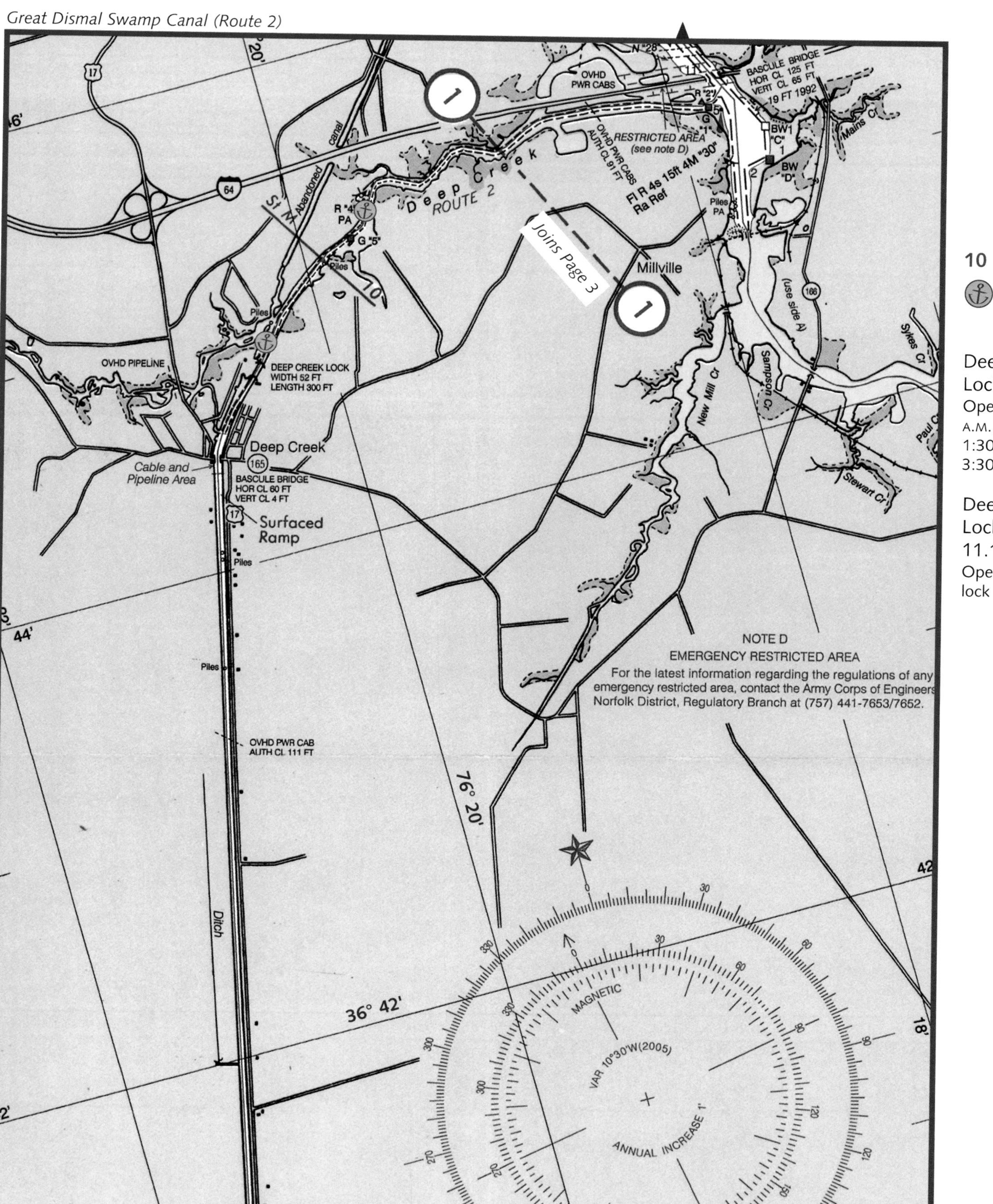

10

10 and 10.5

Deep Creek Lock 10.6
Opens: 8:30 A.M., 11 A.M., 1:30 P.M., and 3:30 P.M.

Deep Creek Lock Bridge 11.1
Opens with lock

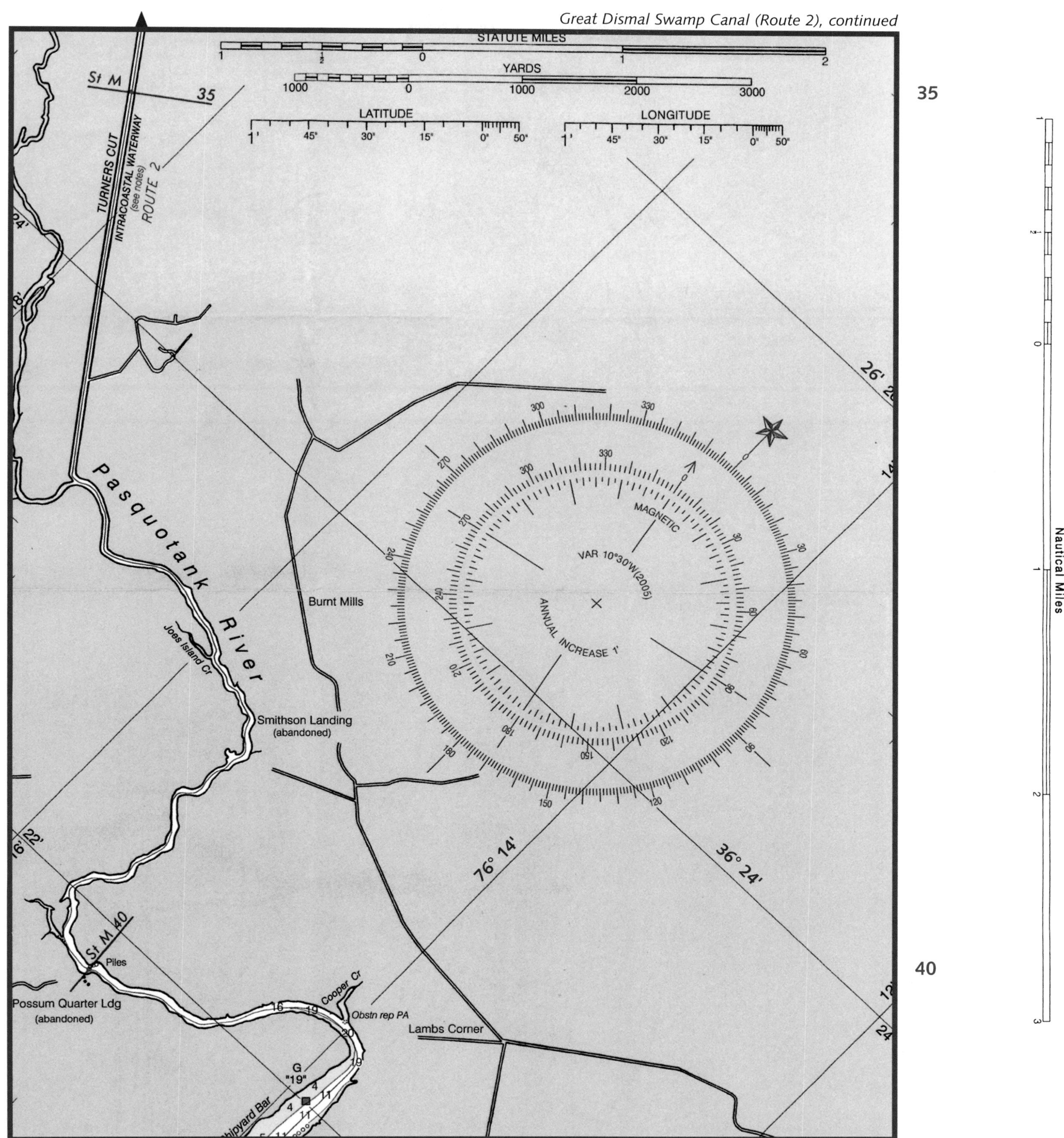

Inlets and Side Channels, Great Dismal Swamp Canal, NC

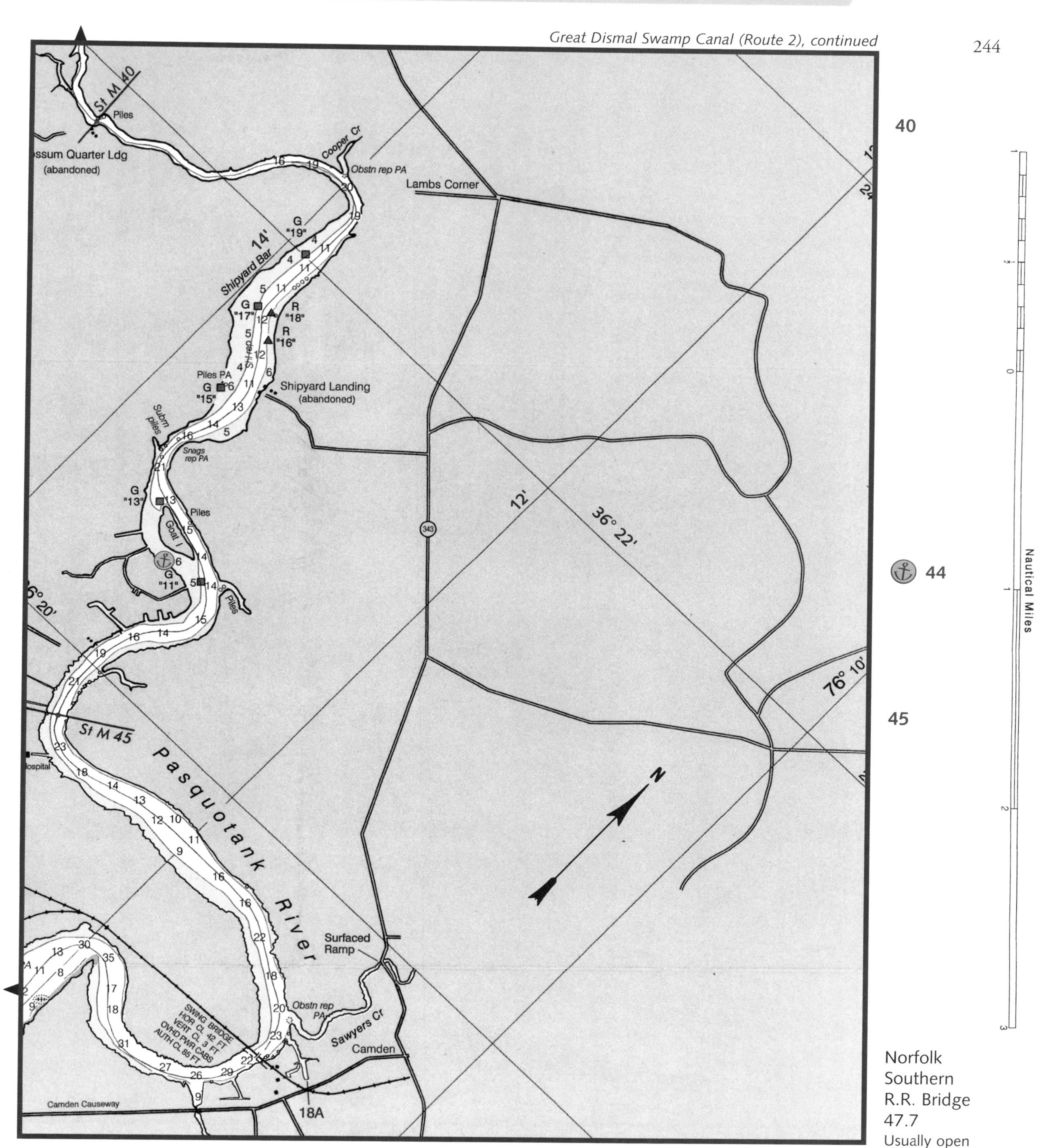

St M 40
Piles
ssum Quarter Ldg
(abandoned)
Cooper Cr
Obstn rep PA
Lambs Corner
G "19"
14'
Shipyard Bar
G "17"
R "18"
R "16"
Piles PA
G "15"
Shipyard Landing
(abandoned)
Subm piles
Snags rep PA
G "13"
Piles
Goat I
G "11"
Piles
343
12'
36° 22'
76° 10'
St M 45
Pasquotank River
Hospital
Surfaced Ramp
Obstn rep PA
Sawyers Cr
Camden
SWING BRIDGE
HOR CL 42 FT
VERT CL 3 FT
OVHD PWR CABS
AUTH CL 85 FT
Camden Causeway
18A
N
40
44
45
Nautical Miles
Norfolk
Southern
R.R. Bridge
47.7
Usually open

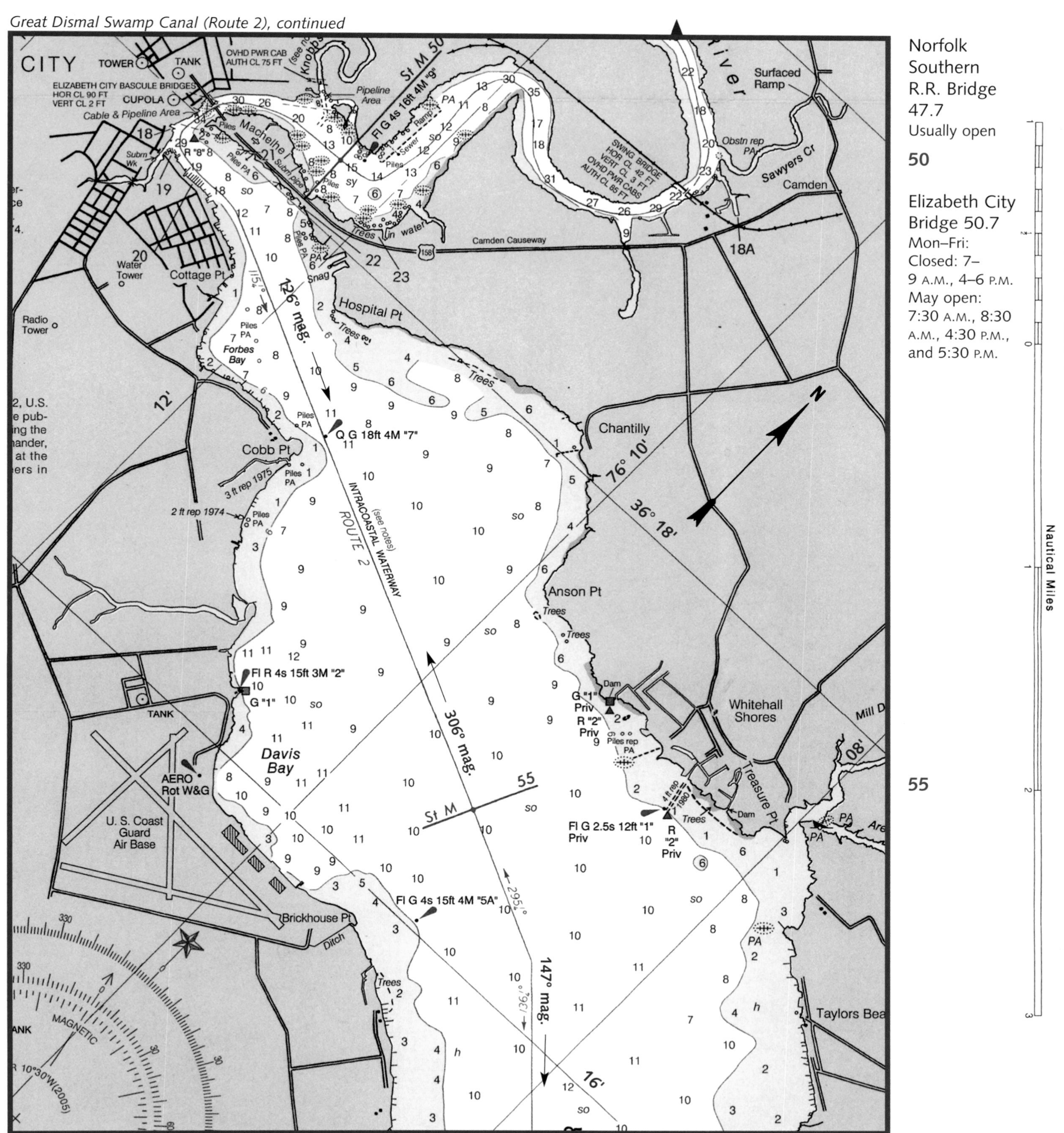

Norfolk Southern R.R. Bridge 47.7
Usually open

50

Elizabeth City Bridge 50.7
Mon–Fri:
Closed: 7–9 A.M., 4–6 P.M.
May open: 7:30 A.M., 8:30 A.M., 4:30 P.M., and 5:30 P.M.

55

Inlets and Side Channels, Great Dismal Swamp Canal, NC

Great Dismal Swamp Canal (Route 2), continued

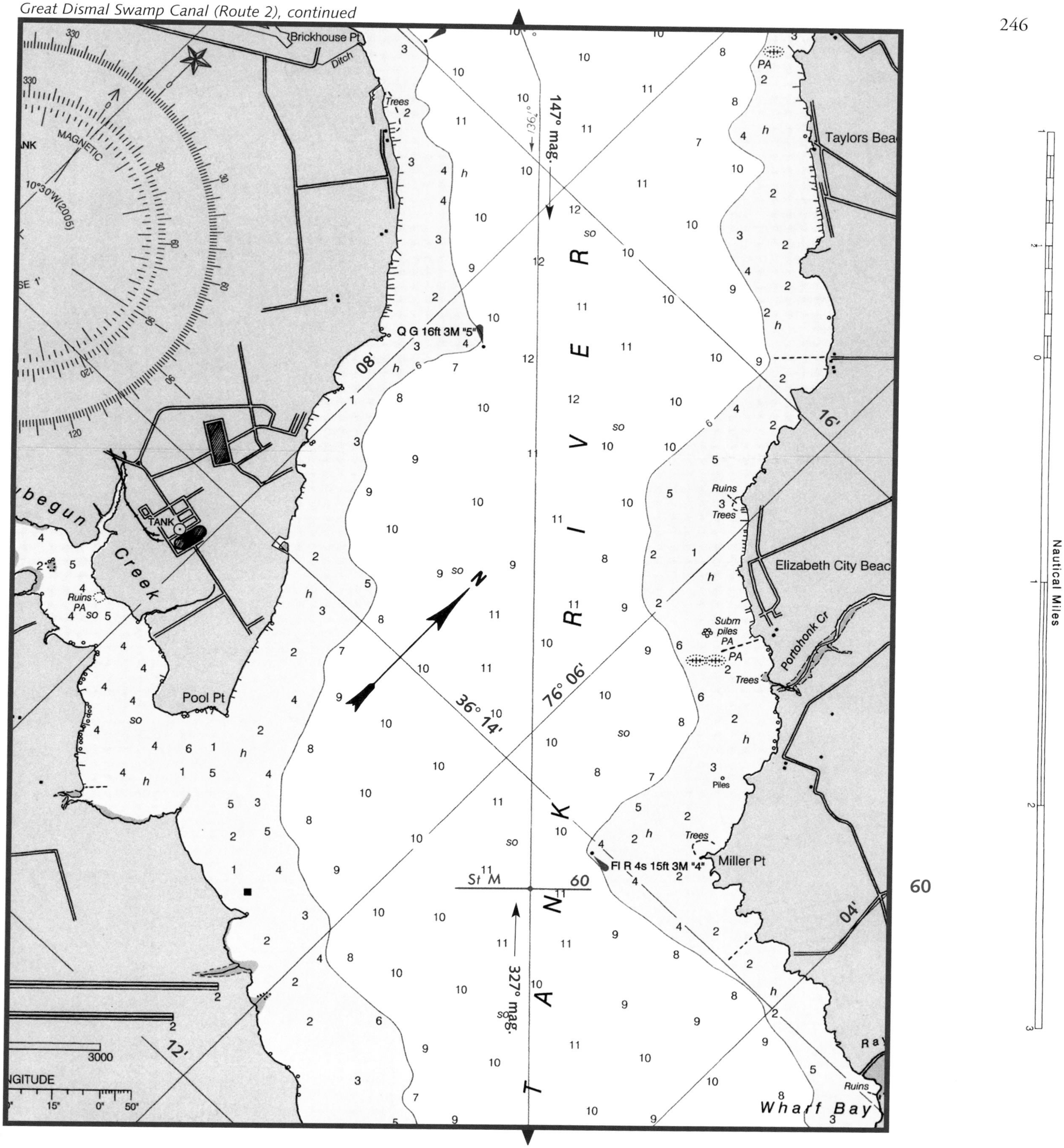

Brickhouse Pt
Ditch
MAGNETIC
10°30'W(2005)
Trees
Q G 16ft 3M "5"
TANK
Creek
Ruins
PA
Pool Pt
147° mag.
327° mag.
PASQUOTANK RIVER
36° 14'
76° 06'
St M
Taylors Beach
Elizabeth City Beach
Subm piles
Portohonk Cr
Piles
Fl R 4s 15ft 3M "4"
Miller Pt
Wharf Bay
LONGITUDE
3000
Nautical Miles
60

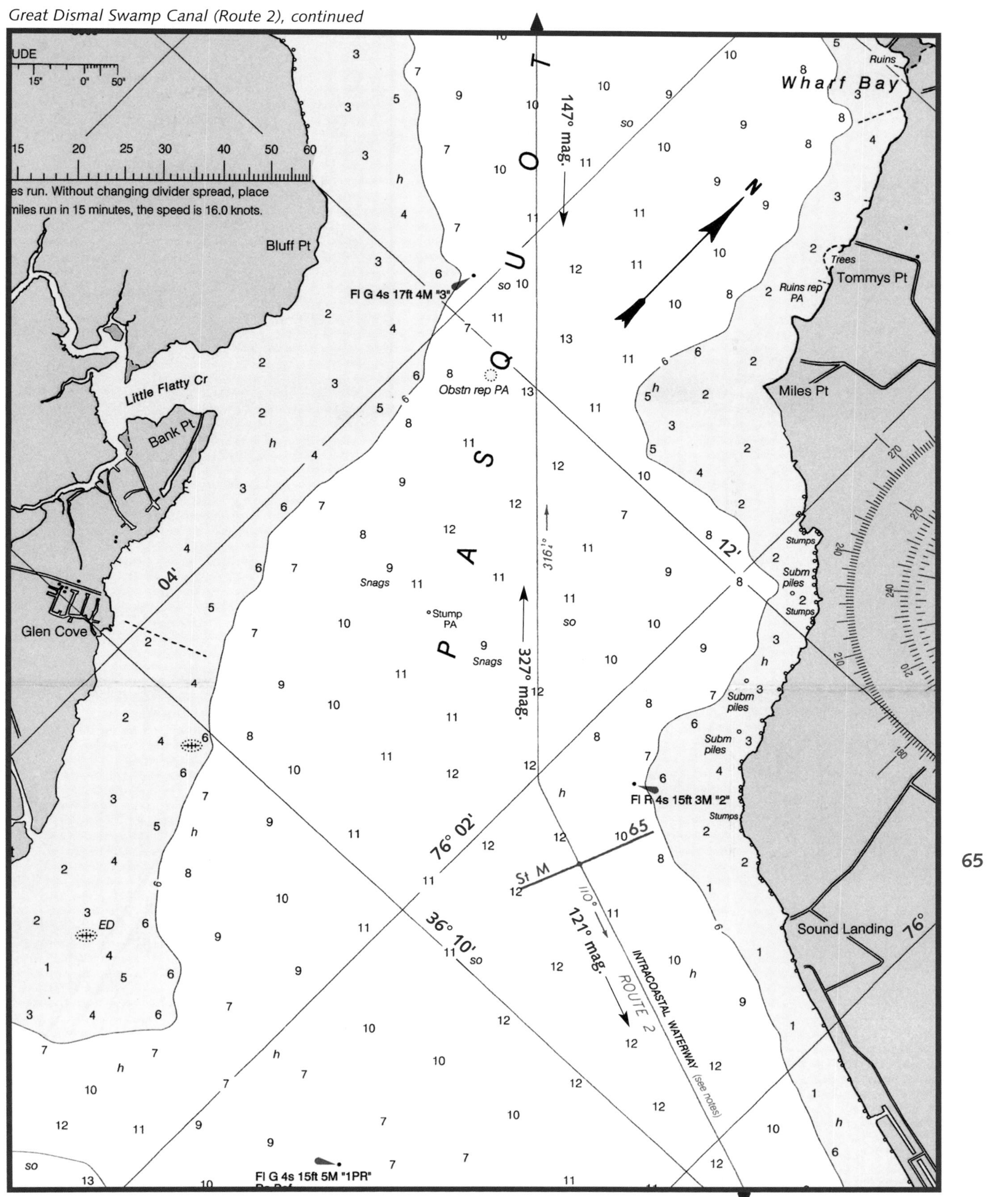

65

Inlets and Side Channels, Great Dismal Swamp Canal, NC

Great Dismal Swamp Canal (Route 2), continued

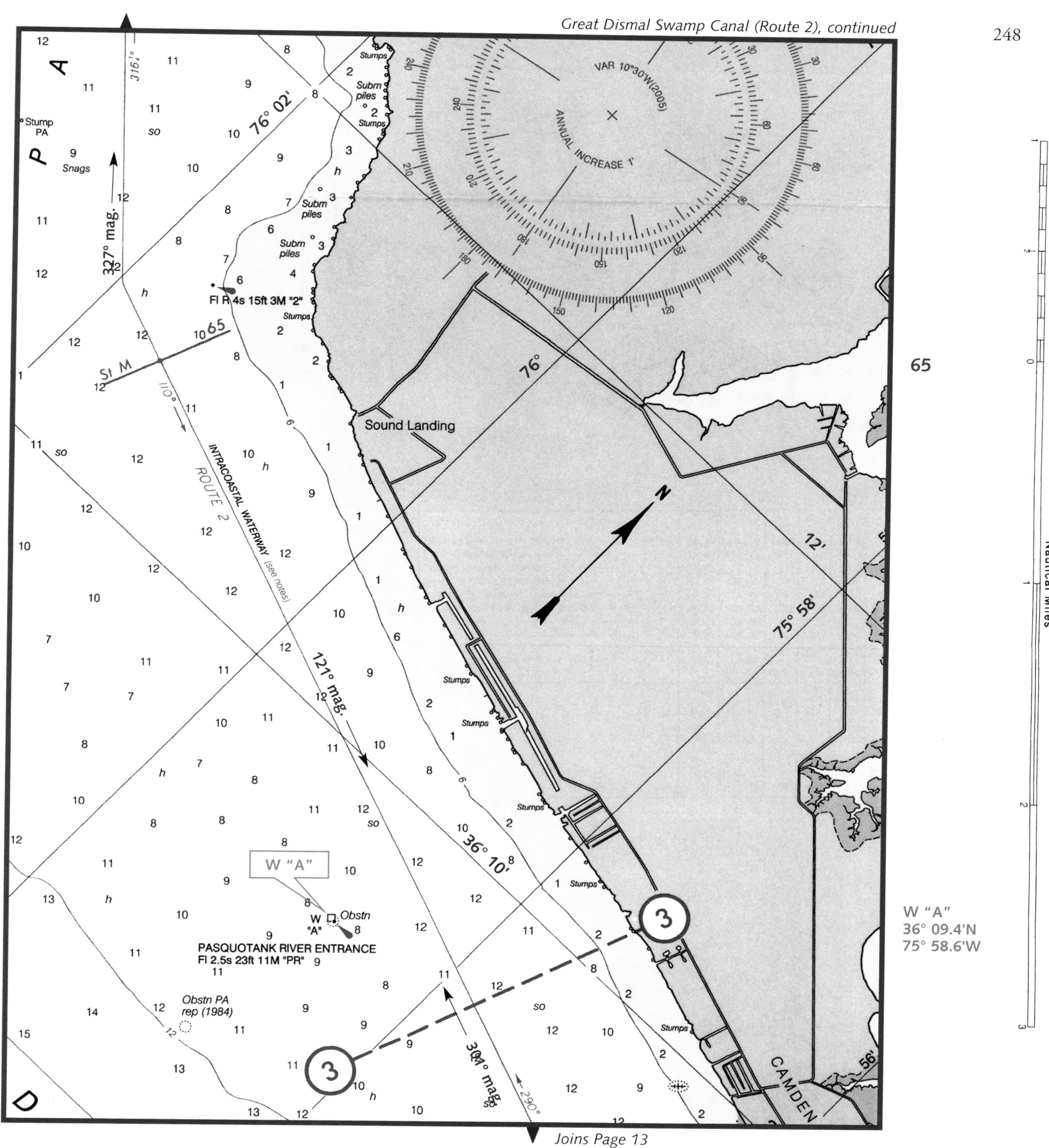

Joins Page 13

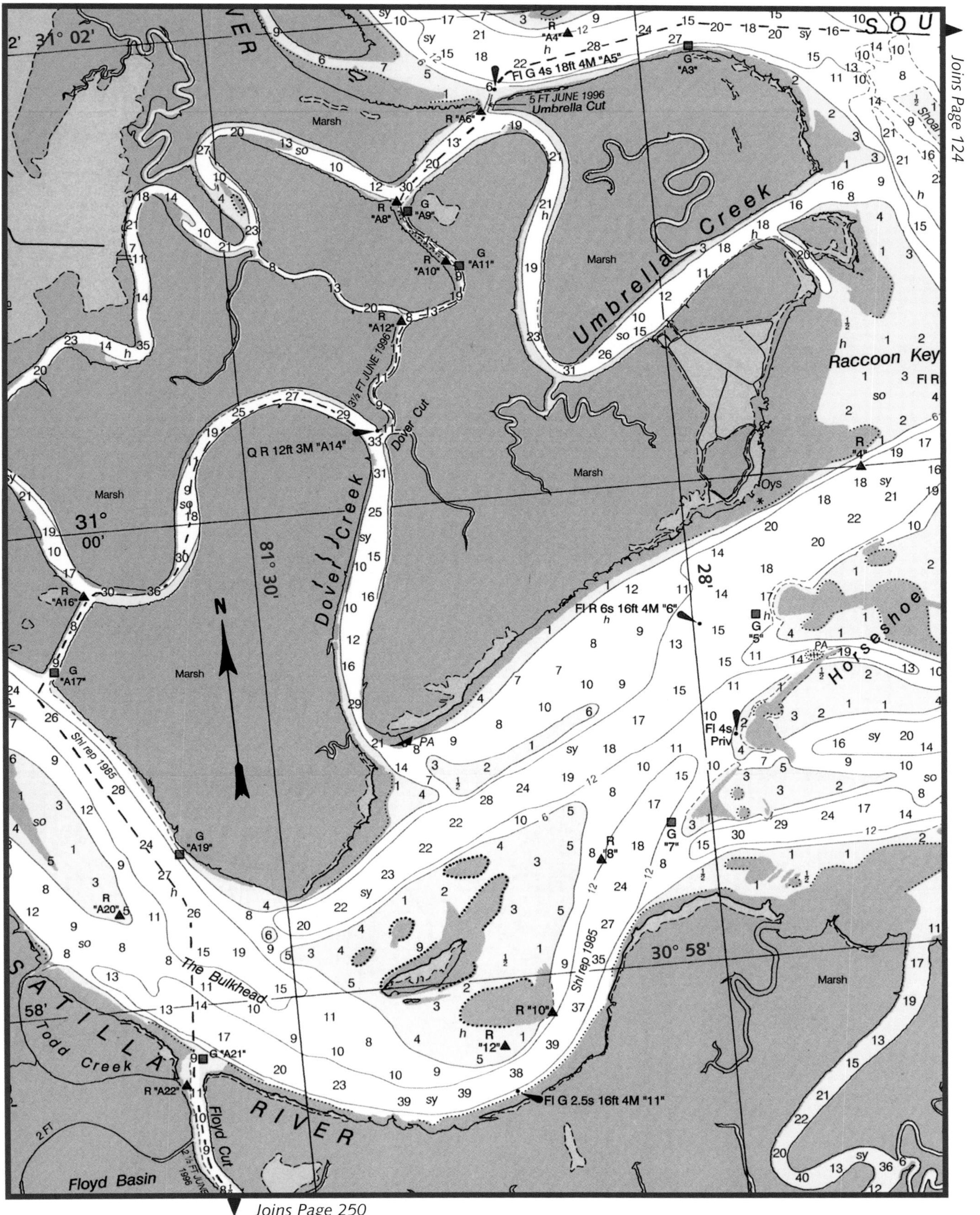

Joins Page 124

Joins Page 250

Inlets and Side Channels, Umbrella Cut, GA

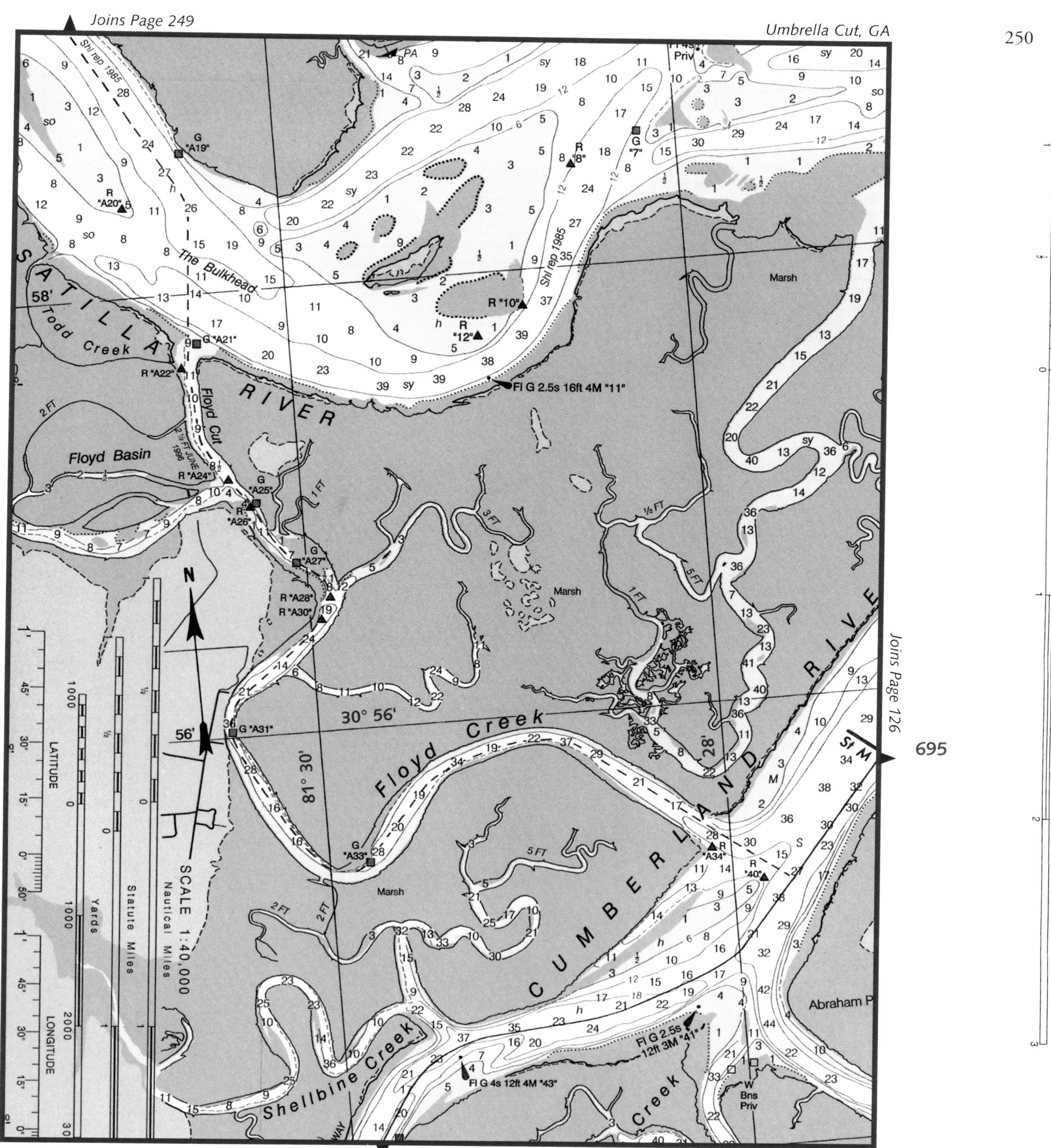
Joins Page 249
Umbrella Cut, GA
Satilla River
Todd Creek
Floyd Cut
Floyd Basin
The Bulkhead
Floyd Creek
Cumberland River
Shellbine Creek
Abraham P
Marsh
30° 56'
81° 30'
SCALE 1:40,000
Nautical Miles
Statute Miles
Yards
LATITUDE
LONGITUDE
Joins Page 126
695
Joins Page 126
Nautical Miles

APPENDIX A

Bridges and Locks on the Intracoastal Waterway

This list includes all of the bridges on the ICW with vertical clearances of less than 65 feet, several fixed bridges with clearance problems, and all of the locks. Operating characteristics of each bridge and lock are based on the latest information available as of August 2007. These regulations change frequently. For the latest updates obtain *Local Notices to Mariners*. See Appendix E for contact information.

The mile number in the left column matches the number on the appropriate chart where the bridge or lock is shown. A mileage number in parentheses indicates a bridge located off the main ICW channel.

The name of the bridge or lock is the commonly used name, which may be different than the name shown on the chart.

Clearances are in feet from mean high water to the lowest part of the span over the channel (there may be more clearance available below some portion of the span, usually near the center).

The "Restricted Period" column lists the months of the year and/or the days of the week when a bridge will not open *on demand.* However, restrictions usually do not apply on Federal holidays.

"Regulated Hours" are the times of the day, *during the restricted period only,* when openings are limited. When a bridge is "on demand" it should open in a reasonable period of time when the proper signal is given or a request is made via VHF radio. NOTE: Do not enter a lock until given the green light to enter.

Example: The Centerville Turnpike (Rt. 170) Bridge at Mile 15.2 in Virginia is a swing bridge with an overhead clearance of four feet (above mean high water) when closed. Openings are restricted every day during the "regulated hours."

The bridge will not open at all between 6:30 and 8:30 in the morning, and between 4:00 and 6:00 in the evening. In between those times, the bridge only opens on the hour and the half-hour.

MILE	BRIDGE OR LOCK NAME	TYPE	CLEARANCE	RESTRICTED PERIOD	REGULATED HOURS
	VIRGINIA Call Virginia bridges on VHF channel 13.				
2.6	Belt Line R.R.	Lift	6'		Usually open
2.8	Jordan (Rt. 337)	Lift	15'	Monday–Friday	Closed: 6:30–8:30 A.M., 3:30–5:30 P.M.
3.6	Old Virginia R.R.	Lift	10'		Usually open
5.8	Gilmerton (Hwy.)	Bascule	11'	Monday–Friday	Closed: 6:30–8:30 A.M., 3:30–5:30 P.M. **CAUTION: Channel bends at bridge and approaching traffic may not be visible.**
5.8	Norfolk Southern 7	Bascule	7'		Usually open
7.1	I-64 Highway	Bascule	65'		Opens with 24 hours' notice (800-305-5799)

MILE	BRIDGE OR LOCK NAME	TYPE	CLEARANCE	RESTRICTED PERIOD	REGULATED HOURS

VIRGINIA (MAIN ROUTE)

Call Virginia bridges and locks on VHF channel 13.

MILE	BRIDGE OR LOCK NAME	TYPE	CLEARANCE	RESTRICTED PERIOD	REGULATED HOURS
8.8	Steel Bridge (Rt. 104)	Bascule	12'	Daily	On hour: 6 A.M.–6 P.M. Closed: 7–9 A.M., 4–6 P.M.
11.5	Great Bridge Lock	Lock	Approx. 2.7' max. lift	Daily	On hour: 6 A.M.–7 P.M.
12.0	Great Bridge (Rt. 168)	Bascule	6'	Daily	On hour: 6 A.M.–7 P.M.
13.9	Norfolk Southern R.R.	Bascule	7'		Usually open
15.2	Centerville Turnpike (Rt. 170)	Swing	4'	Daily	On hour and half-hour: 8:30 A.M.–4 P.M. Closed: 6:30–8:30 A.M., 4–6 P.M.
20.2	North Landing (Rt. 165)	Swing	6'	Daily	On hour and half-hour: 6 A.M.–7 P.M.

NORTH CAROLINA

(Route 2 joins main route near Mile 80)

Call North Carolina bridges on VHF channel 13.

MILE	BRIDGE OR LOCK NAME	TYPE	CLEARANCE	RESTRICTED PERIOD	REGULATED HOURS
84.2	Alligator River (Rt. 64)	Swing	14'		On demand (will not open if wind speed is over 34 knots)
125.9	Wilkerson (Rt. 264)	Fixed	64'		**CAUTION: Bridge is charted at 64 feet but at times may offer less clearance.**
203.8	Beaufort & Morehead R.R.	Bascule	4'		Usually open.
(204)	Beaufort (Gallants Channel, Rt. 70)	Bascule	13'	Monday–Friday	On hour and half-hour: 6 A.M.–10 P.M. Closed: 7–7:30 A.M., 5–5:30 P.M.
206.7	Atlantic Beach	Fixed	65'		**CAUTION: At times height may be less than 65 feet.**
240.7	Onslow Beach (use NW draw)	Swing	12'	Daily	On hour and half-hour: 7 A.M.–7 P.M.
260.7	Surf City (Rts. 50 and 210)	Swing	12'	Daily	On hour: 7 A.M.–7 P.M.
278.1	Figure Eight Island	Swing	20'	Daily	On hour and half-hour
283.1	Wrightsville Beach	Bascule	20'	Daily	On hour: 7 A.M.–7 P.M. **CAUTION: Heavy boat traffic and current at bridge**
337.9	Sunset Beach	Pontoon	No clearance when closed	April 1–Nov. 30 (weekdays) June 1–Sept. 30 (weekends and holidays)	Weekdays on hour: 7 A.M.–7 P.M. Weekends and holidays on hour: 7 A.M.–9 P.M.

SOUTH CAROLINA

Call South Carolina bridges on VHF channel 09.

MILE	BRIDGE OR LOCK NAME	TYPE	CLEARANCE	RESTRICTED PERIOD	REGULATED HOURS
347.3	Little River (Rt. 17)	Swing	7'		On demand
354.3	Barefoot Landing	Swing	31'		On demand
365.4	Seaboard Coast Line R.R.	Bascule	16'		Usually open
371	Socastee (Rt. 544)	Swing	11'		On demand
462.2	Ben Sawyer (Rt. 703)	Swing	31'	Monday–Friday Weekends and holidays	Weekdays closed: 7–9 A.M., 4–6 P.M. Weekends and holidays on hour: 9 A.M.–7 P.M.

MILE	BRIDGE OR LOCK NAME	TYPE	CLEARANCE	RESTRICTED PERIOD	REGULATED HOURS
	SOUTH CAROLINA				
	Call South Carolina bridges on VHF channel 09.				
(469)	Ashley River (Charleston)	Fixed	56'		**CAUTION: This low fixed bridge crosses the Ashley River near the marinas and anchorage area.**
470.8	Wappoo Creek (Rt. 171)	Bascule	33'	April 1–Nov. 30	Weekdays on hour and half-hour: 9 A.M.–4 P.M. Weekends and holidays on hour and half-hour: 9 A.M.–7 P.M.
				June 1–Sept. 30, Dec. 1–Mar. 30 Monday–Friday	Closed: 6:30–9 A.M., 4–6:30 P.M.
				April 1–May 31, Oct. 1–Nov. 30 Monday–Friday	Closed: 6–9 A.M., 4–6:30 P.M.
536	Ladies Island (Rt. 21)	Swing	30'	Monday–Friday	On hour and half-hour: 9 A.M.–4 P.M. Closed: 7–9 A.M., 4–6 P.M.
	GEORGIA				
	Call Georgia bridges on VHF channel 09.				
579.9	Causton Bluff (Rt. 26)	Bascule	21'	Monday–Friday	On hour: 6:30–9 A.M. On demand: 9 A.M.–4:30 P.M. From 4:30–6: 30 P.M. opens only at 5:30 P.M.
592.8	Skidaway Narrows	Bascule	22'	Monday–Friday	On hour: 7–9 A.M. On demand: 9 A.M.–4:30 P.M. On half-hour: 4:30–6:30 P.M.
	FLORIDA				
	Call Florida bridges on VHF channel 09.				
720.7	Kingsley Creek R.R.	Swing	5'		Usually open. **CAUTION: Strong currents.**
739.2	Sisters Creek (Rt. 105)	Bascule	24'		On demand
747.5	McCormick (Rt. 90)	Bascule	37'	April 1–May 31, Oct. 1–Nov. 30	Weekdays on hour and half-hour: 7–9 A.M., 4:30–6:30 P.M. Weekends and holidays on hour and half-hour: noon–6 P.M.
777.9	Bridge of Lions (Rt. A1A) at St. Augustine	Temp. lift bridge	(ask for current clearance)	Daily	On hour and half-hour: 7 A.M.–6 P.M. Closed weekdays: 8 A.M., noon, 5 P.M. **CAUTION: Construction in progress and strong currents.**
788.6	Crescent Beach (Rt. 206)	Bascule	25'		On demand
816	L.B. Knox	Bascule	15'		On demand
829.7	Main St., Daytona Beach	Bascule	22'		On demand
830.6	Memorial, Daytona Beach	Bascule	21'	Monday–Saturday	From 7:45–8:45 A.M., only at 8:15 A.M. On demand: 8:45 A.M.–4:45 P.M. From 4:45–5:45 P.M., only at 5:15 P.M.
845	George E. Musson, Coronado Beach	Bascule	14'	Daily	On hour and every 20 minutes: 7 A.M.–7 P.M.
869.2	Haulover Canal, Allenhurst	Bascule	27'		On demand

MILE	BRIDGE OR LOCK NAME	TYPE	CLEARANCE	RESTRICTED PERIOD	REGULATED HOURS

FLORIDA

Call Florida bridges on VHF channel 09.

MILE	BRIDGE OR LOCK NAME	TYPE	CLEARANCE	RESTRICTED PERIOD	REGULATED HOURS
876.6	NASA, Florida East Coast, R.R.	Bascule	7'		Usually open. Automatic bridge will close for trains. Green light turns red and horn sounds four blasts before bridge closes after an eight-minute delay.
878.9	Titusville, Max Brewer (Rt. 402)	Swing	9'	Monday–Friday	Closed: 6–7:15 A.M., 3:15–4:30 P.M.
885	Addison Point, NASA Parkway (Rt. 405)	Bascule	27'	Monday–Friday	Closed: 6:30–8 A.M., 3:30–5 P.M.
(914)	Mathers Bridge, Eau Gallie	Swing	7'		On demand
964.8	Fort Pierce North (Rt. A1A)	Bascule	26'		On demand
984.9	Indian River, Ernest Lyons (Rt. A1A)	Fixed	65'		New high-rise fixed bridge completed 2007.
995.9	Hobe Sound (Rt. 708)	Bascule	21'		On demand
1004.1	Jupiter 707 (Rt. 707)	Bascule	25'		On demand
1004.8	Jupiter Federal (Rt. 1)	Bascule	26'		On demand
1006.2	Indiantown Rd. (Rt. 706)	Bascule	35'	Daily	On hour and half-hour
1009.3	Donald Ross	Bascule	35'	Daily	On hour and half-hour
1012.6	PGA Blvd. (Rt. 74)	Bascule	24'	Daily	On hour and half-hour
1013.7	Parker (Rt. 1)	Bascule	25'	Daily	On quarter and three-quarter hour
1017.2	Blue Heron Blvd. (Rt. A1A)	Fixed	65'		**CAUTION: Bridge is charted at 65 feet but at times may offer less clearance.**
1021.9	Flagler Memorial (Rt. A1A)	Bascule	17'	Daily	On quarter and three-quarter hour
1022.6	Royal Park (Rt. 704)	Bascule	21'	Daily	On hour and half-hour
1024.7	Southern Blvd. (Rt. 700/80)	Bascule	14'	Daily	On quarter and three-quarter hour
1028.8	Lake Ave.	Bascule	38'		On demand
1031	Lantana	Bascule	13'	Daily	On hour and half-hour
1035	Ocean Ave.	Bascule	21'	Daily	On hour and half-hour
1035.8	Southeast 15th Ave.	Bascule	25'		On demand
1038.7	George Bush Blvd.	Bascule	9'		On demand
1039.6	Atlantic Ave. (Rt. 806)	Bascule	12'	Daily	On quarter and three-quarter hour
1041	Linton Blvd.	Bascule	30'	Daily	On hour and half-hour
1044.9	Spanish River Blvd.	Bascule	25'	Daily	On hour and half-hour
1047.5	Palmetto Park Rd. (Rt. 798)	Bascule	19'	Daily	On hour and half-hour. **CAUTION: Very strong currents.**
(1048)	Boca Raton Inlet	Bascule	23'		On demand
1048.2	East Camino Real	Bascule	9'	Daily	On hour and every 20 minutes. **CAUTION: Very strong currents.**
1050	Hillsboro Blvd. (Rt. 810)	Bascule	21'	Daily	On hour and half-hour
(1054)	Hillsboro Inlet	Bascule	13'	Daily	On the hour and every 15 minutes
1055	Northeast 14th St.	Bascule	15'	Daily	On quarter and three-quarter hour
1056	Atlantic Blvd. (Rt. 814)	Bascule	15'	Daily	On hour and half-hour
1059	Commercial Blvd.	Bascule	15'	Daily	On hour and half-hour
1060.5	Oakland Park Blvd.	Bascule	22'	Daily	On quarter and three-quarter hour
1062.6	Sunrise Blvd. (Rt. 838)	Bascule	25'	Daily	On hour and half-hour
1064	Las Olas Blvd.	Bascule	31'	Daily	On quarter and three-quarter hour

MILE	BRIDGE OR LOCK NAME	TYPE	CLEARANCE	RESTRICTED PERIOD	REGULATED HOURS

FLORIDA

Call Florida bridges on VHF channel 09.

MILE	BRIDGE OR LOCK NAME	TYPE	CLEARANCE	RESTRICTED PERIOD	REGULATED HOURS
1065.9	S.E. 17th St., Brooks Memorial	Bascule	55'	Daily	On hour and half-hour. **CAUTION: Heavy boat traffic in vicinity.**
1069.4	Dania Beach (Rt. A1A)	Bascule	22'	Daily	On hour and half-hour
1070.5	Sheridan St.	Bascule	22'	Daily	On quarter and three-quarter hour
1072.2	Hollywood Blvd. (Rt. 820)	Bascule	25'	Daily	On hour and half-hour
1074	Hallandale Blvd. (Rt. 824)	Bascule	22'	Daily	On quarter and three-quarter hour
1078	Sunny Isles, N.E. 163rd St. (Rt. 826)	Bascule	30'	Daily	Weekdays on quarter and three-quarter hour: 7 A.M.–6 P.M. Weekends and holidays on quarter and three-quarter hour: 10 A.M.–6 P.M.
1081.4	Broad Causeway (N.E. 123rd St.)	Bascule	16'	Daily	On quarter and three-quarter hour: 8 A.M.–6 P.M.
1084.6	79th St. Causeway	Bascule	25'		On demand
1087.1	Julia Tuttle Causeway (36th St.)	Fixed	56'		**CAUTION: This fixed bridge is only 56 feet high.**
1088.6	Venetian Causeway	Bascule	12'	Monday–Friday	Opens on hour and half-hour: 7 A.M.–7 P.M.
1089.4	Dodge Island R.R. and Hwy. bridges (two bridges)	Two Bascules	22'		Usually open

APPENDIX B

Anchorage List

The following is an annotated list of more than 130 anchorages on the ICW. Cruisers are urged to use great caution when venturing outside of the main ICW channel. Unless noted otherwise, the editors (or other reliable reporters) have found at least six feet of water in the approaches and main anchorages. However, all parts of the ICW are subject to shoaling, and many areas outside the main channels have snags, wrecks, or other obstructions. Keep in mind that conditions change frequently and quickly. There are hundreds of other possible places to anchor.

The mile numbers on the left side of this list correspond to the mile numbers accompanied by anchor symbols in the right-hand borders of the chart pages. The geographic names of the anchorages correspond to the place names found on the charts.

Unless noted otherwise, all anchorages have a depth of at least six feet.

MILE	LOCATION	DESCRIPTION
		VIRGINIA
0	Hospital Point, Norfolk	Anchor as far west of the channel as you dare—the area shoals rapidly toward shore.
		Great Dismal Swamp Canal (Route 2)
10	Deep Creek	Just outside the channel east of G5 in 10 feet of water.
10.5	Deep Creek	Tie up to the dolphins just outside of the Deep Creek Lock.
33.5	South Mills	Anchor immediately after the lock in the narrow channel if darkness is approaching.
44	Pasquotank River	Anchor behind Goat Island in the Pasquotank River. Approach from the south near G11.
		NORTH CAROLINA
29	Pungo Ferry	A wide spot in the ICW near marker 42 is the last shelter until Coinjock, but the area is very busy with small boat traffic.
41	North Landing River	Exit the marked channel either east or west around marker 93, staying clear of the ferry route that passes near marker 95. Wide open.
45	Currituck Sound	Emergency anchorage in 4 to 6 feet. Proceed cautiously east from marker G115.
56	Buck Island	Anchor in the loop of deep water east of G153. Watch for crab trap floats and shoaling.
57	Buck Island	Anchor in deeper water east of G157 for some protection in a norther, but open to the south.
61	Broad Creek	Head in as far as you dare; well sheltered, especially in a blow from the northwest.
81.5	Little Alligator River	Rather exposed to the weather with lots of snags.
102	Deep Point	North of the channel opposite G43, where there used to be a mooring buoy for tugs and barges.
104.8	Tuckahoe Point	Feel your way in slowly from east of R52 to deep water, but watch for snags.
127	Pungo River	Anchor north of light 23. Deep water extends well into the river. Lots of crab floats.
135	Belhaven	Anchor inside the breakwater, to the west of the channel.
136	Pungo Creek	Anchor west of Windmill Point.
153	Eastham Creek	Anchor west of channel in deeper water opposite G11.
154	Eastham Creek	Well sheltered and very peaceful, but shallow out of channel. Watch for crab traps.

MILE	LOCATION	DESCRIPTION
		NORTH CAROLINA
154	Campbell Creek	Anchor to west of channel inside Huskie and Pasture points with good shelter and plenty of room.
174	Broad Creek	Well marked and easy to enter both day and night. Watch for crab traps and fish stakes.
182	Oriental	Anchor inside the breakwater south of the town, or up Greens Creek past the 45-foot high bridge.
187	Cedar Creek	Those drawing less than 4 feet can go way in, but most anchor near G9. Wrecked sailboat in anchorage 2007.
203	Town Creek, Beaufort	Avoid the marked shoals and rocks. Keep the marina channel clear. Anchor just east of green channel markers. Not much room.
204	Taylor Creek, Beaufort	Use two anchors in the strong reversing current, and keep the channel clear. Crowded. Dinghy dock near Post Office.
205	Morehead City	Anchor just south of turning basin and marker G1. This is supposed to be a No Wake Zone.
229	Swansboro	Anchor west of R2 and 4 in strong reversing currents—two anchors required.
231	Queens Creek	A narrow, shallow marked channel starts near the label "Subm pile" on the chart. May be less than six feet of water.
244.5	Mile Hammock Bay	Square basin adjoins the Marine Corps' Camp Lejeune. Poor holding and often crowded, and don't be surprised to see landing craft, helicopters, and tanks.
264.5	Topsail Sound	Several places to anchor off the channel, but many shoals to avoid.
283.1	Wrightsville Beach	Anchor in the 10- to 20-foot deep basin south of the bridge, with lots of room.
295.5	Carolina Beach	Anchor south of marker G5. The water is very deep, but shoals rapidly at the edges.
305	Cape Fear River	Anchor east of channel in deep water entered near R22 buoy. Exposed.
309	Southport	Very tight, but room for a couple of boats to anchor in public basin at east end of Southport waterfront.
		SOUTH CAROLINA
342	Little River	Anchor north of the ICW in the bend of the creek, past marker R2 for the Calabash River. May be shallow. **CAUTION: There are two R2s near each other: one for the Calabash River, and one for the ICW.**
377	Bucksport	Anchor north of the docks at Bucksport Landing, but watch for snags.
381	Prince Creek	Narrow waterway is deep, but unmarked. Shelter is excellent.
381.5	Bull Creek	Nice spot in the mouth of the creek. Other good anchorages can be found.
402.5	Georgetown	Anchor along the waterfront, opposite the marinas or the dinghy float at a town park.
410	Winyah Bay	Anchor south of the turn into the Estherville Minim Creek Canal.
416	Minim Creek	A good spot to wait if it is blowing hard in Winyah Bay.
430	Five Fathom Creek	Anchor northeast of the junction of Town and Five Fathom Creeks. Strong reversing currents.
436	Harbor River	Anchor in the deep water opposite marker R48.
448	Price Creek	Beautiful anchorage located in the Cape Romain Wildlife Refuge.
450	Mark Bay	Anchor west of channel and marker R90.
452	Whiteside Creek	Deep water and strong currents, as in many of the creeks in the area.
455	Dewees Creek	Anchor east or west of channel.
461	Inlet Creek	Head north of the Waterway, staying alert for shoaling in the entrance to the creek.
469	Charleston	Designated anchorage is across the river from City Marina, between C5 and the range markers. Lots of debris on the bottom, strong currents, and exposed.

MILE	LOCATION	DESCRIPTION
		SOUTH CAROLINA
471	Wappoo Creek	Anchor behind the little island marked by G9 at its western end. Tight.
487	Church Creek	This creek is wide and surrounded by low marsh and mud flats—not much shelter.
504	South Edisto River	Head northwest of the ICW and proceed around the bend in the river, then watch for shoals.
509	South Edisto River	Anchor near the end of Alligator Creek with little shelter from the ICW or southerly winds.
516	Rock Creek	Anchor north of the Ashepoo Coosaw Cutoff, but watch for shoaling in the entrance. Proceed cautiously around bend (shoal on inside) for best shelter.
521	Bull River	The river is too wide and open to offer excellent shelter, but good when calm.
524	Sams Point	Anchor in the small cove before the bridge (14-foot vertical clearance). Lots of current.
535	Beaufort	Anchor in deep patch west and south of R232, watching out for charted sandbar.
536	Beaufort	Anchor up Factory Creek or 200 yards minimum off the Beaufort marina. Town dinghy dock.
542	Port Royal Landing	Anchor beyond the turning basin in Battery Creek.
544	Cowen Creek	Deep water extends for several miles up Cowen Creek, but there are no navigation aids.
563	Broad Creek	Go in as far as you like. See the inset chart on page 104.
564	Bryan Creek	When Harbour Town lighthouse bears about 172° magnetic, head 352° to the creek mouth, but watch for shoaling.
565	Bull Creek	Enter northeast of light 34.
570	New River	Do not turn into the river until well south of marker 39. Entrance has shoaled to less than 6 feet in spots.
573	Wright River	Head south from marker 43 to anchor west of Turtle Island.
		GEORGIA
578	St. Augustine Creek	A deep, wide anchorage—possibly too deep, and there will be tour boat traffic.
585	Herb River	Beware of shoaling outside the ICW channel in this area, and proceed around bend for best shelter.
586	Turner Creek or Wilmington River	The latter is very wide and open, but easy to enter. Expect heavy boat traffic.
590	Isle of Hope	There is a small designated anchorage south of the marina. The anchorage may be full of moored boats.
595	Moon River	Entrance has shoaled to less than 6 feet in spots—proceed cautiously.
607	Redbird Creek	Good depths prevail well into the creek. Anchor around the first bend to the west. Very narrow.
608	Buckhead Creek and Cane Patch Creek	Go to any spot.
614	Big Tom Creek or Kilkenny Creek	There is a small marina well up the latter creek.
620	Walburg Creek	Nice alternate route to the main ICW. Shoals at south end near ICW.
625	Cattle Pen Creek	Anchorage is rather narrow between marshy banks.
643	Crescent River	Show an anchor light, as many large fishing vessels transit this area.
646	New Teakettle Creek	Creek is deep and wide open to the south so head further in for better shelter.

MILE	LOCATION	DESCRIPTION
		GEORGIA
651–653	North River, Back River, Darien River, and Rockdedundy River	All are open, marshy anchorages and good places to wait for the tide to help you through the very shoal (less than six feet at MLW) Little Mud River.
653	South River	When entering, swing well to the south to avoid the charted shoal area at the first bend.
664	Hampton River	Enter the creek north of marker G223. The Hampton River Club Marina is upstream.
665.5–673	Frederica River	Good depths all along this pretty, alternate route. Lots of boat traffic.
666	Wallys Leg	Enter from near marker 231.
673–665.5	Frederica River	Good depths all along this pretty, alternate route. Lots of boat traffic.
675	Lanier Island	A Special Anchorage area south of Golden Isles Marina.
685	Jekyll Island	Possible to anchor south of bridge near markers 23 and 24. Open and right on the channel.
694	Cumberland Island	Anchor between marker G37 and the shore.
696–704	Brickhill River	Another deep alternate to the main ICW route.
703	Plum Orchard Dock	Anchor in the Brickhill River north of the Plum Orchard Dock that provides access to Cumberland Island. Keep clear of ferry dock.
710	Cumberland Island National Seashore	Deep water along the shore of Cumberland Island north of latitude 30°46'.
		FLORIDA
717	Fernandina Beach	Anchor in Bells River or across the channel from Fernandina Harbour Marina.
720	Amelia River	Anchor east of the ICW before entering Kingsley Creek.
725	Alligator Creek	Enter the area north of marker R36. Anchor off the mouth of Alligator Creek.
735	Ft. George River	The river is well marked and fairly deep.
740	St. Johns River	Emergencies only. Anchor temporarily just outside of the ICW, near marker R2.
765	Pine Island	Enter south of G25 and proceed cautiously to a spot south of the island, or proceed around to anchor near Booth Landing.
775	Vilano Beach	Possible to anchor outside of channel near moored boats, but lots of traffic and wakes.
778	St. Augustine	Anchor south of the St. Augustine Municipal Marina or north of bridge. Keep outside of channel markers. Beware of shoals and currents. Two anchors are advised.
781	Matanzas River	Anchor west of markers R18 and R20.
821	Tomoka State Park	Shallow-draft boats can follow a locally marked channel west toward the park with 3 to 5 feet of water.
831	Daytona Beach	Anchor in deep water south of Memorial Bridge and east of ICW and marker G39. Enter opposite city marina basin using marina channel as a back range.
832	Daytona Beach	Anchor in the deep water extending northwest from marker 44. Avoid the charted cable and pipeline areas.
843	Rockhouse Creek	Enter mouth of creek cautiously. Plenty of current and boat traffic.
844	Coronado Beach	Anchor west of channel and south of marker 22. Feel your way in from near 22.
846	New Smyrna Beach	Anchor in deeper water near marker G45. Swing to current.
877	NASA R.R. Bridge	Anchor in deeper water south of causeway.
878	Titusville	Anchor north or south of the marked entrance channel, as close to shore as depths allow, or anchor south of marker R26 near ICW.
883	Merritt Island	Anchor near the island in a patch of deep water. You can watch space shuttle launches from here.

APPENDIX D

Distance Tables and Mileage Conversion Tables

COASTWISE DISTANCES NORFOLK, VA., TO KEY WEST, FLA.

(Nautical Miles)

Figure at intersection of columns opposite ports in question is the nautical mileage between the two. Example: Norfolk, Va., is 503 nautical miles from Savannah, Ga.

Port	CHESAPEAKE BAY ENTRANCE 36°56. 3'N., 75°58. 6'W.	Norfolk, Va. 46°50. 9'N., 76°17. 9'W.	DIAMOND SHOALS 35°08. 0'N., 75°15. 0'W.	Morehead City, N.C. 34°42. 8'N., 76°41. 8'W.	Southport, N.C. 33°54. 8'N., 78°01. 0'W.	Wilmington, N.C. 34°14. 0'N., 77°57. 0'W.	Georgetown, S.C. 33°21. 4'N., 79°16. 9'W.	Charleston, S.C. 32°47. 2'N., 79°55. 2'W.	Port Royal, S.C. 32°22. 3'N., 80°41. 6'W.	Savannah, Ga. 32°05. 0'N., 81°05. 7'W.	Brunswick, Ga. 31°08. 0'N., 81°29. 7'W.	Fernandina Beach, Fla. 30°40. 3'N., 81°28. 0'W.	Jacksonville, Fla. 30°19. 2'N., 81°39. 0'W.	St. Augustine, Fla. 29°53. 6'N., 81°18. 5'W.	Cape Canaveral, Fla. 28°24. 6'N., 80°36. 5'W.	Fort Pierce, Fla. 27°27. 5'N., 80°19. 3'W.	Stuart, Fla. 27°12. 2'N., 80°15. 6'W.	Port of Palm Beach, Fla. 26°46. 1'N., 80°03. 0'W.	Port Everglades, Fla. 26°05. 6'N., 80°07. 0'W.	Miami, Fla. 25°47. 0'N., 80°11. 0'W.	Key West, Fla. 24°33. 7'N., 81°48. 5'W.
Norfolk, Va.	27																				
DIAMOND SHOALS	117	144																			
Morehead City, N.C.	222	249	105																		
Southport, N.C.	315	342	198	133																	
Wilmington, N.C.	336	363	219	154	21																
Georgetown, S.C.	365	392	248	184	87	108															
Charleston, S.C.	402	429	285	220	130	151	79														
Port Royal, S.C.	465	492	348	284	191	212	141	90													
Savannah, Ga.	476	503	359	295	206	227	154	102	51												
Brunswick, Ga.	527	554	410	346	260	281	210	156	110	104											
Fernandina Beach, Fla.	533	560	416	352	265	286	216	166	120	115	50										
Jacksonville, Fla.	560	587	443	379	294	315	247	197	152	145	82	53									
St. Augustine, Fla.	557	584	440	377	296	317	246	199	157	152	90	61	56								
Cape Canaveral, Fla.	612	639	495	438	367	388	324	283	251	251	195	169	167	120							
Fort Pierce, Fla.	647	674	530	476	407	428	368	329	298	298	242	216	214	167	69						
Stuart, Fla.	666	693	549	497	423	444	391	353	324	324	268	242	240	192	91	32					
Port of Palm Beach, Fla.	678	705	561	509	443	464	407	369	341	340	285	262	259	211	110	52	36				
Port Everglades, Fla.	720	747	603	550	485	506	449	411	383	382	327	304	301	253	152	94	78	46			
Miami, Fla.	743	770	626	573	508	529	472	434	406	405	350	327	324	276	175	117	101	68	27		
Key West, Fla.	881	908	764	711	646	667	610	572	544	543	488	465	462	414	313	255	239	207	165	151	
STRAITS OF FLORIDA 24°25. 0'N., 83°00. 0'W.	942	969	825	772	707	728	671	633	605	604	549	526	523	475	374	316	300	267	226	211	73

Chesapeake Light (36°54. 3'N., 75° 42.8'W.) to: Norfolk, 42 miles; Baltimore, 165 miles.
Cape Fear River entrance buoy 2CF (33°49. 5'N., 78°03. 7'W.) to Wilmington, 28 miles.
Charleston Harbor entrance buoy 2C (32°40. 7'N., 79°42. 8'W.) to Charleston, 12.3 miles.
Savannah Light (31°57. 0'N., 80°41. 0'W.) to Savannah, 25 miles.
St. Johns River entrance buoy STJ (30°23. 6'N., 81°19. 2'W.) to Jacksonville, 23 miles.
Entrance lighted whistle buoy (24°27. 7'N., 81°48. 1'W.) to Key West, 6.3 miles.

Each distance is by shortest route that safe navigation permits between the two ports concerned. The navigator must make his own adjustments for non-direct routes selected to run with or avoid the Gulf Stream. For example, the table shows a distance of 561 miles by direct route from Diamond Shoals to Port of Palm Beach; distances via the routes shown in Chapter 3, Coast Pilot 4, are: Outer route, 572 miles; Gulf Stream route, 593 miles; Inner route, 628 miles.

INSIDE-ROUTE DISTANCES
NORFOLK, VA., TO FERNANDINA BEACH, FLA.

(Nautical and Statute Miles)

Figure at intersection of columns opposite ports in question is the nautical/statute mileage between the two. Example: Morehead City, N.C., is 445 nautical miles (512 statute miles) from Fernandina Beach, Fla.

Statute Miles

Port	Elizabeth City, N.C.	Hertford, N.C.	Columbia, N.C.	Edenton, N.C.	Plymouth, N.C.	Manteo, N.C.	Belhaven, N.C.	Washington, N.C.	Ocracoke, N.C.	Oriental, N.C.	New Bern, N.C.	Beaufort, N.C.	Morehead City, N.C.	Swansboro, N.C.	Jacksonville, N.C.	Wrightsville, N.C.	Wilmington, N.C.	Southport, N.C.	Little River, S.C.	Bucksport, S.C.	Georgetown, S.C.	McClellanville, S.C.	Charleston, S.C.	Beaufort, S.C.	Savannah, Ga.	Thunderbolt, Ga.	Brunswick, Ga.	Fernandina Beach, Fla.
Norfolk, Va. 36°50.9'N., 76°17.9'W	89*	102	102	113	121	92	138	180	151	184	207	204	205	230	266	283	314	308	344	377	405	430	467	536	585	583	685	717
Elizabeth City, N.C. 36°18.1'N., 76°13.0'W		45	45	55	64	45	91	131	105	136	160	154	157	182	217	235	266	260	296	329	358	382	419	488	536	535	636	669
Hertford, N.C. 36°11.6'N., 76°28.0'W			30	40	48	53	91	132	112	137	160	158	158	184	219	236	267	261	298	330	358	383	421	489	537	536	638	670
Columbia, N.C. 35°55.0'N., 76°15.4'W				29	38	52	90	131	110	136	159	157	157	182	217	235	266	260	296	329	357	382	419	488	536	535	636	669
Edenton, N.C. 36°03.3'N., 76°36.6'W					16	62	100	142	120	145	168	166	167	191	227	245	276	270	306	338	366	391	429	497	547	545	647	678
Plymouth, N.C. 35°51.8'N., 76°45.6'W						70	109	150	130	154	178	175	175	201	237	254	285	280	315	349	376	402	438	508	556	555	656	688
Manteo, N.C. 35°54.6'N., 75°40.2'W							81	121	70	105	127	127	127	152	186	205	236	231	267	299	326	352	388	457	506	505	606	639
Belhaven, N.C. 35°32.1'N., 76°37.4'W								45	49	49	72	70	70	96	131	150	181	175	211	243	270	296	334	402	451	450	551	582
Washington, N.C. 35°32.6'N., 77°03.7'W									69	64	87	85	85	110	146	163	194	189	224	258	285	311	348	417	465	464	565	597
Ocracoke, N.C. 35°06.8'N., 75°59.1'W										47	71	68	68	93	129	147	178	173	208	241	268	293	331	399	449	448	549	580
Oriental, N.C. 35°01.5'N., 76°41.8'W											26	25	25	51	86	105	136	130	166	198	226	251	289	357	406	405	506	537
New Bern, N.C. 35°06.1'N., 77°02.1'W												44	44	69	105	123	154	148	184	216	245	270	307	376	425	423	525	557
Beaufort, N.C. 34°43.1'N., 76°40.2'W													3	28	63	81	112	107	143	175	203	229	266	334	383	382	483	514
Morehead City, N.C. 34°42.8'N., 76°41.8'W														25	61	79	110	105	140	173	200	226	264	331	381	380	481	512
Swansboro, N.C. 34°41.0'N., 77°07.3'W															36	53	84	79	115	147	175	200	238	306	356	353	456	487
Jacksonville, N.C. 34°44.7'N., 77°26.3'W																55	86	81	116	148	177	203	239	308	357	356	457	489
Wrightsville, N.C. 34°13.1'N., 77°48.8'W																	31	25	61	94	122	147	184	253	302	300	402	434
Wilmington, N.C. 34°14.0'N., 77°57.0'W																		24	60	93	121	146	183	252	300	299	402	433
Southport, N.C. 33°54.8'N., 78°01.0'W																			36	69	97	122	159	228	276	275	376	409
Little River, S.C. 33°52.2'N., 78°36.6'W																				32	61	86	123	192	241	239	341	373
Bucksport, S.C. 33°39.0'N., 79°05.6'W																					28	53	91	159	208	206	308	339
Georgetown, S.C. 33°21.4'N., 79°16.9'W																						28	64	133	183	181	283	314
McClellanville, S.C. 33°04.7'N., 79°27.6'W																							37	106	155	153	255	287
Charleston, S.C. 32°47.2'N., 79°55.2'W																								69	120	119	220	251
Beaufort, S.C. 32°25.6'N., 80°40.2'W																									49	47	150	181
Savannah, Ga. 32°05.0'N., 81°05.7'W																										16	117	150
Thunderbolt, Ga. 32°01.5'N., 81°02.8'W																											101	133
Brunswick, Ga. 31°08.0'N., 81°29.7'W																												40

Nautical Miles

Port	Norfolk, Va.	Elizabeth City, N.C.	Hertford, N.C.	Columbia, N.C.	Edenton, N.C.	Plymouth, N.C.	Manteo, N.C.	Belhaven, N.C.	Washington, N.C.	Ocracoke, N.C.	Oriental, N.C.	New Bern, N.C.	Beaufort, N.C.	Morehead City, N.C.	Swansboro, N.C.	Jacksonville, N.C.	Wrightsville, N.C.	Wilmington, N.C.	Southport, N.C.	Little River, S.C.	Bucksport, S.C.	Georgetown, S.C.	McClellanville, S.C.	Charleston, S.C.	Beaufort, S.C.	Savannah, Ga.	Thunderbolt, Ga.	Brunswick, Ga.
Elizabeth City, N.C. 36°18.1'N., 76°13.0'W	77*																											
Hertford, N.C. 36°11.6'N., 76°28.0'W	89	39																										
Columbia, N.C. 35°55.0'N., 76°15.4'W	89	39	26																									
Edenton, N.C. 36°03.3'N., 76°36.6'W	98	48	35	25																								
Plymouth, N.C. 35°51.8'N., 76°45.6'W	105	56	42	33	14																							
Manteo, N.C. 35°54.6'N., 75°40.2'W	80	39	46	45	54	61																						
Belhaven, N.C. 35°32.1'N., 76°37.4'W	120	79	79	78	87	95	70																					
Washington, N.C. 35°32.6'N., 77°03.7'W	156	114	115	114	123	130	105	39																				
Ocracoke, N.C. 35°06.8'N., 75°59.1'W	131	91	97	96	104	113	61	43	60																			
Oriental, N.C. 35°01.5'N., 76°41.8'W	160	118	119	118	126	134	91	43	56	41																		
New Bern, N.C. 35°06.1'N., 77°02.1'W	180	139	139	138	146	155	110	63	76	62	23																	
Beaufort, N.C. 34°43.1'N., 76°40.2'W	177	134	137	136	144	152	110	61	74	59	22	38																
Morehead City, N.C. 34°42.8'N., 76°41.8'W	178	136	137	136	145	152	110	61	74	59	22	38	3															
Swansboro, N.C. 34°41.0'N., 77°07.3'W	200	158	160	158	166	175	132	83	96	81	44	60	24	22														
Jacksonville, N.C. 34°44.7'N., 77°26.3'W	231	189	190	189	197	206	162	114	127	112	75	91	55	53	31													
Wrightsville, N.C. 34°13.1'N., 77°48.8'W	246	204	205	204	213	221	178	130	142	128	91	107	70	69	46	48												
Wilmington, N.C. 34°14.0'N., 77°57.0'W	273	231	232	231	240	248	205	157	169	155	118	134	97	96	73	75	27											
Southport, N.C. 33°54.8'N., 78°01.0'W	268	226	227	226	235	243	201	152	164	150	113	129	93	91	69	70	22	21										
Little River, S.C. 33°52.2'N., 78°36.6'W	299	257	259	257	266	274	232	183	195	181	144	160	124	122	100	101	53	52	31									
Bucksport, S.C. 33°39.0'N., 79°05.6'W	328	286	287	286	294	303	260	211	224	209	172	188	152	150	128	129	82	81	60	28								
Georgetown, S.C. 33°21.4'N., 79°16.9'W	352	311	311	310	318	327	283	235	248	233	196	213	177	174	152	154	106	105	84	53	24							
McClellanville, S.C. 33°04.7'N., 79°27.6'W	374	332	333	332	340	349	306	257	270	255	218	235	199	196	174	176	128	127	106	75	46	24						
Charleston, S.C. 32°47.2'N., 79°55.2'W	406	364	366	364	373	381	337	290	302	288	251	267	231	229	207	208	160	159	138	107	79	56	32					
Beaufort, S.C. 32°25.6'N., 80°40.2'W	466	424	425	424	432	441	397	349	362	347	310	327	290	288	266	268	220	219	198	167	138	116	92	60				
Savannah, Ga. 32°05.0'N., 81°05.7'W	508	466	467	466	475	483	440	392	404	390	353	369	333	331	309	310	262	261	240	209	181	159	135	104	43			
Thunderbolt, Ga. 32°01.5'N., 81°02.8'W	507	465	466	465	474	482	439	391	403	389	352	368	332	330	307	309	261	260	239	208	179	157	133	103	41	14		
Brunswick, Ga. 31°08.0'N., 81°29.7'W	595	553	554	553	562	570	527	479	491	477	440	456	420	418	396	397	349	349	327	296	268	246	222	191	130	102	88	
Fernandina Beach, Fla. 30°40.3'N., 81°28.0'W	623	581	582	581	589	598	555	506	519	504	467	484	447	445	423	425	377	376	355	324	295	273	249	218	157	130	116	35

*51 statute miles via Dismal Swamp Canal

*44 nautical miles via Dismal Swamp Canal

INSIDE-ROUTE DISTANCES
FERNANDINA BEACH, FLA., TO KEY WEST, FLA.
(Nautical and Statute Miles)

Figure at intersection of columns opposite ports in question is the nautical/statute mileage between the two. Example: St. Augustine, Fla., is 271 nautical miles (312 statute miles) from Miami, Fla.

Nautical miles (below the diagonal) / Statute miles (above the diagonal)

Port	Norfolk	Fernandina Beach	Jacksonville	St. Augustine	Marineland	Daytona Beach	New Smyrna Beach	Titusville	Cocoa	Eau Gallie	Melbourne	Vero Beach	Fort Pierce	Salerno	Stuart	Port Mayaca	Clewiston	Moore Haven	Fort Myers	Jupiter	Port of Palm Beach	Fort Lauderdale	Port Everglades	Miami	Tavernier	Matecumbe Harbor	Marathon	Flamingo	Key West
Norfolk, Va. 36°50.9'N., 76°17.9'W.		717	758	778	796	831	846	879	898	915	918	952	966	990	995	1026	1053	1066	1122	1005	1018	1064	1067	1090	1150	1170	1203	1208	1244
Fernandina Beach, Fla. 30°40.3'N., 81°28.0'W.	623		41	60	79	114	130	162	181	198	201	235	249	273	278	310	336	349	406	289	302	348	350	373	435	453	486	491	527
Jacksonville, Fla. 30°19.2'N., 81°39.0'W.	659	36		56	75	109	124	158	176	193	197	230	244	268	274	305	331	344	402	284	297	344	345	368	430	449	481	486	522
St. Augustine, Fla. 29°53.6'N., 81°18.5'W.	676	53	49		18	53	68	101	120	137	140	174	188	212	217	248	275	288	344	227	241	287	289	312	373	392	425	430	466
Marineland, Fla. 29°40.1'N., 81°13.0'W.	692	69	65	16		35	51	83	102	119	122	157	170	194	199	230	257	270	327	209	222	269	270	293	356	374	407	412	448
Daytona Beach, Fla. 29°12.6'N., 81°00.7'W.	722	99	95	46	30		16	48	67	84	87	121	135	159	165	196	222	235	292	175	188	235	236	259	321	339	372	377	413
New Smyrna Beach, Fla. 29°01.7'N., 80°55.1'W.	735	113	108	59	44	14		32	52	68	72	106	120	144	150	181	207	220	276	159	173	219	220	243	305	323	356	362	397
Titusville, Fla. 28°37.3'N., 80°47.9'W.	764	141	137	88	72	42	28		20	36	39	74	87	112	116	147	174	188	244	127	139	186	188	211	273	291	323	329	365
Cocoa, Fla. 28°21.3'N., 80°43.1'W.	780	157	153	104	89	58	45	17		16	21	54	68	92	98	129	155	168	224	107	121	167	168	191	253	273	304	311	346
Eau Gallie, Fla. 28°07.9'N., 80°37.1'W.	795	172	168	119	103	73	59	31	14		3	38	52	76	81	112	138	152	208	91	104	151	152	175	237	257	288	293	329
Melbourne, Fla. 28°05.0'N., 80°35.5'W.	798	175	171	122	106	76	63	34	18	3		34	47	71	77	108	135	148	205	87	100	147	148	171	234	252	284	290	326
Vero Beach, Fla. 27°39.0'N., 80°22.4'W.	827	204	200	151	136	105	92	64	47	33	29		14	38	44	75	101	114	170	53	67	113	114	137	199	219	250	257	292
Fort Pierce, Fla. 27°27.5'N., 80°19.3'W.	839	216	212	163	148	117	104	76	59	45	41	12		24	30	61	87	100	157	39	53	99	100	123	185	205	236	243	278
Salerno, Fla. 27°08.8'N., 80°11.6'W.	860	237	233	184	169	138	125	97	80	66	62	33	21		9	40	67	81	137	20	32	79	80	104	166	185	216	222	258
Stuart, Fla. 27°12.2'N., 80°15.6'W.	865	242	238	189	173	143	130	101	85	70	67	38	26	8		31	58	70	128	25	38	85	86	109	171	190	222	228	264
Port Mayaca, Fla. 26°59.1'N., 80°36.8'W.	892	269	265	216	200	170	157	128	112	97	94	65	53	35	27		26	40	96	56	69	116	117	141	203	221	253	259	295
Clewiston, Fla. 26°45.6'N., 80°55.2'W.	915	292	288	239	223	193	180	151	135	120	117	88	76	58	50	23		13	70	83	96	143	144	167	229	247	280	285	321
Moore Haven, Fla. 26°50.0'N., 81°05.3'W.	926	303	299	250	235	204	191	163	146	132	128	99	87	70	61	34	11		56	96	108	155	156	180	242	261	292	298	334
Fort Myers, Fla. 26°38.9'N., 81°52.3'W.	975	353	349	299	284	254	240	212	195	181	178	148	136	119	111	83	61	49		152	166	212	213	236	298	318	349	356	390
Jupiter, Fla. 26°56.8'N., 80°05.4'W.	873	251	247	197	182	152	138	110	93	79	76	46	34	17	22	49	72	83	132		14	60	61	84	146	166	197	204	239
Port of Palm Beach, Fla. 26°46.1'N., 80°03.0'W.	885	262	258	209	193	163	150	121	105	90	87	58	46	28	33	60	83	94	144	12		47	48	71	133	152	184	190	226
Fort Lauderdale, Fla. 26°06.8'N., 80°07.2'W.	925	303	299	249	234	204	190	162	145	131	128	98	86	69	74	101	124	135	184	52	41		1	24	86	106	137	144	178
Port Everglades, Fla. 26°05.6'N., 80°07.0'W.	927	304	300	251	235	205	191	163	146	132	129	99	87	70	75	102	125	136	185	53	42	1		23	85	105	136	142	177
Miami, Fla. 25°47.0'N., 80°11.0'W.	947	324	320	271	255	225	211	183	166	152	149	119	107	90	95	122	145	156	205	73	62	21	20		62	82	113	120	154
Tavernier, Fla. 25°00.7'N., 80°31.3'W.	999	378	374	324	309	279	265	237	220	206	203	173	161	144	149	176	199	210	259	127	116	75	74	54		22	54	60	96
Matecumbe Harbor, Fla. 24°51.1'N., 80°44.5'W.	1017	394	390	341	325	295	282	253	237	223	219	190	178	161	165	192	215	227	276	144	132	92	91	71	19		33	40	75
Marathon, Fla. 24°42.2'N., 81°06.7'W.	1045	422	418	369	353	323	309	281	264	250	247	217	205	188	193	220	243	254	303	171	160	119	118	98	47	29		39	48
Flamingo, Fla. 25°08.5'N., 80°55.4'W.	1050	427	423	374	358	328	315	286	270	255	252	223	211	193	198	225	248	259	309	177	165	125	123	104	52	35	34		84
Key West, Fla. 24°33.7'N., 81°48.5'W.	1081	458	454	405	389	359	345	317	301	286	283	254	242	224	229	256	279	290	339	207	196	155	154	134	83	65	42	73	

Conversion Tables

INTERNATIONAL NAUTICAL MILES TO STATUTE MILES

1 nautical mile = 6,076.12 feet or 1,852 meters   1 statute mile = 5,280 feet or 1,609.35 meters

Nautical miles	0	1	2	3	4	5	6	7	8	9
0	0.000	1.151	2.302	3.452	4.603	5.754	6.905	8.055	9.206	10.357
10	11.508	12.659	13.809	14.960	16.111	17.262	18.412	19.563	20.714	21.865
20	23.016	24.166	25.317	26.468	27.619	28.769	29.920	31.071	32.222	33.373
30	34.523	35.674	36.825	37.976	39.126	40.277	41.428	42.579	43.730	44.880
40	46.031	47.182	48.333	49.483	50.634	51.785	52.936	54.087	55.237	56.388
50	57.539	58.690	59.840	60.991	62.142	63.293	64.444	65.594	66.745	67.896
60	69.047	70.197	71.348	72.499	73.650	74.801	75.951	77.102	78.253	79.404
70	80.554	81.705	82.856	84.007	85.158	86.308	87.459	88.610	89.761	90.911
80	92.062	93.213	94.364	95.515	96.665	97.816	98.967	100.118	101.268	102.419
90	103.570	104.721	105.871	107.022	108.173	109.324	110.475	111.625	112.776	113.927

STATUTE MILES TO INTERNATIONAL NAUTICAL MILES

Statute miles	0	1	2	3	4	5	6	7	8	9
0	0.000	0.869	1.738	2.607	3.476	4.345	5.214	6.083	6.952	7.821
10	8.690	9.559	10.428	11.297	12.166	13.035	13.904	14.773	15.642	16.511
20	17.380	18.249	19.118	19.986	20.855	21.724	22.593	23.462	24.331	25.200
30	26.069	26.938	27.807	28.676	29.545	30.414	31.283	32.152	33.021	33.890
40	34.759	35.628	36.497	37.366	38.235	39.104	39.973	40.842	41.711	42.580
50	43.449	44.318	45.187	46.056	46.925	47.794	48.663	49.532	50.401	51.270
60	52.139	53.008	53.877	54.746	55.615	56.484	57.353	58.222	59.091	59.959
70	60.828	61.697	62.566	63.435	64.304	65.173	66.042	66.911	67.780	68.649
80	69.518	70.387	71.256	72.125	72.994	73.863	74.732	75.601	76.470	77.339
90	78.208	79.077	79.946	80.815	81.684	82.553	83.422	84.291	85.160	86.029

FEET TO METERS

Feet	0	1	2	3	4	5	6	7	8	9
0	0.00	0.30	0.61	0.91	1.22	1.52	1.83	2.13	2.44	2.74
10	3.05	3.35	3.66	3.96	4.27	4.57	4.88	5.18	5.49	5.79
20	6.10	6.40	6.71	7.01	7.32	7.62	7.92	8.23	8.53	8.84
30	9.14	9.45	9.75	10.06	10.36	10.67	10.97	11.28	11.58	11.89
40	12.19	12.50	12.80	13.11	13.41	13.72	14.02	14.33	14.63	14.93
50	15.24	15.54	15.85	16.15	16.46	16.76	17.07	17.37	17.68	17.98
60	18.29	18.59	18.90	19.20	19.51	19.81	20.12	20.42	20.73	21.03
70	21.34	21.64	21.95	22.25	22.55	22.86	23.16	23.47	23.77	24.08
80	24.38	24.69	24.99	25.30	25.60	25.91	26.21	26.52	26.82	27.13
90	27.43	27.74	28.04	28.35	28.65	28.96	29.26	29.57	29.87	30.17

METERS TO FEET

Meters	0	1	2	3	4	5	6	7	8	9
0	0.00	3.28	6.56	9.84	13.12	16.40	19.68	22.97	26.25	29.53
10	32.81	36.09	39.37	42.65	45.93	49.21	52.49	55.77	59.06	62.34
20	65.62	68.90	72.18	75.46	78.74	82.02	85.30	88.58	91.86	95.14
30	98.42	101.71	104.99	108.27	111.55	114.83	118.11	121.39	124.67	127.95
40	131.23	134.51	137.80	141.08	144.36	147.64	150.92	154.20	157.48	160.76
50	164.04	167.32	170.60	173.88	177.16	180.45	183.73	187.01	190.29	193.57
60	196.85	200.13	203.41	206.69	209.97	213.25	216.54	219.82	223.10	226.38
70	229.66	232.94	236.22	239.50	242.78	246.06	249.34	252.62	255.90	259.19
80	262.47	265.75	269.03	272.31	275.59	278.87	282.15	285.43	288.71	291.99
90	295.28	298.56	301.84	305.12	308.40	311.68	314.96	318.24	321.52	324.80

APPENDIX E

NOAA Chart Cross-Reference and Notices to Mariners Information

NOAA Chart Cross-Reference

Pages 1–12 NOAA chart #12206, 31st ed., March 22, 2005
Pages 13–33 NOAA chart #11553, 29th ed., August 1, 2006
Pages 34–56 NOAA chart #11541, 37th ed., March 13, 2007
Pages 57–82 NOAA chart #11534, 34th ed., August 8, 2006
Pages 83–101 NOAA chart #11518, 35th ed., April 18, 2006
Pages 102–122 NOAA chart #11507, 33rd ed., October 24, 2006
Pages 123–139 NOAA chart #11489, 37th ed., May 8, 2007
Pages 140–166 NOAA chart #11485, 34th ed., April 5, 2005
Pages 167–191 NOAA chart #11472, 32nd ed., April 19, 2005
Pages 191–207 NOAA chart #11467, 40th ed., May 15, 2007
Pages 208–209 NOAA chart #11537, 37th ed., November 28, 2006
Pages 210–211 NOAA chart 11532, 21st ed., June 27, 2006
Pages 212–213 NOAA chart #11521, 28th ed., February 7, 2006
Pages 214–218 NOAA chart #11513, 25th ed., April 18, 2006
Pages 219 NOAA chart #11512, 61st ed., October 3, 2006
Page 220 NOAA chart #11513, 25th ed., April 18, 2006
Page 221 NOAA chart #11512, 61st ed., October 3, 2006
Pages 222–224 NOAA chart #11509, 30th ed., December 5, 2006
Pages 225–226 NOAA chart #11502, 31st ed., January 23, 2007
Page 227 NOAA chart #11490, 19th ed., November 28, 2006
Pages 228–231 NOAA chart #11478, 21st ed., May 17, 2005
Page 232 NOAA chart #11476, 21st ed., July 11, 2006
Pages 233–234 NOAA chart #11467, 40th ed., May 15, 2007
Page 235 NOAA chart #11466, 37th ed., August 2, 2005
Pages 236–237 NOAA chart #11467, 40th ed., May 15, 2007
Pages 238–248 NOAA chart #12206, 31st ed., March 22, 2005
Pages 249–250 NOAA chart #11489, 37th ed., May 8, 2007

U.S. Coast Guard *Local Notices to Mariners*

Local Notices to Mariners for this chartbook area may be obtained by contacting the U.S. Coast Guard at the following addresses:

For Virginia and North Carolina:
Commander, Fifth Coast Guard District
431 Crawford Street
Portsmouth VA 23704
757-398-6486/6552
www.navcen.uscg.gov/lnm/d5

For South Carolina, Georgia, and Florida:
Commander, Seventh Coast Guard District
909 SE 1st Avenue
Miami FL 33131
305-415-6730/6751
www.navcen.uscg.gov/lnm/d7

INDEX

Adams Creek, NC, 37–39
Addison Point, FL, 162
Albemarle and Chesapeake Canal, VA, 3–5
Albemarle Sound, NC, 12–15
Alligator Bay, NC, 49–50
Alligator Creek, FL, 130
Alligator River, NC, 16–20
Alligator River–Pungo River Canal, NC, 20–25
Altamaha River, GA, 120
Amelia River, FL, 129
Anastasia Island, FL, 142
Ashepoo Coosaw Cutoff, SC, 97–98
Ashepoo River, SC, 97
Ashley River, SC, 90–91
Atlantic Beach, FL, 134–135
Atlantic Beach, NC, 41
Back Creek, NC, 37
Back River, GA, 119
Bakers Haulover Inlet, FL, 202–203
Bald Head Island, NC, 60, 208
Bal Harbour, FL, 202–203
Banana River, FL, 164–167, 228–229
Battery Creek, SC, 101
Bay River, NC, 32–33
Bear Cut, FL, 207, 235
Bear River, GA, 112–113
Beaufort, NC, 40
Beaufort, SC, 100–101
Beaufort River, SC, 101–103
Belhaven, NC, 27
Bells River, FL, 129
Berkley, VA, 2
Big Tom Creek, GA, 112
Biscayne Bay, FL, 202–207
Biscayne Channel, FL, 235, 237
Boca Raton, FL, 196
Bogue Sound, NC, 41–45
Boynton Beach, FL, 193
Boynton Inlet, FL, 193
Brickhill River, GA, 126–127
Brickyard Creek, SC, 100
Broad Creek, NC (Neuse River), 34–35
Broad Creek, NC (North River), 11–12
Brunswick River, GA, 123
Bryan Creek, SC, 105
Buckhead Creek, GA, 112
Buck Island, NC , 10–11
Bucksport, SC, 74
Bull Creek, SC (Calibogue Sound), 106
Bull Creek, SC (Waccamaw River), 74
Bull River, SC, 98–99
Burnside River, GA, 110
Buttermilk Sound, GA, 120
Calabash Creek, SC, 67
Calibogue Sound, SC, 104–106, 218
Camden Mill, VA, 3
Campbell Creek, NC, 30
Camp Lejeune, NC, 47–48
Canaveral Barge Canal, FL, 163–164, 228–231
Cane Patch Creek, GA, 112
Cape Canaveral, FL, 228–231
Cape Fear River, NC, 58–60, 208
Cape Florida Channel, FL, 207, 235, 237
Cape Romain National Wildlife Refuge, SC, 82–86
Carolina Beach, NC, 57–58
Casino Creek, SC, 82–83
Catfish Point, NC, 18, 23
Cattle Pen Creek, GA, 114
Cedar Creek, NC, 37
Charleston, SC, 90–91, 212–213
Chesapeake, VA, 2
Church Creek, SC, 93
Cocoa, FL, 164
Coconut Grove, FL, 207, 236
Coinjock, NC, 9–10
Combahee River, SC, 98
Cooper River, SC (Calibogue Sound), 106
Cooper River, SC (Charleston), 90
Coosaw River, SC, 98–100
Core Creek, NC, 38–39
Coronado Beach, FL, 153
Cowen Creek, SC, 102
Creighton Narrows, GA, 117–118
Crescent Beach, FL, 143
Cumberland Dividings, GA, 126
Cumberland Island, GA, 125–128, 226
Cumberland River, GA, 125–126, 250
Cumberland Sound, GA, 127–128
Currituck, NC, 8
Currituck Sound, NC, 8
Dania, FL, 200
Dania Cut-Off Canal, FL, 200, 233
Darien River, GA, 119
Daufuskie Island, SC, 106, 218
Dawho River, SC, 95
Daytona Beach, FL, 151
Deep Creek, VA, 3, 238
Deep Point, NC, 19–20
Delegal Creek, GA, 110–111
Delray Beach, FL, 194
Dewees Creek, SC, 88
Dinner Key, FL, 207, 236
Dismal Swamp Canal, VA/NC, 238–248
Doboy Sound, GA, 119
Dover Creek, GA, 249
Dover Cut, GA, 249
Dragon Point, FL, 167
Dumfoundling Bay, FL, 202
Dutchman Creek, SC, 61
Eastham Creek, NC, 30
Eau Gallie, FL, 167
Elba Island Cut, GA, 107–108
Elizabeth City, NC, 245
Elizabeth River, VA, 1–3
Elliott Cut, SC, 91
Enterprise Landing, SC, 73
Estherville–Minim Creek Canal, SC, 80–81
Faber Cove, FL, 177
Factory Creek, SC, 101
Fairfield, NC, 22
Fenwick Cut, SC, 97
Fernandina Beach, FL, 129, 226
Fields Cut, SC, 107
Figure Eight Island, NC, 54
Fisher Island, FL, 205, 206, 234
Fishermans Channel, FL, 206, 234
Five Fathom Creek, SC, 83–84
Flagler Beach, FL, 147
Florida Passage, GA, 111–112
Floyd Creek, GA, 250
Fort George River, FL, 132–133
Fort Lauderdale, FL, 198–200, 233
Fort Pierce, FL, 177–178
Fourmile Creek Canal, SC, 81
Fox Cut, FL, 146
Frederica River, GA, 121–122
Fripp Inlet, SC, 215
Front River, GA, 117
Gale Creek, NC, 31–32
Gallants Channel, NC, 40
Georgetown, SC, 78–79
Gilmerton, VA, 2–3
Goat Island, NC, 244
Goose Creek, NC, 30
Government Cut, FL, 234–235
Grant, FL, 170
Great Bridge, VA, 3–4
Great Dismal Swamp Canal, VA/NC, 238–248
Great Pee Dee River, SC, 77–78
Guana River, FL, 139–140
Gunnison Cut, FL, 132
Halifax Creek, FL, 148
Halifax River, SC, 148–152
Hamlin Creek, SC, 89
Hampton River, GA, 120
Harbor River, SC, 84
Haulover Canal, FL, 158–159
Hell Gate, GA, 111
Herb River, GA, 108–109
Hillsboro Inlet, FL, 197
Hillsboro River, FL, 196–197
Hilton Head Island, SC, 103–105, 218
Hobe Sound, FL, 184–185
Hobucken, NC, 35
Hog Inlet, SC, 68
Holden Beach, NC, 64–65
Hole in the Wall, FL, 173
Hollywood Beach, FL, 200–201
Hospital Point, VA, 1–2
Hunting Island, SC, 215
Hurricane Harbor, FL, 207, 237
Hutchinson Island, FL, 178–183
Indialantic, FL, 168
Indian Creek, FL, 202–205
Indian Harbor Beach, FL, 167
Indian River, FL, 170–183
Indian River City, FL, 161
Indian River North, FL, 154–156
Inlet Creek, SC, 89
Isle of Hope, GA, 109–110
Isle of Palms, SC, 88–89
Jacksonville Beach, FL, 135
James Island, SC, 90–91
Jekyll Island, GA, 123–124
Jekyll Sound, GA, 124
Jensen Beach, FL, 181
John F. Kennedy Space Center Bridge, FL, 162
Johns Island, SC, 92–93
Johnson Creek, GA, 114–115
Jonaquin Creek, NC, 37
Jupiter Inlet, FL, 186
Jupiter Island, FL, 184–186
Key Biscayne, FL, 207, 235, 237
Kilkenny Creek, GA, 112
Kings Bay, GA, 127

Kingsley Creek, FL, 129
Lake Boca Raton, FL, 196
Lake Sylvia, FL, 199
Lake Worth, FL, 188–193
Lake Wyman, FL, 195
Lanier Island, GA, 122
Lantana, FL, 192
Lauderdale-by-the-Sea, FL, 198
Little Alligator River, NC, 16
Little Mud River, GA, 119
Little Ogeechee River, GA, 110–111
Little River, SC, 67–68
Lockwoods Folly, NC, 63–64
Long Beach, NC, 62–63
Loxahatchee River, FL, 186
Mackay River, GA, 121–122
Mad Inlet, NC, 67
Manatee Pocket, FL, 182
Marineland, FL, 144
Marine Stadium, FL, 205
Mark Bay, SC, 87
Masonboro Inlet, NC, 55–56
Matanzas Inlet, FL, 144
Matanzas River, FL, 141–144
Maule Lake, FL, 202
Maw Point, NC, 32–33
Mayport, FL, 133, 227
May River, SC, 105
McClellanville, SC, 83
Melbourne, FL, 168
Merritt Island, FL, 158–167
Miami, FL, 202–207, 234–235
Miami River, FL, 206
Mile Hammock Bay, NC, 48
Milltail Creek, NC, 17
Millville, VA, 3
Minim Creek, SC, 81
Money Island, NC, 41
Moon River, GA, 110
Morehead City, NC, 41
Mosquito Lagoon, FL, 156–158
Mount Pleasant, SC, 89–90
Mud River, GA, 116–117
Myrtle Beach, SC, 69–72
Myrtle Grove Sound, NC, 56–57
NASA Parkway Bridge, FL, 162
NASA R.R. Bridge, FL, 160
Nassau River, FL, 130–131
Neuse River, NC, 33–36
New River, FL, 199, 233
New River, NC, 49
New River, SC, 106–107
New Smyrna Beach, FL, 153–154
New Teakettle Creek, GA, 118
Nixon Crossroads, SC, 68
No Name Harbor, FL, 237
Norfolk, VA, 1–2
North Biscayne Bay, FL, 202–204
North Carolina Cut, NC, 9–10
North Edisto River, SC, 95
North Lake Worth, FL, 187–188
North Landing River, VA, 5–9
North Miami Beach, FL, 202
North Myrtle Beach, SC, 69
North Newport River, GA, 113–114
North Palm Beach, FL, 188
North River, GA, 119
North River, NC, 10–12
North Santee River, SC, 81
Oak Island, NC, 60–62
Ocean Isle Beach, NC, 66
Ogeechee River, GA, 111
Old Teakettle Creek, GA, 118
Onslow Beach, NC, 48
Orchard Creek, NC, 35
Oriental, NC, 36
Ormond Beach, FL, 150
Ossabaw Island, GA, 111–113
Palm Bay, FL, 169
Palm Beach, FL, 187–192
Palm Coast, FL, 145–146
Palm Shores, FL, 167
Palm Valley Landing, FL, 137
Pamlico River, NC, 29–30
Parris Island, SC, 102–103
Parrot Creek, SC, 99
Pasquotank River, NC, 243–248
Peanut Island, FL, 189
Peck Lake, FL, 183–184
Peletier Creek, NC, 41–42
Pelican Island National Wildlife Refuge, FL, 172–173
Pinckney Island, SC, 104
Pine Island, FL, 138–139
Pine Knoll Shores, NC, 42
Plum Orchard Dock, GA, 126
Pompano Beach, FL, 197
Ponce de Leon Inlet, FL, 153
Ponte Vedra Beach, FL, 136
Port Canaveral, FL, 229–231
Port Everglades, FL, 199–200
Port Orange, FL, 152
Port Royal, SC, 101
Port Royal Sound, SC, 103, 216
Portsmouth, VA, 2
Price Creek, SC, 87
Prince Creek, SC, 74–75
Pungo Creek, NC, 27
Pungo Ferry, VA, 6
Pungo River, NC, 25–29
Queens Creek, NC, 46
Ramshorn Creek, SC, 106
Redbird Creek, GA, 111
Riviera Beach, FL, 188–189
Rock Creek, SC, 98
Rockdedundy River, GA, 119
Rockhouse Creek, FL, 153
"Rockpile," SC, 69–72
Salt Run, FL, 141
Sampit River, SC, 78–79
Sams Point, SC, 99
San Sebastian River, FL, 141
Sapelo River, GA, 116–117
Sapelo Sound, GA, 115–116, 224
Satilla River, GA, 124–125, 249–250
Savannah River, GA, 107–108, 219
Sawpit Creek, FL, 131
Sears Landing, NC, 51
Sebastian, FL, 172
Sebastian Inlet, FL, 171
Second Creek, NC, 22
Shallotte Inlet, NC, 65
Shellbluff Creek, GA, 118
Sisters Creek, FL, 133
Skidaway Narrows, GA, 109–110
Skidaway River, GA, 108–109
Skull Creek, SC, 104
Snows Cut, NC, 57–58
Socastee, SC, 73
South Amelia River, FL, 130–131
South Edisto River, SC, 96–97, 214
South Mills, NC, 242
South Newport River, GA, 115
South Palm Beach, FL, 192
South River, GA, 119
South Santee River, SC, 81–82
Southport, NC, 60–61
Spooner Creek, NC, 42
St. Andrew Sound, GA, 124–125
St. Augustine, FL, 141
St. Augustine Creek, GA, 108
St. Catherines Sound, GA, 113, 223
St. Helena Island, SC, 98, 214–215
St. Helena Sound, SC, 214–215
St. Johns River, FL, 133, 227
St. Lucie River, FL, 182
St. Marys River, GA, 128, 226
St. Simons Sound, GA, 123, 225
Stono River, SC, 91–93
Stump Sound, NC, 51
Sullivans Island, SC, 89
Sunny Isles, FL, 202
Sunset Beach, NC, 67
Swansboro, NC, 45–46
Taylor Creek, NC, 40
Thunderbolt, GA, 108
Titusville, FL, 160–161
Tolomato River, FL, 138–141
Tomoka Basin, FL, 148–149
Topsail Beach, NC, 52–53
Topsail Sound, NC, 52–53
Town Creek, NC, 40
Tubbs Inlet, NC, 66
Tuckahoe Point, NC, 20
Turner Creek, GA, 108
Tybee Roads, GA, 219–220
Umbrella Cut, GA, 249–250
Vernon River, GA, 110–111
Vero Beach, FL, 174
Vilano Beach, FL, 141
Virginia Key, FL, 205, 207, 235
Wabasso, FL, 173
Waccamaw River, SC, 73–78
Wachesaw Landing, SC, 75
Wadmalaw River, SC, 93–95
Walburg Creek, GA, 113–114
Wallaceton, NC, 240
Wallys Leg, GA, 121
Wappoo Creek, SC, 90–91
Wassaw Sound, GA, 221–222
Watts Cut, SC, 96
West Landing, VA, 5
West Palm Beach, FL, 190–191
Whiskey Creek, NC, 56
Whitehall Shores, NC, 245
White Point, SC, 95
Whiteside Creek, SC, 87
Whittaker Creek, NC, 36
Wilkerson Creek, NC, 25
Wilmington River, GA, 108, 221–222
Winyah Bay, SC, 79–80, 210–211
Wright Creek, NC, 28–29
Wright River, SC, 107
Wrightsville Beach, NC, 5

ABOUT THE EDITORS

John and Leslie Kettlewell have been traveling the Intracoastal Waterway for more than 20 years. They recently returned from a two-year, 7300-mile family cruise, with their two children, from New England to the southwest Caribbean and back. They are also the authors of International Marine's *Intracoastal Waterway Chartbook: Miami to Mobile.* John is currently Publications and Marketing Director of the Adirondack Mountain Club and Leslie teaches dance at Saratoga City Ballet. John is the former editor of *Reed's Nautical Almanacs*, *Chart Kits*, and *Boating Industry International* magazine. They are rear commodores in the Seven Seas Cruising Association and members of the Cuttyhunk, Massachusetts, Yacht Club.